CW00543023

NEUROPOWER
GROUP
TOOLKIT

The Neuroscience of Building High Performance Teams

Understanding the First Principle of NeuroPower:
Learn the Brain's Six Social Cognitive Needs and
How to Satisfy Them for Yourself and Others

R   E   L   I   S   H

Relatedness   Expression   Leading the Pack   Interpersonal Connection   Seeing the Facts   Hope for the Future

Peter Burow

The material contained in this book is not intended as medical advice. If you have a medical issue or illness, consult a qualified physician.

NeuroPower – The Neuroscience of Building High Performance Teams

Published by:

Copernicus Publishing Pty Ltd
10 Grosvenor Street, Blackburn North VIC 3130 Australia
PO Box 125, Balwyn North VIC 3104 Australia
Ph +61 3 9017 3162
Fx +61 3 9923 6632

Copyright (c) 2010 Copernicus Publishing Pty Ltd, edition 4.0.1 2012.

All rights reserved. No part of this publication may be reproduced, stored in a retrieval system, transmitted in any form or by any means, electronic, mechanical, photocopying, recording or otherwise, without the prior written permission of the publisher.

COMMENTS ABOUT NEUROPOWER

Being a business of nearly 50 psychologists in a very successful consultancy, we are hard to impress on the topic of how to use the mind and brain effectively to enhance performance. Despite this, the NeuroPower team and information not only impressed us, our business is noticeably better as a result. The information was insightful and revolutionary. It has been a long time since I have been this impressed, both professionally and personally.

Jonathan Lincolne (Managing Director, Sentis Pty Ltd)

Having studied many different psychological and behavioural models and frameworks over the past 40 years, I was impressed by Peter's work in weaving together some of the most significant theorists and writers, from Freud and Jung through to those of ancient cultures, into one cogent system. NeuroPower is an informed, integrated and - above all - practical model for understanding and facilitating human development. In my experience, it is a powerful asset, not just for practitioners working in therapeutic or counselling contexts, but for anyone who either works with people or is looking for an empowering tool to further their own development.

Dr Daniele Viliunas (Senior Psychiatrist)

Don't judge a book by its cover, or in the case of this one by its size! When I first saw the NeuroPower book, I was horrified by its size but I quickly learnt that it's actually the modern day version of the holy grail! Understanding Core Beliefs and the emotional resistances that emerge in people's response to change has been invaluable for us. The entire framework gives you such insight into who you are as a leader and how you can influence and inspire your people and stakeholders around you. NeuroPower has enabled us to fast forward strategically and has helped us stay ahead of the curve. Its value to our business comes through at all different levels from formulating strategies to engaging personal relationships – it definitely exceeds the investment.

Sophie Crawford-Jones (Principal, Strategic Sales and Marketing, PricewaterhouseCoopers Australia)

In working with leadership teams in major financial and professional service organisations, I have found NeuroPower to be profoundly insightful, especially in helping clients with motivation, engagement and ensuring their communications hit the mark. In my experience, the insights that

the NeuroPower framework brings have been pivotal in helping our client leaders and their teams achieve that elusive top 20% of performance.

Tim Rossi (Director, Symphony Leadership)

I've been using the six Intelligences to help high performance teams understand their audiences, both internally and externally, for about ten years now. In terms of corporate and media engagement, understanding and application, the practical insights of the NeuroPower framework provide a quantum leap in cut-through impact messaging. It provides the tick-tock to my messaging clock.

Warren Clarke (Director, Executive Media Coaching)

I commend Peter for his courage in integrating ancient philosophies such as those of my people with modern scientific understandings, and for his commitment to excellence that has driven his approach. His resulting work is insightful, practical, integrative and powerful.

HRH Leonel Antonio Chevez (Crown Prince of the Maya Lenca People)

Acknowledgements

Since 1988 many people have made significant contributions to this publication as the RELISH method has been researched, tested, refined and finally published.

Wade McFarlane has worked tirelessly with me, conducting and analysing a staggering amount of field research with more than 10,000 respondents.

Andrew Burow and Anna Byrne have demonstrated their professionalism, discipline, commitment and enthusiasm as my editorial team. They have laboured over sentences, diagrams and book structure to significantly enhance comprehension and flow. I'd also like to acknowledge Misha Byrne for his work bringing and integrating the insights of social cognitive neuroscience into the RELISH method, and thank Shelley Evans-Wild for her idea of creating icons or 'buttons' for each of the intelligences. Zane Harris also made an important contribution to the commercial application of the RELISH method as he has applied it in numerous leadership teams and coaching assignments across many industries.

I would like to acknowledge the significant contribution made to the NeuroPower framework by both the last Royal Maya Lenca living treasure, Her Excellency Francisca Romero Guevara, and her grandson Leonel Antonio Chevez. The Maya Lenca insights into the Six Intelligences have given the framework a practical understanding that wisdom built on more than 10,000 years of learning brings.

My thanks also go to Warren Clarke, Kerrin Edwards, Joe Foster, Victoria Hinge, Susan Nixon, Tim Rossi, Toni Scoble, Daniele Viliunas and Markus Von der Leuhe for their support and encouragement.

To everybody who has made this book possible, I offer my sincere heartfelt thanks to you all.

Peter Burow
October 2013

Contents

Contents

Tables and Diagrams

Tables and Diagrams

Tables and Diagrams

How to Use This Book

The NeuroPower framework offers profound insight into the complexity of human behaviour and how you and others around you think, feel and operate in the world. It provides an insightful map for personal, career and organisational development and can be practically applied to:

- Help individuals grow and develop into effective team members through personal development;
- Develop leaders' ability to build High Performance Teams through more effective management, leadership and emotional engagement of others; and
- Build organisations into coordinated teams that are agile and responsive, with team members who are engaged with highly effective marketing and communication that aligns their behaviours with the organisation's strategic priorities and desired culture.

USING THIS BOOK FOR BUILDING HIGH PERFORMANCE TEAMS

Your success as a leader is directly linked to your ability to create a working environment that enables each team member to use each of their six Intelligences to achieve the team's objectives. Without exception, all six are present in High Performance Teams.

This book will do two things. Firstly, it will help you identify which of the Intelligences are functioning well in your team. Secondly, it will show you where, as a leader, you can most wisely invest your time, energy and resources to increase team functioning and performance by developing the others. For each of the Intelligences, there is a Career Toolbox at the end that focuses on how to apply NeuroPower for career development. This includes:

- Tools to develop the function so that it becomes a driver of team performance; and
- A list of Questions for High Performance Teams which can be used as workshop exercises or discussion starters with your team.

Using these tools will support the healthy functioning of the Intelligences in your team and will build the six characteristics of High Performance Teams: team trust through personal loyalty, team agility through personal spontaneity, shared drive through personal vitality, team connection through personal empathy, team knowledge through a personal love of learning and forward-thinking and openness to new ideas through individual wonder.

USING THIS BOOK FOR PERSONAL DEVELOPMENT

Nature has equipped us with six Intelligences (also known as 'functions') that ensure we win the race in the great evolutionary competition for survival. When these Intelligences are highly functioning, we feel integrated, motivated and happy. When they are not, we don't.

This book will help you map the relative strengths of your Intelligences and highlight the areas that will benefit the most from conscious attention and work. For each of the functions, there is a list of Questions for Personal Development in the Personal Toolbox at the end of the chapter. Working through these questions, as well as the exercises in the text of the chapter, will provide you with a game plan for strengthening and integrating all six of your Intelligences. This will enable you to access the full benefit of the Intelligences and feel secure, spontaneous, motivated, connected, informed and optimistic.

USING THIS BOOK FOR ORGANISATIONAL DEVELOPMENT: TWO CASE STUDIES

If individuals are to embrace change, each of their six Intelligences must give the go ahead, confirming that the change will support them personally. This is reflected in key questions the individual asks themselves that must be answered in a sequenced and structured way. The RELISH method, which is explained later, is a great way to remember these six Intelligences and the order they need to be introduced.

This book explains how these questions can be addressed at a corporate level in order to successfully drive behavioural change. We bring this to life by exploring two case studies in the Organisational Toolbox at the end of the chapter.

Case Study #1: In 2007, an Australian state health department wanted to address the serious threat that health-associated infections posed to hospital patients. Micro-organisms are readily transmitted on the hands of health care workers. In Australia alone, health officials estimate that up to 7,000 people die annually from hand hygiene-related infections in hospitals. The economic burden is also considerable, costing millions each year.

Hand hygiene has been proven to substantially reduce the transmission of micro-organisms. However, despite well-established guidelines, compliance with hygiene standards throughout the world is concerningly low. International and national health agencies have been grappling with how to deal with the issue for some time, and few interventions have had any impact whatsoever (despite both European and US hospitals and governments spending tens of millions of dollars on communications, incentives, closed circuit TV and education).

Since research demonstrated that the hand hygiene issue centred around human behaviour, one state health department decided on an innovative, behaviour-changing approach using the NeuroPower framework to drive the solution. Working with the NeuroPower Consulting Team, the department implemented a behaviour change program called Clean Hands are LifeSavers that engaged the health workers and increased compliance from 18 to 60 per cent. A key driver of this behaviour change involved effectively addressing each of the six Intelligences in the correct sequence. How these progressive steps were taken is outlined in the Organisational Toolbox Case Study at the end of each Intelligence chapter.

Case Study #2: The second case study outlines how one of Australia's leading equity derivatives leadership teams improved employee engagement from 54 to 94 per cent and significantly improved their tangible business performance results by effectively addressing the six drivers of team performance in the way that NeuroPower recommends.

In 2006, at the height of the financial boom, one of Australia's leading equity derivatives teams was operating in an environment that was fast-paced and demanding with a high level of stress. In order to handle large volumes of work in a very volatile market, the team needed to be highly functional and collaborative. Growth was nearly

200 per cent over the previous year so the enormous strain was evident. This was mainly caused by a leadership team in crisis.

The Leadership Team was fractured, non-collaborative and driven by their own individual agendas. There was both a lack of respect and a lack of honesty between members which led to highly reactive responses and conflict. The broader team could see this occurring and they felt they were part of a warring tribe with all the insecurities that brought with it.

NeuroPower consultants devised a program which focused on addressing the splintered leadership team. The intervention involved a series of group structured processes which were embedded by individual coaching sessions. The process undertaken by the team at each phase is outlined at the end of each chapter.

Chapter 1

NeuroPower –
Leading with NeuroIntelligence

If our brain were so simple we could understand it,
we would be so simple we couldn't.
Lyall Watson

**The *NeuroPower* framework offers actionable insight into the complexity of who
we are and how we all think, feel and behave in the world.** Drawing not only on the
latest neuroscientific findings about the brain[1], it also draws on more traditional schools
of thought to map a practical pathway for personal and professional development.
This approach enables a deep dive into the complex world of how we are shaped by the
groups to which we belong - including families, communities and corporate cultures.
Leaders in particular find the *NeuroPower* framework a helpful lense to more accurately
see how their thoughts, words, emotions and behaviour positively or negatively impact
the people they lead.

In striving to understand human consciousness, learning and decision-making
broadly there are two different bodies of knowledge (illustrated in Diagram 1.1). The
first bundles traditional fields that apply practical insights based on behaviour, but
which have had to treat the brain like a black box. This has meant that even in highly
researched areas like perception psychology, it's been slow and incremental progress
with multiple competing theories and few ways to determine which is most accurate.

Some of the great historic minds such as Jung, Blake and Freud couldn't look inside
a working brain, and so had to assume or invent complex models to explain what they

---

1   In 2013, U.S. President, Barack Obama, approved the biggest ever investment in neuroscience
- rivalling the billions spent on the human genome project. The new area of neuroeconomics,
which combines neuroscience (the study of the brain) and behavioural economics (the study
of how psychology informs economic decisions), is also booming. Many businesses are using
neuroeconomic findings and evolved psychographics to predict and influence consumer
behaviour and increase customer intimacy. The commercial world is benefitting from
understanding that how people feel and think links to how they behave - including what they
choose to purchase. Perhaps even more importantly, applied neuroscience is being used to
shape employee experiences in more positive ways, through increased employee engagement,
leadership development, cultural change and the building of high performance teams.

heard and saw. Some of these - like Descartes' view that the mind and the body were fused together in the pineal gland - may seem quaint today, and yet many traditional theories have held up remarkably well.

In contrast, the second and more recently emerged body of knowledge is the world of neuroscience. Whereas traditional approaches have been limited to looking at behaviour and working backwards, the benefit of neuroscience has been the growing ability to look inside the black box and start to tease out what's actually going on in someone else's mind. Starting from the most basic level of cells and tiny molecules, neuroscientists are working to build a picture of how the physical structures of our brain support - and sometimes dictate - how, when and why we think and feel what we do. These advances hold the promise of giving us powerful insight into what drives our human experience and the seemingly infinite complexity of human behaviour.

NEUROSCIENCE IS CHALLENGING OUR UNDERSTANDING OF HOW THE WORLD WORKS

The most successful organisations have already worked out that neuroscientific understandings have huge implications for the commercial world. Using new insights

Diagram 1.1 Integrating the Many Different Approaches to Understanding the Human Condition

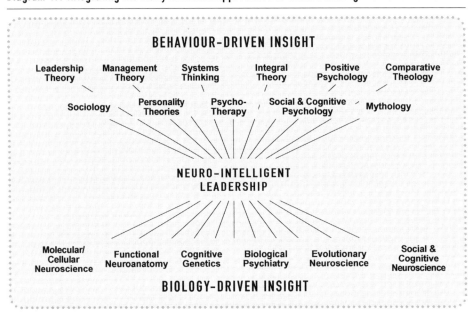

One of my consultants, Misha Byrne, uses the above diagram to illustrate the point that *NeuroPower* draws on both behaviour-driven insight and biology-driven insight to help understand the foundations of human experience, motivation and both personal and professional development.

© Mykolas (Misha) Byrne and Peter Burow, 2013

about how and why people make decisions, these businesses are revolutionising the way that they approach, relate to and communicate with stakeholders, both internally and externally. The new area of Neuroeconomics, which combines Neuroscience (the study of the brain) and Behavioural Economics (the study of how psychology informs economic decisions) is booming. Many businesses are using neuroeconomic findings and evolved psychographics to predict and influence consumer behaviour and increase customer intimacy. The commercial world is beginning to benefit from the reality that how people feel and think is critical to how they behave—including what they choose to purchase or invest in. Perhaps even more importantly, these successful organisations are using Applied Neuroscience to shape the experiences of their employees in more positive ways through increased employee engagement, leadership development, cultural change and the building of high performance teams.

Human behaviour—our own and others—is often a mystery. Why do some people forge ahead with ease or super-human effort and succeed at whatever they put their minds to while others potter about, just managing to hold the threads of life together? Why do you think, feel and view life one way, while those around you can have a totally different take on the world? Why do some people excel at engaging and persuading those around them, while others just seem to make them irate and oppositional?

NeuroPower offers profound insight into the complexity of who you are and how you and others around you think, feel and behave in the world. Drawing on the latest neuroscientific findings about the brain and its influence on behaviour, it also integrates developmental psychology, psychotherapy, philosophy, integral thinking and social research insights into how people behave in their personal, professional and business lives. This integrated approach opens a fascinating pathway for exploration and development—both personally and at work with others. It can also be applied to understand the complex human behavioural terrain of organisations and how your thoughts, words, emotions and behaviour positively or negatively impact the people who work with you.

APPLYING THE INSIGHTS OF NEUROSCIENCE THROUGH THE FOUR PRINCIPLES OF NEUROPOWER

Whether you are a leader trying to engage people in your organisation, a therapist looking for ways to engage your clients, a parent wishing to bring the best out in your kids, or you simply want to achieve more in your personal or professional life, understanding how your brain functions—your NeuroIntelligence—can help you better understand yourself and others at every practical level.

To make this digestible, I've broken the content of *NeuroPower* (Burow, 2013) into four sections, each dealing with a key principle or objective.

- **PRINCIPLE #1: Learn the brain's Six Social Cognitive Needs and how to satisfy them for yourself and others**. (Explored in the RELISH Method.)

- **PRINCIPLE #2: Know how to manage your emotional reactivity.** (Explored with a description of the nine Neuro-Limbic Types and the keys to managing them.)

- **PRINCIPLE #3: Know your genius, and when and how to use it.** (Explored with the eight Neuro-Rational Types and their eight Geniuses.)

- **PRINCIPLE #4: Know how to hardwire character and wisdom into your personality.** (Explored with the Inventory of Human Nobility and the four types of Patron Leaders.)

This handbook explores the first *NeuroPower* principle and how it can be applied in three key areas:

- **Personal Development:** Applying *NeuroPower* to help individuals (yourself or others) grow and develop through the process of integration

- **Leadership Development:** Applying *NeuroPower* to develop your own capability to manage, lead and emotionally engage others

- **Organisational Development:** Applying *NeuroPower* to build organisations that are strategically aligned, agile and responsive, with highly effective marketing and communication that builds trust and aligns the attitudes and behaviours of those receiving the messages with the desired position.

NEUROINTELLIGENCE CAN UNLOCK YOUR 'PHYSIS'

The ancient Greeks had a special word – physis – to describe the drive that compels all living things to grow into all that they can be. Physis is what enables an acorn to become a mighty oak. It also drives humans to become all that they are capable of being. When the force of physis is impeded, it results in mental, emotional and physical frustration.

One objective of the *NeuroPower* framework is to provide a clear road map for directing the inner longing of individuals, teams and organisations to follow the lead of physis towards wholeness and health.

Neuroscience 101

With the development of a range of technologies to study the brain (including e.g. fMRI and EEG) the whole field of neuroscience has exploded in the last decade. It is now regarded as one of the most rapidly advancing areas of scientific research and is helping us understand the complexities of our human behavioural responses.

These have significantly added to our understanding of the brain and how it affects our behaviour. To begin with, here are three foundational insights about the brain to get us started on our learning journey together:

1. **The physical structure of your brain supports and enables your human experience;**

2. **Your brain has two systems—one rational and the other emotional—that drive your decision-making;**

3. **You can change the physical structure of your brain and how you think, emote and behave in life.**

Let's look at each of these in more detail.

FOUNDATIONAL INSIGHT #1: THE PHYSICAL STRUCTURE OF YOUR BRAIN SUPPORTS AND ENABLES YOUR HUMAN EXPERIENCE

In 1848, American rail worker Phineas Gage was injured in a construction accident, when a tamping iron was forced up through his left cheek bone and out the top of his skull. Amazingly, he survived - but a changed man. The bar had damaged much of his brain's frontal lobe (particularly the left frontal lobe) and while at first doctors thought he had escaped disaster - still able to move, communicate and see through his remaining eye - over time it emerged that his personality had changed significantly. This is often cited as the first concrete example of how different parts of the brain might impact personality. The next 130 years saw medical science collect numerous examples of selective deficits in behaviour, thinking or emotion following damage to specific areas of the brain (in so-called 'lesion studies'). Only in the last three decades or so have new technologies like fMRI, PET and EEG helped us look inside undamaged brains to discover how we function at our best.

Thanks to these technologies, for example, we now know that the parts of the brain damaged in Phineas Gage's accident include areas responsible for many of the abilities that we see as central to what makes us human: our executive functions, including our ability to plan, strategise, reason about what other people are thinking, and - importantly - to control our own behaviour.

This is the part of our brain that has developed most in the last few hundred thousand years. Whereas our ancient ancestors relied almost exclusively on their 'limbic' or emotional brain (Diagram 1.2), allowing their emotions to drive their behaviour e.g. through our 'fight/flight' coping response, today we have more of a choice. Certainly we still have an emotional system - and sometimes it gets the better of us (as you may know

Diagram 1.2 Getting Your Bearings in the Brain

a. Key Landmarks

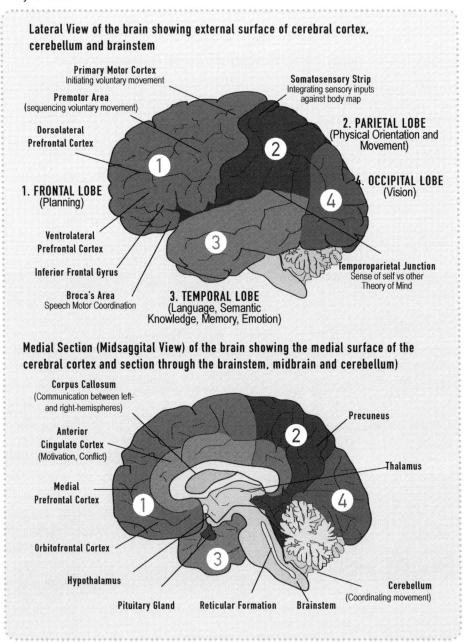

Lateral View of the brain showing external surface of cerebral cortex, cerebellum and brainstem

Primary Motor Cortex
Initiating voluntary movement

Premotor Area
(sequencing voluntary movement)

Dorsolateral
Prefrontal Cortex

Somatosensory Strip
Integrating sensory inputs
against body map

2. PARIETAL LOBE
(Physical Orientation and
Movement)

4. OCCIPITAL LOBE
(Vision)

1. FRONTAL LOBE
(Planning)

Ventrolateral
Prefrontal Cortex

Inferior Frontal Gyrus

Broca's Area
Speech Motor Coordination

Temporoparietal Junction
Sense of self vs other
Theory of Mind

3. TEMPORAL LOBE
(Language, Semantic
Knowledge, Memory, Emotion)

Medial Section (Midsaggital View) of the brain showing the medial surface of the cerebral cortex and section through the brainstem, midbrain and cerebellum)

Corpus Callosum
(Communication between left-
and right-hemispheres)

Anterior
Cingulate Cortex
(Motivation, Conflict)

Medial
Prefrontal Cortex

Precuneus

Thalamus

Orbitofrontal Cortex

Hypothalamus

Pituitary Gland   Reticular Formation   Brainstem

Cerebellum
(Coordinating movement)

b. Directions in the Brain*

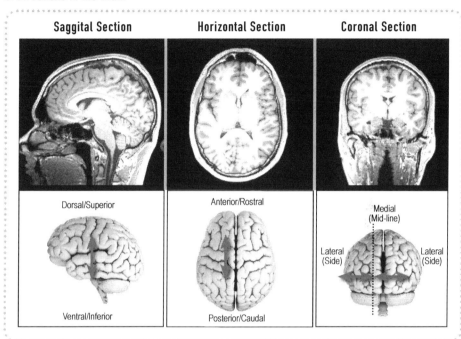

Saggital Section	Horizontal Section	Coronal Section

Dorsal/Superior — Ventral/Inferior

Anterior/Rostral — Posterior/Caudal

Medial (Mid-line) — Lateral (Side)

c. Some Important 'Hidden' Structures

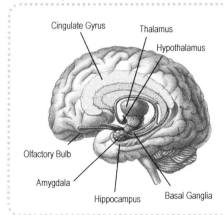

Cingulate Gyrus
Thalamus
Hypothalamus
Olfactory Bulb
Amygdala
Hippocampus
Basal Ganglia

The Limbic System is the name given to a set of connected structures buried within the brain that regulate emotion and memory. These structures directly connect the lower and higher brain functions and influence emotions, visceral responses to those emotions, motivation, mood, and sensations of pain and pleasure. The limbic system is also the name used to distinguish the brain's 'emotional processing' (also sometimes referred to as System 1 or System X) and the brain's 'rational' system (System 2 or System C).

---

* At the time of printing, a great tutorial for learning the different naming conventions in the brain is available at http://www.getbodysmart.com/ap/nervoussystem/cns/brain/brainviews/tutorial.html.

from bitter experience). But today, our neocortex—the front-most part of the brain that includes most of the frontal lobes – acts as a control centre. It allows us to observe, interpret and manage our emotional system. Perhaps most importantly - it can help stop us from 'whacking' our boss, even if they are annoying us.

FOUNDATIONAL INSIGHT #2: YOUR BRAIN HAS TWO SYSTEMS-ONE RATIONAL AND THE OTHER EMOTIONAL-THAT DRIVE YOUR DECISION-MAKING

Nobel Laureate Daniel Kahneman (2003), a psychologist from Princeton University, worked with fellow psychologist Amos Tversky in coming to the initially radical conclusion that there are two modes of cognitive functioning that influence behaviour:

- System 1[2] is the intuitive or emotional brain; and
- System 2 is the reasoning or rational brain.

These two systems differ in terms of both speed, flexibility and operation. According to Kahneman:

> [T]he operations of System 1 are typically fast, automatic, effortless, associative, implicit (not available to introspection), and often emotionally charged; they are also governed by habit and are therefore difficult to control or modify. The operations of System 2 are slower, serial, effortful, more likely to be consciously monitored and deliberately controlled; they are also relatively flexible and potentially rule governed. (Kahneman, 2003, p. 698)

As Diagram 1.3 shows, both systems influence our judgements and choices—meaning that how you feel about something is equally as important as what your common sense or reasoning tells you about it. While this may conflict with your sense of yourself as a sensible being who can divorce emotion from the realities of a situation, it probably aligns with your experiences of others' behaviour as occasionally (perhaps often) irrational and emotional.

FOUNDATIONAL INSIGHT #3: YOU CAN CHANGE THE PHYSICAL STRUCTURE OF YOUR BRAIN AND HOW YOU THINK, EMOTE AND BEHAVE IN LIFE

Our brains are wonderfully complex, adaptive systems that are capable of astounding growth and change—a property referred to as neuroplasticity. This concept has been popularised by books such as Dr Norman Doidge's best-selling *The Brain That Changes Itself* (2007), which includes the almost unbelievable story of a woman born with half a brain that rewired itself to work as a whole. We now know that

2   The neutral terms 'System 1' and 'System 2' were coined by Stanovich and West (2000).

Diagram 1.3 The Two Systems Involved in Decision-Making

1. Input enters brain and the limbic system reacts emotionally, based on existing Core Beliefs – System 1.

    a. If the situation is not 'out of the ordinary' (or 'novel'), an habitual response is invoked and translates into immediate behaviour.

    b. If the situation *is* novel, then the information moves to System 2. Here it is assessed and matched against the individual's conscious world view and analytical style to reach a decision.

2. The trial decision from System 2 is checked by the limbic system:

    a. If it lines up with past experience (i.e. a similar decision has been made previously and the outcome is familiar) the individual will feel 'comfortable' with the trial decision, which will be embraced and translated into action.

    b. If no similar decision has been made previously and the anticipated outcome is unfamiliar, a feeling of discomfort will arise and the trial decision will then be sent back to System 2 for further thought.

3. This moving between the two systems will continue until a balance is reached and both systems are comfortable with the trial decision. Only then will it be translated into behaviour.

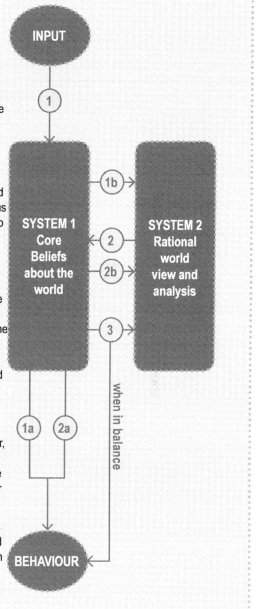

each time we attempt a new task, our brain creates or strengthens a new neural pathway. Every time we repeat the task, more connections are added and the task becomes easier. Some - like Malcolm Gladwell - have argued that after 10,000 hours of practice, we reach a level of mastery—both practically and neurobiologically—and have built a neural superhighway in our brain. Our brain is then hardwired for that activity.

In the same way, you can also hardwire your brain for certain states, which then translate into personality traits. All it takes is 10,000 hours. Scientifically validated studies bear this out, showing us, for example, that regular meditation practice changes some individuals who spend many hours practising different emotions, such as anger, fear, happiness or anxiety. Others have instead practiced and mastered more conscious, higher-order attributes—we call them Noble Qualities—such as integrity, courage or discernment. Whatever it is that you've focused on will become automatic and this will be reflected in your personality.

The Biology of the Dual-Process Model

In the growing field of social cognitive neuroscience, Kahneman's model has been further developed by Lieberman, Gaunt, Gilbert and Trope (2002). They use the terms 'X-System' and 'C-System' to describe two different types of social cognitive processes:

The X-System
- Reflexive, intuitive processes that are subsymbolic, fast and effortless
- Feels like the reality we experience directly
- Often more perceptual or affective (can be non-conscious)
- Produces a "continuous stream of consciousness that each of us experience[s] as 'the world out there'" (Lieberman et al., 2002, p. 204)
- Includes the ventromedial prefrontal cortex, lateral temporal cortex, amygdala, basal ganglia and dorsal anterior cingulate

The C-System
- Reflective processes that are slow, effortful and based on symbolic logic
- Feels like self-generated thought (typically linguistic)
- Produces "conscious thoughts that we experience as 'reflections on' the stream of consciousness" (Lieberman et al., 2002, p. 204).
- Includes the lateral prefrontal cortex, lateral parietal cortex, medial prefrontal cortex, medial parietal cortex, rostral anterior cingulate and the medial temporal lobes

Six Social Cognitive Needs Underpin Our Human Experience

The Six Social Cognitive Needs (described in this book using the acronym 'RELISH') are the neurobiological building blocks of human personality and human experience. These functional systems, which form the basis of the *NeuroPower* approach, each have a distinct focus of cognitive attention, and specific emotions which give rise to very clear behaviour. We all have access to these six functions but, through conditioning during our early lives, we each develop a preference for certain functions over others, and our favouring of these functions translates into habitual use. The variations in the mix of these functions we habitually use give rise to different personality profiles at different levels of integration (see Diagram 1.5). Each of these personalities has a distinct world view and way of operating in life. Once you understand the six Intelligences you'll be able to explore how the simultaneous accessing of particular combinations of Intelligences predictably gives rise to very different thinking, feeling and behaviour. This becomes the external manifestation of the different aspects (i.e. System 1 and System 2) of human personality. Let's take a closer look at Diagram 1.5 to understand how all the different pieces fit together.

THE SIX INTELLIGENCES

At the bottom of Diagram 1.5 you'll find six coloured buttons. Each relates to a neurobiological functional system or building block of human personality. These are Intelligences which enable the individual to understand and respond to the world.

For linguistic ease, the *NeuroPower* **framework has given each of the Intelligences a short-hand descriptor comprising a letter and a number.** These reflect the reality that the brain has six different ways in which it processes things, receives information and manifests creatively in the world.

The six Intelligences can therefore be grouped into three pairs of functions as shown in Table 1.4: The Ps (P1 and P2), the Cs (C1 and C2) and the Is (I1 and I2).[3]

Table 1.4 The Six Intelligences

P - Processing	C - Creativity	I - Information Gathering
P1 - Logical sequencing based on experience	C1 - Spontaneous self-expression and adaptation	I1 - Pattern recognition and external data
P2 - Goal-oriented drive and focus	C2 - Visionary downloading of new paradigms	I2 - Empathic attunement and intuition

---

3 Neuroscientists estimate there are more than 600 functional circuits in the brain. Of these, the *NeuroPower* framework identifies just 18 (six sets of three: a thinking, feeling and behaviour component of each Intelligence) that have the most significant influence on the manifestation of personality.

Our Biases Towards Each of the Six Intelligences Explain the Diversity of Insight Embedded across Many Professional Tools

Each of us tends to favour one of each pair (e.g. P1 rather than P2) more than the other, and we tend to value some Intelligences but not others. **It's not surprising, therefore, that the myriad of different tools and frameworks of leadership, management, marketing, coaching, personality (and many other fields) focus on achieving some or all of these needs. A cross-section of these tools are mapped out in Table 1.6.** The six Intelligences are helpful in professional practice and personal development because they help us understand why - and in what situations - different tools are effective or ineffective.

More broadly, however, understanding that you need to be highly functioning in all six Intelligences—regardless of whether your focus is individual, career or organisational development—is the first step of your *NeuroPower* awareness.

The easiest way to remember the six Intelligences, and their order, is to remember the acronym RELISH which stands for **R**elatedness (P1), **E**xpression (C1), **L**eading the Pack (P2), **I**nterpersonal Connection (I2), **S**eeing the Facts (I1) and **H**ope for the Future (C2).

In this handbook, we'll be exploring each of the Intelligences in detail, including the neurobiology of each system. For now, let's take a brief look at the characteristics of each of these functions.

P1 | THE AUTOMATIC FUNCTION (R - RELATEDNESS)

P1 Intelligence houses our implicit procedural memory—the parts of our brain that enables us to operate in the absence of conscious attention. This is our 'automatic pilot' mode and the seat of our habitual patterns. Driven by our personal values, this system encodes the rules that we were taught as children and symbolises the part of our mind that thinks as a member of the collective—our family or tribe. P1 is therefore culturally determined and heavily impacted by our family of origin and primary caregivers early in life, although the extent to which these factors continue to influence us are often largely outside our conscious awareness. The P1 Intelligence can also be referred to as 'Relatedness' because the brain loves being part of a group that is cohesive, fair and safe. The evolution and growth of the prefrontal cortex was driven by the need to survive and thrive by remaining secure within our social groups. People define themselves by the groups they belong to and are highly sensitive to social rejection and exclusion.

P1-Related Research Terms in Neuroscience:

Prenatal learning; procedural memory; moral behaviour and moral judgements; fairness; values; self-control; compliance; social inclusion and exclusion (social isolation); ingroup-outgroup; social value orientation; infant attachment; fear-learning; trust; security; certainty vs risk preference; obsessive passion; prevention regulatory focus; 'ought' goals; 'should' goals; extrinsic goal motivation.

Diagram 1.5 The Map of Human Personality

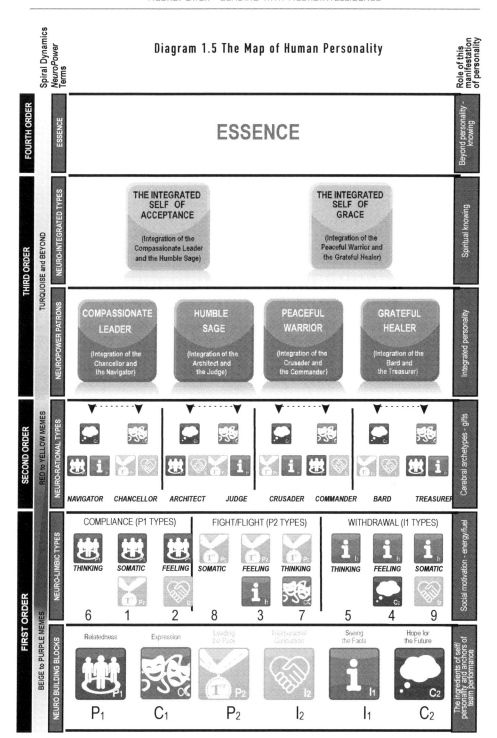

Table 1.6 How Contemporary Frameworks Address the Six Social Cognitive Needs

FRAMEWORK	RELATEDNESS (P1)	EXPRESSION (C1)	LEADING THE PACK (P2)	INTERPERSONAL CONNECTION (I2)	SEEING THE FACTS (I1)	HOPE FOR THE FUTURE (C2)
Myers Briggs Type Indicator[1]	Thinking	Extraversion	Feeling	Intuition	Sensing	Introversion
Herman Brain Dominance Index (HBDI)	Quadrant B	-	-	Quadrant C	Quadrant A	Quadrant D
Hogan Assessment System[2]	*Low* Ambition, *High* Prudence	*High* Sociability	*High* Ambition, *Low* Prudence	*High* Interpersonal Sensitivity, *Low* Learning Approach	*Low* Interpersonal Sensitivity, *High* Learning Approach	*Low* Sociability
Five Dysfunctions of a Team (Lencioni)	Lack of Trust	Fear of Conflict	Lack of Commitment	Inattention to Results	Avoidance of Accountability	-
Situational Leadership	Low Directive (S3, S4)	-	High Directive (S1, S2)	High Supportive (S2, S3)	Low Supportive (S1, S4)	-
S.C.A.R.F (David Rock)	Certainty, Relatedness, Fairness	-	Status, Autonomy	-	-	-
C.O.R.E (Jan Hills)	Certainty, Equity	-	Options, Reputation	-	-	-
'Engaged' (Holbeche & Mathews)	Connection, Support	Voice	Scope	-	-	-
Agile Principles	Value	Flexibility, Simplicity	Speed, Teamwork	Collaboration	Continuous Improvement	-
Agile Practices	Social contract	Stand-ups	Sliders, Progress walls	Co-location, Showcase	Planning poker, Retrospectives	BVCs
Lean Problem Solving	Define the Problem	Grasp the Situation	Plan, Do	-	Check, Act	Conclusions, Lessons Learned
Product Management (e.g. Black Blot)	Value proposition/ Unmet needs	Customer segmentation, Pain points	Competitor analysis	Customer personas	Product features matrix	Product roadmap
Design Thinking (d school)	Focus on human values	Embrace experimentation	Bias towards action	Radical collaboration	Show, don't tell, craft clarity	Be mindful of the process
4Q Integral (Ken Wilber)	Collective	-	Individual	Interior	Exterior	-
Neuro-Linguistic Programming Techniques	e.g. Anchoring	e.g. Reframing, State Management	e.g. Goal-setting	e.g. Matching & Mirroring	e.g. Chunking Down, Chunking Up, Meta Models	e.g. Shifting Perceptual Positions
Demartini 7 Areas of Life	Physical, Family, Social	Physical	Physical, Vocational	-	Financial, Mental	Spiritual

Vertical section labels (left margin): PERSONALITY · LEADERSHIP FRAMEWORKS · PROCESS METHODOLOGIES · DEVELOPMENT TOOLS

1   The MBTI dimensions 'Judging' and 'Perceiving' indicate a preference for either processing (P1/P2) or information (I1/I2), respectively.
2   The 'Adjustment' dimension in the Hogan Assessment System is predominantly Relatedness (P1) with aspects of Hope for the Future (C2).
    The 'Inquisitive' dimension describes a focus on a creative style, with a bias towards Expression (C1) and elements of Hope for the Future (C2).

C1 | THE EMOTIONAL FUNCTION (E - EXPRESSION)

C1 Intelligence helps us remember what happens to us emotionally so that we keep doing what we enjoy and stop doing what causes us pain. It houses our central emotional position that we develop in early childhood and which, if unquestioned, often dictates the future course of our emotional lives. If the C1 Intelligence is not functioning well, we are destined to repeat the same emotional and behavioural patterns we learned as children. However, when C1 is highly functioning, it fosters spontaneity, experimentation, lateral thinking and fun. The C1 Intelligence can also be referred to as 'Expression' because the brain loves expressing emotions. Unexpressed emotion and activity in the amygdala is related to a significant decrease in cognitive ability and can seriously reduce performance. Labelling emotions appropriately reduces this load. (Labelling is enabling!)

C1-Related Research Terms in Neuroscience:

Emotion regulation; affect labelling; addiction; innovation; dopamine; endorphins; hedonic motivation (pleasure); sexuality; positive affect; emotion reappraisal; extroversion; distraction; ADHD; affective experience; homeostasis; alliesthesia; pleasure paradox; affective neuroscience.

P2 | THE INTERVENTION FUNCTION (L - LEADING THE PACK)

P2 Intelligence enables us to interrupt the habitual process of automatic behaviour and navigate in the external world to get what we individually want or desire. This is the part of the brain that is the seat of motivation, drive and ego. By intervening to break old habits and patterns, P2 enables us to go that extra mile to achieve our goals. It also gives us the energy to aim for what we truly desire. This is the part of your mind that values independence and drives personal accomplishment. The P2 Intelligence can also be referred to as 'Leading the Pack' because the brain loves status and once basic needs have been met, status, recognition and independence are key drivers of satisfaction and must be managed to foster healthy passion rather than unhealthy competition.

P2-Related Research Terms in Neuroscience:

Self-esteem; agency; autonomy; status; social comparison; fight/flight; HPA axis; testosterone; aggression; competition; power; harmonious passion; approach motivation; promotion regulatory focus; 'ideal' goals; 'want' goals; intrinsic goal motivation.

I2 | THE RELATING FUNCTION (I – INTERPERSONAL CONNECTION)

I2 Intelligence is based on several parts of the brain that work together to enable us to empathise with others through attuning to their experiences and 'best guessing' their thoughts and feelings. This paves the way for genuine heartfelt connection and minimises the amount of needless pain caused by prejudice and misunderstanding. I2 also enables us to connect meaningfully with ourselves and to find what we love in the world—be it a vocation, an activity or others to share the journey. This is the seat of our authenticity and enables us to have lasting and meaningful relationships. The I2 Intelligence can also be referred to as 'Interpersonal Connection' because the brain is naturally focused on connections with other people and needs to feel genuinely understood by others. The brain's mirror neuron system is dedicated to helping us interpret and understand others. This system helps us feel what other people feel and is intrinsically linked to the positive relationships we form with others.

I2-Related Research Terms in Neuroscience:

Empathy; Theory of Mind; mentalising; mindsight; mirror neuron system; default mode network; altruism; generosity; emotional intelligence (EQ); empathising; empathising quotient (EQ); E-S theory; oxytocin; pain perception; facial mimicry; synchronicity; autobiographical memory; episodic memory.

I1 | THE OBJECTIVE LEARNING FUNCTION (S – SEEING THE FACTS)

I1 Intelligence draws on our brain's ability to recognise and learn patterns and recall factual information. This includes patterns of behaviour, cause and effect patterns and all forms of data. Our capacity to learn is directly linked to our ability to interpret the information that is available to us in all aspects of life. We are able to do this through our explicit declarative memory—the part of our brain that wants to understand the world through quantifiable fact. The brain loves feedback and having all the information at hand. The I1 Intelligence can also be referred to as 'Seeing the Facts' because the brain is a complex self-regulating machine that adapts constantly to external feedback. The primary source of this feedback is through the eyes and large regions of the brain associated with visual processing. Often we need to see it to believe it and the brain is always looking for continuous feedback.

I1-Related Research Terms in Neuroscience:

Systemising; Systemising Quotient (SQ); E-S theory; explicit semantic memory; spatial memory; 'place cells'; hippocampus; visual discrimination; pattern recognition; feature discrimination; expertise hypothesis of facial recognition; alexithymia; autism; extreme male brain theory; foetal androgen exposure.

C2 | THE OPEN FUNCTION (H - HOPE FOR THE FUTURE)

C2 Intelligence is much more expansive than the other systems. It acts as the modem for the brain, downloading new paradigms, concepts, big picture and fresh vision. It draws on parts of the brain that enable us to be open to a completely new way of looking at things. C2 is also the part of our brain that thinks about tapping into higher consciousness, and is frequently accessed by experienced meditators and forward-thinking strategists. C2 Intelligence can also be referred to as 'Hope for the Future' because the brain loves moving forward based on hope for the future. The brain is an anticipation machine - constantly projecting into the future the consequences of staying on its current path. Importantly, our level of hope is directly linked to our sense of whether our current path will lead to a positive future.

C2-Related Research Terms in Neuroscience:

Neurotheology; spiritual neuroscience; out-of-body; unitary experience; mystical experience or mystical state (including 'timelessness', 'union', 'spacelessness'); alpha-theta state; openness; introversion; prayer *and* health; religion; global precedence; affective forecasting.

As we progress from infancy through childhood, we move through the Intelligences in a sequential order—bottom row, from left to right in Diagram 1.5. Many contemporary psychiatrists have documented this progressive development of self, including Piaget, Erikson, Maslow, Kohlberg and Berne. These, together with two ancient philosophies held by the Maya Lenca and the Indians, are summarised in Table 1.7.

If the development of highly functioning Intelligences is impeded in childhood, there are long-term impacts on the personality of the individual in later life. It also affects their ability to access the capabilities associated with the less developed Intelligences, which will affect their ability to function, both at home and at work. This, in turn, shapes the habitual characteristics that the individual will demonstrate (i.e. their personality).

The Nine Neuro-Limbic Types

In the second row of Diagram 1.5, we start to see how the Intelligences combine to create childlike, emotional personalities. Along the bottom of the row, there are a series of numbers. Each number represents a particular combination of Intelligences (the ones that appear directly above it). These are the personalities that sit in System 1 of our brain and are reactive and emotional. Housed in the more primitive part of our brain, the limbic system, these personalities are essentially habitual patterns that we've developed in response to our early experiences, a default setting for survival.

Table 1.7 Comparative Theories of Development

THEORY OF DEVELOPMENT	RELATEDNESS (P1)	EXPRESSION (C1)	LEADING THE PACK (P2)	INTERPERSONAL CONNECTION (I2)	SEEING THE FACTS (I1)	HOPE FOR THE FUTURE (C2)
Piaget	Sensory-Motor (stages 1 and 2)	Sensory-Motor (stages 3 to 6)	Pre-operational	Pre-operational	Formal operations	Formal operations
Erikson	Trust vs mistrust	Autonomy vs Shame and Doubt	Initiative vs Guilt Industry vs Inferiority Identity vs Role Confusion	Intimacy vs Isolation	Generativity vs Isolation	Integrity vs Despair
Maya Lenca Energetic Symbol	Armadillo	Rabbit	Jaguar	Turtle	Monkey scribe	Eagle
Chakra	Base (Muladhara)	Sacral (Svadhisthana)	Solar Plexus (Manipura)	Heart (Anahata)	Brow (Ajna)	Crown (Sahasrara)
Maslow	Physiology	Safety	Self-esteem	Belonging	Trans-cendence	Trans-cendence
Kohlberg	Punishment/ obedience	Instrumental/ hedonism	Good boy/ nice girl	Law and order	Universalism	Universalism
Berne	Parent	Child	Adult	–	–	–

In *NeuroPower*, we call these the Neuro-Limbic Types (NLTs). At best, the NLTs provide us with the emotional fuel we need to get through life, but hamper us with predictable cognitive biases. At worst, they are reactive, disruptive and cause chaos in our lives. The NLTs are discussed in detail in **Principle #2** of *NeuroPower* (Burow, 2013).

In total there are nine NLTs, each consisting of either one or two of the Intelligences. Each NLT can be broadly described according to how it reacts to stress: by complying, fighting or withdrawing. This relates to whether the type is formed around the P1 Automatic System (which results in *compliance*), the P2 Intervention System (which results in *fighting* or moving against something) or the I1 Objective Learning System (which results in *withdrawal* to reconsider the situation). The impact of these three limbic or emotional reactions on the psychological health of an individual were first quantified in 1945 by the renowned German psychiatrist Karen Horney. These nine personalities can be seen in action in yourself and others. They have been written about extensively in the Enneagram personality system made popular by US researcher and psychologist Helen Palmer (1988, 1995, 1998) and Stanford Professor David Daniels (Daniels et al., 2000). This handbook provides readers with an overview of the nine types rather than an in-depth analysis. This is because many other authors have written excellent material that we would be simply repeating.

We each have access to three of these Neuro-Limbic Types: one compliance type, one fighting type and one withdrawal or flight type. These personalities provide us with our limbic connection to the world and provide the emotional energy or fuel for our more rational, noble Self (see *The Eight Adult Neuro-Rational Types*) to function. When we lose our connection with our Neuro-Limbic Type, we lose our motivation, interest in others and much of our 'gut reaction' to life. Conversely, if we are a slave to them, we lose all human nobility and perceive everyone around us, even those closest to us, as either competition or food.

In Principle #3 of *NeuroPower* (Burow, 2013) outlines the specific method required to convert this primitive drive into human nobility. This third principle of

What is the Low Road?

The Neuro-Limbic Types are sometimes described as the Low Road because they are driven by the brain's more primitive limbic system whose function is to keep us alive through quick, automatic responses to the world around us. The structures of the limbic system (including the now popularly infamous amygdala and other parts of the mid-brain basal ganglia) work constantly to scan our environments, filtering out most information and attending only to things that we have learned, through past experience, are most relevant.

When we are under stress and we have a panic response our system floods and the limbic system (our Neuro-Limbic Type) can take over. While a healthy functioning limbic system is critical to our survival, UCLA neuroscientist Matthew Lieberman and others have observed that this system is closed, reflexive, uncontrolled and - largely - unconscious. It also focuses exclusively on self-survival (selfish). So when your limbic system is calling the shots about your behaviour it will tend to be repetitive, narrowly focused and selfish. Philosophers and theologians have historically referred to this as the Low Road.

(Consequently, throughout this handbook we have referred to an overreliance on the Neuro-Limbic System as the Low Road or the Lower Self.)

In contrast, the brain's rational system (largely seated in the cerebral cortex and in particular the frontal lobe) is more dynamic, responsive, open and creative. While much slower than the limbic system, it is able to recognise and work through complexity to resolve difficult challenges. Our best decisions, therefore, are made when these two systems work together in harmony. Many traditions of meditation (including techniques like yoga) are thought to be beneficial at least in part because they help us practice using the executive functions of the brain's rational system to manage and control the impulses of the emotional system. This then helps us mediate the impulses of the limbic system in the rest of our lives.

NeuroPower is a central competency for each human life to master if they are to reach their full potential.

The Eight Adult Neuro-Rational Types[4]

The third row of Diagram 1.5 shows eight combinations of the Intelligences called Neuro-Rational Types (NRTs). Each is made up of three of the Intelligences: one of the Ps, one of the Is and one of the Cs.

Personality at this level manifests when the individual can hold the tension between the P (Processing) and the I (Information) Intelligences and transform this into nobility through the C (Creativity) Intelligence. The Neuro-Rational Types can manifest only when the individual has the ability to **contain** the tensions between the P and I (Intelligences) and unify this through C1 or C2. This takes strength of character because when confronted with a difficult situation it is much easier to disintegrate into one of the Neuro-Limbic Types than to stay in the Neuro-Rational Type and manifest human nobility. This containment requires the use of the large, more evolved part of the brain, the cerebral cortex, rather than the primitive limbic system that gives rise to the Neuro-Limbic Types. The higher levels of human consciousness are accessible only when the individual can access their adult Neuro-Rational Type.[5]

Each Neuro-Rational Type[6] has a way of interpreting the world and has access to a Genius that it can use in their daily life. Knowing and using our Genius is one of the keys to a satisfying life because it results in a flow or optimal experience. While each one of us has a genius, it is only when we discover and apply it that we become a genius. It's also the key to creating wealth in a satisfying way.

All eight Areas of Mastery are needed in teams if they are to perform at an optimum level and avoid blind spots that could impede success. Similarly, the most healthy individuals are able to move flexibly and access Areas of Mastery other than their own.

Each Neuro-Rational Type also has a specific process for moving from one level of consciousness to the next. *NeuroPower* refers to this as transformation through integration. (This is the basis of the NeuroPower Integral Coaching System™.)

---

4   Sometimes referred to as Archetypes.
5   For those well versed in the language of Spiral Dynamics, the Neuro-Limbic Types rarely move the individual beyond the Red meme, whereas the Neuro-Rational Types enable the individual to move up to second-tier consciousness. Each Neuro-Rational Type manifests a different and specific noble quality at each meme. This makes up the comprehensive Map of Human Nobility in Principle #4, Table 20.2, *NeuroPower* (Burow, 2013).
6   *NeuroPower* gives each of the Neuro-Rational Types names from the Celtic Arthurian Legend. These names are simply tags for generic archetypes and so are not restricted to the Celtic tradition. For a description of the Celtic tradition refer to Appendix 9, The Arthurian Legend, *NeuroPower* (Burow, 2013).

Each of the eight Neuro-Rational Types has a hidden personality which is made up of three of the six Intelligences not used by the Master (*NeuroPower* refers to this as the individual's Mirror). In Diagram 1.5, each Master and its corresponding Mirror are next to each other. While we are all aware of and are attached to our Master personality, we prefer to keep our Mirror personality hidden because it represents the parts of us that we do not like or accept. The Mirror is usually underdeveloped relative to the Master. As we grow and develop we learn to integrate the viewpoints of both the Master and the Mirror. This enables us to have a more complete and integral understanding of the world.

THE FOUR PATRONS

The fourth row of Diagram 1.5 has four turquoise buttons which represent the four Patron Types. These leaders manifest when the individual has successfully integrated their Master and Mirror. Very rarely do we experience this level of personality, but when we do, it gives us access to an even higher level of consciousness.[7] The term Patron has been borrowed from the ancient Maya Lenca people of Central America who have a similar tiered approach to the manifestation of personality. Like *NeuroPower*, the Maya Lenca system argues that integration is the key to accessing higher levels of consciousness. It is the only system I have found which accurately describes personality at this level of cognitive, emotional and spiritual development. The four Patrons focus not only on living responsibly free, but also on making a difference through a combination of being and doing. The Patron still has internal work to do, however, and this takes the form of integrating the Patron's Mirror.

THE INTEGRATED SELF

When the Patron has integrated its Patron Mirror, one last personality type manifests. These are represented by the two yellow buttons on the very top row of Diagram 1.5. These Neuro-Integrated Types are very rare indeed and when they do manifest they change the world. Jesus Christ and the Buddha are two well known spiritual leaders who *NeuroPower* recognises as falling into this category.

Weaving Ancient Philosophies with Contemporary Science

Dan Siegel, author of *The Developing Mind* (1999), a brilliant and ground-breaking book on neuroscience and human development, made the point that much of his work involved encouraging different university departments to share information. This is because the fields of medicine, neurobiology, psychiatry and psychology historically

---

7   Spiral Dynamics would refer to this higher level of consciousness as the Turquoise meme.

have had no acquaintance with one another's research or conclusions. In the same way that Western scientific schools do not interact, ancient wisdom is often relegated to the school of history and is not seen as relevant to contemporary scientific discussion.

However, ancient cultures like the Celts, the Central American Maya, the Chinese, the Indians and the Tibetans, just to name a few, are rich in insights that can make a substantial contribution to our understanding of developmental psychology, personality and consciousness.

The *NeuroPower* framework explores important insights offered by these traditional cultures and validates elements of these philosophies with cutting-edge neurobiological research.

This text begins the process of distilling the data from the divergent perspectives of science, mythology, medicine and the ancient and primitive oral traditions into an elegant, cohesive and practical system which defines human personality, consciousness and nobility, and can be applied to individual, team and organisational performance.

THE NEUROINTELLIGENCE OF INTEGRAL THEORY

Coincidentally, key research relating to neurobiological functional systems aligns with integral theory as outlined by Ken Wilber (1996). Wilber's *Four Faces of Truth* makes an important link between the world of causality and the higher road of harmony by showing how the integration of four of the Intelligences creates a higher order of awareness. The *Four Faces of Truth* matrix suggests that all living and non-living substance has an interior-exterior dimension. (Neurobiologically, these can be equated to I2 and I1.) It also has an individual-communal dimension (P2 and P1). Wilber argues that along a continuum of complexity, from an individual to a family, to a tribal group, to a nation-state, and to the United Nations, or in the other direction, from an individual to their digestive systems, to each of the organs in the digestive systems all the way down to the sub-atomic particles of the tissues that constitute the organ, there is both an interior-exterior dimension and an individual-communal dimension. For example, a quark, a sub-atomic particle, has an interior-exterior dimension and an individual-communal dimension just as the United Nations has an interior-exterior dimension and an individual-communal dimension. This is certainly true of the brain, where we have one functional system for the communal P1 and one for individual P2, and one system for external I1 and another for internal I2.

To explore this at a deeper level, let us start with a consideration of the interior (I2) and exterior (I1) dimension. This dimension refers to the relationship between the inner world of subjectivity (I2) and the outer world of objectivity (I1). This dimension is a fundamental source of tension within many schools of scientific and philosophical thought. The difference is that the interior perspective represents the subjective interpretation of

Diagram 1.8 Wilber's Four Faces of Truth

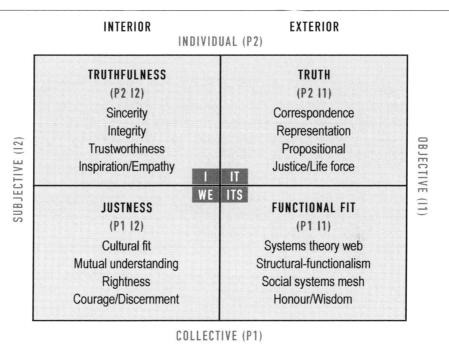

events, whereas the exterior perspective represents the 'rational scientific' approach that bases perception on external and quantifiable details in the external world. We can see this tension in every aspect of life. For example, in the Western theological tradition, we can see the tension in the totally different perspectives of the Christian theologians of St Aquinas and Augustine. St Aquinas argues the existence of God from certain natural facts and then attempts to show that these facts demand an Author. In contrast, Augustine turns attention within, arguing that a subjective and introspective approach reveals the existence of God. If understanding of the world is sought through external sources, material details and empirical observations, it is said to follow the rational path to understanding (I1); if it is sought through interpretive assessment and subjective experience, then it is said to follow the intuitive path to understanding (I2).

The other critical dimension that Wilber describes is the division between individual and communal understanding. This dimension tracks understanding in terms of agency (P2) or communion (P1); that is, understanding can be derived through the experience of individual agency or it can be derived through the experience of collective communion. Along this dimension one can study experience either through the perspective of the individual (P2) or the perspective of the group (P1), the movement of an individual electron (P2) or the understanding of the atom as a whole (P1), the health and functioning of the stomach (P2) or the health and functioning of the entire digestive system (P1).

Neither the dimensions I1/I2 nor P1/P2 are sufficient in themselves to completely understand a situation. What is needed is to combine the two dimensions and the knowledge from the resultant four quadrants (Wilber, 1995). When plotted on a matrix (see Diagram 1.8) four distinct perspectives emerge. Wilber calls these *The Four Faces of Truth*: truthfulness, justice, truth and functional fit.

I, Upper Left Quadrant, Truthfulness: The interior and subjective experiences from an individual perspective place the individual in quadrant I of the matrix. As you read this book, this aspect of your mind will focus on how you, as an individual, are feeling right at this very moment as you begin to understand this knowledge. From this base of truth you may be asking questions like, 'How am I reacting to this knowledge? How am I feeling about this? How is this fitting into my wider life story?' If the ideas have been neither relevant nor appropriate within your life, then they will have no truthfulness for you (I).

WE, Lower Left Quadrant, Justness: The lower left quadrant, the subjective and collective quadrant (WE), comprises, among other things, the fact that the book is written in English. Not only does the book subjectively feel right, but the concepts fit with you and those with whom you are associated. Our collective ability to read and understand the concepts in the book, and to be able to arrive at any assessment as to their personal validity, must be based on a shared cultural perspective that enables these ideas to be communicated. As your mind considers the concepts in this book according to the WE quadrant, you will consider the level of relevance both for yourself and within the broader social groups to which you belong. While these concepts may be useful for you, they may have no cultural fit and so may not represent the collective construct of knowledge that you share with others. Using this face of truth as a filter, the ideas may or may not be fair and reasonable, and if they have no sense of justness about them (WE) they will be rejected.

IT, Upper Right Quadrant, Truth: The aspect of your mind in the exterior-individual quadrant (IT) focuses on the specific knowledge that you are reading here and how you can personally benefit from it. This quadrant would ask, 'What are the concepts that this book has been discussing? Are the frameworks accurate from my understanding? Do they actually represent the truth?' 'How can I use this insight to achieve my goals?' As you study each individual component of the book and assess whether it is accurate, you will make an assessment about the truth of the book (IT). 'Is the concept of the *Four Faces of Truth* itself true?'

ITS, Lower Right Quadrant, Functional Fit: The aspect of your mind in the objective and collective quadrant (ITS) may consider how this concept will fit with all the other ideas discussed within the book. You may be considering the implications of the concept being explored and be wondering how you will form a complete understanding of the *NeuroPower* framework. As you build a complete understanding about how each thought and idea builds into the entire system of integration contained within this book, you will make an assessment of the functional fit of the constituent parts and their collective arrangement (ITS). 'How does the concept of the *Four Faces of Truth* sequentially build towards an understanding of how truth is assessed?'

ADDING CREATIVITY TO THE INTEGRAL MODEL

The *Four Faces of Truth*, however, excludes a very significant neurobiological axis. This additional dimension is centred about the two types of creativity found in the functional systems dedicated to creative expression, C1 and C2. The C1 dimension refers to lateral creativity that is externally focused and gregarious in nature. C1 finds innovative applications and solutions to the problems of life and is referred to in Greek literature as the Dionysian approach from the Greek god Dionysus. The C2 dimension, in contrast, involves adopting a reflective, introverted and visionary approach to resolve issues. Greek mythology refers to this as the Apollonian approach from the Greek god Apollo. When these axes are inserted into Wilber's matrix, each quadrant is broken into halves (shown in Diagram 1.9). These eight segments each perceive a different aspect of truth and describe the eight Neuro-Rational Types.

NEUROPOWER AND THE JOURNEY OF INTEGRATION

Each of us has a dominant Neuro-Rational Type, however, the story doesn't end there. Throughout our lives, we can each integrate or disintegrate depending on the choices we make and where we choose to focus our attention. Moving through the process of integration can be described as both simple yet difficult. Each of us can see what we need to do but it means breaking our comfortable pattern of avoidance in order to do it.

In contrast, disintegration is complex yet remarkably easy. In disintegration we misuse our creativity to justify and reframe the situation so that we avoid having to do the hard work of internal awareness, pain and integration. In this way, we cling to our habits, neuroses and entrenched games.

We find the process of integration stressful. We usually make the hard step only when the alternatives—which are to do nothing or to continue on the path of disintegration—are even more painful.

Diagram 1.9 NeuroPower's Eight Strategic Mindsets

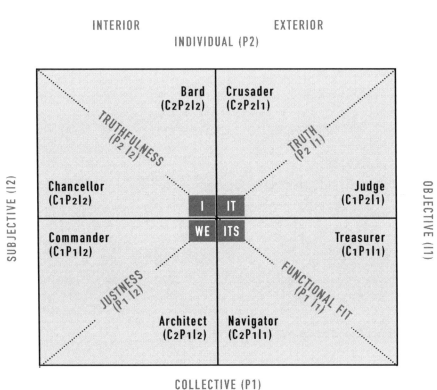

Understanding the processes of integration is essential when leading, managing, coaching, counselling, encouraging or motivating clients, partners, children or friends. This is explored in more detail in Principle #3, *NeuroPower* (Burow, 2013).

YOUR TASK: CONVERTING INSIGHT INTO ACTION (OR 'HOW TO USE THIS BOOK')

Before we start exploring each of the Intelligences in more detail, it may be helpful to consider how you want to apply the framework in your life. Having a clear idea of how you intend to use the information—be it with yourself, your team or your organisation—will help focus your mind on the parts that are most relevant to you and ensure that you convert your new found insight into action.

As we explore each Intelligence, for those who are interested, this book includes some detailed neuroscience behind why people behave the way that they do, including the different neural correlates involved in different responses. If you are new to neuroscience and would like to become more familiar with the different neural structures and how the brain works, you might consider finding a basic neuroanatomy text. One good option, used in many first year neurophysiology courses, is Professor John Pinel's *Biopsychology* (2009).

Chapter 2

Our First Social Cognitive Need:
RELATEDNESS &
The Automatic Function (P1)

RELATEDNESS (P1) AT A GLANCE

Relatedness is our Brain's First Social Cognitive Need

The brain loves being part of a group that is cohesive, fair and safe. The evolution and growth of the prefrontal cortex was driven by the need to survive and thrive by remaining secure within our social groups. People define themselves by the groups they belong to and are highly sensitive to social rejection and exclusion.

Characteristics of the Relatedness (P1) Functional Network

Process and Logic

STRENGTH	WEAKNESS
Consistent and stable, takes one step at a time	Can be slow to reach an outcome through rigid adherence to process

OPPORTUNITY	THREAT
Can lack prioritisation and enthusiasm - may seem disorganised or disinterested	Can get bogged down or paralysed by obstacles

Management Style

- Ordered and logical thinking
- One step at a time
- Process focused and incremental
- Balanced and even-handed

TRIBAL LOYALTY

P1 THINKING
Learned logic

P1 FEELING
Calmness and Stability

P1 SOMATIC
Compliance to learned rules

COMMUNICATION STYLE

- Often feels frustrated if others take the discussion off-track - even if it's a beneficial discussion
- Makes a good impartial chairperson or mediator
- Will logically clarify people when they speak, listen for a lack of logic and highlight it
- Will not understand why people are irrationally angry or moody

KEYWORDS INCLUDE

- Logic
- Control
- Order
- One Step at a Time
- Team before Self
- Family

Relatedness (P1) Helps Us to Survive

Relatedness (P1) helps us both as individuals and the group to survive and thrive by motivating and enabling us to learn and comply with specific social roles and understood social rules.

Relatedness &
The Automatic Function (P1)

RELATEDNESS: OUR BRAIN'S FIRST SOCIAL NEED

Humans are herd animals. From our earliest ancestors, humans have evolved to be part of groups, not only to satisfy needs for interaction and companionship, but most importantly, in order to ensure our own physical survival. The ones who survived were those who could work together to hunt and gather, warn each other about dangers and maintain knowledge by learning from each other. The infants that instinctively stayed in the middle of the group were safer than those that went wandering.

It is not surprising that neuroscientists have discovered our brains are hardwired to keep us safe within our social groups and are wired to raise the alarm at the mere possibility of social exclusion. Studies in the lab of Professor Matthew Lieberman at UCLA have revealed that experience of social exclusion activates the same regions within the brain that are activated when a person experiences physical pain, with the alarm signals just as strong. The brain's interpretation of social exclusion mirrors its interpretation of physical danger.

From an organisational or community perspective, for leaders looking to build a high performance team, their first task is to make sure that each member of the team feels secure in the value they add to the group. This isn't about being liked, it's about being respected and valued for the contribution a person makes to the group. When team members don't feel safe or are unclear on how they add value, they may resort to playing politics in order to maintain their position in the group. These divisive strategies can destroy group cohesion and dramatically reduce the team's performance.

Within the brain, a diverse range of structures and neuronal networks drive us to satisfy our need for Relatedness. Within the *NeuroPower* framework, this set of structures is called the 'P1 Automatic System' (or sometimes the 'P1 network' or 'P1 function') and gives rise to a particular thinking style referred to as 'P1 Intelligence'. The rest of this chapter explores the characteristics, development and maintenance of this P1 functional network in detail.

THE EVOLUTIONARY SOCIAL BRAIN FUNCTION OF RELATEDNESS (P1)

The P1 system enables the individual to survive through:

- Membership of a community (kinship) through compliance with a specific social role and understood social rules, socially known as moral behaviour (Ciaramelli et al., 2007)

- Movement of behaviour from a conscious action to a habitual response, freeing up mental energy for novel situations requiring creative thought (Saling & Phillips, 2007)

- Control of behaviour in terms of thoughts and physical reactions (Lieberman & Eisenberger, 2004)

- Sequencing events and behaviours (Ratey, 2002)

- The sense that we are the author and controller of our actions (Frith, 2002)

BUILDING BELONGING IS A PRIORITY FOR LEADERS

Our brains are wired to enable us to survive by becoming valued members of groups. Members of these tribes tend to put a premium on leaders that are willing to do what is right to protect follower's interests. This is a key role of leadership in all environments although what is in the best interests of the team members changes according to the type of group. Leadership, therefore, is contextual to the work of the group. That is to say, the role of the leader changes depending on the role of the group. In all groups, the effectiveness of the teamwork is directly proportional to the importance of the work needing to be done by a team. If there is no work to be done by the team, there will be no teamwork. From this perspective, the greatest single priority for a leader is to establish the critical nature of the team's work and clarify, from team members, the role they need the leader to play to enable the team to deliver on this work. Nowhere is this more evident than in the military and other uniformed organisations where the life and death of team members is largely determined by the decisions made by leadership. In these organisations it quickly becomes evident just how important it is that team members can trust that the leader will play their role in keeping team members safe. This is critical to team performance.

In teams, before this trust is established, team members display both aggressive and passive aggressive behaviour as they jostle for power and influence for personal gain and security.

In their groundbreaking book *Leadership in Dangerous Situations*, authors Patrick Sweeney, Michael Matthews and Paul Lester (2011) articulate it like this: "To risk their lives and safety, first responders must firmly believe in their leaders, know those leaders care for them, and have confidence that they can make good decisions quickly. This unique set of skills is called dangerous context leadership. Understanding how to operate and inspire in extreme circumstances greatly strengthens any organisation whether military or civilian."

This underpins the idea that of all the social cognitive needs held by both teams and individuals, the most foundational is trust. Trust between leaders and their followers and between members of the group is only achieved when group members feel they are valued by, and belong to, the group. The neural correlates of this social cognitive need link to some of the earliest functional networks established in the infant human brain. Research published by the Society for Personality and Social Psychology (Shnabel et al., 2013) and reported by the Scientific American showed that when ethnic minority students felt they didn't belong to their cohort, their cognitive capacity was significantly compromised. By increasing their feeling of belonging, these under-performing students were able to lift their academic performance by a massive 70 percent over three years. These findings suggest that 'reminders of relational connections boost one's ability to perform well academically'.

As babies we are hardwired from before the dawn of consciousness to do what it takes to belong to a group because, at the most primitive level, group belonging means individual survival.

Recognising the Characteristics of Relatedness (P1)

P1 mental processing has distinct features: it is logical and strives to be objective, analytical and impersonal. It follows accepted procedures, thinks one step at a time, and displays intellectual, emotional and physical control. P1 urges us to obey the desire for calm, social order and structure. P1 is in time (rather than through time), steady, focused and in the present. 'What next?' is the cognitive question of P1.

When accessed, P1 feels grounded. The pace of P1 is measured, even, slow, steady and unhurried. Music to access P1 is a march or a steady beat.

The primary fears assessed by P1 are related to issues that could logically challenge physical survival, abandonment by the group, loss of physical order, tribal conflict or individual selfishness that could threaten the tribe. The primary strengths of P1 are related to tribal/family identity, bonding and the tribal honour code, as well as tribal support and loyalty that give the individual a sense of safety and connection to the physical world.

Early neurobiological research linked many of the characteristics of P1 with the 'dorsal pathway' on the left side of the brain, the left prefrontal cortex and the implicit memory systems that are established immediately following birth (Siegel, 1999). In particular, the rigidity of P1 rules correlates with the formation and characteristics of implicit memory.

Brains with highly functioning P1 have three elements that integrate to deliver a greater sense of stability, security and belonging. The thinking function incorporates learned logic, the feeling state centres around a sense of calmness and belonging, and somatically P1 relates to behavioural compliance with tribal authority or, in contemporary cultures, with the 'rules' of society.

Without an integrated P1, the individual may never experience true contentment or belonging.

From an evolutionary perspective, the social cognitive role of P1 is to maintain the survival of the tribe. This means when an individual accesses the P1 function there is a focus on minimising intra-tribal conflict. The P1 injunction is that conflict within the tribe threatens survival and must therefore be removed. There are three ways individuals respond to the issues around the maintenance of tribal rules. Firstly, they can focus on ensuring rule compliance and playing the role of enforcer; secondly, they can focus on maintaining the social order through strong connection with and loyalty to the leader (or if they are the leader, demanding loyalty from others) or finally, they can ensure the tribe is aware of any danger facing it so that it can prepare for the worst.

The first step of adult integration involves taking tribal rules from the unconscious implicit memory and carefully and consciously examining which are relevant and which need to be discarded. Emotional patterns, world views, rituals, interpersonal relationship rules, spiritual beliefs and even food intake all fall into tribal or family patterns and need examination and re-interpretation.

P1 THINKING – LOGIC, MORAL REASONING, FAIRNESS AND SECURITY

The thinking style associated with P1 is logic. Logic enables the brain to apply previously learned rules of cause and effect to predict the future consequences of current behaviour. As such, P1 thinking draws heavily on brain structures associated with working memory (frontal lobe), mathematical reasoning (frontal and parietal lobes) and socially driven self control (frontal lobes, particularly the lateral prefrontal cortex[1]).

The focus of P1 thinking is to help maintain stability in our external environment (including our social environment). P1 thinking is primarily focused on avoiding disruption to the status quo through compliance with social rules, roles and expectations and has been linked to increased activity in the right prefrontal cortex (Amodio et al., 2004). It provides our motivation to follow rules to avoid being 'in trouble' and experiencing others' anger. It is also the same circuit that motivates us to follow the rules or decisions of our own, that we have etched into our memories after experiencing fear. This 'prevention regulatory focus' has been associated with increased activity in the

---

1   Recent reviews suggest that when we comply with and apply 'if-then' rules recently given to us by others (P1 thinking) these rules are represented in more lateral areas of the prefrontal cortex (Berkman & Lieberman in Moskowitz & Grant, 2009). When these rules are repeated over time, they then become progressively embedded into implicit procedural memory, mediated by both the orbitofrontal cortex and subcortical structures including for example, the basal ganglia (Pascual-Leone et al., 1996; Saling & Phillips, 2007).

Social Pain and Social Cognitive Neuroscience

It hurts to be excluded - and around 10 years ago, there was already a large amount of psychological and social sciences research to indicate that feeling left out can lead to anxiety, depression and self-esteem issues. But focusing on social inclusion was still regarded by many in business as a 'soft' topic that didn't apply to the corporate world.

Then, in 2003, Naomi Eisenberger and Matthew Lieberman at UCLA published a powerful study looking at what happens in the brain when we are excluded.

They found that when you are excluded from a group - even in a simple computer game as part of a lab experiment - the same parts of your brain are activated as if we are in physical pain.

This study sparked a whole series of studies over the following decade and in many ways marks the beginning of the field of social cognitive neuroscience, which seeks to explore and understand human experience based on the foundation observation that our brains are hardwired to think and operate in groups.

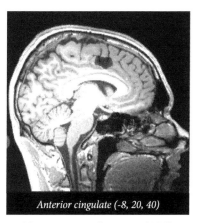

Anterior cingulate (-8, 20, 40)

The anterior cingulate cortex (ACC), indicated here on a structural scan of one of our team member's brains, acts as a 'conflict detector' in the brain and, among other things, is highly sensitive to signs of social exclusion.

precuneus and posterior cingulate cortex (Strauman et al., 2013). A key aspect of this is an aversion to risk and uncertainty, linked to activity in the dorsal medial prefrontal cortex (dMPFC; Xue et al., 2009).[2] P1 thinking is slower, repetitive and more conservative compared to P2 thinking (Crowe & Tory Higgins (1997).

Moral reasoning, which helps us understand and apply moral rules also seems to be linked strongly to activity in both the frontal lobes and areas surrounding the temporoparietal junction (TPJ); Moll et al., 2005). However, more recent research suggests that these different areas are playing quite different roles. Whereas simple moral

2   Xue et al. (2009) found that the dMPFC was activated whenever we make risky decisions, especially if individuals have a bias towards avoiding risk. Conversely, a positive preference for risk (dominant P2) correlated parametrically with increased activation in the ventral MPFC.

judgements based on social norms (Relatedness - P1) draw heavily on the ventromedial prefrontal cortex, the more posterior areas like the TPJ (which is an important part of the brain for integrating complex social information and theory of mind[3]) get called on when there is no clear answer and we need to simulate multiple options and consider their impact on other people before we reach a decision (FeldmanHall, Mobbs & Dalgleish, 2013).

Following on from work done in Professor Matthew Lieberman's lab at UCLA, we also know that the dorsal anterior cingulate, which acts like the brain's 'error detector', is quick to respond at signs of social exclusion.

P1 FEELING – SOCIAL ACCEPTANCE/REJECTION

The feeling states associated with P1 range from positive emotions associated with social acceptance and belonging to feelings of loneliness or panic if isolated from the group. The main neurotransmitters for brain chemicals associated with the P1 system are serotonin, corticotrophin-releasing hormone (CRH) and endorphins (see Appendix 1).

Several groundbreaking studies over the last decade have shown that when an individual's safety within the group is challenged, they typically respond with high levels of distress, anxiety and anger. These correspond with activation in the brain's emotional or limbic system, including those areas associated with the experience of physical pain (Lieberman & Eisenberger, 2004).

In 1998, affective neuroscientist, Jaak Panksepp described in detail a neurobiological mechanism for the emotional experience for this kind of 'FEAR' or 'PANIC', which he observed as common to all mammals. He called it the FEAR Circuit. This circuit spans from the temporal lobe to the anterior and medial hypothalamus through to the lower brainstem and spinal cord. The circuit's temporal lobe includes the central and lateral areas of the amygdala. The circuit's lower brainstem areas include the periventricular gray substance of the diencephalon and mesencephalon and connects to specific autonomic and behavioural output components of the lower brainstem and spinal cord.

Interestingly, the neurochemical mechanisms that help regulate the P1 system are similar to those that are targeted by modern psychiatric drugs used to treat anxiety. GABA receptors are one of the brain's most widespread 'braking mechanisms' (like the brakes in your car) and are found on the surface of neurons throughout the brain and particularly in the cerebral cortex. When GABA binds to GABA receptors it opens channels that allow chloride ions to flow into neurons, which slows down their firing. GABA receptors are highly expressed throughout most of the brain areas that support the P1 system. They exist from the cerebral cortex, right down along the nucleus reticularis, pontis

---

3   These abilities are discussed more in the I2 thinking (Seeing the Facts) section in Chapter 5.

caudalis, the periaqueductal gray and substantia nigra, and continue to the anterior and medial hypothalamus, the ventral amygdalofugal pathway, and the central amygdala. In healthy brains, GABA receptors are activated to inhibit the P1 system to modulate the level of fear or anxiety we experience in daily life. One widespread treatment for anxiety disorders is the use of benzodiazepines (BZs), which enhance the activity of GABA and GABA receptors. Effectively, BZs help hyperpolarise the neuronal fear message carriers to suppress fear. Interestingly, another 'natural' drug - alcohol - also directly activates GABA receptors to sedate the brain.

GABA is the brain's most common inhibitory neurotransmitter and is just one decarboxylation step away from glutamate, the most common excitatory neurotransmitter, and investigations into neuroplasticity suggest that glutamate is a probable excitatory neurotransmitter for this circuit and mediates the learning of fears (Panksepp, 1998).

P1 SOMATIC - HABITUAL BEHAVIOUR

The P1 somatic circuit involves our implicit procedural memory which enables us to complete tasks without needing to give them conscious attention. This is the part of the brain involved when activities become second-nature or habitual.

Our understanding of P1 implicit memory was significantly driven by the case of HM, a young man who underwent radical brain surgery in 1953 in an attempt to treat intractable epilepsy. Unfortunately, the surgery (which removed most of his hippocampus, parahippocampal gyrus and amygdala) had unforeseen consequences.

HM was unable to form new long-term explicit memories and also suffered from temporally graded retrograde amnesia – he could not remember most events in the three to four days before the surgery and some events up to 11 years before then. However, he was able to form new long-term procedural memories, such as motor skills, despite not being able to remember them. HM's personal tragedy was the first evidence that different types of memory involve different parts of the brain. Subsequent research on HM until his death in 2008 enabled scientists to use fMRI to explore his intact implicit procedural memory, particularly in the motor regions of the brain. On 2 December 2009, the Brain Observatory at the University of California, San Diego began an unprecedented anatomical study that aims to create a complete microscopic survey of HM's entire brain. This may well provide further insights about the neurological basis of HM's historical memory impairment, and assist us in gaining an even better understanding of the neural correlates of implicit procedural memory.

P1 and the Link Between Politics and Riding a Bicycle

According to social cognitive neuroscientists, political thinking and bike riding have more in common that you might think. It seems that both involve flexing a common set of mental 'muscles' that support the development and expression of habits (i.e. P1 patterns). Lieberman, Scheiber and Ochsner (2003) identified three common characteristics of habitual behaviours that suggest parallels between the political thinking and cycling:

(1) Both can become routinized and automatic with behavioral repetition.

(2) Once formed, these behaviors are difficult to explain. Just as it is difficult to consciously access and describe the coordinated movements that underlie riding a bike, the bases for decision-making in many domains become less accessible to conscious inspection over time.

(3) We have imperfect introspective access to the mechanisms supporting habitual behaviors; hence, we can lose sight of the forces that trigger and guide their automatic expression. Indeed, decades of social-psychological research have revealed many ways in which thoughts, preferences, and attitudes are influenced by subtle contextual factors, prior habitual thought patterns, and current mood... Similarly, many factors that shape the way we ride a bike—including tire size and inflation, handlebar position, weather, and terrain—can change how we ride, but may do so without any blip on our conscious radar (p. 682).

The link between the two activities is that both involve the implicit procedural memory of the P1 Intelligence.

The Development of Healthy Relatedness (P1)

RELATEDNESS (P1) IS HARDWIRED TO PROMOTE THE CHILD'S SURVIVAL

In the middle of the twentieth century a psychoanalyst and psychiatrist, John Bowlby, turned to animal behaviour studies to develop an idea that profoundly challenged the traditional analytic views of child development (Bowlby, 1969; George and Solomon, 1996). He argued that the nature of the relationship with a child's primary caregiver becomes internalised within the child and, for the infant's lifetime, will determine the degree to which it feels safe, worthy and secure. This breakthrough resulted in a shift in the care of institutionalised children throughout the Western world. (From this time on these children were assigned specific individuals to care for them rather than whoever was available.)

Bowlby's insights were appropriate from a neuroscientific perspective, because the P1 system emerges in the developmental period from the womb to about twelve months. This is the pre-ego stage. The infant is totally dependent and so their identity is merged primarily with their mother and with their environment. The basic needs of infancy are the instinctual needs for survival: holding and nurturing, food and physical comfort, continuity and safety. If the mother is healthy and happy and the environment is safe and nourishing, the child can be expected to emerge with a healthy, strong and integrated P1.

Importantly, the strength of the bond developed between the child and the mother in the first twelve months powerfully shapes the child's brain and has a lasting impact on the nature of the child's P1. Amazingly, researchers have also found that the P1 network can be influenced even before the child is born. For example, Anthony DeCasper (University of North Carolina, Greensboro), has demonstrated that our attachment through voice recognition begins before we are born. In the now famous 'Cat in the Hat' experiment, mothers read to their unborn children in the weeks before birth. After birth, most of these children sucked faster and more enthusiastically when they heard their mothers voice rather than that of a stranger. This suggests that they remembered the sound of their mother's voice from in utero. Once born, the level of emotional synchrony developed within mother-infant pairs during their first year is predictive of the infant's level of self-control (P1) at two years, even after taking into account temperament, IQ and maternal style (Feldman, Greenbaum and Yirmiya, 1999).

The P1 functional network is developed during the stage referred to by German psychologist and psychoanalyst, Erik Erikson as the Trust versus Mistrust stage.

Attachment Provides a Secure Base

Repeated experiences of treatment by parents become encoded in implicit memory as expectations and then as mental models or schemata of attachment, which serve to help the child feel an internal awareness of what Bowlby referred to as a 'secure base' in the world (Bowlby, 1969, 1988). These neurally encoded representations serve as the core of the social brain. While the development of attachment schemata occurs predominantly in children, adults continue to manifest attachment throughout their life span (Parkes, Stevenson-Hinde & Marris, 1991). Particularly under periods of stress an adult will monitor the whereabouts of a few selected 'attachment figures' and seek them out as sources of comfort, advice and strength.

The Importance of Eye Contact

Eye contact is a powerful medium through which a parent translates their internal world to the child. As a child gradually moves away from their parent, they will check back visually to see the expression on a parent's face. If the parent appears calm, then the child will feel confident to explore further, whereas a frightened look will decrease exploration. The process through which the parent's internal world is automatically transferred to the child is referred to as social referencing (Gunnar and Stone, 1984).

If the infant develops a sense of trust that their needs will be met by their primary caregivers, as they grow they will typically trust the world and himself or herself. With a healthy P1, the child can confidently move on to the next phase of exploring the world, confident that it is a safe place to be (Sigelman and Rider, 2006).

As discussed before, many of the attributes of the P1 Intelligence arise from its developmental process. Bowlby's proposition in the late 1960s has since been extensively studied and given rise to the field of *Attachment Theory*, which explores the complex relationship between an infant and its caregivers, and the ramifications of that relationship on the infant's future development. Even from before birth, Attachment Theory argues that our interpersonal experiences become organised into schemas (or basic templates) for attachment (Bowlby, 1969) that form implicit procedural memories incorporating sensory, motor, affective and cognitive memories. These attachment schemas direct our attention by providing ongoing and often unconscious input about dangerous situations. Furthermore, the interactions with attachment figures contribute to the organisation and integration of neural networks that give the child the capacity for self-regulation (Siegel, 1999).

Mary Ainsworth, a professor in developmental psychology at the University of Virginia, collaborated with Bowlby at the Tavistock Clinic in the 1950s (Bowlby, 1969; Bretherton, 1992). Her idea was to study mother-infant interactions over the first year of life, and then to place the child within situations that would trigger their attachment system. This was achieved by bringing each mother-infant pair into a laboratory setting. At various times in the twenty-minute procedure, the infant stayed with the mother, with the mother and a stranger, with only the stranger, and then on its own for up to three minutes. Her theory was that separating a one-year-old from their attachment figure within a strange environment should activate the infant's responses to separation. Ainsworth found that the infants' behaviour at reunion fell into specific patterns of response that reflected how securely the infant was attached to its mother (Ainsworth et al., 1978) and that these categories corresponded to the independently performed home observation ratings for the year prior to the laboratory assessment. This laboratory measure is called the Ainsworth or Infant-Strange Situation (Ainsworth et al., 1978). Ainsworth's Baltimore study has been replicated throughout the world with consistent results.

Another study that explores the P1 social cognitive need through the lens of infant attachment was conducted using a process called the Adult Attachment Interview (AAI) (George and Solomon, 1996). The AAI is a 'narrative assessment of the interviewee's state of mind with respect to attachment' (Main and Goldwyn, 1998; Main, 1995; Hesse, 1999). The AAI is undertaken by an interviewer asking open-ended questions about an adult's childhood relationships and experiences. Their responses enable researchers to conduct a linguistic analysis of the coherence of the narrative's organisation and presentation (Hesse, 1999). Four categories result from research with the AAI, correlating with the results of both in-home observations of mother-child dyads and of the Infant-Strange Situation. The AAI reflects an ingrained state of mind within the interviewee that has a significant impact on later character and archetype development.

Of all available measures – including intellectual functioning, personality assessments, and socioeconomic factors – the AAI is the most robust predictor of how effectively infants have become attached to their parents (van Ijzendoorn, 1992, 1995; Sagi et al., 1994; Hesse, 1999). To contextualise the rates of attachment security, it has been found that in low-risk, non-clinical populations, 55-65 percent of infants are securely attached (Ainsworth et al., 1978).

A wide range of attachment studies have found that by 12 months old, a child will have formed deeply encoded attachments with its parents. The nature of these attachments results in significant differences in behaviour when the child is around its mother or father (Siegel,

---

Infant P1 Injunctions Can Impact Our Adult Lives

We all have absolute P1 injunctions that we unconsciously apply to the way we live our lives. ('**Always** eat everything on your plate,' for example.) Many of these deeply held practices come from our earliest experiences. With repeated feedback, the infant's brain detects similarities and differences across experiences. From these comparative processes, the infant makes generalised representations that are encoded within the brain. These generalisations form the basis of prototypal 'mental models' that help the child to interpret present experiences and to anticipate future ones. These mental models are important because they allow the brain to act as an 'anticipation machine', constantly scanning the environment, trying to determine what will come next and to avoid pain (Freyd, 1987). In many cases they also provide a level of certainty that save us from learning everything from first principles every time.

1999). By 18 months, the child's brain will have developed explicit memory. It is thought that this enables the child to bring forward in its mind the sensory image of the parent in order to help calm and regulate its emotional state (Schore, 1994; Hofer, 1994). If the child is securely attached, they will be calmed by an image of their parent; if the attachment is insecure, they are likely to be anxious, distant or fearful. In adult life this reaction is often projected onto mother and father figures, authority figures and leaders.

Infants seek proximity to their attachment figures because this provides them with a sense of security. Bonding activity, such as proximity seeking, cooing, cuddling or gazing into the eyes, between a mother and an infant involves a biochemical cascade (including the secretion of oxytocin, prolactin, endorphins and dopamine) that not only produces positive and rewarding feelings in the pair but also stimulates the structural development of the brain (Panksepp, 1998; Schore, 1994). The release of these opiates serves to strongly reinforce and shape preferences from early in life (Kehoe and Blass, 1989). These chemicals help us feel safe and relaxed, which are two emotional hallmarks of a well-functioning P1. When naltrexone, a drug that blocks the effect of many endogenous opioids released through attachment activity, was administered to infant primates their clinging behaviour increased (Kalin, Shelton and Lynn, 1995). This same effect has been demonstrated in rodents (Panksepp, Nelson and Siviy, 1994) and also in dogs (as measured by increases in tail wagging) (Knowles, Conner and Panksepp, 1989). As children grow they internalise their relationships with their attachment figures. This process is facilitated by release of these opioids, which reinforce the network of visceral, motor, sensory and emotional memories that will be evoked in times of stress and can support the ability to regulate emotion.

PHYSICALITY AND A SENSE OF SAFETY HELP BUILD RELATEDNESS

Infants sense the world through their body. Johnson (1987) suggests that it is the experience which our bodies provide that forms the internal basis for meaning and reasoning. He even argues that the physical experiences of the body provide an orientation for mental processing.

Various studies have suggested that physical touch may also have a significant influence on the establishment of stress modulating functions in adulthood (Meaney et al., 1989; Plotsky and Meaney, 1993). Research has shown that rats stroked and nurtured during infancy show more open field activity (i.e. are more inclined to explore new environments; Levine, Haltmeyer, Karas and Denenberg, 1967), increased gene expression and higher levels of stress inhibitors in the hippocampi than control rats that are not handled (Meaney et al., 1989, 2000). These changes remained well into the rats' lives, indicating that the early establishment of these physiological setpoints relating to the individual's ability to emotionally cope with life's stresses and surprises may continue

What is Implicit Memory?

The manifestation of P1 links the individual with their implicit memories from childhood. These implicit memories provide a structured and understandable explanation of the world around us in the form of behavioural, perceptual and emotional learning (Bauer, 1996; Schachter, 1996; Emde, 1990; Fivush and Hudson, 1990). Since this implicit memory is encoded within parts of the brain that do not require conscious processing during retrieval (Bauer, 1996; Schachter, 1996; Emde, 1990; Fivush and Hudson, 1990) the individual accessing P1 may be unaware that they are accessing models of reality based on a child's understanding. Consequently, when the adult is enforcing P1 rules, it is the equivalent of enforcing a view of reality which is seen as 'ultimate truth' and as timeless. Any threat to these mental models triggers unconscious defence mechanisms within the body.

over a lifetime.[4]

Unfortunately, it is often forgotten that the body has an intelligence of its own and that touch is essential to calm young children. As a result, children who are raised without touch and other somatic expressions of reassurance and safety can develop a dissociation between mind and body, focusing only on the intellectual need for safety but never experiencing a sense of security. As adults, these individuals are often highly anxious. Until the child learns how and when to focus their attention on their somatic P1 they will feel unsafe in the world.

High-functioning somatic P1 can be actively developed through tailored physical exercise. One example of a yoga exercise to access and balance P1 is aptly called 'planting the stump', which involves steady and strong movements. The exercise starts by planting your feet firmly on the ground and imagining wrapping your arms around a huge vertical log and heaving it down while simultaneously exhaling with a 'huh'. Exercises like this are designed to evoke and strengthen the mind's ability to access somatic P1.

---

4   More recently, researchers have shown that when female rats are stressed by isolation before mating, their offspring are also affected, showing blunted neurohormonal responses to painful physical stimuli (Pisu et al., 2013). This and many other studies are now starting to show us that in addition to our own environment and the DNA that makes up our genes, our parents' lives may also directly influence basic aspects of our temperament and our own experience.

Tribal Beliefs (P1) Have Strengths and Weaknesses

The P1 Intelligence enables the individual to apply faith, a belief in community, and control, to maintain a sense of stability. When somebody is accessing P1 they assess others by asking themselves, 'Do you look, smell or sound like those of my tribe?' P1 asks 'who?', 'when?', 'how?' and 'what?' but never 'why?' The role of this Intelligence is to not challenge the wisdom of the tribe.

The infant is born into a family from which it absorbs the collective consciousness and willpower as it absorbs the family's strengths and weaknesses, beliefs, superstitions and fears. These influences can be both positive and negative. Later in life, an important integration task is to contextualise this implicit tribal world in their current life. This involves moving beyond literal implicit thinking to symbolic explicit thinking.

The beliefs of the tribe form the emerging child's world view; the world is either safe or dangerous, abundant or poverty stricken, educated or ignorant, a place to take from or to give to. Tribal power protects the tribe from damaging external influences (just as the immune system does for the body). There is a sense of power in sharing and acting on the beliefs of the family or community. The consequences of such actions can be either for the greater good or they can be destructive or vengeful. One downside to this social immunity is that no individual takes responsibility for their own actions. At a trial the perpetrator of P1 violence will claim they were only doing what was 'right'.

It is a task of adult P1 integration to become conscious of actions which are prompted by unconscious, outdated family or tribal beliefs. We need to take responsibility for our own behaviour and not excuse it with 'tribal reasoning'. We need to re-examine our family beliefs in the light of our current context, insight, responsibility and values. It is important for our physical and mental health to include in our examination beliefs about our life expectancy, the time we should retire, where we should live, whether to save or spend and even where to invest our money.

If our conscious plans are unconsciously based on family or tribal beliefs, our assumptions can prevent us from changing and expanding our horizons. Adult maturity involves breaking belief patterns that have limited relevance but still have a seemingly inexplicable power over us.

LOYALTY, HONOUR AND JUSTICE — THE UPSIDE OF ATTACHMENT

As we have explored, the human infant has an inbuilt system within the brain that influences and organises emotional, motivational and memory processes with respect to significant caregiving figures. At the most basic level these systems increase the chances of the infant's survival. Neurologically, attachment establishes an interpersonal relationship that helps the immature brain of the infant to use the mature functions of the parent's brain to organise its own processes (Hofer, 1994).

From the healthy family or tribe the developing child learns the virtue of Tribal Loyalty. This virtue is important to the health and security of both the tribe and the individual members. Tribal Loyalty is the human bond in the family or group which ensures reliability, especially in a crisis. It implies keeping one's word and acting with integrity, and imbues strength, dignity and pride in oneself, which is a good basis for further development. The child learns to trust society and to respect themselves, and so see the world as a trustworthy place. Of course, if the child sees in its family a lack of commitment and respect, they will grow up with this code of (mis)behaviour.

In this way, tribal justice is learned in the family or tribe. This, too, is specific to the tribe. The tribe's justice might dictate, 'Do unto others as you would be done by', or it might say 'an eye for an eye'. We see this noticeably in international relations, where a whole nation will call for aggression in the name of justice.

Exploring and understanding implicit junctions and P1 tribal reasoning can help an outsider make sense of what seems to be strange or illogical in an individual or a group. It can also help you as an individual to free yourself from unconstructive patterns of behaviour that are based on tribal logic rather than contextual insight based on your own personal wisdom.

EMOTIONS RELATED TO FOLLOWING RULES

While the tribal rules are being followed, the person accessing P1 feels safe, grounded, cheerful, certain and self-confident. They appear calm, unhurried and controlled. These emotions stem from the groundedness and certainty of the tribe or family. It is important to remember that rule following is essential for the survival of the tribe. The impulse to survive is instinctual; it is built into the brain and tells the infant that to defend itself it must connect to its environment.

Our P1 emotional state often changes according to whether the tribal rules are being upheld. If the rules are broken, the emotion changes to anger, self-righteousness, rule-bound intolerance and a need to control.

However, when the P1 individual is relaxed and confident that their rules are being upheld, P1 can feel free to be sanguine and tolerant.

P1 RULE FOLLOWING AT WORK

At its best, P1 Intelligence fosters consistency and stability. However, at its extreme, P1 Intelligence can become a weakness, entrenching us into inflexibility and a need to control at the first sign of instability or conflict. Conflict triggers P1 into personal and group control, using the childhood family as its source of rules.

As the individual matures, rule-following behaviour is extended from the family to work, where the rules are the accepted practices of the organisation. Here, individuals high in P1 assume that 'If only everyone would follow the rules we would be fine.' Conflict within the tribe or organisation is seen by P1 as a threat to the tribe's survival and so the person accessing somatic P1 will naturally try to control the situation by demanding everyone follow the rules.

Organisational culture is so embedded in employees' P1 that P1-driven behaviour resembles something Dr Herbert Spiegel, leading New York psychiatrist and author, calls a 'Compulsive Triad', which is not dissimilar to an individual who has been hypnotised. This Compulsive Triad has three characteristics:

1. *The individual commits an act resulting from post-hypnotic suggestion* (i.e. we do things because the cultural environment cues us to do so);

2. *The individual has amnesia to the signal that triggers the action* (i.e. we are not aware of these cues); and

3. *The individual shows post-event rationalisation of the act* (i.e. when challenged, we recruit the brain's reasoning and narrative-making areas to reconstruct a justification for our behaviour).

In this way it is often virtually impossible for culturally hypnotised employees to see the culture of their own organisation or check whether it is helping achieve corporate objectives - but it is much easier to see the culture of another organisation and the apparent hypnotism acted out by others.

When confronted with tasks without structure or procedure, P1 encourages behaviour that either freezes – not knowing where to start – or mindlessly follows instructions even when they are clearly failing to deliver their intended outcomes.[5] Furthermore, P1 completes tasks one at a time, so will not want to start a new task before completing the existing one. This can be an issue when the new task has a higher priority for the needs of the workplace.

P1 appears calm and dispassionate, excellent for settling down others. But P1's lack of passion and a lack of contextual prioritising can be misinterpreted by others as a lack of interest or commitment.

People who rely heavily on their P1 function have an opportunity for growth if they are able to learn how not to get bogged down or paralysed by obstacles that fall outside the solutions provided by precedent.

P1'S INFLUENCE ON OTHER INTELLIGENCES AND ROLES

P1 rules may include those determining how an individual expresses the other Intelligences. P1 rules dictate when it is appropriate to use C1, P2, I2, I1 and C2. For

---

5   Throughout more than twenty years of working with middle managers right up to senior executives, I consistently hear complaints from team leaders complaining that 'I am the only one doing the thinking' or 'My team act like children - everything needs to be constantly supervised.' These are classic signs of a team that has collapsed into P1-driven compliance (obsessive passion). This obsessive passion stands in stark contrast to what social researcher Robert J. Vallerand (2003) described as harmonious passion, where an individual is achieving their own objectives with a sense of autonomy and control. These are discussed more in Chapter 4 on the social need of Leading the Pack (P2).

P1 Affect and Social Standing

Serotonin, a chemical in the brain that is linked with the absence of anxiety, seems to be critical to the functioning of P1. Male monkeys who have made it to the leadership position in their tribe show increased serotonin in the left prefrontal lobes and a corresponding lift in mood. In contrast, monkeys who are still fighting to get to the leadership position (and higher in Leading the Pack (P2), *discussed in Chapter 4*) show decreased levels of serotonin in the left prefrontal lobes and experience much higher levels of stress (Siegel, 1999).

example, in some cultures (P1), self-expression (C1) is not encouraged; in others (such as Australia) it is promoted almost to excess. In this way P1 has a disproportionately large influence on the formation of the infant's personality. This blurs the distinction between nature and nurture when considering how our Neuro-Limbic Type personalities are formed.[6]

Poorly Functioning P1 and Neurotic Compliance

Our research suggests that approximately 30 percent of the population default to accessing their P1 rules in a crisis. If their P1 is functioning poorly, this can lead quickly from crisis into personal neurosis. In her book, *Our Inner Conflicts* (1945), Dr Karen Horney gives a detailed description of the traits of co-dependent neurotic patients she treated as a psychiatrist. She also explains the thinking which produced their behaviour, which she classifies as *moving towards* people. People such as these clients have compulsive, neurotic needs for affection and approval, especially the need to be important to a special partner, who they expect will make them happy. This need is indiscriminate; they disregard their own feelings, desires and discrimination regarding the worth of the other, seeing only what they have in common. Indeed, they see everyone as 'nice'.

These needs arise from the person's world view; they see themselves as helpless in a hostile world, and so they seek affection from someone who they hope will protect and guide them. The person most attractive to them is usually therefore the most aggressive one.

Horney (1945) argues that this neurotic behaviour arises directly from a person's inner conflict. For the compliant type of person with a poorly functioning P1, she sees the inner conflict as having a distinct dynamic. Firstly, the person denies their need

6   For more detail on Neuro-Limbic Types, see Principle #2, *NeuroPower* (Burow, 2013).

for affection, approval and acceptance. This denial is a way of dealing with their fear of becoming vulnerable or emotionally involved with others. This disconnection inevitably leads to a profoundly selfish, aggressive and 'egocentric' world view, which directly conflicts with their belief that they are loving, giving and affectionate people who turn themselves inside out to love whatever the cost. Finally, unaware of this internal conflict they look outside themselves for resolution. Believing that all their frenetic demands for attention and approval is authentic love and affection, the neurotically compliant type develops three dysfunctional characteristics.

Poorly Functioning P1 Thinking

The first set of characteristics initially appear to be endearing. They display sensitivity to the needs of others (especially when the needs are similar to their own), and self-denial and compliance, which they justify as unselfishness. This need is also undiscriminating. However, denying their own feelings and judgement (which may tell them that the people they pursue are untrustworthy), they make themselves believe everyone is 'nice'. This sets them up for disappointment when they become victims, which in turn fosters more insecurity.

Poorly Functioning P1 Somatic

The second set of characteristics associated with the person with a poorly functioning P1 are related to an attitude of appeasement – peace at any price. This person is too afraid and too 'nice' to show egotism, aggression or even assertion, too 'nice' to steal the limelight or compete, or even to follow their own selfish goals. They are self-effacing and sweet to everyone. If conflict arises, they avoid attack by becoming conciliatory and apologetic, and will even take the blame themselves, rather than accuse others. Once again they deny their own feelings of innocence, criticism, resentment or aggression since these are 'bad qualities'. All this appeasing is designed to draw fire away from themselves. In practice, they are setting themselves up for exploitation.

Poorly Functioning P1 Feeling

The third set of characteristics relate to a sense of worthlessness and helplessness. The neurotic person is so self-effacing and dependent on others that they are unable to enjoy their own company or their own pursuits (this is often accompanied by a poorly functioning P2 – we will look at that Intelligence later). They sense themselves as empty, as having nothing inside them. They feel weak and helpless, which becomes a self-fulfilling prophecy. They also use this stance to stave off attack, along the lines of, 'You wouldn't hurt or desert/blame/not love poor little helpless me!'

As well as feeling helpless, Horney argued that this person has a pervading sense of their own inferiority and incompetence, even in areas of obvious competence. Around aggressive or arrogant people they feel even more stupid. We have seen how childhood abuse sets people up for feelings of low self-esteem. As a result of their belief that they are worthless, such a person depends on others for their feelings of self-worth. Their self-esteem, therefore, see-saws with the feedback they get from others. Worse, any criticism or rejection by others is seen as a disaster and the poor 'victim' will turn themselves inside out to regain the person's regard. Of course this neurotic's attitudes of self-abasement and consequent insecurity and dependence on others invites exploitation and makes them particularly vulnerable when others do exploit them or even simply fail to give them all the support, appreciation and affection they crave.

It is important to remember that although we suppress unwanted emotions, they are still there and surface in subconscious behaviour. Therefore, while this neurotic type of person suppresses their inevitable feelings of egotism and self-will – their criticism, resentment, aggression and so on – these feelings are still manifested, but usually in ways which are acceptable to this person's strict code of P1 behaviour. So they will, for example, make demands out of helplessness, or control out of 'love'. Repressed anger may surface as irritability or temper tantrums, or if totally denied may affect the person's health. Occasional lapses of temper can be justified, of course, because as we have seen, the person's self-abasement and dependence can invite abuse.

Horney's research explains that the neurotic's 'good' behaviour is motivated by a desire either to avoid hostility or to avoid their need to excel[7]. In some cases, if they let others exploit them, they may be motivated by a reactive fear of their own capacity to exploit others themselves.

The sad thing about the neurotic with a poorly functioning P1 is that they mistake their compliant, affectionate feelings – which are really based on need – as real love.

They never realise how excessive and egocentric their constant demands are, and how controlling they can be in their loving. Yet for them love is everything. Nothing has meaning without it.

The reality is that because of the irrational and compulsive nature of the neurotic's drive, this 'love' which can never be satisfied becomes the sole focus of the person's attention.

There is a strange logic in the reasoning of the neurotically compliant person's world view. Love as an attachment answers all their conscious and unconscious needs: the need to like and be liked; the need to dominate (in the guise of love); the need to use their initiative and work off their aggression (on behalf of the other and so for a 'good' cause); even the need to excel (in the lover's eyes) without the stress of being out in front; and above all, the need not to have to be assertive (after all, the beloved should know

---

7   This drive is part of the Leading the Pack (P2) social cognitive need, described in Chapter 4.

what they need), or to defend themselves (because the beloved will love them for their helplessness and protect them).

All this, of course, is a vain hope. At best they will find a co-dependent relationship, which is intrinsically unhealthy anyway. Usually they remain unaware of their neurosis, and their relationships end in great pain. Feeling that they are nothing when they are alone, solitary pursuits are meaningless. This person seeks love or, if desperate, sexual intimacy, yet in reality they remain detached; they are afraid of being emotionally involved (Horney, 1945).

The only way out for the compulsively compliant person is first of all to recognise their inner conflict – their repressed attributes of aggression and even destructiveness, their egocentricity (the repressed P2 Intelligence) and 'victim' mentality versus their kindness and caring thoughtfulness for others. They need to be aware and observe the polarities, and hold them, both 'good' and 'bad' in their awareness – not with a view to resolving the conflict, but to reconcile the two opposite intentions, to accept them and live with them and the energy they generate.

From Cradle to Grave: The Impact of P1 Over a Lifetime

How can rules embedded in the P1 Intelligence so young have such a strong impact on adult life? I have found one of the most effective lenses to help understand this is an approach which first became popular in the mid 1970s, called Transactional Analysis or TA. In 1976, Thomas Harris published the book *I'm OK You're OK* , which popularised the Transactional Analysis school of thought that had been developed by renowned New York Freudian psychiatrist, Dr Eric Berne. In many ways this book was one of the first attempts to translate insights from neuroscience into a practical interpretation of internal conflicts and lived experience.

In his book, published long before neuroscientists had access to today's sophisticated fMRI brain imaging technologies, Harris argued that there is an information highway that connects the left prefrontal lobe (which early evidence suggested was linked to P1) and the right temporal lobe (which had been linked to immediate emotional experience). This, was how he explained the observation that family rules stored in the P1 Intelligence don't feel to the individual like an injunction or a memory from the past; instead, they feel as if they are happening right here, right now. He then proposed that scripting, dreams or direct downloading, and experience feel equally immediate and real because they are experienced through parts of the right temporal lobe that are focused on the present moment. To explore this a little deeper, it is useful to have a high level of understanding of the principles of the theory of Transactional Analysis.

In his clinical work, psychiatrist and author Dr Eric Berne observed that every person carries inside them three parts (or aspects of themselves) that seem to emerge quite separately in real time as the person interacts with others. As Harris (1976) explains:

> *[A]s you watch and listen to people you can see them change before your eyes. It is a total kind of change. There are simultaneous changes in facial expression, vocabulary, gestures, posture and body functions, which may cause the face to flush, the heart to pound, or the breathing to become rapid ...*

> *Changes from one state to another are apparent in manner, appearance, words, and gestures... Continual observation has supported the assumption that these three states exist in all people. It is as if in each person there is the same little person he was when he was three years old. There are also within him his own parents. These are recordings in the brain as actual experiences of internal and external events, the most significant of which happened during the first five years of life. There is a third state, different from these two. The first two are called Parent and Child, and the third, Adult.*

> *These states of being are not roles but psychological realities. Berne says that Parent, Adult, and Child are not concepts like superego, ego, and id but phenomenological realities. The state is produced by the playback of recorded data of events in the past, involving real people, real times, real places, real decisions and real feelings.* (pp. 16-18)

This concept has direct relevance to three of the Intelligences. Briefly, the Parent state is the articulation of P1. The Child state is the articulation of C1 and the Adult is the articulation of the adult Neuro-Rational Type[8] (which starts to emerge as the child individuates and develops their P2 Intelligence). Harris explains the P1 Parent in more depth:

> *The Parent is a huge collection of recordings in the brain of imposed, unquestioned external events perceived by a person between birth and age five (a taught concept of life).*

> *The name Parent is most descriptive of this data inasmuch as the most significant 'tapes' are those provided by the example and pronouncements of a person's own parents or parent substitutes. Everything the child saw his parents do and everything he heard them say is recorded in the Parent.*

---

8   The Neuro-Rational Types are our higher order, conscious personalities that form when we access three Intelligences simultaneously (a phenomenon known as parallel processing). This gives rise to a unique world view and Area of Mastery that is invaluable in the team context. For more detail about the Neuro-Rational Types, see Principle # 2, *NeuroPower* (Burow, 2013).

Everyone has a Parent and each Parent is specific for every person, being the recording of that set of early experiences unique to him. Interestingly the data was recorded straight without editing. (1976, pp. 18-19)

The child takes in all the information uncritically because he or she is too young, too dependent and does not possess the language skills to be able to analyse, edit or explain its meaning critically.

Harris continues:

In the Parent are recorded all the admonitions and rules and laws that the child heard from his parents and saw in their living. They range all the way from the earliest parental communications, interpreted non-verbally through tone of voice, facial expression, cuddling or non-cuddling, to the more elaborate verbal rules or regulations espoused by the parents as the little person became able to understand words. In this set of recordings are the thousands of 'nos' directed at the toddler, the directed 'don'ts' that bombarded him. They are recorded as the truth from the source of all security, the people who are six feet tall. A time when it is important to a two foot tall child that he please and obey them. It is a permanent recording. A person cannot erase it. It is available for replay throughout life. This replay is a powerful influence throughout life. These examples – coercing, forcing, sometimes permissive but more often restrictive – are rigidly internalised as a voluminous set of data essential to the individual's survival in the setting of a group, beginning with the family, and extending throughout life in a succession of groups necessary to life.

(1976, pp. 19-21)

However, when the recording in the Parent is inconsistent, as when the child's parent says one thing and does the opposite, or when the two parents disagree in their rules, and the recording is discordant, the child becomes confused or fearful. In these cases the P1 is weakened or fragmented, and the rules in this area will not be a strong positive influence in the person's life (Harris, 1976).

Included in the vast amount of Parent data are all the 'how to' instructions: how to hit a nail, eat soup, shake hands or pretend no one's at home. This data is useful as long as it is relevant to the real world of the person. It is our task as adults to take another look at and sift through these instructions for relevance to our current world view.

Throughout life, whenever a person consciously focuses on something, the brain lays down memories as vivid, specific and detailed as a video tape recording, often stored in the unconscious mind. These memories are stored in the temporal cortex, which is the part of the brain used when the person is making meaning of current events. That's why past

Do Babies Pick Up Stress?

An infant will experience trauma if they are separated from parents, looking into the eyes of a depressed mother, or are in a household with a high level of marital tension (Cogill, Caplan, Alexandra, Robson and Kumar, 1986; Lupien et al., 2009). This was discovered by monitoring the chemical changes within an infant's body that indicate a stress response (Gunnar, 1992).

More recently, neuroimaging studies have confirmed that even when asleep, infants' brains showed distinct patterns of activity corresponding to different emotional tones and that tension at home has a lasting impact on brain responses. Compared with babies raised in healthy homes, infants in high-conflict homes (as reported by their mothers) had a greater response to angry voices in brain regions involved in stress and emotion regulation — the rostral anterior cingulated cortex, the caudate, the thalamus and the hypothalamus (Graham et al., 2013). Children from chronically high-conflict families have less gray and white matter in the anterior cingulate cortex (an important area for social cognition and regulating our stress responses), and this reduction predicted poorer performance on spatial memory tasks (Hanson et al., 2012).

events can impact on the meaning given to present events. The memory is complete and intact even if the person is unaware of and unable to voluntarily recall it. Amazingly, these memories can be involuntarily evoked at any time by stimuli such as sound, sight or smell.

For example, if the event was recorded when the person was five years old, if it is later triggered, they relive the event as a five-year-old. This means they simultaneously experience the past event together with the current event with all the feelings of the five-year-old. For that moment, the person is back in the original event with exactly the same feelings they had at the time the brain recorded it. Further, the person gives the event the same meaning as they did when the tape was laid down. So when accessing P1, the reason the rules seem vital is because the event relating to the source of the rules feels as if it is happening in real time – right now (Harris, 1976).

P1 AND TRANSACTIONAL ANALYSIS (TA)

Transactional Analysis (TA) also provides a useful and accurate model for analysing our interactions with others. Harris (1976) outlines Berne's definition of TA as follows:

The Attachment Window

The repeated activation of specific neuronal pathways creates, reinforces and strengthens connections between groups of neurons and consequently macro systems within the brain. Neurons that do not get activated are not reinforced and can eventually die away completely.

Researchers learned early on that there are critical periods in development, like 'windows of opportunity', during which our environment has a vital impact on the development of specific functions. For instance, when kittens are raised in an environment that gives them no exposure to horizontal lines within a specific critical period of their development, then their visual cortex does not develop the capacity to process such visual input later in life (Hubel, 1967). Similarly, infants who are not exposed to any spoken language are dramatically impaired in their ability to acquire normal linguistic functions after the first few years of life (Schuman, 1997).

In a similar way, infants who have poor or absent attachment relationships (such as an infant in an orphanage that lacks sufficient staff so that attachments do not develop) before the end of their third year of life may find it extremely difficult to form attachments later in life and ever feel secure (Bowlby, 1988; Colin, 1996).

The unit of social intercourse is called a transaction. If two or more people encounter each other.... Sooner or later one of them will speak, or give some indication of acknowledging the presence of others. This is called the transactional stimulus. Then another person will say or do something which is in some way related to the stimulus, and that is called a transactional response.

Transactional Analysis is the method of examining this one transaction wherein 'I do something and you do something back' and determining which part of the multiple-natured individual is being activated.

As we have seen, the three parts of the individual are the Parent (P1), the Child (C1), and the Adult (the Neuro-Rational Type).[9] It is a useful exercise to analyse our incidents

---

9   In some cases, however, the individual's narrative about themselves is focused not around their Neuro-Rational Type but rather on their more reactive selves. When this happens, the Adult part of the self is more likely to reflect the individual's P2 Intelligence than their Neuro-Rational Type, and the content of this P2 reaction will depend on how the individual unconsciously

of conflict by using TA. In this way we can discern when we lapse into our Parent (P1) or our Child (C1) or are accessing our Adult.

TRAUMAS AND ABUSE IN INFANCY CAN IMPACT P1 DEVELOPMENT

If the infant's basic needs are not met – if they are not nurtured and nourished and they don't feel safe – the child will have a sense that the world is hostile and not to be trusted. This can negatively impact on subsequent stages of their development.

Childhood traumas such as abuse, accidents or even illnesses can damage a formerly highly functioning P1, since the child's survival is threatened.

Early traumatic experiences also impact on biochemical levels and neuroanatomical networking. Prenatal stress may result in permanent alterations in dopamine activity and cerebral lateralisation, making infants more susceptible to anxiety and limiting their functioning well into adulthood (Field et al., 1988). This can create a tendency to dissociate and disconnect various elements of processing, and a bias towards unintegrated information processing across conscious awareness, sensation, affect and behaviour. General dissociative defence mechanisms result in an aberrant organisation of neural networks of memory. If the child is frightened, it results in deficits of affect regulation, attachment and executive functioning (van der Kolk et al., 1996). The malfunctioning of these interdependent mental systems results in many disorders. Compulsive disorders related to eating or gambling, borderline personality disorder, and self-harm can all reflect complex adaptation to infant trauma (Saxe et al., 1994; van der Kolk et al., 1996).

Judith (1996) argues that the survival instinct is part of being human and that when an infant's needs are satisfied, they can develop a well-functioning P1. In this situation, their survival instinct, instead of putting their senses on red-alert, will retreat into the background of their consciousness.

However, when the developing infant's survival instinct is constantly threatened, as happens when they live in a violent or chaotic environment, their P1 is damaged. Hence they grow up with a pervasive sense of insecurity. They may have recurring issues related to survival, such as housing, work, health or money. Judith's research suggests that the following traumas suffered in childhood can affect the individual's development, even into adulthood:

Birth traumas: There is a whole generation of people for whom the birth experience was traumatic. Born under glaring lights, they were immediately separated from their mother for the first week of life, except for the brief periods of

balanced the competing needs and scripting of their Parent and Child selves. Regardless of how sophisticated this management strategy was, a key developmental step for the individual involves shifting from a reactive 'Adult' position (which is emotional and driven by the limbic system) to the more considered, rational and mature world view of their Neuro-Rational Type.

feeding. Worse, baby boys were circumcised without being anaesthetised. Children who experienced a traumatic birth almost always have increased P1-related issues, such as being more likely to cry, being needy and having various health issues. If the parent does not respond to the pleas and cries from the child, the child may not learn to invite the positive support it needs.

Incubators: If an infant is put into an incubator from birth they are denied the mother's touching and suckling. This can result in an adult feeling a sense of distance and isolation in relation to others.

Abandonment: Physical or emotional abandonment influences the infant's survival. A child needs the mother's touch. Institutionalised babies who have been deprived of touch often die. However, any separation from parents is traumatic for a young child, especially if it is for more than a day or so. A lengthy time in hospital, long holidays or divorce can be traumatic, especially if the child does not receive extra attention. Similarly, adopted babies are abandoned for a time and the new parents should give them more than the usual amount of care to compensate.

Abandonment in the formative years often creates an over-reliance on P1, with the individual overcompensating by clinging to security, food, loved ones or routine. The person will cling to money or an unsatisfactory situation for fear of being alone or desperate. Without trust in life, they fear change. For others, abandonment as a child causes them to abandon themselves as adults. For instance, they abandon a course, a project, or even their body, forgetting to care for it. Abandonment can also be seen as including neglect, which often results in an inability to trust others or treat oneself well.

Feeding difficulties: Poor nourishment or difficulty with breast feeding or eating can have a lasting impact. It can result in adult problems with food, allergies, addictions or avoidance, or digestive problems. It can also cause wider nourishment issues such as lack of partaking in friendships or intellectual or creative stimulation.

Physical abuse: Since the abuse usually comes from the home, physical abuse leads to the child living in fear. This can stimulate stress hormones, which in turn may lead the child to become addicted to abnormally high levels of these hormones in order to overcome the numbness from the body. In extreme cases, the person may become accident-prone or create crises in order to feel the familiar pain, sense of stress and chemical response.

Accidents, surgeries and illnesses: These traumatic events can seriously damage a previously highly functioning P1. They can cause problems with P1 issues such as sleeping, eating, concentrating and persevering or even sitting still, or may lead to an unconscious but pervasive sense of fear.

Inherited traumas: These can be passed unconsciously from parents to their children through injunctions or the child's vicarious experience of the parent's responses to the world. Hence, even though they have not experienced the traumas directly, the children can grow up with pervasive insecurity or lack a sense of trust in the world.

Depressed parents: Chronically stressed or depressed mothers give birth to depressed children. Tiffany Field and colleagues found that infants of mothers who were depressed during the baby's first year of life demonstrate biochemical, physiological and behavioural dysregulation. These infants show more neurophysiological and behavioural signs of stress and depression, including greater activation in their right frontal lobes, higher heart rates, higher levels of norepinephrine, lower vagal tone, and higher cortisol levels (Field, 1997; Field et al., 1988).

THE LEGACY OF TRAUMAS AND ABUSES

Doctors and counsellors are constantly working with unhappy or dysfunctional people damaged by childhood traumas or abuses. Judith (1996) offers a compelling list of P1-related issues that arise from poorly functioning P1:

The Impact of Poorly Functioning P1

Impulsive behaviours and thoughts, disconnected from self-reflective processes, often serve the purpose of avoiding awareness of unaddressed feelings and needs (Miller, Alvarez and Miller, 1990). For those with poorly functioning P1, the experience of the inner world is paired with discomfort, sadness, isolation and shame from a time before conscious awareness. Psychologist Louis Cozolino (2002) describes imperfect attachment formation as resulting in individuals with an inability to be alone. These adults come to therapy with reports of despair and emptiness unconnected to any event, and often is despite a seemingly successful life. Their lives show patterns of insecure attachments, based on achievement, which of course, had to be continually increased. Constant activity meant they never relaxed. Time alone or unoccupied allowed the return of uneasy feelings, so they kept themselves distracted by busyness.

- **Poor boundaries (P1 Feeling):** One general effect is an inability to create appropriate boundaries – to know, for example, when one has had enough food, or drink, or time with another person. The person is unable to leave, because they never had enough closeness as a child and they are still trying to fill the gap. Co-dependence is another example of an inability to set appropriate boundaries.

- A second general effect of childhood trauma is a mind-body split (**P1 Thinking**). The mind concentrates on intellectual, creative or imaginative engagement and does not listen to the body or the person's own emotions. Consequently the individual ignores their own needs, often while experiencing an ongoing sense that something is wrong.

- A third general effect of a damaged P1 is to make **the body an object (P1 Somatic)** alienated from the self. In this case the body is seen as a thing to be mastered and controlled, to be shaped even as an ornament, rather than a living expression of who we are.

Early trauma results in the adult questioning the value of life. This cynicism extends to their attitude to accepted norms and values.

The key underlying theme, however, for all P1 issues is a sense of fear or terror. This is the antithesis of highly functioning P1, which provides the individual with a sense of safety and security. If a person is living amidst danger or impoverishment, they must be constantly vigilant. If this state continues over time, it is likely to affect the stressed person's health, resulting in such ailments as high blood pressure, insomnia, chronic fatigue or problems with heart, stomach, adrenal glands and their immune system (Judith, 1996).

ISSUES WITH P1 FUNCTIONING

Poorly functioning P1 is caused by either insufficient or excessive use of the Intelligence:

Under-reliance on P1: A person with a deficiency or under-reliance on P1 is not much interested in their body. They are primarily focused on activities of their mind – fantasies, dreams, knowledge or spirituality. Consequently they may have little interest in daily life, including grooming, hygiene or dress, and are likely to be restless and have difficulty concentrating. Their mind is often not present in the here and now. In short, they have a mind-body split. This person will benefit from grounding exercises.

Over-reliance on P1: A person with excess or over-reliance on P1 likes routine to the point of being so afraid of change that they are inflexible. They are interested in security, possessions and incremental financial gain. They are likely to be interested in their appearance and meticulous in habits and grooming. In their thinking they prefer to focus on the concrete rather than abstract ideas. They are likely to have strict boundaries. This person will benefit from physical movement, such as dancing, swimming or yoga.

Further insight can be gathered by identifying which component of the Intelligence the individual relies on to excess: the somatic, feeling or thinking aspects.[10]

Somatic Over-Reliance on P1: Those who have an over-reliance on somatic P1 tend to obsess about doing things the way they have always been done. This is linked to implicit procedural memory and is largely outside conscious awareness.

Feeling Over-Reliance on P1: Those who have a high degree of focus on the feeling aspect of P1 concentrate on being accepted within the group and focus on drawing the group together in a way that maintains the current power structure. This individual can be particularly obsessed with bonding with and looking after the leader of the tribe.

Thinking Over-Reliance on P1: If an individual focuses more on thinking P1 than the feeling or somatic aspects, they can become obsessed with the risks facing the group. This can lead to paranoia and anxiety and is accompanied by heightened awareness of the internal social politics of the group. The combination of these two characteristics often results in the development of sophisticated but nonetheless spurious conspiracy theories.

Strengthening your Relatedness (P1) as an Adult

REVISITING OUR ANCESTRAL BASE

The P1 Intelligence, our first stage of development, is grounded firmly in our roots, which my ancestral heritage, the Celts, associated with the element earth. Our roots are our family or our tribe, which give us nurture and care. Also, according to many traditional cultures, we are rooted in the earth, which gives us sustenance and shelter. These constitute our primary needs for survival. As we grow up, in order to develop autonomy and the free will to follow our own goals, we feel the need to distance ourselves from our family. For some people, there needs to be a time of complete separation.

However, although we may believe we have severed ourselves from our roots, they

---

10 Each of these reflects a particular Neuro-Limbic Type; the One, Two and Six respectively. These relate to *NeuroPower* Principle # 2 and are explored in detail in Principle #2, *NeuroPower* (Burow, 2013).

are still there in our unconscious and this can affect our behaviour. We need to bring our roots into our conscious awareness, to uncover and examine our past and reclaim our ancestral base in order to again feel the groundedness of the tribe.

Grounding brings us into the here and now and connects us to the environment, giving us focus and strength. Judith's (1996) research found that the basic rights of P1 are the right to be here and to have what we need for survival. We need to reclaim our right to be here, to learn to ground ourselves and to nourish ourselves if we are to do the work of reclaiming our roots.

A significant finding of the Adult Attachment Interview (AAI) is that exposure to trauma or loss during childhood is not the key determining factor in attachment. What does appear to matter more critically is the coherence of the narrative created. This strongly suggests that the processing, working through and integration of childhood experiences is the most significant variable in a parent's ability to provide a safe haven for their children. It is through this *earned autonomy*, by a parent healing their own wounds, that the transmitting of negative attachment patterns is stopped from one generation to the next (Siegel, 1999).

Judith suggests that it is important to realise that with the security and grounding that P1 gives, comes the acceptance of our own personal limitations and the strength of family or community.

CREATING A HIGHLY FUNCTIONING P1

Diagram 2.1 shows the three aspects of P1 that require integration so that true Tribal Loyalty can form.

Due to family upbringing, socialisation, genetic disposition or individual tendencies, you may have a thinking, feeling or somatic understanding of P1 rather than a highly functioning P1 that shows on all three aspects.

Compare your own experience with Diagram 2.1. Which aspects of P1 are you more aware of – the thinking, feeling or somatic? Is there one that you tend to focus on above the other two?

- The P1 somatic element is expressed in even, measured movements and a strong sense of physical *grounding* or being present.
- The P1 feeling element involves a sense of contentment and pride.
- The P1 thinking element is one of logic and sequential thinking, overriding unacceptable social responses, and anticipating and managing risk for the tribe.

INTEGRATION TASK

It is the task of the adult to examine and update their P1 data file. However, when

Diagram 2.1 Healthy P1 Intelligence — Noble Quality: Tribal Loyalty

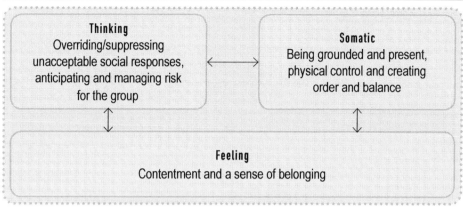

Thinking
Overriding/suppressing unacceptable social responses, anticipating and managing risk for the group

Somatic
Being grounded and present, physical control and creating order and balance

Feeling
Contentment and a sense of belonging

For the Neuroscience of Tribal Loyalty see Table 2.2

the rules given by the child's parents were reinforced with words such as 'never' and 'always', and accompanied by a high degree of intensity, it may be too uncomfortable and stressful for the person to revisit them. In this case, the imperatives may persist long after the rules have become archaic, resulting either in prejudices, or quirky or compulsive adult behaviour.

When you have an over-reaction to an event it could be that you have triggered some unresolved event from childhood. You may need to examine these unconscious P1 beliefs from the adult experience of your conscious Neuro-Rational Type.[11]

According to Myss (1996), key questions to ask yourself are:

- 'Do these rules all hold water and are they aligned with my new level of awareness?'

- 'Where are these rules coming from?'

- 'Are they coming from my parents, or history, or are they relevant now?'

In first-order consciousness the whole personality forms around one or two Intelligences. When P1 is at the lowest level of consciousness, rules are to be taken literally and obeyed, not interpreted. At second-order consciousness (i.e. from the perspective of your Neuro-Rational Type), the objective is to contextualise the P1 Intelligence, not ignore it or let it run rampant.

The task of integrating P1 involves embracing your family heritage and unifying it with your chosen life path. Whenever you feel unreasonably aggressive, it is advisable to consider whether someone is breaking your family or tribal rules. Whenever you

---

11 To explore your Neuro-Rational Type, see Principle #3, *NeuroPower* (Burow, 2013).

Table 2.2 The Neuroscience of Tribal Loyalty

The table below details the Neuroscience of P1. Refer to Appendix 1 for more details.

Somatic Aspect	Feeling Aspect	Thinking Aspect
• **Embedding learned rules into implict (unconscious) procedural memory** (orbitofrontal cortex, dorsolateral prefrontal cortex and striatum; Pascual-Leone et al., 1996; Saling & Phillips, 2007)	• **Feelings of loneliness or panic if isolated from the group (either physically or socially)** (dorsal anterior cingulate cortex and anterior insula; pituitary-induced increases in cortisol and progesterone (Eisenberger & Lieberman, 2004; Brown et al., 2009)	• **Suppressing/ disrupting unwanted cognitive, affective or behavioural responses** (frontal cortex and left prefrontal cortex)
• **Automatic habitual response without thought** (ACC, posterior rostral cingulate zone and dorsolateral prefrontal cortex)	• **Aversion to risk and uncertainty** (dorsal prefrontal cortex; Xue et al., 2009)	• **Applying 'if-then' rules given to us by others** (lateral prefrontal cortex; Berkman & Lieberman in Moskowitz & Grant, 2009)
• **Coordination of smooth, timed and rhythmic movements** (primary motor cortex, basal ganglia)	• **Preference for fairness** (midbrain dopaminergic reward regions; Tabibna & Lieberman, 2007)	• **Focusing on 'ought' goals based on social roles and expectations** (precuneus and posterior cingulate cortex, in particular right prefrontal cortex; Strauman et al., 2013; Amodio et al., 2004)
• **Selection and coordination of movements** (basal ganglia)	• **Homeostasis/Neutrality** – maintained by serotonin; influenced by e.g. valium and other anti-anxiety drugs which increase the ability of GABA inhibitory neurons to prevent excitatory transmission (sent by the cortex to settle down the amygdala)	
• Making **associations that may promote our survival** (anterior insula and orbitofrontal cortex)	• **Positive emotions** associated with social acceptance and belonging – through endorphins (opium-like hormones that stimulate well-being; Eisenberger, 2008)	• **Applying simple moral rules** to determine socially appropriate behaviour (ventromedial prefrontal cortex; Moll et al., 2005; FeldmanHalll, Mobbs & Dalgleish, 2013)
• **Priming, conditioning and skill-learning** (striatum, cerebellum and brainstem)	• Emotion is **felt by the body, monitored** by brain areas placed at several levels of the central nervous system (e.g. singular cortices, hypothalamus, tegmentum) and **interpreted by the cortex** (lateral and polar parts of frontal lobe). Activity in the prefrontal cortex increases and decreases respectively with feelings of acceptance and rejection	
• **Somatic markers – access to information about the best way forward based on past experience, focusing on safety** (circuits linking posterior sensory cortices, temporal and parietal regions with prefrontal circuits)		

experience that unmistakable sense of knowing something is absolutely right, beware! The source may well be unexamined family rules.

Highly Functioning P1 in Adult Life

The noble quality of Tribal Loyalty requires the integration of the thinking aspect of cultural logic, the feeling aspect of calmness and the somatic aspect of physical strength and control.[12] This sense of Tribal Loyalty is critical in teams and is a key characteristic of High Performance Teams.

Tribal Loyalty arises from a sense of membership of a tribal group or community. This is expressed when the individual identifies with and feels a sense of obligation to the common good of the tribe. This will include a sense of the individual's own good, but will stretch beyond the self and encompass the interests of others in the group.

An individual with these strengths has a strong sense of duty, works for the good of the group rather than for personal gain, is loyal to the tribe or collective, and can be trusted to pull his or her weight. This capability will be expressed through active involvement in civic affairs in the community. This noble quality embraces public interest over self-interest.

There are three elements of Tribal Loyalty:

1. **Social responsibility** to members of the 'tribe': An orientation to helping others even when there is nothing to be gained from them.

2. **Loyalty:** An unwavering commitment to and a bond of trust with the members of the group.

3. **Team work:** An ability to work with others in a group for a common purpose – to collaborate and cooperate.

Aristotle, writing in ancient Greece about small city-states comprised mostly of related individuals, describes this Tribal Loyalty as a network of friends bound together by the pursuit of a common good. According to Aristotle:

> *The man who is isolated – who is unable to share in the benefits of political association, or has no need to share because he is already self-sufficient – is no part of the polis, and must therefore be either a beast or a god.*

Embedded in this noble quality there is a sense of reciprocity, an implicit understanding that if the community cares about an individual, that individual will

---

12 Peterson and Seligman's meta-study of the most widely influential traditions of thought and religion in human history found Tribal Loyalty to be a significant human strength (Peterson and Seligman, 2004).

respond by respecting the cultural norms and adhering to the common good of the community. Eccles and Gootman (2002) found empirical evidence to support the importance of loyalty with troubled youth whose expression of the noble quality positively changed their personal behaviour towards their community.

HOW P1 TRIBAL LOYALTY MEETS THE NOBILITY CRITERIA

Tribal Loyalty can answer key questions of existence related to the right of the individual to live. This noble quality also enables the individual to accept that their own survival is no more important than the survival of their family. The individual learns how to be valued for who they are, their heritage, their family's future and the unconditional love that this commitment brings.

Tribal Loyalty is appealing to express. Individuals yearn to be a valued member of their family and the community. To be unconditionally loved by family members and to be able to contribute rates highly on life satisfaction surveys. Individuals report that using loyalty to resolve an internal tension has a paradigm shift impact on their lives.

When leaders are able to create an environment in which Tribal Loyalty flourishes, team members feel safe, secure and committed to a team on which they know they can rely. This is the first characteristic of a High Performance Team.

I got support from this community and I decided to chip in,
to help my community change with the times.
If you don't serve your community,
then you don't plow anything back.

Sam Nzima,
a South African freedom fighter

P1 Toolbox

THE IMPORTANCE OF P1 IN BUILDING HIGH PERFORMANCE TEAMS

P1 Tribal Loyalty, ensures the survival of the organisation even at the cost of personal autonomy or individual status.

When Tribal Loyalty is absent, individuals in the team think only of themselves. In the absence of highly functioning P1, personal agendas replace organisational aspirations and objectives. The workplace becomes a 'dog eat dog' world – every person for themselves, preoccupied with watching their own backs. No one is safe and the survival of the organisation is threatened.

However, when P1 is functioning highly in the organisation, team members think beyond their own personal survival to provide genuine help to others in the team. In this way, standards of organisational welfare are established and individuals can feel secure in the knowledge that they are safe and valued.

Leaders looking to increase the functioning of P1 in their team can increase Tribal Loyalty by applying the following P1 techniques and tools.

P1 QUESTIONS FOR PERSONAL DEVELOPMENT AND SELF REFLECTION

The best high performing teams are made up of individuals who have focused on their own personal development. The following questions can be used as a starting point for those leaders looking to improve their P1.

In this exercise, you can survey how rules functioned in your family's life. Many of these rules will be implicit (i.e. not top of mind). Your task is to recall them and then, if necessary, update them.

1. Make a list of five rules, spoken or unspoken, that you remember from your childhood and adolescence.

2. Write your responses to these rules, giving examples or recounting vivid incidents:

    a. Who made the rules in your family?

    b. How were the rules enforced?

    c. How easy or hard was it to change the rules?

    d. How were you affected by your family's rules as a child? How have you either kept them or changed them as an adult?

3. Write directly and simply whatever message you most want to convey about trust, hope, and possibility to the child you were somewhere between birth and three. Notice and express whatever you feel as you write, and finish with some comments and reflections about the short message you've written.

4. How important is control to you? (Do you thrive on chaos?)

5. Was your family life chaotic and out-of-control, fairly stable and orderly, or overly controlled and rigid?

6. Did you learn as a child that keeping control of a situation was one way to be safe? Explain.

7. Has your family life stance about control worked well for you?

P1 TOOL #1:
DEVELOP YOUR TEAM'S VALUE PROPOSITION

HOW THIS RELATES TO P1

If there is no shared understanding of the value of your team, members are not secure that the team, as a group, will survive. This results in limited commitment. Conversely, when the value of the team is clear and shared, team members feel the team's future is secure and are willing and wanting to commit to achieving the team's objectives.

PROCESS

1. Write a **list of the benefits** – technical, economic, service and social benefits – that your team brings to your customers (virtual or actual customers).

2. **Classify each benefit** as either a:

   a. **Point of parity:** Elements that have essentially the same performance or functionality as those of the next best alternative (i.e. your closest competitors);

   b. **Point of difference:** Elements that make your offering either superior or inferior to the next best alternative; or

   c. **Point of contention:** Elements about which there might be some debate about how your performance or functionality compares with the next best alternative. You might see it as a point of difference in your favour, but your customers might see it as a point of parity. The reverse may also be true.

3. If necessary, conduct an **opinion audit** to validate your initial assessment regarding how your team compares with others.

4. Once you've consolidated your team's value proposition (VP) (based on your main points of difference), you may need to conduct **shareholder research** in your key target markets to assess whether your team's VP resonates with others and is commercially appealing. Review and revise the team VP as necessary.

5. Use this VP as the basis for communication with all stakeholders. **Review the ongoing appropriateness** of your team's VP at least every six months.

DOS

✓ Do be prepared to use the VP development process as an opportunity for review. Chances are, if you don't have clear points of differences between your team and others, your commercial viability may be uncertain. Use the process to think laterally about how you might expand your operations to increase points of difference hat matter to your internal or external customers.

DON'TS

✗ Don't assume either that your customers will automatically presume the benefits of your team, or that it will be enough simply to state the benefits. This may work sometimes, but the gold standard you should aim for is to demonstrate to your internal or external customers how you offer superior value compared to the next best alternative.

P1 TOOL #2:
CLARIFY EACH TEAM MEMBER'S ROLE AND GIVE FEEDBACK ON HOW THEY ARE GOING

HOW THIS RELATES TO P1

If the individual has poor attachment, this exercise enables them to feel they have a legitimate right to be a member of the team - and that they are valued for the role they play.

PROCESS

1. **Identify the format of the meeting** – decide whether you will conduct individual one-on-one meetings, or review with the wider team as a whole.

2. **Prepare for the meeting**:

   a. **Schedule the meeting** with the employee(s). Allocate between one hour and two and a half hours, depending upon your observations of how things have been going and how much clarification is needed.

   b. **Arrange a venue**. Make sure there's enough room for comfort, and that you'll have access to a whiteboard and flip chart.

   c. Inform the employee that in preparation for the review, they'll need to conduct an **employee self-assessment of their work performance** and bring with them a list of the things that they would like to either keep doing, stop doing and start doing in relation to their job (a 'Keep, Stop, Start').

   d. **Review the employee's role and responsibilities document**. If there isn't one, write one so that you can bring it with you to the meeting.

   e. Based on both their role document and your observations, prepare your own **Keep, Stop, Start** suggestions.

3. **Conduct the meeting**. Use the roles and responsibilities document and the Keep, Stop, Starts (yours and theirs) as a starting point for the discussion. The aim of the meeting is to ensure that there is mutual clarity about what is expected of the employee, how they are currently tracking against those expectations, what needs to change for them to fulfil their role and responsibilities and how that performance can be tracked. Make sure that you provide positive feedback about their performance (include those items in the 'Keep' list) as well as areas for improvement. By the end of the meeting, there should be agreement about all aspects of the employee's role and a documented action plan for making any necessary changes moving forward.

4. **Set a date for review**. When you inform the employee of the review date, simultaneously provide them with a copy of the record from the review session.

5. **Track progress** to ensure that there are no holes in the process (i.e. the individual team member's performance is not being impeded by other external factors).

DOS

✓ Do use the employee's roles and responsibilities document to highlight any ways in which they are not performing their role.

✓ Do use the review meeting as an opportunity to explore the hidden talents and aspirations of your staff.

✓ Do consider conducting a skills audit if you are concerned about competency levels. You might also consider this option if you suspect the employee is overqualified by their current position, and may contribute more value in another role.

DON'TS

✗ Don't use hearsay comments as the basis for negative feedback. Either comment from first-hand experience or investigate all issues thoroughly before raising them with the employee.

✗ Don't allow the aspirations of the employee to become the focus of the meeting. Although it's helpful information for you to have as their leader (particularly if they have a specific plan for moving either sideways or upwards), the aim of the session is for them to leave with clarity about what's expected of them now, not where they'd like to be in the future.

P1 TOOL #3:
DEVELOP YOUR OWN LEADERSHIP CODE OF CONDUCT

HOW THIS RELATES TO P1

Every member of your team comes from a different family background with different rules. It is important to have one set of explicit rules encoded in a code of conduct to create a sense of tribal loyalty and minimise unnecessary conflict. Start with your own code of conduct as a leader and then facilitate a session to create one for the team.

PROCESS

1. **Write a list of your strengths and weaknesses.** Then write a paragraph summarising your **signature gift** and how you use it in daily life.

2. Write a list of your **top 10 current key objectives**.

3. **Identify your six key leadership behaviours** – the qualities you want to establish as foundational attributes of your leadership style.

4. **Link your leadership behaviours to the achievement of your objectives**. Use the following sentence construction: 'I will ... (behaviour) ... so that ... (outcome)...'. For example, 'I will focus my attention and keep the end goal in mind so that I can reduce my wasted time and complete my Tax Return by July 7'. This creates a very clear cause and effect statement with results that can be measured.

   Make sure that all your leadership behaviours link to your objectives. Although there may be many other 'nice' qualities that you want to embody, they don't belong on this list. As a team leader, you need to learn how to be both a person of character and a yielder of great results – and your Leadership Code of Conduct needs to reflect both.

5. **Focus on cultivating these qualities** over the next three months. Place your Leadership Code of Conduct in a prominent place – somewhere that you'll see it a number of times each day (e.g. noticeboard, ruler insert in a filofax, screensaver on your computer or mobile). Continually review the extent to which you are embodying these qualities in daily interactions and remind yourself that they are the key to helping you achieve your objectives.

P1 Tool # 3

DOS

✓ Do see your six key behaviours as the life principles you've chosen as your 'true north'.

✓ Do remember that, as the saying goes, *'If you're not achieving your own objectives, you're probably achieving someone else's.'*

DON'TS

✗ Don't rush this process. Make sure you give yourself enough time to identify the six key qualities that genuinely reflect the leader you want to be.

✗ Don't forget about your Code of Conduct once it's written. Review it on a daily basis, and constantly self-assess how well you measure up against the standard you've set for yourself. Develop strategies for how you could incorporate these qualities more fully into your daily life.

KEY RELATEDNESS QUESTIONS FOR BUILDING A HIGH PERFORMANCE TEAM

1. What is the purpose of your team? What value does it add to the business?

2. How does your team interact with the rest of the organisation?

3. What is your own role within the team? How do you contribute to the team?

4. If the team is to deliver its work, what role do you want your leader to play? What should s/he keep doing, stop doing, start doing?

5. For the team to deliver on its purpose, what ground rules do you need to have in place for working together? What needs to go in the team's Code of Conduct?

6. How will you keep each other accountable and provide feedback on behaviour that is outside of the Code of Conduct? How might this work on a practical level?

Key P1 Questions for High Performance Teams

THE IDEA IN ACTION

ORGANISATIONAL CASE STUDY #1: STATE HEALTH HAND HYGIENE PROJECT

The Task: To improve compliance by health workers with hand hygiene practice.

Recap:

In 2007, an Australian state health department wanted to address the serious threat that health-associated infections posed to hospital patients. Micro-organisms are readily transmitted on the hands of health care workers. In Australia alone, health officials estimate that up to 7000 people die annually from hand hygiene-related infections in hospitals. The economic burden is also considerable, costing millions each year.

Hand hygiene has been proven to substantially reduce transmission of micro-organisms. However, despite well-established guidelines, compliance throughout the world with hygiene standards is concerningly low. International and national health agencies have been grappling with how to deal with the issue for some time, and few interventions have had any impact whatsoever, despite both European and US hospitals and governments spending tens of millions of dollars on communications, incentives, closed circuit TV and education.

Since research demonstrated that the hand hygiene issue centred around human behaviour, one state health department decided on an innovative, behaviour-changing approach using the *NeuroPower* framework to drive the solution. Working with the *NeuroPower* Consulting Team, the department implemented a behaviour change program called Clean Hands are LifeSavers that engaged the health workers and increased compliance from 18% to 60%. A key driver of this behaviour change involved effectively addressing each of the six Intelligences in the correct sequence. How these progressive steps were taken is outlined in the Organisational Toolbox Case Study at the end of each Intelligence chapter.

Action: Create Safety and Security in the Hospital Environment

Attitudes to hand washing are culturally determined on one level but also heavily impacted by the individual's primary caregivers in their early life. *NeuroPower* consultants undertook extensive research with doctors, nurses and other health workers to determine their core views and values about hand hygiene and uncovered the resistance strategies being used by different profiles.

To implement the program, we embarked on establishing Hand Hygiene LifeSavers in each hospital. Their key role was to be on the front line making sure all their colleagues – doctors, nurses, orderlies or caterers – adhered to their specialised roles as guardians of the community's health. The LifeSavers ensured everyone agreed to the code of conduct that was expected of them around safety and security in the hospital environment.

ORGANISATIONAL CASE STUDY #2: MERCHANT BANK EQUITY DERIVATIVES LEADERSHIP TEAM

The Task: Improve employee engagement and tangible business performance.

Recap:

In 2006, at the height of the financial boom, one of Australia's leading equity derivatives teams was operating in an environment that was fast-paced, demanding and with a high level of stress. In order to handle large volumes of work in a very volatile market, the team needed to be highly functional and collaborative. Growth was nearly 200 percent over the previous year so the enormous strain was evident. This was mainly caused by a leadership team in crisis.

The Leadership Team was fractured, non-collaborative and driven by their own individual agendas. There was both a lack of respect and a lack of honesty between members which led to highly reactive responses and conflict. The broader team could see this occurring and they felt they were part of a warring tribe with all the insecurities that brought.

NeuroPower consultants devised a program which focused on addressing the splintered Leadership Team. The intervention involved a series of group structured processes which were embedded by individual coaching sessions.

Action: Repairing and Embedding P1

The first task was to repair the fractured P1 in the Leadership Team. To set the stage, a Leadership Team Code of Conduct was developed and agreed upon to establish the rules the team would play by – how they would treat each other and interact as a group.

The most powerful session followed – Role Clarification. Much of the interpersonal conflict came from the confusion around overlapping roles and responsibilities within the Team. This workshop had been scheduled for two hours but was extended to a whole day because the members found it so invaluable. It was during this session that the Team relaxed, opened up and began to work together in a more harmonious manner. By day's end, there was an expanded sense of safety and openness as the P1 had been repaired and stabilised.

P1 Tool #1

Chapter 3

Our Second Social Cognitive Need:
EXPRESSION &
The Emotional Function (C1)

EXPRESSION (C1) AT A GLANCE

Expression is our Brain's Second Social Cognitive Need

The brain loves expressing emotions. Unexpressed emotion and activity in the amygdala is related to a significant decrease in cognitive ability and can seriously reduce individual and team performance. Labelling emotions appropriately reduces this load.

Characteristics of the Expression (C1) Functional Network

Spontaneity and Innovation

STRENGTH	WEAKNESS
Open to new experiences and ideas	Easily bored; tactical rather than strategic

OPPORTUNITY	THREAT
Recognising that new doesn't mean better; learning to endure pain	Can become easily bored, distracted or manic

Management Style

- Great for adapting concepts and designs
- Innovative and can think on the run
- Can frustrate with too many new ideas

SPONTANEITY

C1 THINKING	C1 FEELING	C1 SOMATIC
Brainstorming and innovation	Excitement, fun and extroversion	Body sensations, pleasure and fun

COMMUNICATION STYLE

- Witty and humorous
- Conversational and tangential (easily side-tracked)
- Loves brainstorming
- Highly animated
- Loves interacting with others
- Playful

KEYWORDS INCLUDE

- Flexibility
- Spontaneity
- Laughter
- New ideas
- Child-like and Playful
- Self-Expression

Expression (C1) Helps Us to Survive

Expression (C1) helps us both as individuals and the group to survive and thrive by motivating and enabling us to move rapidly towards pleasant (constructive) experiences and away from painful (unconstructive) experiences.

Expression &
The Emotional Function (C1)

EXPRESSION: OUR BRAIN'S SECOND SOCIAL NEED EXPLAINED

Our emotions - and expressing them to others - seem to be core to our human experience. We become excited when things improve and frustrated when things just won't change, anxious when things are uncertain and self-righteous when we feel we're being unfairly criticised. These emotions colour our experience, and the more intense the emotion, the more driven we seem to let others know about it! (Those people who thrive on expressing their emotions to others are usually referred to as 'extroverts'.) Now neuroscience is confirming that emotions are central to our lives because they are powerful tools that our brain - through Expression (C1) - uses to keep us alive and help us thrive.

Our understanding of emotions has come a long way since Cicero, Seneca and the Roman Stoic thinkers described the 'perturbatio' (their word for emotions), which they believed distracted us from our virtues, caused our suffering and were to be avoided at all costs (Schmitter, 2010). Instead, we now know that emotions are core to how we make sense of the world and - when functioning appropriately - the emotional system is the brain's way of giving us rapid access to our past experiences - both positive and negative. The brain's limbic system[1] is the seat of our emotional experience. It constantly scans the environment and our internal state to help us notice the 'important stuff' and filter out everything else. As a rapid decision-making system, our emotions help us move towards pleasant, positive experiences and away from painful, negative experiences.

When we feel emotional, whether it is a positive or negative emotion, our bodies become flooded with neurochemicals that change our breathing, heart-rate and muscle responses. In the brain, these neurochemicals affect what we can remember, how we perceive the outside world and how we process information. In times like these it is all

---

1   In the past, emotional processing was thought to be supported by contiguous structures in a dedicated 'limbic lobe', but contemporary neuroscience evidence now points to a more loosely connected set of structures within the midbrain, described as the 'limbic system'. The limbic system includes some popularly known brain areas including the amygdala (which pop culture frequently, though inaccurately, describes as the 'fear' part of the brain) and the hippocampus (associated with memory formation and consolidation) as well as other less well known but important structures such as the areas closely associated with our experience of pain like the insula and dorsal anterior cingulate cortex (dACC). Areas like the striatum, rich with cells producing dopamine, play a crucial role in the experience of pleasure and reward, while the ventral tegmental area and periaqueductal gray are thought to be critical to our behavioural responses to emotionally charged experiences.

Table 3.1 At a Glance – The Benefits of Healthy C1 Expression

Five reasons to develop C1 Expression for yourself and others	
1. Effectively labelling emotions in the moment can reduce their intensity.	Lieberman et al.,(2011)
2. In contrast, unexpressed, intense emotions significantly reduce cognitive performance by shifting activity from the frontal lobes to lower-level emotional parts of the brain.	Oei et al.,(2012)
3. Expressive flexibility is an important contributor to personal resilience over time.	Westphal, Seivert and Bonanno (2010)
4. Self-expression activates the mid-brain dopamine reward system and can in itself be rewarding and motivating.	Tamir & Mitchell (2012)
5. Emotional states have a strong impact on creativity and innovation, particularly for individuals high in C1 (extroverts)	Stafford, Ng, Moore and Bard (2010)

too easy to find yourself carried away by instinctive emotional responses because our emotions prepare our bodies to run when we are afraid, fight when we are angry and rest and heal when we are relaxed.

Although strong emotional reactions were critical to the survival of our ancestors, they create a lot of conflict and can often be disruptive. Workplaces often expect employees to try to eliminate, suppress or ignore their emotional responses. But neuroscience research is now confirming that this is exactly the wrong approach if you're looking to create high performance in yourself and in others.

Studies conducted by Matthew Lieberman at UCLA show that being asked to control our emotional responses (what he calls 'masking') can dramatically reduce performance on even simple cognitive and physical tasks. When we ask individuals to 'control their emotions' at work instead of expressing them constructively, we force them to use parts of their frontal lobes (the 'higher thinking' part of the brain) to keep the brain's emotional system under control so they can focus on the task at hand (Anticevic et al., 2010). This competing challenge significantly reduces the brain's available capacity for complex thinking.

Perhaps, even more importantly, unacknowledged or unexpressed emotions can bias our performance. Emotions have the powerful ability to shape what we perceive, what we remember, and how we interpret and respond to the world. For example, anxiety leads us to be more pessimistic when making judgements about the future, whereas anger makes us more optimistic so that we downplay risks (Lerner & Keltner, 2000). This means that, when unexamined and unexpressed, our emotions drive cognitive biases. As individuals, our judgements are clouded by emotions, and in teams their collective impact leads to flawed decision-making.[2]

So what's the alternative? Studies by Lieberman and others show that one highly constructive way to manage our emotions is not only to become aware of them but also to find the right word to describe them. This approach (called 'labelling') leads to big decreases in activity in the amygdala (the brain's 'danger detector'). This in turn reduces the intensity of the emotion so we can get a better grip on the situation. While there are many useful tools and techniques for building your personal emotional awareness, a key role of leadership is to create a culture that fosters healthy emotional expression.

In high-risk environments, expression can mean the difference between life and death

Effective leaders are able to create an environment where emotions can be expressed. In their book *Leadership in Dangerous Situations*, authors Patrick Sweeney, Michael Matthews & Paul Lester (2011) make the compelling point:

> "Strong cohesive bonds between members serve to form an effective social support network within an organisation. Support networks are important in assisting group members in managing stress because they provide a forum to voice concerns, receive guidance, and get information about how to more effectively manage problems. Thus, support networks enhance members' perceptions of their ability to handle dangerous situations and also to formulate realistic expectations of the demands involved, which helps members manage stress."

EXPRESSION, FLEXIBILITY AND FUN – THE CHALLENGE FOR LEADERS

From a community or organisational perspective, to build effective teams, leaders need to understand that emotional responses are an inevitable part of working in teams. If team members are emotionally triggered by each other or by external inputs but are unable to express this within the group in a constructive way, their agility, creativity and overall mental capacity for completing complex tasks will diminish. As a leader, creating a culture that enables the team to identify and label their emotions appropriately can liberate a surprising amount of enthusiasm and creativity that will then fuel their performance.

2   In Principle Two, we explore each of the nine patterns of emotion (the nine Neuro-Limbic Types) and the core bias associated with each one.

SET POINTS DEFINE OUR CHARACTER BY RETURNING THE BRAIN TO EMOTIONAL HOMEOSTASIS (ALLIESTHESIA)

Our brain has a simple operating principle which goes something like this: what has got us here, will keep us here. This simple principle is informed through past emotional experience. This primitive system is in the brains of most of the more advanced living things because it underpins learning, adaption and agility which are important to survival. Creatures without this aspect of adaption intergenerationally adhere to the principles of natural selection but the species requires mutation and multiple generations to achieve what more advanced brains can do with surprising speed.

Each of the social cognitive needs has a set point based on repeated experience which is rewarded by the C1 system (emotional alliesthesic homeostasis). For example, if during the consolidation of the P1 system, the child has positive attachment, feels comfortable with their caregiver and experiences many of the positive feelings associated with belonging and self value this encodes in the child's brain as reality. In this way, when the child feels wanted, supported, loved and connected, the brain will release a reward to reassure the baby that it is on the right path. Later in life the child will not always experience this sense of belonging in every group they are members of, however, their brain will let them know that this is the exception rather than the rule and the individual will do whatever it takes to become a trusted and valued member of the team knowing that this is how it 'should be'. Conversely a child that has poor attachment, that has never really felt they belonged or was valued, may experience anxiety, rejection and isolation. If this state is experienced for a long enough time it moves from being a state into being a trait. The brain treats our own emotional traits as set points that need to be maintained for survival. In the brain of this child, anxiety, rejection and isolation become the 'norm'

Diagram 3.2 The Functional Neural Architecture of Emotional Labelling

Directing attention to the affective response Dorsomedial Prefrontal Cortex	←→	Categorising the response (Verbalising) Ventrolateral Prefrontal Cortex	CONSCIOUS INTERPRETATION
↕		↕	
Intensity of the emotion Limbic regions, including the anterior insula, amygdala			EMOTION

Based on Satpute, Shu, Weber, Roy & Ochsner, (2012)

Talking – Even When You Don't Feel Like It

Research in Professor Matthew Lieberman's lab at UCLA has confirmed something that we all seem to get wrong: talking about unpleasant feelings makes us feel better. Lieberman and his team have found that accurately labelling both positive and negative emotions dampens their intensity by reducing amygdala-related responses, but that even when we experience this directly, we keep on mistakenly believing that talking about negative emotions will make us feel worse (Lieberman et al., 2007, 2011).

Lieberman's research indicates the positive impact of labelling comes when parts of the frontal lobe (including the ventrolateral prefrontal cortex (VLPFC) and the ventromedial PFC) increase their activation and help to interpret and reduce activation in the amygdala and other emotional areas of the brain. This lines up with a number of other studies into emotional reappraisal which similarly found that reappraising our emotions increases prefrontal activity and reduces limbic activity and emotional distress (Ochsner & Gross, 2005).

Applying this insight, researchers at Oxford have recently shown that training smokers to be aware of their cravings (through mindfulness practices) when they see images of smoking successfully reduced their cravings, and that this corresponded with a decrease in activity in craving-related regions of the brain (particularly the subgenual anterior cingulate cortex; sgACC) and reduced the functional connectivity between the sgACC and other craving-related regions in the brain (Westbrook et al., 2013).

Such studies reinforce the powerful impact awareness of activity of the emotional system has on the frontal lobe's ability to manage our emotions and, therefore, associated behaviour.

and represent the world, as it actually is for them. Every time they feel this pattern of emotions the brain will reward them with a mix of positive neurotransmitters the predominant of which is dopamine. Rewards like this feel as if everything is right with the world – "I am on track. This is right." So for this poorly attached child, the world feels right when he or she is anxious, feeling rejected and isolated. This emotional alliesthesic set point becomes a homing system, a script or a repeating pattern which is encoded into the individual's sense of self and emotional identity. This process is true for all six of the social cognitive needs and explains how character traits emerge. **The unusual aspect of this process is that in this way the brain has the ability to sometimes make us feel**

good about feeling bad if feeling bad is our set point. There are two other important characteristics of this reward system that it's useful to understand:

Firstly, the brain does not establish an emotional set point according to what is right or wrong but rather according to the number of times you have experienced that emotion. In this way the brain can reward the individual for things that are not healthy. This explains why we keep following patterns of behaviour that are plainly no longer serving us.

Emotional alliesthesic homeostasis (C1) means that depressed people are rewarded for being depressed, angry people feel good about exploding and strange people feel good about demonstrating behaviour that is strange.

C1 is the system that rewards us for maintaining the status quo by reliving the same emotions again and again. Our C1 also does one more thing. It rewards us for expressing these emotions, which we do through a rehearsed narrative or story. To explore this space further, therefore, we need to look at the nature of self-expression, its benefits and explore further the evolutionary benefits of emotion itself.

Within the brain, a diverse range of structures and neuronal networks help us satisfy our need for Expression. Within the *NeuroPower* framework, this set of structures is called the 'C1 Emotional System' (or sometimes the 'C1 network' or 'C1 function') and gives rise to a particular thinking style referred to as 'C1 Intelligence'.

THE EVOLUTIONARY SOCIAL BRAIN FUNCTION OF C1

The C1 system enables an individual to survive through:

- Aversive motivation (pain) or getting away from hedonically unpleasant experiences of food, recreational drugs, sex and the like (Esch & Stefano, 2004).

- Motivation to repeat constructive activities. Natural rewarding activities are necessary for survival and appetitive motivation ('pleasure'), usually governing beneficial biological behaviours like eating, sex and reproduction, and behaviour directed towards hedonic or pleasurable processes. Social contacts can further facilitate the positive effects exerted by pleasurable experiences (Esch & Stefano, 2004).

- Adaptation to novel situations by thinking laterally or creatively, using creativity to problem-solve and resolve conflict with others.

- Maintaining positive expectations for the future (Klein, 2006).

- The experience of pleasure, the state of feeling happiness and satisfaction resulting from an experience that one enjoys (Esch & Stefano, 2004).

- The experience of extraversion and subjective well-being (Pavot et al., 1990).

- Satisfaction of the body returning to homeostatic conditions ('sensory alliesthesia'; Burgdorf & Panksepp, 2006).

Recognising the Characteristics of Expression (C1)

Thomas Edison, whose mind was very high in the Expression (C1) function, is famous for having once explained, "I'm not discouraged, because every wrong attempt discarded is another step forward."

This seemingly inexhaustible energy to try something new, to give it another go in a different way, is characteristic of the C1 function at work. Levels of motivation are at their peak when new ideas and solutions are being sought, new people are being met or new experiences are at hand. They love anything new, fun or novel. This extroverted, emotional, associative part of the brain also gives our brain the ability to create unusual, previously unthought of 'creative' ideas which, in Edward de Bono's language, would be thought of as lateral thinking or practical creativity. C1 most often plays out as a 'hands on' practical creation of new things, adaptability and an ability to change course mid-way.

C1 THINKING

On a daily basis we use this C1 kind of creativity when we think outside the square to solve problems. In this process, we integrate feelings of freedom, play and novelty-seeking with the hands-on touching of objects and curiosity about how things work in practice. Added to this is a fluidity of focus, which canvasses a spectrum of disparate thoughts then selects one for the task at hand.

C1 Thinking is nicely described by Dr Joel Robertson[3], who observes that thinking related to excitement, risk-taking, sex, gambling, fear, anxiety, frightening scenarios or stories, or concerns about a challenging or difficult future is all linked to the release of dopamine in the brain. How we experience each of these is bundled up in the mental frameworks that each of us use to describe the relationship between us and the world. These manifest in the layered and complex thoughts, behaviours and emotions that make up our core beliefs about the world. According to Robertson, this system of core beliefs determines the individual's baseline chemistry and, to a large extent, establishes a range of automatic behaviours or even addictions. This is because if the individual believes that he or she is under any kind of threat their dopamine levels will be raised.

This also works in reverse; if we have a particular view about the world and dopamine is linked to rewarding the brain for returning to a homeostatic set point, any well-worn narrative will result in the release of dopamine. Either way – if we respond to stress in a way that has become habitual, we will be chemically and therefore emotionally reassured and even rewarded with the release of dopamine. That's why so many counterproductive core beliefs are so difficult to change.

3   Dr Joel Robertson is an internationally acclaimed clinician, lecturer, consultant, author and director of the Robertson Institute in the USA, which provides neurochemical evaluations and treatment techniques for corporations, athletes and mental health facilities.

C1 FEELING

C1 is characterised by a great sense of extroversion and spontaneity, which is facilitated by both the expression of feelings and emotions and fluid, flexible and fluent movement of mind, body and emotions. When accessing C1, individuals experience a range of characteristics including rapidly changing moods; a sense of freedom from boundaries and from rules; a seeking for pleasure, play and novelty; a sense of adventure and engagement in the real world; a fascination with the here and now; and a focus on exploring the world through the senses. There is a sense of timelessness and of playing with whatever is at hand. Add to this the creative life force and the stage is set for the individual to adapt whatever they find to make a new plaything. This is the cradle of a practical kind of creativity using lateral thinking.

C1 SOMATIC

C1 intelligence is the domain of spontaneous emotional expression in the physical world. Individuals high in C1 tend to have a wide range of expressions, move quickly, smile, laugh, cry and express their emotions facially and using gestures.

Equally, the C1 system is highly influenced by the emotional expressions of others in the immediate surroundings, mediated by our emotional reactivity to our own bodily states. For example, studies have found that simulating a frown (negative) or a smile (positive) using simple facial exercises creates negative and positive biases in interpreting otherwise neutral data (Larsen, Kasimatis and Frey, 1992). Neurologist Antonio Damasio (1994) argued that these arose because our brains recognise our body states as 'somatic markers' which it interprets to judge our emotional state. In particular, he argued, muscle changes in our limbs and faces send information directly to the brain and are represented in the somatosensory cortex, and are very sensitive components of emotional reactions. Meanwhile, less clearly defined - but arguably more intense - bodily responses in the viscera (such as the stomach, intestines, heart and lungs) are registered in the orbitofrontal cortex and related areas. These bodily responses are the C1 somatic markers of our emotional experience.

The correlation between how the physical body is feeling and how we're thinking is very clear to the C1-dominated brain. Hollywood is a testimony to being able to change people's mood and thinking through the use of explicitly expressed emotion. The old truism 'Smile and the world smiles with you', encapsulates the C1 somatic obsession with using emotion to actively frame the way messages are interpreted and the ways others perceive experiences.

Those high in C1 are highly aware of how expressed emotion directly shapes their emotional state: they dance to happy music to raise their mood, find humorous videos to diffuse tension, and their faces tend to default back to looking for physical expressions of fun and interaction. For those low in C1, this bodily feedback also occurs but largely without awareness (Porges, Donssard-Roosevelt and Maiti, 1994; Ehlers, Margraf, Roth, Barr and Birbaumer, 1988).

Highly Functioning Expression (C1) has Both Strengths and Weaknesses

Those who enjoy accessing their C1 are energised by brainstorming new ideas and are practical, quick-witted, energetic, adaptable, flexible thinkers who hop from one idea to another. These strengths are inevitably accompanied by inherent weaknesses, ranging from a short attention span through to a strong discomfort with negative emotions (either personally or in others). The lesson to learn for those high in C1 is that life is more than an addiction to fun, novelty, change and fast movement.

Expression (C1) and Childhood Development

In the Relatedness (P1) chapter, we looked at the issue of attachment and how the pattern of a child's emotional relationship with its primary caregiver at age one has significant predictive power for their future relationships (Ainsworth et al., 1978). Specifically, this relationship determines how the child sees the world (i.e. whether it is safe or not) and whether they are entitled to be in it. Attachment also affects the development of the C1 Intelligence by shaping how the child views themselves and others. This becomes their central emotional position (i.e. I'm OK, Not OK; You're OK, Not OK) (Harris, 1976). These are described in Table 3.1.

The same interactions that stimulated excitement, exhilaration and brain growth within an infant during its first year of life now include information on the recognition of disapproval and disappointment. During early socialising experiences, disapproval and disappointment reflect a loss of connection with the attachment figure, which is a powerful socialising experience given the primal requirement of staying connected for personal survival. Prolonged and repeated experiences result in physiological dysregulation and produce a negative result for the development of networks that affect regulation and attachment located within the medial prefrontal areas (Schore, 1994). In other words, the C1 Intelligence can be damaged from these very early experiences which later can have a very negative impact on adult personality.

Several key developmental theories have explored how Expression (C1) matures in early life.

In 1990, Henry Wellman proposed that at about two years of age a child's theory of mind first takes shape as a desire psychology (Sigelman and Rider, 2006). At this age toddlers communicate what they want and justify their own behaviour and the behaviour of others based on this (Sigelman and Rider, 2006).

According to Judith (1996), the emergence of C1 occurs within the child between six and twenty-four months. Developmentally, this aligns with Freud's oral stage, Piaget's sensory-motor stage and Kohlberg's Instrumental Hedonism stage. Developmental psychology assumes that there are specific facets of the child to be developed at each stage and specific knowledge to learn. It also assumes that the strength of the emerging facet for each stage depends on how effectively the work has been done in the preceding stage.

From a neurological perspective, the early emotional environment (C1) of an infant may become imprinted within the human brain through the shaping of their narrative and, in turn, their neural networks, and by establishing biochemical setpoints for circuitry dedicated to memory, emotion and attachment. These structures and processes then serve as the infrastructure for later-developing intellectual skills (I1), affect regulation, attachment (I2) and the sense of self (P2) (Schore, 1994; Siegel, 1999).

Neurobiologist Joseph (1996) refers to implicit memories relating to early childhood experiences as our human 'childlike central core'. This reflects the C1 Intelligence, which encapsulates the individual's C1 central emotional position, involving their emotional core beliefs about themselves.

To determine the strength of the attachment script, the AAI (Adult Attachment Interview as discussed in P1) was administered to parents when their children were at different ages: in utero; at the same time as the Strange Situation interaction (age one) and five years later (when the child is six) (Fonagy et al., 1991; van Ijzendoorn, 1995). In each situation the AAI was associated with the specific classification of the infant-parent attachment. This means that the findings from the AAI are strong, seem to be stable across time, and have predictive power even before an infant is born. Even when the child reaches late adolescence, the classifications made in the Strange Situation interactions generally remain predictive of AAI classifications (Benoit and Parker, 1994; Main, 1995; van Ijzendoorn, 1995; van Ijzendoorn and Bakermans-Kranenburg, 1996; Hesse, 1999). This suggests that the central emotional position encoded in the C1 Intelligence is stable and predictive into adulthood.

While an infant will have a different attachment pattern with different caregivers, and so may have different central emotional positions, it seems the primary caregiver exerts the strongest influence over the adult's narrative and attachment status (van Ijzendoorn and Bakermans-Kranenburg, 1996). This supports Berne's theory that men inherit their C1 (child ego state) from their mothers. Why women tend to inherit their C1 (child ego state) from their fathers is still unclear.

EXPRESSION (C1) PROBLEMS AT SCHOOL

In training for creative problem-solving, many teachers in Western schools have trained children to develop this flexibility and fluency of thought with lateral thinking

Table 3.3 The table below shows the Emotional Positions manifested in childhood and corresponding adult behaviour, based on Ainsworth et al.'s (1978) Strange Situation experiments

Emotional Position Expressed In Childhood Behaviour	Emotional Position Expressed In Adult Behaviour	Central Emotional Position	Response to Psychosocial Challenge Test
Secure The infant will explore the room and toys with interest during pre-separation. Displays signs of missing parent during separation with frequent crying by the second separation. Infant has an obvious preference for parent over stranger. Greets parent actively, typically initiating physical contact. By the second reunion the infant will maintain contact but will then settle and return to play.	**Secure/Autonomous** Coherent and collaborative discussion. Valuing their attachment, but appears objective regarding any particular event/relationship. Description and evaluation of attachment-related experiences is consistent, regardless of whether experiences are favourable or unfavourable.	I'm OK. You're OK.	• **Low** level of reported stress • **Moderate** HPA response (ACTH and cortisol); • **High** level of oxytocin release
Avoidant The infant fails to cry on separation, then actively avoids and ignores parent on reunion (for example, turning away, leaning out of arms when picked up, moving away). Little or no proximity or contact seeking, and no anger or distress. Response to parent appears very unemotional. The infant focuses on toys or environment throughout the procedure.	**Dismissing** Lacks coherence. They dismiss attachment-related experiences and relationships. They use normalising descriptions ('fine', 'nice' and 'typical mum') with generic statements invalidated through specific episodic recall. There is a tendency to have very brief statements of childhood.	I'm OK. You're not OK.	• **Moderate** level of reported stress • **High** HPA response (ACTH and cortisol); • **Moderate** level of oxytocin release
Resistant or ambivalent May be wary or distressed even before parent leaves. The infant explores very little, is preoccupied throughout procedure, and may seem angry or passive. Fails to settle and take comfort in parent on reunion, and usually continues to focus on parent and cry. Infant does not return to exploration after reunion.	**Preoccupied** No coherence. They will be preoccupied with past attachment relationships/experiences, and will appear angry, fearful or passive. Their sentences are often long, grammatically entangled, or containing vague phrases ('and so on').	I'm not OK. You're OK.	• **Moderate** level of reported stress • **Moderate** HPA response (ACTH and cortisol); • **Low** level of oxytocin release
Disorganised or disorientated Infant shows disorganised and/or disorientated behaviours in the parent's presence. This suggests a temporary collapse of behavioural strategies. For instance, infant may pause with a trance-like expression, with hands raised in the air; may rise up at their parent's entrance, then they fall prone and huddled on the floor; or may cling to their parent while bawling and leaning away with their gaze averted. Otherwise the infant will fit within the other three categories.	**Unresolved/Disorganised** While discussing abuse or loss within the attachment they will show surprising lapses in the monitoring of reasoning or discourse. This may be through a sudden belief that the person who is being spoken of is still alive in the physical sense even though they have been dead for years, or that this attachment figure was killed as a result of a childhood thought. They may lapse into prolonged silence or eulogistic speech. They will otherwise ordinarily fit within the other categories.	I'm not OK. You're not OK.	• **High** level of reported stress • **Suppressed** HPA response (ACTH and cortisol); • **Moderate** level of oxytocin release

Note: This table is adapted from Hesse (1999). The descriptions of infant classification (secure, avoidant, resistant or ambivalent) are summarised from Ainsworth et al. (1978) while the descriptions of the disorganised or disorientated category is summarised from Main and Solomon (1990). The descriptions of adult attachment classification system are summarised from Main, Kaplan and Cassidy (1985) and from Main and Goldwyn (1984, 1998). The descriptions of the central emotional positions are from Harris (1976). Responses to the Psychosocial Challenge Test are from Pierrehumbert et al., (2012).

exercises. Unfortunately, the rest of the time these same teachers often chastise and 'correct' their naturally C1-dominant students for being off task, not concentrating, making smart comments or 'fooling around'. Indeed, children whose C1 is highly activated and who have an understimulated brainstem are often labelled as having Attention Deficit Disorder (ADD) or Attention Deficit Hyperactivity Disorder (ADHD) and given drugs to calm them, such as Ritalin (a drug which stimulates the brain so the child doesn't need to use C1 to keep themselves awake).

As they mature and C1 Intelligence is mediated by the development of other Intelligences, these children usually learn to balance and moderate their tendency to create chaos, but C1 is still a powerful force which can be creative, light-hearted, vivacious and witty. However, this childish C1 energy is so pleasurable that it can become addictive, even when the child grows into an adult. After all, who wants to be serious and take responsibility when life can be so much fun? This may be why the C1 inner child within us refuses to grow up, continues to run towards pleasure and avoid pain, and may prefer not to take responsibility throughout our lives.

THE IMPORTANCE OF NARRATIVE

One of the most powerful ways parents and caregivers shape the brains of the children they have in their care is wrapped up in the way they make sense of the events the child experiences.

The way in which parents construct narrative descriptions of events creates scripts by shaping their children's sense of self and the world (Ochs and Capps, 2001). This is because the self is a combination of learning and memory, reflective of, and constantly being influenced by, social interactions (Cacioppo and Berntson, 1992). Narrative is important in establishing our sense of self because storytelling is the primary method for integrating activity in a sequential and meaningful manner (Oatley, 1992). Narratives are a means of explaining behaviour and defining both the social and private selves. They are emotionally meaningful, causally linked sequences of actions and consequences that help in the organisation, maintenance and evaluation of behaviour (Fivush, 1994). They also serve to educate children in the tales, myths and legends of their families and cultures (Howard, 1991; Malinowski, 1984).

As the child begins to verbalise, parents and children work together to co-construct the child's narrative. Miller and Sperry's (1988) research showed that when the child is around two-and-a-half, co-construction of narrative descriptions of events occurs at the rate of 2.2 per hour in everyday conversation. This dialogue helps the child form their C1 emotional life script.

C1 Expression and the Facebook Effect

Have you ever wondered why social networking sites like Facebook are so addictive? Recent research from Harvard provides some insight into why sharing so much of our personal lives can be so satisfying.

On the one hand, there's the positive reinforcement we get from our friends every time they 'like' something we've shared. But in addition, recent evidence suggests that the act of sharing may itself be an instant reward.

Researchers Tamir and Mitchell (2012) recently reported that expressing your own opinions activates dopamine-related reward systems in the brain. As part of a range of experiments, they offered participants small cash rewards for answering easy, factual questions based on things they observed, or lower rewards for offering their own views about a subject. To their surprise, more than two thirds of the time participants chose smaller rewards for talking about themselves, even when it meant a smaller financial reward. *"Just as monkeys are willing to forgo juice rewards to view dominant groupmates and college students are willing to give up money to view attractive members of the opposite sex, our participants were willing to forgo money to think and talk about themselves,"* the researchers wrote.

In a separate experiment, Tamir and Mitchell used fMRI to observe the brains of their participants. They found that when participants were disclosing their own attitudes they had significantly greater activation in the nucleus accumbens and the ventral tegmental area (both part of the dopaminergic reward system) than when they were evaluating other people's opinions.

Little surprise, then, that platforms like Facebook have unleashed an avalanche of sharing. It looks more than likely that each post we make and photo we share gives us another hit of one of the brain's favourite drugs.

DEVELOPING AN EMOTIONAL IDENTITY[4]

C1 enables us to feel and emotionally connect to the world. Piaget observed that young children learn this at the sensory-motor stage of development when the body first starts accessing the C1 Intelligence. This is when the child is beginning to separate from, and move independently of, its mother and connect to the outer world. Since children

---

4   An in-depth analysis of the nine emotional identities (Neuro-Limbic Types) that form during the sensory-motor stage is outlined in Principle #2, *NeuroPower* (Burow, 2013).

at this age have not yet developed language, they have no ability to name the things they sense, and consequently cannot categorise or reason about them. They explore their world by sensing and expressing emotion through their bodies. At this age, the child's focus is on seeking pleasure, avoiding pain and acquiring knowledge of the world (Harris and Butterworth, 2002).

If all goes well, the little person will integrate the cognitive, emotional and physical aspects of C1 and will be able to feel, know and validate what they want. They will also decide how they feel about the world (based on scripting embedded in their P1), including whether it is a place of pain to be avoided or pleasure to be embraced. Further, the child will know whether or not they have valid needs and desires, which can be gratified without guilt (Judith, 1996).

From the C1 stage the child's emotional identity emerges. Reality is felt and translated through the senses, and since the child has no sense of time, now is forever. As a result, their many experiences combine to form the dominant sense of reality.

To cement this belief about themselves and the world, the child receives explicit training and implicit teaching through modelling. The impact of this interaction is boosted by face-to-face interactions which activate an infant's sympathetic nervous system and increase oxygen consumption and energy metabolism. High levels of C1 activity correlate with increased production and availability of norepinephrine, endorphins and dopamine, serving to enhance the infant's energy and enjoyment (Schore, 1997). Once embedded in the C1 Intelligence, this results in what psychologist Eric Berne called a 'life script'.

Diagram 3.4 Healthy C1 Intelligence – Noble Quality: Spontaneity

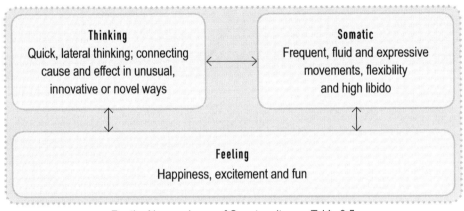

Thinking
Quick, lateral thinking; connecting cause and effect in unusual, innovative or novel ways

Somatic
Frequent, fluid and expressive movements, flexibility and high libido

Feeling
Happiness, excitement and fun

For the Neuroscience of Spontaneity see Table 3.5

Table 3.5 The Neuroscience of Spontaneity

The table below details the Neuroscience of C1. Refer to Appendix 1 for more details.

Somatic Aspect	Feeling Aspect	Thinking Aspect
• Increases in **skin temperature, dampness** and the rate at which blood pulses, as well as trembling fingers	• Dominated by **dopamine**, but also affected by oxytocin and beta-endorphone	• **Cheerfulness and optimism** (left prefrontal cortex)
• **Relaxation of muscles and increased flexibility**	• The dopamine pathway to the nucleus accumbens:	• **Positive emotional/ arousal states**, including those induced by taste, sight, touch and sound (orbital frontal cortex, prefrontal and cingulate cortices, the nucleus accumbens and its mesolimbic projection, the lateral hypothalamus, the ventral pallidum and the brainstem, especially the parabrachial nucleus)
• **Slight tensing of zygomatic muscle** (which pulls the mouth upward), **contraction of the orbicularis oculi muscle** ('crow's feet') and **relaxation of the corrugator supercilii** (responsible for expressions of disgust, sadness and fear)	– 'The Pleasure Pathway' can be activated by amphetamines (e.g. cocaine, crack, heroin, opium etc.) (tegmentum-nucleus accumbens). Anticipation of pleasure ultimately leads to addiction	
• **High activity in the midbrain:** including processing impulses from the brainstem and sending instructions to the muscles (cerebellum), releasing emotional excitement (diencephalon) and conversion of emotions to plans and actions (prefrontal cortex)	– Stimulation also leads to the sudden onset of mirth	• **Decrease in amygdala activation** with positive arousal-inducing stimuli (such as music, odour, self-generated positive arousal and male orgasm)
• **Activation of the 'pleasure and pain centres'** linked to the limbic system (cingulate gyrus, hippocampus, dentate gyrus, amygdala, hypothalamus, septal area and thalamus)	• Emotion is **felt by the body, monitored** by brain areas placed at several levels of the central nervous system (e.g. cingulate cortices, hypothalamus, ventral tegmentum) and **interpreted by the cortex** (lateral and polar parts of frontal lobe). Activity in the prefrontal cortex increases with feelings of anticipation	• **Divergent or creative thinking** (increased complexity of brain activity in the frontal cortex)
• **Somatic markers** – access to information about the best way forward based on previous experience (circuits linking posterior sensory cortices, temporal and parietal regions with prefrontal circuits)	• The anticipation of an **eminent and highly predictable reward** elicits positive feelings	

A script is an ongoing life plan formed in early childhood under parental pressure. It is the psychological force which propels the person toward his destiny, regardless of whether he fights it or says it is his own free will. A real person may be defined as one who acts spontaneously in a rational and trustworthy way with decent consideration for others. One who follows a formula is a not-real, or unreal, person ... these seem to constitute the bulk of humanity. (Berne, 1975, p. 32)

In describing those who follow scripts, Berne uses the image of a player sitting at a pianola, pedalling for all he is worth, believing he is autonomous, but really just following a set piece. Every so often he will improvise, but most of the time he plays out the script. As we have seen, the child has no way of reasoning about events that happen to and around them in their early family life so they lay down these life scripts uncritically.

[By the end of the nursing period] *the child already has certain convictions about himself and the people around him, especially his parents. These convictions are likely to stay with him the rest of his life, and may be summarized as follows: (1) I'm OK or; (2) I'm not OK; (3) You're OK or; (4) You're not OK. On the basis of these he makes his life decision. 'It's a good world, some day I'll make it a better one' – through science, service, poetry, or music. 'It's a bad world. Some day I'll kill myself' – or kill someone else, go crazy, or withdraw. Perhaps it's a mediocre world, where you do what you have to do and have fun in between; or a tough world, where you make good by putting on a white collar and shuffling other people's papers; or a hard world, where you sweep or bend or deal, or wiggle or fight for a living; or a dreary world, where you sit in a bar hoping; or a futile world, where you give up.* (Berne, 1975, pp. 84-85)

However, these scripts can be augmented or revised later through reasoning or experience. Berne (1975) explains that though they 'are usually based on childlike illusions which may persist throughout a whole lifetime ... in more sensitive, perceptive, and intelligent people these illusions dissolve one by one' (p. 26) as the person is faced by life's crises and deals with them according to their own judgement. These crises can include 'the adolescent reappraisal of parents; the protests, often bizarre, of middle age; and the emergence of philosophy after that' (Berne, 1975, p. 26).

C1 IS THE EMOTIONAL CHILD STATE

You will recall from our discussion of P1 that parents' rules and data are embedded in the memory of the child exactly as the little person hears them and sees them. As the parents' data is being observed, heard and recorded, the child is simultaneously recording internal

---

The Importance of Self-Expression

C1 enables you to take in new ideas, think conceptually and work collaboratively in an innovative and spontaneous way. However, when we are emotionally charged, our brain becomes 'full' of emotion and prevents our C1 from fully functioning. The key to getting back on track is to vent some of the emotions that are clogging up the system. This self-expression is like turning on a tap that is connected to an over-pressurised pipe system – it releases the pressure and enables the ideas and creativity to flow freely once more.

---

events as their individual responses to what is perceived. Harris (1976) makes a good point:

It is this seeing and hearing and feeling and understanding body of data which we define as the Child. Since the little person has no vocabulary during the most critical of his early experiences, most of his reactions are feelings. (pp. 24-25)

Harris' research shows that these feelings are generally positive.

However, for most children of loving and well-intentioned parents there is also much positive data recorded. Creativity, curiosity, the desire to explore and know, the urges to touch and feel and experience, and the recordings of the glorious, pristine feelings of first discoveries. In the child are recorded the countless, grand a-ha experiences, the firsts in the life of the small person. (1976, p. 27)

The *feelings* that accompany all of these delightful experiences are recorded as emotional memories in the C1 Intelligence, and include the many delicious feelings of the happy, carefree child. Importantly, this happy child can re-emerge at any time in the grown person's transactions.

The OK, not OK world view of our C1 child ego remains with us throughout life and it can emerge any time we feel helpless or overwhelmed by life's circumstances. Harris explains:

As in the case of the Parent, the Child is a state into which a person may be transferred at almost any time in his current transactions. There are many things that can happen to us today which create the situation of childhood and bring on the same feelings we felt then. Frequently we may find ourselves in situations where we are faced with impossible alternatives, where we find ourselves in a corner, either actually or in the way we see it. These 'hook the child' as we say, and cause a replay of the original feelings of frustration, rejection, or abandonment, and we relive a latter day version of the small Child's primary depression. Therefore, when a person is in the grip of feelings, we say his Child has taken over. When his anger dominates his reason, we say his Child is in command. (1976, p. 26)

If we prefer C1 to the C2 Intelligence (which we will explore in due course), we may habitually want to seek pleasure and avoid pain. This is the C1 Child – the life of the party, the seductive lover, the cute little girl, the charmer; all are accepted and sometimes encouraged in our culture.

But children are not always charming. In this situation, the Child's negative feelings far outweigh the positive. When they do not get their way, they usually throw a tantrum; even senior executives do this when they are accessing C1 in a Child state and have their wants thwarted. They rant, and rave and yell, and I have even seen some stamp their feet! Sometimes they bully, or scream, or become helpless and cry or wail. Others pout and sulk. All this behaviour reflects the inner Child (C1) wanting to avoid pain and responsibility, and trying to exert power over others to get their own way. For example:

Example one: You are at a dinner party. The lady of the house (your hostess) has cooked a dish containing herbs she knows her husband dislikes but does it anyway. When they are served, the husband demands very loudly, 'What's this got in it? It tastes mouldy! It's disgusting! etc.' He gets a win when all the guests stop eating and push their plates away.

Example two: A conversation becomes too dull (C1 cannot bear slow, ponderous talk) or too depressing, as in someone's heartfelt sad story. The person accessing C1 takes control by simply and blatantly changing the topic (e.g. 'Did you hear the great news about ...').

INTEGRATING C1 INTO THE OTHER INTELLIGENCES

If the child's needs are felt, expressed and met, the person will grow up with the capacity to feel and gratify their own emotional needs and fulfil the desires of their own soul. As the child grows they pass through each of the Intelligences, and at every stage, the C1 Intelligence interacts with a specific emotional need to be met.

The needs of each stage are as follows: P1 needs control (we have already explained how the family meets this need of belonging, security and control); C1 needs fun; P2 needs achievement and recognition; I2 needs connection and love; I1 needs to learn and experience new things; and C2 needs freedom.

Well-functioning C1 will help the individual to meet each of these needs in turn. The members of the family, the source of P1, interact with the little child and teach them to have appropriate expression of emotions. At the emergence of P2, C1 emotions fuel the passion to achieve. Next, C1 gives the emerging I2 Intelligence the courage to connect with others. Then, C1's energy and love of novelty spur on the developing I1 Intelligence to seek out new knowledge and experiences. Finally, C1's free Child gives C2 the freedom to dream and so develop.

Poorly Functioning C1

If the child's needs are not heard, acknowledged or gratified, the C1 Intelligence will not develop strongly. In fact, the grown adult may find it difficult or even impossible to understand their own emotional needs, and so may operate some or much of the time with a child-like level of emotional maturity. The adult following a Child script may depend on family, spouse, partner or friends to tell them what they need, how they should feel and what they should do. The dependent person relies on someone else to look after them. Hence, they plead and charm, wheedle, cry, or throw tantrums to ensure this happens. If the C1 script is unpleasant, it will often be suppressed and pushed out of conscious awareness.

As well as not knowing what they need, an individual with poorly functioning C1 does not understand the link between external stimulus and internal emotional gratification. In this case if they like something, they will often assume more is better, and that even more is even better. This is the genesis of the addictive personality that has an inability to gauge limits.

OVER-RELIANCE ON C1

If you have an over-reliance on C1, you are likely to be conscious of your feelings but express them as a child. The task of integration is to learn to recognise and express your feelings when appropriate, using an Adult mode of communication. Be mindful that our feelings often spring from the scripting of our little Child and so may no longer be relevant to the current situation. Make sure you consciously filter for whether the feelings are appropriate.[5]

Whenever you catch yourself acting like a child, remind yourself that you have the option to behave as an adult instead. It is important to listen to your own transactions and practise Transactional Analysis.

---

5   This is done by accessing your Neuro-Rational Type. For more detail, see Principle #3, *NeuroPower* (Burow, 2013).

UNDER-RELIANCE ON C1

Those with a poor awareness of their C1 have difficulty recognising their emotions (their core belief types) and often ignore their body sensations altogether. They may deny them or explain them away, especially if their family scripting says, for example, 'It's bad to get angry' or 'Crying is a sign of weakness'.

Even so, their emotions will still be there, buried in the individual's mind and body, ready to ambush them. These feelings will either come out inappropriately (such as through a petulant sulk), or will be buried so deep that they remain unrecognised and unresolved, until they ultimately affect the individual's health and sense of wellness.

SEXUALITY

Judith (1996) argues that the C1 Intelligence also gives the child a healthy sense of their own body, as they are handled and touched with love and respect. At this age, this bodily pleasure is not associated with good or bad, right or wrong. From here the child can develop a healthy positive sexuality, which Judith aptly calls 'the connecting force that unites and delights' (p. 123). From this libido issues the creation of new life and of procreation. This powerful life force is also associated with a general creativity, of new ideas, and of self-expression.

Creating a Highly Functioning C1

Compare your own experience with what you have learned about C1. Which aspects of your C1 are you aware of? Is there one that you tend to focus on above the other two?

- The C1 somatic element relates to fast and constant physical movements and a heightened sense of libido.

- The C1 feeling element involves happiness, excitement, and the sensation of fun.

- The C1 thinking element focuses on creating multiple options and scenarios. It is about brainstorming.

Diagram 3.2 shows the three aspects of C1 that require integration for the C1 Intelligence to function optimally. While every individual is different, our research suggests that the majority of the population experiences C1 as somatic (i.e. as fast movement and high libido).

To integrate these three aspects, you first need to recognise and acknowledge your body sensations and feelings, be they anger, hurt, fear, envy, guilt, etc. and reconcile them with the meaning you give them and how you think about them.

Begin this process by paying attention to your body. Your voice will provide clear give-away signs if you are in the Child state: a bully roars; a tantrum is full of screams or yells; and a helpless child has a high whining voice. Your body also reflects your emotion; bullying stance, stamping feet, frowning face, pouting lips, seductive looks and smiles, pleading eyes, and coy shoulders are all indicators of different emotions. Once you notice any of these (or other) physical characteristics, stop and ask yourself what are you feeling and how you interpret these feelings.

Emotions are instinctual, unconscious reactions to life, telling us to move and to be fluid. When feelings are habitually ignored or controlled, the body becomes the opposite of fluid and flexible and moving – it becomes stiff and rigid. Habitually unacknowledged anger, for instance, not only makes you stubborn, passive-aggressive and inflexible in your attitudes, but also gives you a rigid jaw, and stiffness in your neck and shoulders. If you hold your anger in long enough it will become painful. So if you develop a stiff neck and shoulders you could ask yourself, 'What am I angry about?' There are two parts to the work you can do to resolve the body pain. One part is to think it through and the other is to move the body. This will help you access your C1 Intelligence and process the emotion that underlies the pain.

YOUR EMOTIONAL SCRIPT

Every family has spoken or explicit rules about expressing emotions. When you were very small, before you could evaluate critically, scripts for emotions were laid down in your memory as you listened to your family and interacted with them. The following exercises will help you investigate your emotional life script. Start by considering anger.

Write a short response to each of the following questions. It can be a sentence, a recollection of an event, a poem, a conversation – however you choose to answer.

a.   When someone in your family was angry, how did you know? How did you feel? Was the anger acknowledged? What was the family's response? Did they respond positively? Did the family try to acknowledge it, control it, ignore it, punish it, or was there an all-out fight?

b.   Do you remember a time when you felt angry? Did you express your anger? How did you express your anger? How did your family respond? How did that make you feel? Was the conflict resolved?

c.   Write a new script for yourself about expressing anger. Now that you have considered anger, go through the same exercise with sadness, fear, guilt, joy, pleasure, sexuality and envy.

The following methodology can be helpful in accessing and integrating the C1 Intelligence.

1. The first step is to recognise the feeling. If you need to, give yourself permission to have the feeling.

2. Acknowledge the emotion and the meaning you give the feeling.

3. Consider the appropriateness of the feeling. If it appears inappropriately strong, it could be you are reliving a past unresolved event.

4. Express your feeling in an adult way to the person involved.

5. If the person is no longer living, one strategy is to write them a letter.

6. Tidy everything up: There may be restitution for you to make if you have hurt someone, or there may be someone you can forgive.

After doing the thinking work, complete the integration work by moving your body to release the emotions – massage and/or exercise will release the frozen parts of the body, restore your wholeness and health, and facilitate increased functioning in your C1 Intelligence.

C1 AND PROJECTION

Projection, a common psychological phenomenon, can also result from poorly functioning C1. An individual who has an under-reliance on C1 and is, for example, unconsciously angry, may be overtly polite while noticing how stubborn, terse and obviously angry others around them are. Projection leads us to notice and criticise in others what we cannot acknowledge in ourselves.

Well-functioning C1 operates under the mantra of 'honour one another'. To do this for others first we need to honour the entirety of ourselves, including our poorly functioning C1. Only then will we have the capacity to accept and respect others. A key component of honouring one another is a sense of fair play. While societal rules are derived from P1, a sense of personal ethics and morals for the individual springs from C1. As these develop, we learn to forgo the need to control, manage ourselves in relationships, and devote time to enjoying life.

Highly Functioning C1 in Adult Life

The first-order noble quality of Spontaneity requires the integration of lateral thinking, childlike feelings and the somatic aspect of kinaesthetic appreciation and pleasure.

Spontaneity[6] enables an individual to generate creative solutions to the various

---

6   Peterson and Seligman's meta-study of the most widely influential traditions of thought and religion in human history found spontaneity to be a significant human strength (Peterson and Seligman, 2004).

problems they encounter at both home and work. When expressing this noble quality, individuals tend to be independent, nonconformist, unconventional, even bohemian, and are likely to have wide interests, greater openness to new experiences and more conspicuous behavioural and cognitive flexibility (Feist, 1998). The noble quality also fosters a certain risk-taking boldness. William James (1890) saw ingenious creativity as an evolutionary tendency because it fostered exploring. Since attention is a limited resource, James suggested that individuals who are curious tend to focus on stimuli fostering excitement or personal meaning. The noble quality of Spontaneity involves a definite attraction to novel stimuli. This is adaptive because it increases the individual's knowledge of the world. Spontaneity is also a fun-loving noble quality that experiences life through the pleasures of the physical body. Strongly associated with humour and the Dionysian pursuit of all earthly things that can be enjoyed by the body, C1 Spontaneity is never stumped for options and can brainstorm solutions quickly and effortlessly.

This noble quality actively seeks novel and exciting experiences to elevate stimulation. This often requires a willingness to endure high levels of risk (for example, rejection when meeting new people, and high-risk sports activity) to obtain the benefits of trying something new. Spontaneity also embraces the childlike capacity to see life as a uniquely pleasurable physical experience that only being alive in human form can bring.

HOW C1 SPONTANEITY MEETS THE NOBILITY CRITERIA

Spontaneity answers questions related to the right of the individual to experience physical pleasure. This noble quality enables the individual to discover that they have the right to independently enjoy their life and their body and can build relationships of integrity while doing it. This noble quality is linked to what the German philosopher Nietzsche called the Dionysian man who is transformed through earthly pleasures.

Spontaneity brings value to the community by facilitating ingenious creativity and enabling the community to solve problems. This creates a sense of fun, right here, right now, and manifests in celebrations, parties, community theatre and comedy.

Being Spontaneous is appealing. Individuals yearn to relax, let their hair down and have fun. Hormonally we 'need' laughter as a medicine to release endorphins and to break free from our reactive selves[7] and reduce stress. Individuals report that using Spontaneity to resolve an internal tension has a paradigm shift impact on their lives.

In teams, Spontaneity leads to ingenious creativity which enables the team to be innovative, agile and able to respond adaptively to changing situations.

---

7   The nine reactive personalities, or Neuro-Limbic Types, are explored in Principle #2, *NeuroPower* (Burow, 2013).

I will tell you something. I love friends, I want more friends. I love smiles. That is a fact. How to develop smiles? There are a variety of smiles. Some smiles are sarcastic. Some smiles are artificial - diplomatic smiles. These smiles do not produce satisfaction, but rather fear or suspicion. But a genuine smile gives us hope, freshness. If we want a genuine smile,
then first we must produce the basis for a smile to come.

14th Dalai Lama

C1 Toolbox

THE IMPORTANCE OF C1 IN BUILDING HIGH PERFORMANCE TEAMS

The emergent cultural impact of C1 is Spontaneity, which enables the organisation to be agile and constructively solve problems as they arise in the course of daily business.

When Spontaneity is absent or suppressed, problems, pessimism and negativity escalate. In the absence of highly functioning C1, workplaces and teams experience low productivity and minimal engagement. Interpersonal conflicts remain unacknowledged and unaddressed, creating either an environment in which everyone feels stifled or a quagmire of emotional tension. Far from bringing joy to employee's lives, work is not a pleasant place to be.

However, when there is highly functioning C1 in the organisation, team members feel comfortable expressing themselves and are able to deal with any potential interpersonal issues constructively. This facilitates the agility of the team and its capacity to think creatively in solving problems that inevitably arise. The team is filled with a sense of optimism – right here, right now! – which is reflected in a fun and lighthearted work environment.

Leaders looking to improve the function of C1 in their team can increase Spontaneity by applying the C1 Tools.

C1 QUESTIONS FOR PERSONAL DEVELOPMENT

The best high performing teams are made up of individuals who have focused on their own personal development. The following questions can be used as a starting point for those leaders looking to improve their C1.

Write a short response to each of the following questions. It can be a sentence, a recollection of an event, a poem, a conversation – however you choose to answer.

1. What do you really enjoy doing?

2. How did your family enjoy themselves?

3. Did you enjoy the same things as your family?

4. What makes you laugh?

5. How much were you encouraged to express your feelings when you were growing up?

6. How did your parents respond to you when you expressed negative emotions? Did the family try to acknowledge it, control it, ignore it, punish it, or was there an all-out fight? How may that still be influencing you today?

7. Do you remember a time when you expressed yourself and it was not accepted well?

8. What did you do?

9. How did your family deal with issues around sexuality?

10. When there was emotional conflict, how did your family resolve it?

11. How did that make you feel?

12. How effectively was the conflict resolved?

13. How can you increase the amount of fun you have in your life?

C1 TOOL #1:
ACTIVELY FOSTER INNOVATION

PROCESS

1. **Identify sources of creativity** – There are many different areas of your business that creative solutions can come from:

   - **Employees:** are the ones who handle the day-to-day problems and are best placed to spot opportunities for devising better ways of doing things
   - **Customers:** listen carefully and explore their comments as they often give good feedback
   - **Relationships with suppliers:** many suppliers are also looking for mutual benefit
   - **Competitors:** gather intelligence on what your competitors are doing

2. **Set an example yourself** – Realise that staff need a space to chat, think and have sessions to explore different ideas in different ways. Encourage new ideas consistently, discuss all the ideas in an open forum, welcome new explorations and different directions. Be willing to think outside the box and not just the way you've always done things.

3. **Foster a climate of creativity** – Provide a sense of dynamism rather than 'quiet time' and provide a feeling of interest and mutual respect when people interact. Create an atmosphere of enthusiasm, open-mindedness and commitment in which conflicting ideas are used positively.

4. **Use techniques for creativity** – Brainstorming involves spontaneous discussion in the search for new ideas and is invaluable in generating large numbers of ideas (See C1 Tool #3). Employee suggestion schemes also gather great ideas but the key to success is to offer feedback and rewards to contributors so that employees realise that management listens and values the ideas. Focus groups can also explore a particular topic in depth and are good for developing related ideas.

5. **Become a team member** – Challenge others in the way they do things, and encourage them to challenge you.

6. **Build in breathing space** – If you want people to be creative, you can't expect them to be 'doing' all the time. Trust people with space and time and generally they will come up with the goods.

7. **Work out inexpensive pilots** – It is important to try out ideas that seem to be promising but be aware that some of these ideas may need significant investment.

Work out how to pilot such ideas on a smaller scale so that you can get feedback on how they can be further developed.

8. **Feedback and reward** – Let employees know how their suggestions are being implemented and the results being achieved because this encourages them to be forthcoming with further ideas. Feedback should be constructive, supportive and should cover all the ideas they have contributed

DOS

✓ Have a customer focus in order to produce goods and services that people want now or may want in the future

✓ Encourage trials and experiments, and use failure to move forwards, not backwards

✓ Weigh up the importance of different ideas whether they be good or bad

DON'TS

✗ Don't accept that good ideas are the privilege of a few

✗ Don't accept that all conflict is negative

✗ Don't accept that creativity takes a second place to order and routine

C1 TOOL #2:
MAKE EMOTIONAL CONFLICT A BUSINESS AS USUAL PROCESS

HOW THIS RELATES TO C1

Spontaneity only occurs when individuals are free to express themselves. This expression, however, can cause conflict within the team that can negatively impact performance if the team doesn't know how to manage it. The Pinch Crunch model is a highly effective way for teams to effectively manage the conflict that free expression engenders.

INTRODUCTION TO THE PINCH CRUNCH MODEL

The key to managing conflict is to understand how to respond rather than react to Pinches. A Pinch is a signal of the possibility of an impending disruption; it describes a sense of loss of freedom within one's current role and translates into a range of emotions including anger, frustration, hurt and shame, just to name a few (for detailed information on the nine Pinch points refer to Principle 2). If not addressed, an emotional Pinch is likely to become a Crunch – a major disruption. If the renegotiation of expectations is raised at the point in the relationship when one of the members feels a Pinch, the parties have more choice and more control over the situation.

It is important that people learn to detect Pinches before Crunches develop so that they can be managed before a full on emotional hijack takes place and the individuals either withdraw from the process, maliciously comply or attack each other.

PROCESS

1. Identify your own Pinch point.
2. Identify what happens when this Pinch turns into a Crunch.
3. Have a discussion about what your and their Pinch point is.
4. Explore what happens when their Pinch turns into a Crunch.
5. Create a contract with every key member in your team that outlines what causes a Pinch for you, how that can be dissolved, and what takes the Pinch to a Crunch and how that can be dissolved.

DOS

✓ Do be honest about your Pinch
✓ Understand how you feel when the Pinch turns into a Crunch
✓ Be aware of what makes other people Pinch
✓ Agree with them on how together, if a Pinch does happen, it can be resolved

DON'TS

✗ Don't assume that other's Pinch and Crunch is the same as yours
✗ Don't intentionally trigger people into a Pinch
✗ Don't turn the Pinch into a Crunch

C1 Tool # 3

C1 TOOL #3:
USE BRAINSTORMING TO DRIVE INNOVATION

THERE ARE FIVE STEPS TO BRAINSTORMING

1. **Set directions**. Describe the situation and define the problem. Help people to understand the problem to be solved and clarify the objectives. Focus on productive objectives and keep group on track. Spend time deciding on what criteria the final solution will need to address.

2. Encourage everyone to say whatever comes into their mind about possible solutions to the problem. **Encourage outside-the-box thinking**. *Challenge assumptions*. Be creative. Go crazy. *Think outside the box*. Sometimes the wildest ideas lead to great ones. The wilder the ideas the better. Step out of your shoes to surface new insights. ('What if you were a cat, or a film scenario writer – how would you solve the problem?'). *Encourage active listening*.

3. **Record and display each idea**. To avoid misunderstanding, make sure each idea is complete – don't use one-word descriptions. Don't edit.

4. **Apply the 80/20 rule and shift thinking styles to select the best ideas**. Look through your list of ideas and circle the 20% that will yield 80% of the results you are looking for. Encourage full-spectrum thinking.

5. **Prioritise the ideas** by evaluating them against the criteria established at the beginning of the session.

DOS

✓ Involve everyone. Encourage everyone to contribute. Control dominating participants. Celebrate diversity. Use different techniques to draw ideas from the group.

✓ Encourage cross-fertilisation. Build on each other. Let others' ideas take you somewhere else. Combine, synergise, and improve upon ideas.

✓ Suspend judgement. No ideas are bad ideas. All ideas are good ideas. (Actually, a minority opinion offered during group decision-making often stimulates more innovative solutions to problem.)

DON'TS

✗ Don't overlook the obvious – the obvious solution is sometimes the best.

✗ Don't fear repetitions. At different moments you see with different eyes. During discussion, afterwards you may find that duplicate ideas are actually different, or that they may trigger different responses.

✗ Don't stop and discuss. Go for quantity, not quality. Keep the momentum going.

KEY EXPRESSION QUESTIONS FOR BUILDING A HIGH PERFORMANCE TEAM

1. How well does your team deal with conflicting points of view?

2. How good is your team at expressing their emotions to each other?

3. How does the team manage the conflict that inevitably comes from expressing emotions?

4. How good are you as a team at being creative and innovative when working together and solving problems?

5. How often does your team encourage new ideas and approaches? How often do you stretch yourselves to try something novel or different?

6. How do you have fun as a team? How could you inject more of this?

NEUROPOWER CASE STUDY

ORGANISATIONAL CASE STUDY #1: STATE HEALTH HAND HYGIENE PROJECT

The Task: To improve compliance by health workers with hand hygiene practice.

Recap:

In 2007, an Australian state health department wanted to address the serious threat that health-associated infections posed to hospital patients. Micro-organisms are readily transmitted on the hands of health care workers. In Australia alone, health officials estimate that up to 7000 people die annually from hand hygiene-related infections in hospitals. The economic burden is also considerable, costing millions each year. Hand hygiene has been proven to substantially reduce transmission of micro-organisms. However, despite well-established guidelines, compliance throughout the world with hygiene standards is disconcertingly low. International and national health agencies have been grappling with how to deal with the issue for some time, and few interventions have had any impact whatsoever, despite both European and US hospitals and governments spending tens of millions of dollars on communications, incentives, closed circuit TV and education.

Since research demonstrated that the hand hygiene issue centred around human behaviour, one state health department decided on an innovative, behaviour-changing approach using the NeuroPower framework to drive the solution. Working with the NeuroPower Consulting Team, the department implemented a behaviour change program called Clean Hands are LifeSavers that engaged the health workers and increased compliance from 18% to 60%. A key driver of this behaviour change involved effectively addressing each of the six Intelligences in the correct sequence. How these progressive steps were taken is outlined in the Organisational Toolbox Case Study at the end of each Intelligence chapter. **Having already:** Created safety and security in the hospital environment by embedding values through a code of conduct

Step 2: Empower People to Express Themselves Spontaneously and Creatively
Historically, programs developed and delivered elsewhere in Australia failed to improve compliance greatly despite pouring millions of dollars into impressive (and expensive) marketing materials.

NeuroPower's approach was to encourage each ward in every hospital to work collaboratively to solve the issue. We showed the LifeSavers how to engage the health workers themselves in the creation and production of communications and marketing materials to support the campaign. As a result, every ward across the state came up with its own individual approach with events, posters, competitions and other inventive ideas for getting the hand hygiene message across.

ORGANISATIONAL CASE STUDY #2: MERCHANT BANK EQUITY DERIVATIVES LEADERSHIP TEAM

The Task: Improve employee engagement and tangible business performance

Recap:

In 2006, at the height of the financial boom, one of Australia's leading equity derivatives teams was operating in an environment that was fast-paced, demanding and with a high level of stress. In order to handle large volumes of work in a very volatile market, the team needed to be highly functional and collaborative. Growth was nearly 200 per cent over the previous year so the enormous strain was evident. This was mainly caused by a Leadership Team in crisis.

The Leadership Team was fractured, non-collaborative and driven by their own individual agendas. There was both a lack of respect and a lack of honesty between members which led to highly reactive responses and conflict. The broader team could see this occurring and they felt they were part of a warring tribe with all the insecurities that brought.

NeuroPower consultants devised a program which focused on addressing the splintered Leadership Team. The intervention involved a series of group structured processes which were embedded by individual coaching sessions.

Having already: Created role clarity

Step 2: Empowering People to Express Themselves using C1

Once the team environment became safe, the next step was to ensure the Leadership Team had permission to express themselves honestly, be creative and use out-of-the-box thinking with no fear. We looked at the Core Belief profiles of the group members (these are the profiles embedded in C1) which revealed each individual's world view and how they interacted with others in the workplace. For many members, the fact that people saw the world differently was a revelation. A key aspect of this session was the Pinch/Crunch model which looked at the resistance strategies and emotional reactions the various Core Belief profiles have and how this underlies all conflict. We helped them develop ways to deal with conflict in this volatile and challenging environment.

Chapter 4

Our Third Social Cognitive Need:
LEADING THE PACK &
The Intervention Function (P2)

LEADING THE PACK (P2) AT A GLANCE

Leading the Pack is our Brain's Third Social Cognitive Need

The brain is competitive and loves status. Once basic needs have been met, money itself has little influence on happiness. Instead, status, recognition and independence are key drivers of motivation and satisfaction and must be managed to foster healthy passion rather than unhealthy competition.

Characteristics of the Leading the Pack (P2) Functional Network

Action and Passion

STRENGTH	WEAKNESS
Committed and focused on doing whatever it takes to achieve the outcome	Can cut corners and ignore processes to achieve the outcome

OPPORTUNITY	THREAT
To detach from their overattachment to outcomes	Can burn out

Management Style

- High energy and passionate
- Results-focused and able to make quick decisions
- Can be argumentative or aggressive

VITALITY

P2 THINKING	P2 FEELING	P2 SOMATIC
Personal goals and priorities	Passion and drive	Physical strength

COMMUNICATION STYLE

- Can often push the conversation in one direction
- Can be totally insensitive to others not in line with their ideas
- Can be very passionate about a cause or topic
- Will talk over others and will not keep to set timeframes unless they believe they should
- Can be bombastic or rude
- Very persuasive and energetic

KEYWORDS INCLUDE

- Passion
- Success
- Drive
- Achievement
- Goals

Leading the Pack (P2) Helps Us to Survive

Leading the Pack (P2) helps both individuals and the group to survive and thrive by motivating and enabling us to break past patterns, challenge the status quo and apply passion to drive towards better outcomes.

Leading the Pack &
The Intervention Function (P2)

LEADING THE PACK: OUR BRAIN'S THIRD SOCIAL NEED

In Chapter 1, we introduced a foundational social need - Relatedness (P1) - which drives us to learn the rules of the groups to which we belong and to then apply them. Relatedness (P1) encourages us to blend into the group and promote our own survival by helping the *group* to sustain itself (using historical knowledge embedded in the group's culture). It encourages us to learn our place in the group and stay there. And yet on a daily basis many of us seem to push back against this Relatedness and the group. Rather than maintaining the status quo, we challenge ourselves and the group and drive towards achieving personal goals that help us differentiate ourselves as individuals. We want to be better than the rest, we want to 'lead the pack' and be respected for it in at least one area. As with Relatedness (P1), this drive to be Leading the Pack (P2) has deep roots in our evolution.

Within the brain, a diverse range of structures and neuronal networks help us satisfy our need for Leading the Pack. Within the *NeuroPower* framework, this set of structures is called the 'P2 Intervention System' (or sometimes the 'P2 network' or 'P2 function') and when we emphasise this social need, we give rise to a particular thinking style referred to as 'P2 Intelligence'. The rest of this chapter explores the P2 Intervention System in detail.

No matter how much some of us deny it, all humans are competitive. We see it on full display- in schools, stadiums, bars and workplaces around the world. Whether we're athletes, spectators, workplace leaders or followers, our brains are constantly comparing ourselves to others. For our ancestors, those at the 'top of the tree' in the group had first choice of food and mates, giving us a definite incentive to reach for the top (Jordan, Sivanathan & Galinsky, 2011). Now, many generations later, social cues about status, recognition and independence can have a powerful impact on our brains. For example, brain imaging studies have shown that praise activates the same reward areas of the brain (the caudate and putamen) as money rewards - and that these areas are highly sensitive even to small changes in your status (Izuma et al., 2008; Zink et al., 2008). The value of money itself seems to diminish when we know someone else is earning more, with less internal reward activity in the brain (Fliessbach et al., 2007). And David Rock[1],

---

1   David Rock's SCARF model draws on neuroscience and other research to effectively explore the impact of social dynamics on workplaces. Within this model, the elements of 'Status' and 'Autonomy' align well with the social need of Leading the Pack (P2). In addition, Rock's 'Certainty', 'Relatedness' and 'Fairness' each describe aspects of the P1 Intelligence (Relatedness) within the *NeuroPower* framework.

who first coined the term NeuroLeadership, has highlighted Japanese research showing that when we see others outperforming us in things that we value then the challenge to our sense of status and self-esteem activates a threat response in the anterior cingulate cortex. Needless to say, the resulting emotional response can be quite unconstructive (Takeushi et al., 2008).

Performance-driven tasks can lead to stress responses when we know that we are being assessed by others, but - importantly - psychology and neuroscience research suggests that our ability to cope depends heavily on our sense of control over the situation; the more autonomy and control we have, the easier it is to cope (Dickersen & Kemeny, 2008). In fact, in 2012, Gary Sherman and his colleagues at Harvard Business School found that amongst senior military and government leaders, individuals who *felt* they had more power showed consistently lower levels of the stress hormone cortisol. And the benefits don't just extend to the individual. Research out of Stanford has shown that giving someone a greater sense of control over their situation increases their optimism and self-esteem, and leads to greater task-related activity and effort (Fast et al., 2009).

Both organisational and neuroscience research point to the benefits of supporting and encouraging this drive (Leading the Pack) for individuals and teams. Driven by greater activity in the left frontal lobe, individuals high in Leading the Pack focus more on achieving the goals of the organisation, show tenacity in the face of early failures and can generate more options (Amodio et al., 2004; Crowe & Higgins, 1997; Markovits et al., 2008; Mehta & Josephs, 2006). And yet, when over-emphasised and misdirected, the drive of P2 can lead to divisive competition and aggression (McAndrew, 2009).

THE P2 CHALLENGE FOR LEADERS

So how can leaders keep 'P2' in their teams within the healthy zone and motivate their teams to brilliant performance? Firstly, as we mentioned earlier, building evidence from research conducted by people such as Dr Caroline Zink and highlighted by authors such as Daniel Pink, show that status, recognition and independence are key drivers of motivation and performance and in many cases have a greater long-term effect than money. In a family, community, team or corporate environment, we all have a need to be personally successful and to be recognised. Leaders can create this in three ways. Firstly, to build energy and drive, leaders need to identify different markers of excellence so that each member of the team has an area in which they Lead the Pack.

Secondly, they need to recognise that central to the P2 system in the brain are two areas, the orbitofrontal cortex and the anterior cingulate cortex, which together work to constantly assess the relationship between what you're doing and the rewards that you are getting. The question they ask: *"Is this course of action still bringing me sufficient reward or do I need to change my behaviour?"* When working with individuals high in P2, leaders need to keep a keen eye on the effort-reward ratio for both the individual and the team as a whole as it works towards its goals.

Finally, to drive high performance, leaders must align individual aspirations and motivation with the team's goals and have the ability to redirect individual competitiveness towards shared competitive advantage.

THE EVOLUTIONARY SOCIAL BRAIN FUNCTION OF P2

The P2 Intelligence enables the individual to survive through:

1. Goal-directed behaviour and independent action (Berkman & Lieberman, 2009)

2. Motivation and drive that keeps the mind and behaviour focused on the achievement of purposeful goals – including those that may involve competition with other members of the group for individual reward. Specifically, this involves attention, motor control, response inhibition and progress monitoring (Decety et al., 2004)

3. Prioritisation of options so that the individual can achieve the greatest benefit with minimum cognitive, somatic or emotional effort (Walton et al., 2006)

4. A sense of urgency and independence; a sense of willpower and ego .

Recognising the Characteristics of Leading the Pack (P2)

The P2 Intelligence gives the mind willpower that drives enthusiastic behaviour aimed at success. P2 is a very high-energy function, and individuals with highly functioning P2 are skilled at energising, striving, convincing and debating. Many of the world's most powerful leaders have highly developed P2.

However, the P2 Intelligence can also drive a person to be so intent on performing and achieving that they become exclusively task-oriented. When this happens they often bully or play favourites because they see people only as a means to achieving their own success and rise to power.

From an Eastern perspective, Judith (1996) argues that in our physical body P2 is associated with the solar plexus or 'the gut'. The childhood development of this Intelligence follows on from that of C1, the pleasure instinct. From the safety of the family (P1) and awareness of their own individuality and emotions (C1), a young person with well-functioning P1 and C1 will develop the motivation to act independently and to address the challenge of P2: to realise their separateness, to establish their autonomy and to establish the right to act. As the child rises to these

P2 in the Brain[*]

Research has revealed that several parts of the brain support the P2 system:

- The left medial prefrontal cortex (PFC) and in particular the orbital PFC, which performs executive functions (Schore, 1994) mediates both the reward value of voluntary actions and calculates the magnitude of reward or punishment values (O'Doherty et al., 2001; Rolls, 2000; Tremblay & Schultz, 1999; Watanabe, 1996). This part of the brain is sensitive to the size of our gains and losses and assesses whether there is enough in it for us to undertake a task (Xue et al., 2009).
- More generally, the medial PFC is consistently implicated when we make evaluations about ourselves (Saxe & Haushofer, 2008), and when we reflect upon our personal goals and aspirations (P2 Thinking; Johnson et al., 2006).[†]
- The anterior cingulate cortex contains many neuron pathways that are also recruited to help process the costs and benefits of different courses of action. Activity in individual neurons in this area predicts whether an individual will choose to compete for a larger reward or settle for a smaller reward without having to compete (Walton & Baudonnat, 2012).
- The insula (in particular the right insula) is strongly implicated in having a sense of agency (Sperduti et al., 2011) and the precuneus (located on the medial surface of the parietal lobe) is associated with first-perspective taking (Cavanna & Trimble, 2006).[‡]

---

[*] Both P1 and P2 can be seen as describing different motivations that produce behaviours. Those behaviours and actions are supported by an extensive set of structures in the somatosensory and motor areas of the brain (including, for example, the primary and supplementary motor areas. Here we focus on brain areas supporting characteristics that distinguish P2 (achievement-focused action, a sense of agency, assessment of status, social competition) from P1 (obligation-focused action, motivation to comply with externally directed rules and behaviours, assessment of safety and security).

[†] By contrast, recent reviews suggest that applying 'if-then' rules given to us by others (P1 thinking) seem to be represented in more lateral areas of the PFC (Berkman & Lieberman in Moskowitz & Grant, 2009).

[‡] Interestingly, however, the precuneus has also repeatedly been implicated in both self-related processes (such as recognising your arms and legs as your own) and other-related processes (such as the ability to recognise actions caused by others, and a focus on duties and obligations; Cavanna & Trimble, 2006; Farrer & Frith, 2002; Mitchell et al., 2009).

Searching for the 'Self' in the Brain

Where are 'you' in your brain? Answering that in any one brain imaging study has many challenges. But as technology increases in speed and capacity, researchers are now combining data collected over years of brain imaging studies to examine similarities between thousands of brains simultaneously - and some, like researchers from the NeuroImaging Data Access Group, have begun sharing this database online to the public.[§]

The images below show the results of an automated, computer-based meta-analysis of 206 different studies that each explored different brain processes involving our sense of 'self'. Each blue dot shows a location where one of these tasks involved greater activation when study participants had to perform tasks that involved thinking about or making decisions related to themselves.

The pattern of activations across all these different studies suggests that processing about the 'self' involves activity predominantly in the left medial prefrontal cortex (which sits just above the eyes) and another midline area further back in the left precuneus. These areas are part of what has become known as the midline default mode system which seems to be critical for understanding our own (and others) internal states.

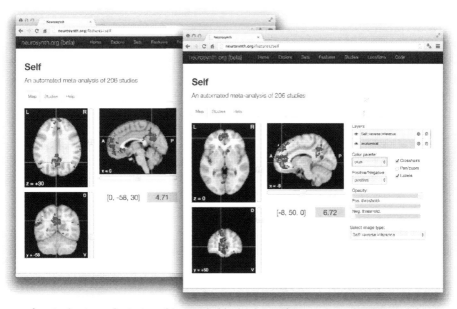

§   At the time of printing, this searchable database of comparisons has been made available at www.neurosynth.org

challenges and begins to take risks, they develop their own individual willpower.

Research focused on the neuroscience of 'promotion-focused' regulatory styles and goal-approach behaviours indicate that P2 is linked to activation in the left prefrontal cortex (Amodio et al., 2004; Eddington et al., 2007; 2009) as well as left and right precuneus and the anterior cingulate cortex (Strauman et al., 2013).

The Development of Leading the Pack (P2)

THE EMERGENCE OF THE EGO

The strengths of P2 include:

- Self-esteem
- Self-respect
- Self-discipline
- Ambition
- A willingness to take risks in order to achieve goals
- Drive
- High energy

The P2 Intelligence relates to the ego, which Jung proposed is made up of the individual's conscious perceptions, memories and thoughts and is responsible for the individual's sense of personal success.

The focus of this Intelligence is on individual action. High functioning P2 reflects the development of a person's autonomy and the ability to take responsibility for themselves. Without this independence, they will act like a victim, blaming others for events in their life, while believing they have no power to influence the direction their life takes. Those with high functioning P2 act in a way that reflects their strong sense of self, even if this risks the disapproval of others or conflicts with the values or beliefs of the tribe.

THE DEVELOPMENT OF AN EGO IDENTITY

During the P1 stage, the child identifies with their body and internalises society's rules. Freud would refer to P1 as the *superego*. As they develop their C1 Intelligence they identify with their emotions and needs – what Freud would refer to as the *id*. The focus of P1 is the internal unconscious world, while C1 focuses on the conscious external world. According to Freud, the child then develops their ego, which consists of the conscious elements of the self. Thus P2 acts as the communicator between the unconscious and conscious parts of self. As the P2 Intelligence develops, the focus shifts from how we relate to others to how we relate to ourselves.

During the P2 stage the child needs to learn to direct the impulses and emotions from P1 and C1 into goal-aligned behaviour. The focus of the ego is self-definition, but the tribe moderates it. As the child develops their ego they step out and take risks. According to the response of the tribe, the more acceptable parts of the individual become the first ingredients for what will later become their conscious personality profile (i.e. their Master[2]). The parts that are rejected by the significant people in the tribe are also rejected by the child's ego and sent into the unconscious. These aspects of the self are the first ingredients for what will later become their unconscious second-order personality profile (also known as their Mirror). This aspect of self, while denied by the person, is quite obvious to those around them, especially during times of stress.

The P2 Intelligence is linked with the hippocampus (in the medial temporal lobe) and the orbitofrontal cortex. The development of these areas allows the child to have 'explicit' memories where they are aware that they are remembering something (Squire & Zola-Morgan, 1991; Perner & Ruffman, 1995; Tulving, 1993; Schachter et al., 1996).

The development of the P2 Intelligence may begin to occur as early as the second year of life. During this sensitive period a 'cognitive mapper' develops (Edelman, 1992; Bauer, 1996). Thought to be located within the hippocampus, this mapper enables the child to recall the order in which events occur. This allows the child to develop a sense of time and sequencing. The child comes to expect what typically comes first and what comes next in a specific circumstance. For example, consider the passionate reaction displayed by a toddler to a visitor sitting in the 'wrong' chair for the family dinner. This hippocampal development is associated with the capacity to generate the spatial representational maps for the locations of things in the world. Loss of hippocampal functioning in rats, for example, leads to loss of memory for running a maze (Squire, 1987).

This cognitive mapper allows the brain to create a four-dimensional sense of the self in the world across time. The ability to link reward with actions through time is particularly important for the development of actions based on positive reinforcement, such as those associated with P2 (Siegel, 1999).

Highly functioning P2 will act as a force that encourages self-expression, rather than one that produces guilt and a feeling that the individual is confined to behaving in certain approved ways. Keeping this in perspective can enable us to have a strong will, while simultaneously transcending it.

Aggression from significant adults for 'bad' behaviour can result in the child developing low self-esteem. This leaves no room for taking risks that may result in further mistakes. The risk-averse ego instead loses power and relies on external success and the approval of others in order to feel good. On the other hand, if the significant adults can support risk-taking and moderate the child's behaviour without shaming, the child will develop a healthy self-esteem (Judith, 1996).

---

2   For more information about the Master and Mirror personalities, and the Neuro-Rational Types, see Principle 3.

'Asian Brains' vs 'Western Brains'

Do cultural differences show up in the brain? Researchers describing themselves as 'cultural neuroscientists' have been exploring this question in recent years, using brain imaging techiques to try to explain interesting differences between Western and Asian styles of thinking.

For example, culturally speaking, anthropologists have observed that individuals in Western cultures tend to have a strong focus on the self (individualistic), and Asian cultures tend to place comparatively more emphasis on family and social groups (collectivist). One easy demonstration of this in the lab is that American individuals are much better at recognising and remembering adjectives related to themselves than those relating to family or strangers; Chinese individuals, on the other hand, seem to remember descriptions of themselves and of their family equally well.

To explain this, cultural neuroscientists looked at brain activity when performing this kind of task. They have found that the ventromedial PFC (a key area for awareness of the 'self') was activated by viewing descriptions of the self for both Americans and Chinese participants, but that the Chinese *also* had activity in this area when viewing descriptions of their family members (Zhu et al., 2007; Han & Northoff, 2012).

As UCLA-based researcher, Dr Meghan Meyer (2009), observes:

> *Taken together, these divergent findings fit with each cultures' conceptualization of the individual — independent in Western-European/American cultures, and intertwined with others in your environment in East-Asian cultures. Of course, this research should not be used to over-generalize differences in thinking across cultures. Indeed, there is also a great deal of research highlighting the commonalities in cognition across cultures. That said, acknowledging the subtle differences may help people in contemporary society — which is increasingly culturally diverse — appreciate the nuances in thought and behavior among the people we come across in our day to day lives.*

Willpower has Both Strengths and Weaknesses

POWER

It is clear when we spend time around people with highly functioning P2 that they are powerful individuals. Our society promotes power over (force), but when an individual with developed P2 becomes more evolved, their power is more akin to the original Latin meaning, which is 'to be able'. This most commonly takes the form of physical power, but also relates to the ability to cause change. To be empowered is to be able to determine our own destiny, to risk and take responsibility for the outcome, to learn from and correct mistakes, and to change our behaviour accordingly.

People with a highly functioning P2 are confident in their own personal opinions. During their development, the child forms opinions and develops the confidence to express them. If the tribe supports this independence, they will grow up to become passionate, persuasive and powerful. With self-confidence, these people can express their individuality while appreciating the opinions and beliefs of others. Respecting both themselves and others, they will willingly cooperate and contribute to their community.

P2 provides us with the means to break through the glass ceiling of performance to be and do whatever it is that we really want. As psychiatrist Dr Brenda Davies (1998) suggests, if your ship hasn't come in yet, use your P2 to take you out to meet it.

However, P2 also has a dark side. With excess P2, individuals can act as insensitive weapons, potentially marring or destroying relationships and the self-esteem of others.

Myss (1996) insightfully outlines the natural evolution of P2 as involving four stages, each of which can take just a short time, months, or years. Each stage challenges the person's character, ethics, morality and self-respect. (This is the same process undertaken by teams as they develop a sense of team identity and compete in the market.)

The first stage is **rebellion**. It starts with an act of revolution or several minor rebellions. This establishes the person's separateness from group authority and signifies they have sufficient inner strength to 'stand their ground' and live according to their own examined values and beliefs. In teams, this is also known as *Forming* and involves establishing the team's separation from the rest of the world. This gives the team permission to operate as a separate unit.

The second stage of P2 evolution is **involution**. The person calls on their 'guts' or internal fortitude to do the internal work of dealing with the consequences of their choices and actions. They acquire the skills of self-inquiry and finding insight, and therefore develop faith in their ability to act in a way that honours themselves. This includes releasing the past and accepting themselves and is like dying to self in order to be reborn. In teams, this phase is also known as *Storming* and reflects a realisation that the team possesses the skills and knowledge needed to get the job done; that is, that it does not need to rely on anyone outside the team.

At this stage, it is important to acknowledge that it takes strength to withdraw from the authority of a group norm. If your spirit is strong enough to go against your support network, it has the potential to change your life. If we look our fears in the face, they will be overcome. As individuals, it is at this stage that bad childhood memories can be used to make good choices as an adult.

The third stage of P2 evolution is a period of **narcissism**, when the person develops the personal strength to create an image of themselves regardless of tribal criticism. Their newly formed self-esteem gives them a strength, stamina and the ability to follow their 'gut' instincts. The individual now feels free to be guided in their choices by more than reasoning; their 'gut' feelings warn them, then direct them towards personal power and encourage them to take control of their life. In teams, this equates with a period of *Norming* in which a team gains a sense that it can compete in the market and deliver on KPIs. The team creates its own sense of true north, through performance management and the celebration of success.

The fourth stage is **evolution**. A person needs to like themselves, or they will continue to attract situations that reinforce their low self-esteem. As they face sequential challenges, they gain strength to make wiser choices – choices which enhance their spirit rather than drain their power. Eventually the person gains a high level of self-esteem and spiritual power and can be whoever they wish. They are empowered to maintain their principles, dignity and passion without compromise, whatever the odds. In teams, this final phase of P2 evolution is called *Performing*; the team is empowered and every member does whatever it takes to smash through glass ceilings.

P2-DRIVEN PERSON AT WORK

The P2-driven person at work is a competitive, formidable powerhouse. A mind with highly developed P2 is a study in proactivity. These individuals set their goals and use their initiative to make things happen, taking responsibility for their own circumstances. This is no helpless victim!

Whereas a P1-driven person is not ego-centred but instead focused on the ways of the team and will cooperate with workmates, the P2-driven person is egocentric and strives to achieve as an individual.

It is a common perceptual bias for those with highly developed P2 to consistently overestimate their control over an outcome and to underestimate the role of chance or

Childhood Experience of Shame
Damages P2 Intelligence

During early infancy, the vast majority of parent-child interactions are positive, affectionate and playful. Due to the very limited skills and mobility of the infant, he or she will tend to stay in close proximity to the caretaker, who provides for the child's bodily and emotional needs. As the helpless infant grows into an exploring toddler, the parent's role expands to include protecting the infant from the many domestic risks of life, like stairwells, cars and the vagaries of pets. As the parent's role increases they begin to say 'No!' on an almost constant basis from the beginning of the second year (Rothbart, Taylor & Tucker, 1989). Now the state of acceptance and attunement with the attachment figure begins to be conditional on specific behaviour. Shame, arising from this loss of attunement, is a powerful inhibitory emotion and a primary means of social control (Schore, 1991). Shame effectively truncates the positive emotions generated within reciprocal interactions through activation of dopaminergic and opioid systems – systems that build the brain and increase tolerance for higher levels of positive affect and arousal. During the second year of life, studies have found that the eyes and facial expressions come to be used to inhibit toddler activities. Looks of disapproval or disgust from an adult, while their infant is in a state of arousal, result in the experience of shame (Schore, 1994). This is in sharp contrast to early infancy where the mutual gaze between attachment figure and child is a primary mechanism for promoting brain growth and organisation.

factors beyond their control (Taylor & Brown, 1988; Langer, 1978).

It is not the *doing* but the *completing* that holds pleasure for the P2 Intelligence. Work is a means of enhancing their own rise to stardom or to look the strongest and the best. Therefore, the P2-driven team member often presents as the most efficient, tireless and achieving member of the team. In this space, there is no time for friendship or play for self or others unless useful to their rise to power or prestige (Horney, 1945).

Of course, there is a price to pay for this self-forgetfulness and denial of feelings. Judith (1996) argues that the gut feelings of our solar plexus are the source of P2. Their domain is in dealing with action as well as integrity and righteousness. The emotions of the gut include anger, rage, jealousy, resentment and guilt. Repressing any of these can cause diseases such as cancer, digestive problems, diabetes, obesity, problems with the pancreas or gall bladder, fatigue, depression and even despair (Judith, 1996).

Poorly Functioning P2 and Ego-Centric Behaviour

Poorly functioning P2 manifests in low levels of energy, passion and self-discipline, and a weak will and ego. The person will be passive, avoiding risks and confrontation by following the rules. They appear to please but resent the demands of others, and yet lack the will to manage their own lives. These individuals do not take responsibility for their situation but blame others. They may have goals, but lack the self-discipline, perseverance and will to bring them to fruition. These people can become passive-aggressive or detached. Shy and withdrawn, they can appear cold. How was this character formed? We can look back to childhood to find the answer.

When the child starts to act according to their own volition, and takes risks to 'do their own thing' independent of directions of their elders, they are working with the emergence of P2. If they are to develop a highly functioning P2, they need guidance without stifling their ego. Of course, the world is not full of wise parents, and so many children fail to effectively develop their ego. This can happen in any number of poor parenting approaches including overindulgence, under-attention, too high expectations, parentification, excess control or sexual over-stimulation (Judith, 1996).

UNDER-RELIANCE ON P2

Not all children grow up with a highly functioning P2. Judith (1996) argues that children with poorly functioning P2 have usually been the victims of inconsistent parental discipline. This parenting approach teaches the child that taking on new or risky things will result in punishment rather than support and guidance. Operating from a space of fear, the child therefore learns to follow the rules without question and not stray into the unknown. Children who have been abused may also interpret their experience as punishment, which can similarly affect the development of the P2 Intelligence. In an attempt to compensate for being 'bad', they continue restricting themselves and feeling unworthy of the reward of pleasure and happiness even into adulthood (Judith, 1996).

The demon at this stage of development is shame. When a child is shamed, their power is destroyed and their ego development is impeded. This involves shaming not

When More is Never Enough

Cozolino (2002) describes the behaviour of minds totally focused on P2 as being manic. This pattern of behaviour involves engaging in constantly escalating levels of activity in order to avoid facing the difficult personal questions that the P2-driven mind has repressed.

only of their ego but also their instincts, which are part of their identity from P1 and C1. As the child tries to control their instincts with their thoughts, their instincts are denied and driven into their unconscious. But of course this isn't the end; their instincts break out in bad behaviour, such as bursts of temper, passive-aggression or procrastination.

From the perspective of the individual, shame is somehow atoned by self-punishment or suffering. The person punishes themselves with misery and failure, and will continue to do so all their life unless they focus on developing their P2 self-esteem. The task of integration is to embrace their P2 and give themselves permission to act on their own behalf.

OVER-RELIANCE ON P2

Some people grow up with an over-reliance on P2. This manifests somatically in high anxiety (hypertension), which makes the person overcharged with energy or hyperactive. Their muscles are tense and their stomach becomes acidic. Because their core self is undernourished, they need to bolster their false self with the approval of others.

This is achieved through constant activity and trying to over-achieve. Indeed, these individuals do not feel alive without this frenetic activity. Their ironclad will appears powerful but is brittle and fragile; when challenged, they retreat out of fear or react with anger. They may also become obsessed with getting everything right.

These people are obsessed with having power over themselves and others. Some people who over-rely on P2 put great energy into pushing their own bodies, treating them like machines in order to look and perform well (thereby bolstering their ego). These people are well advised to find a balance between listening to their body and achieving. At the extreme, people who rely excessively on P2 become like robots. Their ego comprises no body or spirit, only will, and activity. They are what they do and achieve, and are just one small step from abusing their power. This is the dominator, or the bully, who needs to win at all costs – to have power over rather than power *with* others (Judith, 1996).

Karen Horney (1945) suggests that excessive P2 leads to neurotic thinking and behaviour. This can be experienced to some extent by any person with a strongly developed P2 Intelligence, especially if their reactive personality (i.e. Neuro-Limbic Type or Core Belief) is dominated by P2.

To this person, life follows the Darwinian theory of survival of the fittest, where everyone is fighting for survival. Life is seen as a struggle and you have to fight to win. This aggressive type, therefore, 'moves against' people, rejecting compliance or neutrality as foolhardy. Instead, they proactively go out to face the 'enemy' (although this is usually accompanied by a smile or a greeting). These individuals are constantly alert to the fighting strengths of everyone they meet because, of course, they feel they need to be prepared. The demon of P2 is fear and is usually the unrecognised motivation for action. This fear is completely ego-based, usually involving fear of rejection, not looking good or criticism.

However, at the heart of all P2 fear is the fear of death. Facing death, heartbreak or even depression causes panic in the ego-focused individual who relies excessively on P2. In contrast, an individual who prefers the P1 Intelligence feels part of the tribe and can usually accept death as part of life, believing, 'When I die, the tribe or family lives on and I'll leave a legacy if there's time.' However, the P2 ego thinks, 'I'm an individual. When I die nothing survives.'

The P2-driven mind works very hard to overcome its fears and does its best to hide these fears from others, because to show it will weaken their competitive edge. Horney (1945) explains that while aggressive and innately fearful, a P2-dominated person often appears to be a 'good fellow'. In reality, their feelings are a combination of genuine benevolence, pretence and a neurotic need for approval (to bolster their fragile ego). Because of their innate fear about survival, raw P2 has a great need to control, either directly or indirectly. This can take the form of overt use of power or indirect manipulation. In the latter case, the individual may choose to be the power behind the throne while sadistically pursuing their own goals.

Individuals who over-rely on P2 are driven by an endless need to succeed. Success for them means not just a pass, but to surpass the competition. They crave prestige and recognition, as this external affirmation makes them feel strong and powerful. Of course, they can never feel satisfied. They always feel insecure because of their innate belief that the world is dangerous. Therefore, they become and wish to appear hard or tough, giving the message, 'I'm no pushover.'

Unfortunately, in their drive to win at all costs, these people exploit, outsmart and use others. Whenever they form a new relationship they are asking themselves, 'What's in it for me?' This can mar their close relationships as well, as they will choose a life partner who will bring them success, power, prestige, contacts or ideas. Love is often

How Autonomy and Learned Helplessness Relate to the P2 Function

Psychologist Fritz Perls, who founded the Gestalt movement, moved the concept of aggression from the Freudian concept of a purely destructive force to a concept closer to its original root which is 'to reach out'. He wished to re-establish its true biological function, which is not senseless discharge but rather application of one's will to bring about desirable changes in one's environment (Perls, 1969).

In contrast, the psychological condition, termed 'learned helplessness', that results in clinical depression occurs when individuals do not believe they have any influence on their circumstances and lack control over the conditions of their life (Maier & Seligman, 1976; Overmier & Seligman, 1967; Seligman, 1975; Seligman & Maier, 1967).

Interestingly, recent neuroscience research shows that this learned helplessness may be linked to decreased activity in the left prefrontal cortex (PFC). The left medial orbital PFC is usually activated when we focus on the achievement of positive goals, but individuals with major depressive disorder showed much less activity in this region, even when primed to focus on personal goals (Eddington et al., 2009).

considered to be soft or weak.

There is a basic persona versus authenticity conflict for the P2-driven person: whether to ignore or repress their feelings, or alternatively to allow their feelings, show their vulnerability and allow an opening for their enemies to attack.

A person driven by raw P2 can be deceptive. When they interact they appear to be uninhibited because they express their viewpoint with confidence and passion; they say what they want and clearly express any anger. However, because they are inhibited in their emotional world, they have a diminished capacity for friendship, love, affection, sympathy and understanding. All of these feelings are rejected and seen as sloppy sentimentality with no positive impact on the achievement of results. The P2-driven person can therefore send mixed messages; while they may appear friendly and confident and express 'safe' feelings, they must appear strong in order to appear successful.

The inner conflict for neurotic P2 is the need to combat all softer feelings because

Unhealthy Narcissism

Narcissists crave others' admiration more than their love. These people are often innovators and compelled to perform, not because they are working to a high internal standard of excellence but because they want the benefits and accolades that performance bestows. They take the freedom to follow their goals aggressively, irrespective of the cost to and effect on others. In stressful times, narcissistic managers can appear attractive, but only because they have the fight to push through plans that bring radical change (Goleman, 2006, p. 119).

emotions will weaken their ability to fight in a hostile world. Even more challenging is the need to fight the enemy within, which is their desire to be sympathetic and caring. If they do repress their feelings and their desire to be 'good' or compliant, they can become more compulsively aggressive (Horney, 1945). It is important to remember that we all have the potential for aggression, but when we are not neurotic we can integrate this into our conscious personality profile (i.e. Neuro-Rational Type) and so moderate it. Thus, we can let our Master lead us out of our fear.

Individuals who have an over-reliance on P2 somatic, feeling or thinking circuits can be described as follows[3]:

Somatic Over-reliance on P2: If there is an over-reliance on P2 somatic, the individual focuses on feats of strength, physical power and exacting revenge. Using the self-justifying reframe of having a lust for life, they do everything in excess.

Feeling Over-reliance P2: With an over-reliance of P2 feeling, the individual becomes obsessed with success, approval and looking good in everybody's eyes.

Thinking Over-reliance P2: If there is an over-reliance on P2 thinking, the individual focuses on reframing everything so it is positive, motivated by a desire to avoid emotional pain (either their own or that of others).

THE IMPORTANCE OF WILLPOWER

The experience of shame can break a child's will. Any kind of shaming can crush the child's emerging P2, especially if it is related to behaviour they are too young to manage. Shaming includes child abuse, both verbal or physical. At this early stage the child's

---

3   Each of these reflects a particular Neuro-Limbic Type; the Eight, Three and Seven respectively. These relate to *NeuroPower* Principle #2, *NeuroPower* (Burow, 2013).

ego is fragile and grows to include a sense of shame because they believe their 'self' (as opposed to their behaviour) is bad. These children can grow up to believe they will fail at anything they put their hand to, and their lives often become self-fulfilling prophecies.

Receiving insufficient attention can also break a child's will. Some parents mean well but are just too busy to pay attention to what the child feels or wants. They give the child no choices, so provide no chance to develop a sense of will. The child then grows up with a sense of powerlessness and resignation. To compensate for their sense of loss, the child (and later the adult until the deficit is resolved) may become passive-aggressive and resentful, or swing the other way and become a violent bully. Lacking the will, power and freedom of P2 to create their own destiny, they must rely on their other Intelligences to run their life. Under-stimulation can also break a child's will, potentially inducing the child to grow up troubled by fatigue, low energy, a sense of emptiness and low libido (Judith, 1996).

Conversely, an overindulged child learns that any behaviour is accepted without restraint. They grow up with an inflated ego, feeling inferior or superior according to their unrealistic expectations, and lacking the self-confidence and limits to discover their own power. If a child is pushed beyond an appropriate level by supportive parents with very high expectations they can develop a sense of inadequacy, with their achievements

The Difference Between Shame and Guilt

Schore (1994) differentiates between shame and guilt. Guilt occurs later in development and is related to unacceptable behaviour, whereas shame is an emotion about the self that becomes internalised before there is an ability to differentiate between one's behaviour and self. Physiologically, shame is represented in a rapid transition from a positive to a negative affective state and from sympathetic to parasympathetic dominance. This shift occurs when the child has an expectation of attunement in a positive state, only to find disapproval and misattunement in the face of the attachment figure (Schore, 1994). Prolonged and repeated shame states result in physiological dysregulation and negatively impact the development of networks of affect regulation and attachment centred in medial prefrontal areas (Schore, 1994). Since shame is a powerful, preverbal and physiologically-based organising principle, the overuse of shame in the process of parenting can predispose a child to developmental psychopathology related to affect regulation and identity (Schore, 1994).

never being enough. They too will grow up with low self-esteem and may ultimately specialise in failure, regardless of ability.

Some children are parentified and given work or sex roles that are far beyond their age and ability. They can also emerge with a sense of inadequacy and inferiority and are set up for failure.

A child's will can be broken as a result of over-controlling parents. This child submits but still has inner conflicts between their will (inner resistance) and outer compliance. My experience supports Judith's (1996) research that shows that when these children grow up they become reliable, hard working, eager to please and enduring during a crisis. However, in my experience these same adults are often quietly passive-aggressive and likely to sabotage the work environment.

Sexual over-stimulation can also break the will of a child. Physical abuse that overloads the sensory system can cause a heightened resistance to intrusion to develop. Judith (1996) observes insightfully that this can grow into hypersensitivity to other intense sensory stimulations, such as noise, colour or emotions. These children may also attempt to discharge their excess energy through hyperactivity (Judith, 1996).

In summary, if the child risks acting autonomously and the parents respond with shaming, punishment or control, the child becomes either compliant (remaining in P1) or rebellious (over-relying on P2). Either way, they fail to develop an appropriately functioning P2, and lose their ability to match the appropriate P2 response with a problem requiring the application of willpower. Complaining about a situation is the manifestation of a poorly developed P2. Protest and rebellion are reactive positions and stem from repressed P2. A well-functioning P2 is instead proactive and provides the individual with the ability to make their own luck.

Building Your Willpower (P2) as an Adult

DEVELOPING YOUR WILLPOWER

If you wish to strengthen your willpower, you need to develop the courage to take risks and work outside your comfort zone.

If you have learned to habitually follow orders, your weak will is prey to the manipulation of others. Obeying orders without question relinquishes your own sense of responsibility, and so sells a piece of yourself in the process. An alternative is to try to find your own true will. Ask yourself, 'What would I do if there was nothing I was supposed to do?' Then action becomes future-focused and goal-centred. This sounds simple but it requires willpower and the effective management of emotions.

Acknowledge your innate power and decide what you really want. Exercise your will to direct your life with thought, self-discipline and passion, and then apply this willpower to ensure you remain honest and sensitive to yourself and others.

DEVELOPING P2

Poorly developed P2 or an over-reliance on P1 can cause illnesses related to issues of self-responsibility, self-esteem, fear of rejection or an over-sensitivity to criticism. It may also be difficult for an individual who is low in P2 to develop the power, energy and willpower they need to achieve success. Working through the following list of excellent actions suggested by Myss (1996) can build ego strength:

- Build your body health and fitness with a good diet and aerobic exercise.
- Engage in activities you enjoy.
- Plan in your schedule to engage in these activities regularly.
- Meet challenges and difficulties one at a time.
- Start small and build your will and power.
- Set long-term goals: a master plan plus a plan for a routine to include your goals. Then follow the plan, meeting the challenges and difficulties that naturally arise.
- Confront others when necessary.
- Risk new ventures. Each time you meet a challenge, you will gain power and confidence.
- Give up playing safe. Take risks and grow your ego strength.
- Work on your anger, both past (from enduring bad situations) and current.
- Attack the demon shame.
- Engage in an inner dialogue between your caring adult self and your abused child. Give your child permission to rebel against the rules you don't agree with.

HEALING P2 OVER-RELIANCE

If you have an over-reliance on P2 you will have more energy in your system than it can handle. Therefore, it needs to be discharged or rerouted. The following exercise (adapted from suggestions by Judith (1997) and Davies (1998)) can help.

- First, relax. Sit still and let go of control.
- Then do either a guided meditation, Feldenkrais or yoga. A hyperactive person will probably find it easier to start with yoga or Feldenkrais – at least they are active.
- Give yourself regular downtime. That is, take time to do nothing. Just be. You are, after all, a human being, not a human doing.

- As you relax, integrate your body, mind and emotions. Let your internal observer state be aware of your submerged emotions. Listen to your gut feelings.

- Then align your thinking with your relaxed emotions. Understand, respect and accept your feelings. Consider their relevance and appropriateness to the current situation then decide on and monitor your actions.

CREATING A HIGHLY FUNCTIONING P2

Compare your own experience with what you have learned about the P2 Intelligence. What are the aspects of your P2 of which you are aware? Is there one that you tend to focus on above the other two?

- The P2 somatic circuit is high energy and moves towards creating new rules that right injustice for the old rules.

- The P2 thinking circuit experiences high levels of enthusiasm, optimism and excitement.

- The P2 feeling circuit focuses on end results and the means of attaining them.

Diagram 4.1 shows the three aspects of P2 that require integration so that true Vitality can form.

The task involved in creating highly functioning P2 is to integrate the thinking aspect of enthusiasm, personal values and prioritising options, the somatic aspect of passion and justice, and the feeling aspect of moving towards goals. You may start by examining

Diagram 4.1 Healthy P2 Intelligence – Noble Quality: Vitality

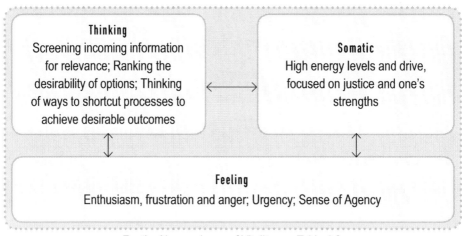

Thinking
Screening incoming information for relevance; Ranking the desirability of options; Thinking of ways to shortcut processes to achieve desirable outcomes

Somatic
High energy levels and drive, focused on justice and one's strengths

Feeling
Enthusiasm, frustration and anger; Urgency; Sense of Agency

For the Neuroscience of Vitality see Table 4.2

your values and beliefs and the degree to which they align with your feelings as well as your actions.

Table 4.2 The Neuroscience of Vitality

The table below details the Neuroscience of P2. Refer to Appendix 1 for more details.

Somatic Aspect	Feeling Aspect	Thinking Aspect
• Motor control through recruitment of P1 motor areas (primary motor cortex, supplementary motor area, premotor cortex, cerebellum and basal ganglia) • Sense of 'self' (integrated in the precuneus and supported by somatosensory areas in the parietal lobe) that orientates us in physical space and time essential to our ability to interact with the physical world (e.g. prevents us bumping into things; orientation association area), filtering out redundant sensory information (e.g. to navigate a crowded railway station; lateral prefrontal cortex)	• High motivation to succeed (left putamen and caudate nucleus, orbitofrontal cortex and the insula, medial prefrontal cortex for social feedback) • Anger and frustration (left orbital cortex, right anterior cingulate cortex affective division, bilateral anterior temporal poles) • Sense of power, perception of strength (leading to dominating behaviour) (testosterone, cortisol and adrenaline) • Urgency or impatience (adrenaline and testosterone) • A sense of what action to take to be successful (through somatic markers relating to success) • Feelings of elation following success or dejection following failure (associated respectively with increases and decreases in activity in the left prefrontal cortex monitored by the cingulate cortices, hypothalamus, tegmentum and interpreted by lateral and polar parts of the cortex in the frontal lobe)	• Ability to focus attention of goal-relevant information (lateral prefrontal cortex), including the ability to focus the mind to single-pointed attention (prefrontal cortex) in contemplative disciplines often developed through mantras, chanting, images and repetitive movement • Intrinsically driven, achievement focused, goal-directed behaviour (both physical and psychological; medial prefrontal cortex) • Filtering of redundant thoughts (prefrontal cortex) (i.e. elements not related to the achievement of the identified goal) enables us to focus on the issue at hand and come up with an appropriate plan of action

AFFIRMATIONS

If you are unaccustomed to it, putting your P2 willpower into play with confidence may feel as if you are unreasonably trusting the unknown. This may feel dangerous. If this is the case, some find that repeating the following affirmations inspired by Myss (1996) can help develop P2 functioning:

- I welcome opportunities to live in the power of the universe, to be self-expressed in my actions, and to fulfil my highest potential.

- I am powerful and I am worthy.

- I am responsible for myself, my life, my health, my welfare and my behaviour.

- I am open to receive prosperity in all its forms.

Highly Functioning P2 in Adult Life

The first-order noble quality of Vitality[4] requires the integration of the thinking aspect of prioritisation, the feeling aspect of goal-oriented passion and enthusiasm, and the somatic aspect of physically moving towards achieving specific objectives even if it is frightening. A primary contributor to Vitality is the exercising of will to achieve objectives and specific results. As the vital individual attains and reaches their goals, they experience a sense of success, achievement, and of having the capability to achieve greater objectives (Tracy, 2004).

Vitality refers to feeling alive; the very word is derived from vita, or 'life'. While Vitality is related to being energetic and passionate, Vitality entails only energy experienced as positive and available to the self (Nix, Ryan, Manly & Deci, 1999). Someone who is tense, angry or jittery may be energised but not imbued with the noble quality of Vitality.

Individuals with a high level of Vitality strongly endorse the following statements:

1. *I feel alive and vital.*　　　　4. *I feel energised.*

2. *I have energy and spirit.*　　　5. *I rarely feel worn out.*

3. *I nearly always feel awake and alert.*

Vitality is an activated positive emotion, which means personal energy is directed towards the attainment of goals. As such, it is different from happiness or contentment, which are undirected.

4　Peterson & Seligman's meta-study of the most widely influential traditions of thought and religion in human history found Vitality to be a significant human strength (Peterson & Seligman, 2004).

HOW P2 VITALITY MEETS THE NOBILITY CRITERIA

Vitality answers questions related to the right of the individual to personally achieve and make the world a better place for themselves and others. This noble quality enables the individual to discover that they have the right to be who they want to be. This is linked to the desire to make things better, to be committed and to stake life itself on an outcome.

Vitality brings value to the community by enabling it to complete projects on time, to strive, to compete and to constantly improve in every aspect of community life. It helps focus the individual on achieving their best and reaching their potential. This in turn enables the community to compete in the wider world. Vitality fosters the sense that, 'Yes, we CAN do this' which is a fundamental aspect of improving community life.

Vitality describes a dynamic aspect of well-being marked by the subjective experience of energy and aliveness (Ryan & Frederick, 1997). Individuals report that using Vitality to resolve an internal tension has a paradigm shift impact on their lives.

In high performance teams, Vitality gives team members confidence in the ability of the team to achieve its goals, exceed expectations and compete against the rest of the world.

P2 Toolbox

THE IMPORTANCE OF P2 IN BUILDING HIGH PERFORMANCE TEAMS

The emergent cultural impact of P2 is Vitality, which enables the organisation to complete projects on time, to strive, to compete and to constantly improve in every aspect towards organisational objectives.

When Vitality is absent in the organisation engagement is low, challenges are passed up, deadlines are missed and opportunities disappear. Without Vitality, personal productivity declines along with a sense of achievement and satisfaction for work.

When there is highly functioning P2 in the organisation there is also a focus on the individual achieving their best and reaching their potential. This in turn enables the organisation to compete with greater effectiveness

Leaders looking to increase the function of P2 in their team can increase Vitality by applying the P2 tools.

P2 QUESTIONS FOR PERSONAL DEVELOPMENT AND SELF REFLECTION

The best high performing teams are made up of individuals who have focused on their own personal development. The following questions can be used as a starting point for those leaders looking to improve their P2.

1. What do you believe about yourself? Do you like and respect yourself? (A healthy P2 has a healthy ego.)

2. Do you trust your ability to make good choices? Describe a time when you forgave yourself when you made a mistake or fell short of your own goals and expectations.

3. What do you want to be famous for having achieved?

4. Have you developed the skill of self inquiry - have you learnt to trust your own insights, and do they help you to act in ways that honour yourself and others? Explain.

5. Do you believe you can make the world a better place? How?

6. Do you often need the others' approval in order to feel good? Explore why this is or isn't so.

7. Do you live according to your own objectives or are you more influenced by others' expectations? When you achieve your objectives do you need another's praise before you feel good about it or able to affirm yourself? Explore this.

8. When you have strong feelings, explore how you are able to express them in ways that respect yourself and others.

9. What is your greatest fear? Is it a fear of failure or of offending others? (When your inner observer notes this, it is valuable to ask yourself if this is appropriate now, or is it a replay of disapproval expressed by others in your childhood?)

10. Do your actions align with your values and principles as well as your feelings?

11. Can you stand up for yourself, and respect yourself and keep your principles, whatever the odds?

12. How do you manage power? Is it power over (force) or an enabling power?

13. What do you feel highly motivated about in life right now?

14. Can you forgive yourself when you make mistakes or fall short of your own goals and expectations or are you plagued by guilt or shame?

P2 TOOL #1:
REFINE YOUR COMPETITIVE STRATEGY

HOW THIS RELATES TO P2

P2 gives the individual the energy required to win. Your competitive strategy will fuel this energy by enabling all team members to work together and agree on an approach. This keeps the P2 function focused on team success rather than individual success achieved at the expense of the team.

PROCESS

1. **Schedule a Strategy Review Workshop** with key thought leaders within your team/ organisation.

2. **Conduct a SWOT analysis** by getting the workshop group to list the team's Strengths, Weaknesses, Opportunities and Threats given its current positioning and existing strategy. (Depending on the size of the group, you may like to split the workshop into smaller tables, then combine the responses to one group analysis). While it is critical that the workshop group drives the process and analysis, make sure that you have given this some thought yourself in advance (so that you can keep things moving with suggestions of your own where needed). You may even like to have some relevant figures and data to share. Another good option is to send each participant details on the SWOT analysis as a pre-workshop exercise, so they will have the chance both to think it through and to informally consult colleagues in advance of the workshop.

3. **Introduce the work of Michael Porter** (1998). Many will be familiar with Porter's work, which is still as useful today as it was when introduced in the 1980s. He identified five competitive forces that affect profitability:

    a. **The entry of new competitors.** New competitors necessitate some competitive response which will inevitably use resources and reduce profits.

    b. **The threat of substitutes.** If there are viable alternatives to your product or service in the marketplace, the prices you can charge will be limited.

    c. **The bargaining power of buyers.** If customers have bargaining power, they will use it. This will reduce profit margins.

    d. **The bargaining power of suppliers.** Given power over you, suppliers will increase their prices and adversely affect your profitability.

    e. **The rivalry among existing competitors.** Competition leads to the need to invest in marketing or Research and Development, or to price reductions.

Explain that the collective strength of these five forces determines the ability of firms in an industry to earn, on average, rates of return on investment in excess of the cost of capital (Porter, 1998).

4. **Assess the existing strategy** based on the extent to which it either currently addresses each of the forces or has the flexibility to do so as needed. Is the organisation/your team currently at the whim of one or more of these forces or is it taking proactive steps to strengthen its competitive edge in the current market? Where possible, relate this analysis back to the SWOT conducted at the start of the session.

5. **Finalise an Action Plan moving forward.** This may involve seeking further information, tweaking the strategy or contacting key stakeholders (internally or externally) to action any changes. The important outcome is to emerge from the workshop with clarity about both how the strategy needs to change to stay competitive and who is responsible for the identified actions moving forward.

DOS

✓ Do set aside enough time to finalise the Action Plan – there's no point spending the day working out what's missing from the existing approach if you don't direct that toward the practical goal of actioning the insights

DON'TS

✗ Don't allow the discussion to get bogged down – focus on the end goal of getting shared clarity about the benefits and weaknesses of the strategy and what needs to change

P2 TOOL #2:
DYNAMISE YOUR GROUP

HOW THIS RELATES TO P2

P2 drops when goals are too distant (there is no urgency) or complex. This tool will lift P2 by simplifying and clarifying the goals and creating a clear deadline (compelling event).

PROCESS

1. **Identify a key new project or operation** (e.g. new product launch or initiative) that can be used as a vehicle around which to dynamise the team.

2. **Assemble a Tiger Team** — a special team to focus on the new project/operation. Find the ablest people and place them under highly motivated, effective leadership that will encourage sub-leadership.

3. **Brief the Tiger Team**

   a. Introduce yourself (if appropriate) and explain the purpose of the team and the project. Emphasise that the group has been put together for a specific purpose/project, and that the particular skills of each individual member are fundamental to the success of the project.

   b. Highlight the team's freedom in choosing how to approach the challenge, emphasising that creativity and innovation are encouraged.

   c. Outline the value of the team and make sure that everyone is clear on their role in achieving these objectives. If possible, identify 'the competition' – whether it is last year's figures, another section within the organisation or an external rival. This will set a benchmark for the team's performance.

   d. Express confidence in the people present and emphasise group/team working and cohesion.

   e. Emphasise that the team's efforts will be fully supported, including outlining the resources that are available to them.

   f. Express confidence in and optimism about the group's ability.

4. **Hold regular meetings** to ensure the team stays focused. Make sure there is clarity about what has been achieved and how much more needs to be done. Use these times to reinforce motivation and purpose, as well as to review progress.

5. **Continue to recruit new talent**, particularly as gaps in the skills base become apparent throughout the project. Encourage the group to be proactive in identifying potential new talent and areas in which they could valuably contribute.

DOS

✓ Make your authority clear, but make sure that the group feels that it also has autonomous power to act. For the group to be dynamised, team members will need to feel a sense of urgency in tackling the challenges that arise.

✓ Be positive and enthusiastic – your energy with inspire confidence and encourage your group to follow your example.

DON'TS

✗ Don't allow the process to be stagnated by 'how things have been done in the past'. Encourage the group to look forwards, not backwards, and to forge its own path towards the end goal.

✗ Don't forget that the ultimate objective is for the group to drive the project. You can be firm about your expectations, but make sure that the energy for the process is coming from the team itself.

P2 TOOL #3:
EFFECTIVELY MANAGE PLATEAUED PERFORMERS

HOW THIS RELATES TO P2

When an individual's P2 drops to counterproductive levels it can be due to a range of issues. Many of these have been outlined in the text. Your role as a leader is to work with the individual to find what has worked in the past and what can be introduced into the current situation to restimulate the P2 function.

PROCESS

1. **Scope the plateau.**
   a. **Diagnose the plateau.** A plateau is an emerging process that doesn't happen overnight. To qualify as a Plateaued Performer, the employee would have been plateaued for at least a year, perhaps two. They are also likely to have been in the same job or department for some time. Ask yourself whether the employee's productivity has declined consistently or sporadically. Have you observed a slackening in interest and commitment? Has the person's behaviour deviated from the norm? Or are they simply not interested in improving?

   b. **Characterise the plateau.** Use the individual's attitude or level of activity to characterise the type of plateau involved. Potential categories include:
      - **Passive:** Low in energy and activity and trapped in personal inaction.
      - **Productive:** Plenty of energy and activity, but the busy-ness is not translating into effectiveness.
      - **Partial:** Concentrates on one small area of responsibility, valiantly keeping a personal spark alive in the absence of prospects for promotion or challenge.
      - **Pleasant:** Happy with the status quo, doing the job well enough, in a comfortable groove but wanting neither challenges nor risks, and showing no desire to improve. Different strategies will be appropriate depending upon the nature of the plateau.

   c. **Get to know the person properly.** Try to understand what makes the plateaued performer tick. Ask about outside interests, whether there's anything stressful happening at home and whether they're content to stay where they are (e.g. an earlier failure to get a promotion had a demotivating effect). Try to find out from the person what their personal and professional ambitions are. Only by knowing the plateaued performer as a person can you hope to improve matters.

2. **Identify the core problem.** Using all the detail obtained in scoping the plateau, be as specific as you can in outlining its root causes. Some of these will be within the control of the individual but others may not. Examples of causes for the plateau may include:

   a. The company has not offered a stimulating environment

b. The person feels written off by you or another superior

c. It's a long time since the person has been given a new challenge

d. Colleagues are largely ignoring the person

e. Problems at home

While there may be many contributing factors, lack of stimulus is likely to feature prominently.

3. **Find out what has worked for them in the past.** By exploring with the employee times in their work history when they have been motivated you can discuss how some of the characteristics of the external environment and their approach can be reintroduced into the current situation.

4. **Work with the individual to develop an Action Plan moving forward.** This will necessarily depend on the individual circumstances, but the solution usually involves providing a new stimulus. This might include: introducing a new challenge within the individual's existing responsibilities; assigning the person to work on a special team or project; or suggesting a sideways shift to a new position within the company. Make sure the plateaued performer has ownership of the Action Plan and understands that they need to take responsibility for their own future.

5. **Continue to show interest, and give support and positive feedback.** While you need to emphasise the plateaued performer's responsibilities, make it clear that they have your support. A plateaued performer may show a short-term improvement and then sink back again. Show continuing interest without being too obtrusive, and be prepared to intervene where needed.

6. **Follow up if there is no improvement.** It is important to recognise that some performers will stay on a plateau. Although you will have some surprising successes, you won't succeed every time. If you can't raise a particular staff member's sights after several attempts, take advantage of the opportunity to alert them that their behaviour is likely to be unsatisfactory to the organisation sooner or later and might risk dismissal.

DOS

✓ Do make identification and support for plateaued performers company policy.

✓ Do assume that something can be done.

✓ Do get to know the person as well as you can and identify what is holding him or her back.

✓ Do remember throughout the process that the employee is not yet a problem – so don't treat them like one! Your only aim is to see if and how they can rise off the plateau.

DON'TS

✗ Don't start with negative assumptions.

✗ Don't underestimate the potential disadvantages of handling the situation poorly.

✗ Don't assume that plateaued performers are incompetent. Often they simply can't channel their energies or abilities into productive performance.

✗ Don't give up too easily.

KEY LEADING THE PACK QUESTIONS FOR BUILDING A HIGH PERFORMANCE TEAM

1. What would you like your team to be famous for?

2. What most motivates you about your role in the team?

3. What do you believe to be the team's greatest strength? How can the team leverage from this strength?

4. As a team, when have you been successful in the past? How might we use the same techniques to deliver in the future?

5. Do you have something against which to benchmark your performance as a team? How do you know when you are doing an excellent job?

6. How do you celebrate success as a team? What is your philosophy towards recognition and reward?

NEUROPOWER CASE STUDY

ORGANISATIONAL CASE STUDY #1: STATE HEALTH HAND HYGIENE PROJECT

The Task: To improve compliance by health workers with hand hygiene practice.

Recap:

In 2007, an Australian state health department wanted to address the serious threat that health-associated infections posed to hospital patients. Micro-organisms are readily transmitted on the hands of health care workers. In Australia alone, health officials estimate that up to 7000 people die annually from hand hygiene-related infections in hospitals. The economic burden is also considerable, costing millions each year.

Hand hygiene has been proven to substantially reduce transmission of micro-organisms. However, despite well-established guidelines, compliance throughout the world with hygiene standards is disconcertingly low. International and national health agencies have been grappling with how to deal with the issue for some time, and few interventions have had any impact whatsoever, despite both European and US hospitals and governments spending tens of millions of dollars on communications, incentives, closed circuit TV and education.

Since research demonstrated that the hand hygiene issue centred around human behaviour, one state health department decided on an innovative, behaviour-changing approach using the *NeuroPower* framework to drive the solution. Working with the *NeuroPower* Consulting Team, the department implemented a behaviour change program called Clean Hands are LifeSavers that engaged the health workers and increased compliance from 18% to 60%. A key driver of this behaviour change involved effectively addressing each of the six Intelligences in the correct sequence. How these progressive steps were taken is outlined in the Organisational Toolbox Case Study at the end of each Intelligence chapter.

Having already:

- Created safety and security in the hospital environment by embedding values through a code of conduct
- Empowered spontaneity and self-expression through collaboration and the development of creative promotional materials

Step 3: Get action happening, establish key goals and motivate by celebrating wins

LifeSavers were encouraged to get action happening and keep motivation high by celebrating wins within each hospital. Wards were encouraged to compete with each other to find creative approaches to keeping hand hygiene top-of-mind so posters, events, barbecues, film tickets and other motivating offers were used. As well, internal observers were sent periodically to watch the health-workers at their tasks, completing a statistical survey on hand-held recording devices. Results from each ward were then posted around the hospital, indicating the results in graphic form. The teams in these wards were then rewarded with the kudos of being most successful.

ORGANISATIONAL CASE STUDY #2: MERCHANT BANK EQUITY DERIVATIVES LEADERSHIP TEAM

The Task: Improve employee engagement and tangible business performance

Recap:

In 2006, at the height of the financial boom, one of Australia's leading equity derivatives teams was operating in an environment that was fast-paced, demanding and with a high level of stress. In order to handle large volumes of work in a very volatile market, the team needed to be highly functional and collaborative. Growth was nearly 200 per cent over the previous year so the enormous strain was evident. This was mainly caused by a leadership team in crisis.

The Leadership Team was fractured, non-collaborative and driven by their own individual agendas. There was both a lack of respect and a lack of honesty between members which led to highly reactive responses and conflict. The broader team could see this occurring and they felt they were part of a warring tribe with all the insecurities that brought.

NeuroPower consultants devised a program which focused on addressing the splintered leadership team. The intervention involved a series of group structured processes which were embedded by individual coaching sessions.

Having already:
- Created role clarity
- Empowered people's self-expression

Step 3: Encouraging Healthy Egos and Passion for Work Through P2

The Equity Team Leaders all had enormous passion for their work and strong ego development. The work here was to show that healthy ego development was fine but they needed to know when to reduce their drive for the betterment of the whole team.

It was important to set clear team goals so the group identified six key competencies they wished to focus on during the intervention and developed 360 degree questions which linked to their performance review. This was an overt way to make the team accountable as a group while offering the end game of individual reward for success.

Chapter 5

Our Fourth Social Cognitive Need:
INTERPERSONAL CONNECTION &
The Relating Function (I2)

INTERPERSONAL CONNECTION (I2) AT A GLANCE

Interpersonal Connection is our Brain's Third Social Cognitive Need

The brain is naturally focused on connecting with and understanding others, and needs to feel that you have been genuinely understood. The brain's oxytocin, mirror neuron and default mode networks work overtime to help us interpret and understand others - at times by helping us literally feel what others feel. Our willingness to be generous, to forgive and to 'think together' are linked to how well we feel we understand and connect with someone else.

Characteristics of the Interpersonal Connection (I2) Functional Network

Empathy and Understanding

STRENGTH	WEAKNESS
Can pick up how others are feeling (emotionally intuitive)	Easily swayed by the emotions or people aspects of a situation

OPPORTUNITY	THREAT
Developing objectivity and discernment	Can be swamped by powerful external emotions

Management Style

- Often socio-emotional leaders
- Decision-making based on avoiding pain for others
- May struggle to manage non-performers

EMPATHY

I2 THINKING

Theory
of mind

I2 FEELING

Connection to
others and self

I2 SOMATIC

Emotionally
responsive to the
environment

COMMUNICATION STYLE

- Will be excellent listeners
- Will focus on how people are feeling and responding to work and personal life
- Excellent counsellors/encouragers/affirmers
- Will respond slowly and need time to go away and think about it - conversations can take days to complete

KEYWORDS INCLUDE

- Awareness
- Collaboration
- Empathy
- Generosity
- Connection
- Feeling

Interpersonal Connection (I2) Helps Us to Survive

Interpersonal Connection (I2) helps both individuals and the group to survive and thrive by helping us be aware of our own internal states, and by motivating us to understand, be generous and collaborate with others.

Interpersonal Connection & The Relating Function (I2)

INTERPERSONAL CONNECTION: OUR FOURTH SOCIAL NEED EXPLAINED

Humans have a rare - possibly unique - advantage over other species: our highly sophisticated ability to understand what another person is thinking and how they are feeling (Saxe, 2006). This ability, which is informed by empathy (feeling what others are feeling), prompts us to care for others (children, parents, employees), make sacrifices for others based on generosity and make us sensitive to the impact of our actions on others. These abilities are supported by highly sophisticated (and overlapping) mechanisms in the brain including the mirror neuron network, the default mode network and the oxytocin system, and are intimately linked with our fourth social cognitive need: to understand others and be understood by them (Interpersonal Connection).

WHEN YOU FEEL WHAT I FEEL

A few years ago, European neuroscientists, Dr Peter Their and Dr Giacomo Rizzolatti, discovered that when you see someone hit their finger with a hammer, something fascinating happens in your brain. As you see that person's pain response, your own brain's pain areas fire up as if you're the one who has been hit.[1] This and many other studies in humans and other primates revealed the existence of a so-called 'mirror neuron' system, which together with parts of the frontal and parietal lobes (notably, the temporoparietal junction), form the biological hardware that we use to understand others and empathise with them.[2] This ability to understand others reduces stress responses and promotes generosity with our time and money, so much so that researchers have argued that "Human altruism derives from our readiness to understand each other in terms of their internal thoughts, feelings and desires" (Waytz, Zaki & Mitchell, 2012).

---

1   Notably, this happens even for individuals with medical conditions that prevent them from having ever experienced pain themselves (Danziger et al., 2009).

2   It's worth noting that while the mirror neuron system has been extensively investigated in primates, exploring the full extent - and limitations - of the human mirror neuron system is the subject of substantial ongoing research. This includes, for example, earnest debate about whether the overlapping areas of brain activation between a person's emotional experience and the observation of another's emotion reflect the same neural circuits or different circuits located close to one another (see e.g. Decety, 2010, for a detailed critique). Nonetheless, substantial accumulating evidence from social cognitive neuroscience supports the idea that so called 'mirror neuron' areas of the brain interact with other areas of the brain focused on understanding our own and other's minds (mentalising; Rameson & Lieberman, 2009) to help us form working models of what others are experiencing.

Simultaneously, neuroendocrinologists have shown us that neurochemicals like oxytocin and progesterone increase our motivation to be close to and focus on others (e.g. Schultheiss et al., 2004; Brown et al., 2009).[3] When the brain releases oxytocin, our social anxiety reduces and our affiliative motivation increases, our heart rate starts to respond more adaptively to our social environment and our awareness of social cues and information increases (Bartz et al., 2011; Kemp et al., 2012). This effect also seems to be uniquely social - oxytocin improves our learning when feedback has a social component; it increases generosity when we're playing a game with another human, but not with a computer.

Interestingly, some studies have suggested that oxytocin's impact on generosity also works in reverse. Research from Paul Zak's lab suggests that when we receive generosity from others that is based on trust, it increases our own levels of circulating oxytocin, increases our own prosocial intentions (Zak, Kurzlban & Matzner, 2005). This is important, because it emphasises that Interpersonal Connectedness (I2), rather than just benefiting the recipient, changes our brain chemistry in a way that helps the group as a whole.

Oxytocin was first discovered through its role in childbirth and when new mothers form attachments with their infants, and then sprang into popular consciousness for its role in romantic love. Today, however, researchers have teased out oxytocin's broader ability to focus our attention on others, to improve our understanding of how they are feeling and to promote generosity and forgiveness.[4] As our understanding of this grows, it's now easy to see that this neurobiological system also has a crucial role in day-to-day work life for establishing strong interpersonal connections between people in all aspects of our lives.

---

3   Oxytocin has swept through popular consciousness in the last decade as the now infamous 'love drug' of the brain, with the frenzy going so far that some have even marketed oxytocin-based products as aphrodisiacs and tools for building trust and love. In reality, oxytocin is likely to be far less of a 'quick fix'. Instead, there is building consensus from the research community that oxytocin's primary effects are to increase our awareness of social information, motivate us to connect with others and reduce social anxiety. See Bartz et al., (2011) for some recent insight into this debate.

4   Given the overlap between the effects of oxytocin and the domains of the mirror neuron system and default mode network, you would expect that the two are intricately linked. However, only in the last few years have the first tentative pieces of evidence for this emerged. Perry et al.,(2010), for example, reported that giving healthy adults a dose of oxytocin changed patterns of brain activity near sensorimotor regions recorded using EEG in a pattern that has been linked to mirror neuron activation. This is the first tentative step I have seen in the neuroscience literature linking oxytocin to the mirror neuron system, but I predict that this link will become stronger over the coming years.

'FEELING THE LOVE' AT WORK - THE CHALLENGE FOR LEADERS

Interpersonal Connection (I2), or our ability to understand and connect with others, is a powerful glue that helps keep groups together and reach high performance. It does this in part by helping us manage stresses and conflict through mutual understanding, generosity and forgiveness. In a corporate setting, then, in order to create high performance a leader needs to learn how to create a sense of connection, empathy and dare we say it...even love...within their teams.

Importantly, recent research has confirmed something I have observed for decades, namely, that the brain areas that support Interpersonal Connection (I2) and our understanding of others' *internal states* are very different - and compete with - the parts of the brain that help us understand the physical, external world (Seeing the Facts, or I1; Jack et al., 2013). Of course, many of our leaders and managers have been promoted for their analytical and technical skills, rooted deeply in their ability to master the complexity of their technical profession. While these strengths are critical, brains that run high in Seeing the Facts (I1) often miss the human impact of objectively justified decisions. This one-sided set of information lies at the heart of many costly 'surprises' for corporate leaders, from failed mergers that looked 'good on paper' and product launches that fell flat, through to the valued team member whose 'sudden resignation' significantly impacts the ability to deliver corporate objectives. Without a healthy Interpersonal Connection (I2), our brains simply miss the people information.

To realise the full potential of their teams (as well as their own potential), effective leaders need to learn to meet the team's needs for Interpersonal Connection (I2). Part of this involves the leader working to build their personal awareness of their own internal world. (This challenging task is a core theme of the many Eastern traditions that describe the longest journey in the world as that 'between the head and the heart'.)

Based on my work with organisations around the world, I have found a useful process for building I2 within teams involves team members getting to know each other for their heartfelt passions, strengths and aspirations (rather than their weaknesses). This is important, because understanding the strengths of your colleagues, and the challenges they have faced to build them, fosters an appreciation of the individual, an increased sense of closeness and an increased willingness to tolerate and forgive their foibles. Learning what people are passionate about doing and where they shine the most, reveals hidden areas of strength that become resources for the team. Having a range of different strengths supports the team's diversity. These diverse teams are not always easier to manage but they make better decisions and get better results.

As we have already discussed, several structures and neuronal networks help us satisfy our need for Interpersonal Connection. Within the *NeuroPower* framework, this set of structures is called the 'I2 Relating System' (or sometimes the 'I2 network' or 'I2

Taking a Closer Look at Mirror Neurons

In the last decade or so, neuroscientists have been trying to understand how human brains make sense of what other people are thinking and feeling. One line of this research has been the investigation of whether 'mirror neurons' in the brain might help us understand others (giving rise to an understanding of their intentions and, perhaps, empathy) by matching their actions and experience back to our own bodies.

Using single-cell recording techniques, early research found individual 'mirror neurons within the premotor areas of a primate's frontal cortex that fire *both* when it performs a specific task (such as grasping an object with a hand) *and also* when it sees another primate or the experimenter engage in the same behaviour (Jeannerod, Arbib, Rizzolatti, & Sakata, 1995; Gallese, Fadiga, Fogassi & Rizzolatti, 1996). Since then, these mirror neurons have been discovered in several areas of the brain, including some in motor areas responsible for controlling, and, it seems, interpreting eye gaze and attention (I2 Thinking; Shepherd et al., 2009).

A range of studies have also attempted to extend these findings to humans and indicated that - as with primates - there are specific areas of the human brain (described by some as the parieto-frontal mirror system) that are strongly activated by both taking specific goal-directed actions and observing those same actions being taken by others (reviewed in Fogassi & Rizzolatti, 2013). Interestingly, the response of these brain areas to an action seems to depend on the context and intention being the same for the actions and there is some evidence that our unconscious body responses may also have mirror-like qualities (I2 Somatic).

To understand the link between mirror neurons and empathy, some have argued that observing the facial expressions, gestures and posture of another individual will activate similar sensory-motor circuits in an observer. Supporting this, Cattaneo et al., (2007) found that a muscle which we use to open our mouths is activated when we reach for food to eat and when we see someone else reach for food to eat, but not when we see someone else reach for food to put it away. These motor systems, in turn, are presumed to activate in the observer networks of emotion associated with such actions. For example, observing a sad child makes us reflectively frown, tilt our heads and make soothing gestures. It is thought that this is one means by which the gap between the sender and the receiver is bridged. In this way mirror neurons allow for the possibility of empathic attunement (Wolf, Gales, Shane & Shane, 2000).

function') and gives rise to a particular thinking style referred to as 'I2 Intelligence'. The rest of this chapter explores the I2 Relating System in detail.

THE EVOLUTIONARY SOCIAL BRAIN FUNCTION OF I2

The I2 system enables an individual to:

1. Survive through understanding and empathising with others, and through connection and loving friends and family.

2. Empathise with others and provide support and comfort during both good and bad times (attachment).

3. Best guess how others will react through Theory of Mind – being able to guess what somebody else is thinking about you and others. This can be described as a process by which most healthy human adults:

   a) attribute unobservable mental states to others (and under certain circumstances, to the self); and

   b) integrate these attributed states into a single coherent model that can be used to explain and predict the target's behaviour and experiences (Saxe & Wexler, 2005).

4. Form lasting and meaningful relationships through romantic (pair bonding) and maternal love (Dêbiec, 2007).

Recognising the Characteristics of Interpersonal Connection (I2)

The purpose of I2 is to connect with, understand others and attune with others. The characteristics of a highly functioning I2 Intelligence include attunement, active listening, love, altruism, peace, balance, trust, generosity, inspiration, dedication, forgiveness, and acceptance of others. These facilitate the noble quality of Empathy.

Empathy is linked with active listening (Rogers & Farzon, 1987). This form of listening involves no value judgements and simply reflects the content of what is being said. Active listening presupposes in the listener an attitude of genuine respect for the other person and an expectation that they have the potential for self-direction. Clinical and research evidence shows that active listening can be expected to produce positive developmental changes in both the listener and the person being listened to (Rogers and Farzon, 1987).

The recipient of active listening receives a respectful, uncritical, sensitive hearing. As a result, they commonly exhibit positive growth in emotional maturity. They listen more openly and carefully to themselves and give more care to expressing their own thoughts and feelings more clearly. They also become more democratic and attentive to others, and are less inclined to be defensive or authoritarian.

Active listening also has a positive effect on groups. When a group of individuals experience attentive and non-judgemental listening, their group discussions tend to become more agreeable and sensitive. Individuals feel their contribution matters and are more likely to see their own ideas more objectively. At a neurobiological level, this settles the amygdala and reduces the experience of stress.

Rogers & Farzon (1987) make the excellent additional point that this active listening can have a profound effect on the listener as they learn to build deep, meaningful and positive relationships by constructively altering their attitudes.

A TRADITIONAL UNDERSTANDING OF THE DYNAMICS OF THE I2 FUNCTION

Most traditional schools of thought and faith argue that connection based on love nourishes our physical, emotional and spiritual bodies. It motivates, controls, inspires and heals us. However, painful experiences of connection can also have a profoundly negative impact on our psychological and physical health. Many of life's challenges result in a lesson on some aspect of love. How we respond often affects our health.

The demon of I2 is sometimes described as grief. Poorly functioning I2 can also bring jealousy, bitterness, grumpiness, anger, hatred, insensitivity, disconnection from others and an inability to forgive oneself or others. Judith (1996) argues that physical malfunctions arising from poorly functioning I2 may include problems with the heart, lungs, thymus, breasts, arms, hands, shoulders or diaphragm. Telltale symptoms include shortness of breath, sunken chest, circulation problems, asthma, immune system deficiency, tension between the shoulder blades and pain in the chest (Judith, 1996)[5].

5   After emerging from the twentieth century's rigid focus on rational thinking and research into brain functioning, work by a range of western-trained researchers has begun to reintegrate an awareness of the role our physical heart might play in understanding and sensing emotional experiences (I2). In doing so, they are re-discovering the philosophies of earlier thinkers. In the nineteenth century, for example, William James posited that an emotion is firstly a physical state that then becomes accessorily a perception in the brain. In more recent times, the apparent relationship between heart and brain has led some cardiologists and neurologists to refer to an indivisible 'heart-brain system' (Servan-Schreiber, 2005). Meanwhile, neuroscientist Antonio Damasio (2003) on somatic markers argues that the work of seventeenth century philosopher Baruch Spinoza, which linked mind and body, fits neatly with modern concepts of neurophysiology. The notion that the heart is an independent centre of information, memories, desires and behaviours is also explored by Paul Pearsall in his book *The Heart's Code* (1999), while Californian researchers at the Institute of HeartMath have for over a decade been using neurophysiological measures like EEG and ECG to help understand how once mysterious 'heart-heart' connections might in fact be mediated by the electromagnetic impulses (generated by calcium-mediated contraction) in the tissue of the heart. These researchers are among the first to publish reports that heart rate variability in one person may directly influence patterns of brain activity in someone nearby, suggesting a

The developmental task for the individual at this stage is to form healthy peer and family relationships. The primary fears associated with I2 are loneliness, commitment, following one's heart, fear of not being able to protect oneself emotionally, emotional weakness and betrayal (Judith, 1996).

SIMULATION THEORY AND THEORY OF MIND

Our ability to empathise with others has recently captured the attention of the neuroscientific world, with two different theories developing about the neural

Diagram 5.1 Some of the Brain Areas Supporting Interpersonal Connection (I2)*

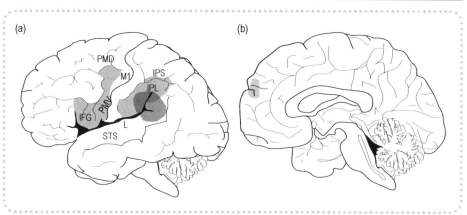

(a) Cortical areas belonging to the parieto-frontal mirror system. Gray shaded regions indicate cortical sectors activated during action observation, that become also active during execution of the same actions. Note that in some studies additional cortical areas (e.g. dorsal premotor cortex and superior parietal lobule) can activate during observation of reaching or body movements. A rostral sector of the superior temporal sulcus also activate during action observation, but not during action execution. IFG, inferior frontal gyrus; IPL, inferior parietal lobule; IPS, intraparietal sulcus; L, lateral sulcus; M1, primary motor cortex; PMD, dorsal premotor cortex; PMV, ventral premotor cortex; SPL, superior parietal lobule; STS, superior temporal sulcus (Adapted from Fogassi and Rizzolatti, 2013). The temporoparietal junction (TPJ, orange), particularly the right TPJ, has been shown to be important for our ability to attributing mental states to others Saxe & Wexler (2005).

(b) Region of dorsomedial prefrontal cortex (DMPFC, green) - known to be important for our ability to 'mentalise' or think about others' mental states. Activity in this region when thinking about other people correlates with altruism as measured by allocation of money and time (Waytz et al., 2012).

* Areas associated with mentalising (I2) as compared to reasoning about inanimate objects (I1) are discussed further in Diagram 6.1 in Chapter 6.

possible physical mechanism for interpersonal 'intuition' and empathy.

underpinnings of empathy. The *Simulation Theory* of empathy proposes that we use our own mind as a model in understanding the thoughts and feelings of others. This theory found support in the discovery of the mirror neuron system, which is thought to allow us to vicariously experience the emotional states of others, thus enabling empathetic feelings (Decety & Jackson, 2004). In seeming contrast, *Theory of Mind* research has focused on the role of the medial prefrontal regions, which enable us to consider that what others think, feel and believe, may differ from our own thoughts, feelings and beliefs. The ability to best guess what another person is thinking or feeling is known as mentalising (Frith & Frith, 1999). *Theory of Mind* work suggests that empathy is based on this deduction about another person's experience.

In 2009, social cognitive neuroscientists Lian Rameson and Matthew Lieberman published an outstanding article about the social cognitive neuroscience of empathy, including a concise but comprehensive review of the literature supporting both theories. They suggest that these two models for explaining empathy are not mutually exclusive and may, in fact, provide a more comprehensive understanding of empathy when considered together. Their analysis supports the view that our ability to have Theory of Mind is an indication of how readily we access *I2 thinking*, while the activity of our mirror neurons reflects the strength of our *I2 somatic* functioning.

In considering reactions to upsetting events that are focused on others, Rameson & Lieberman (2009) argue that responses can be either *experiential* (i.e. feeling like you've taken the place of the other person and are in the situation, experiencing it for yourself)

I2 and the Right Hemisphere

While the idea of 'lateralisation' itself moves in and out of popularity with the neuroscience community, many of us have traditionally seen I2 characteristics as a '*right* brain' quality. This was based on evidence that linked the right hemisphere of the brain with empathetic experiences and emotional awareness. The right hemisphere was found to be superior at comprehending emotionally laden language (Searleman, 1977). Emotions in general, and the ability to evaluate emotional facial expressions and visual-spatial abilities, are predominately right-hemisphere processes (Ahern et al., 1991). When damage occurs to the right hemisphere there is an impairment not only in the ability to assess facial gestures, but also in the ability to comprehend other non-verbal aspects of communication such as hand gestures and tone of voice (Blonder, Bowers & Heilman, 1991). This suggests that the right hemisphere plays an important role in I2 functioning.

or *propositional* (i.e. a controlled cognitive process focusing on the other person's thoughts, feelings or experience). They suggest that while the two modes of processing presumably share some common neural circuitry, each is likely to have a 'unique neural signature' (Rameson & Lieberman, 2009, p. 103). Experiential processing therefore maps very closely onto Simulation Theory, while propositional processing bears striking similarities to *Theory of Mind*. From their perspective, the two modes of processing are complementary rather than contradictory, and may in fact build on each other. For example, seeing a picture of maltreated inmates in a WWII concentration camp may generate an affective response that is magnified by furthering consideration of their circumstances and mental state.

Rameson & Lieberman also note that the two modes of processing are likely to result in qualitatively different motivations and consequent behaviours; experiential processing is likely to engender an affective reaction to the other person's distress that motivates immediate physical engagement, while propositional processing may 'initiate more complex thinking about long-term solutions to problems that might not be immediately gratifying, but might produce systemic changes in the target's situation' (Rameson & Lieberman, 2009, p 103).

Highly Functioning Interpersonal Connection (I2) has Both Strengths and Weaknesses

Bertrand Russell once said, "We know too much and feel too little." Interpersonal Connection (I2) is what helps us to 'feel' and so come to understand ourselves and others' internal states. I2 enables you to empathise and gives you access to your ability to connect with others. I2-dominant minds - sometimes called 'Empathisers' - are sensitive, emotionally aware and naturally focus on others. They easily sense the feeling in a room - including the fears and insecurities of others - and seem to know just how others are feeling in the most difficult situations. Although this ability to empathise is very useful, it can also cause difficulty for the I2-dominant mind.

Most people high in I2 never feel totally confident or in control, and sometimes wonder why they don't seem to be able to be as balanced or consistent as their more 'objective' friends[6]. The primary reason for this is that the I2 function naturally tracks and picks up pain, excitement and pleasure from others - meaning the individual often becomes a passenger on someone else's emotional journey. To function effectively, individuals high in I2 need to learn to detach, and balance their natural empathy for others with an objective perspective on the world.

---

6   Explored in Chapter 6 on Seeing the Facts (I1)

Alexithymia

The inability to consciously experience and describe your own and others feelings (both of which are features of healthy Interpersonal Connectedness (I2)) is referred to as alexithymia. Patients with alexithymia often report being consciously aware that other people have feelings, but not being aware of them themselves. Early research suggested that this condition appears to reflect a lack of transfer or integration of right-hemisphere emotional and somatic information with the linguistic cognitive systems of the left hemisphere (Taylor, 1999), and subsequent studies have shown that alexithymia is linked to reduced activity in the broader network of regions of the brain dedicated to understanding the mental states and emotions of others, including the DLPTF, anterior insula and temporoparietal junction. This alexithymia, which can be interpreted as a deficit in Interpersonal Connection (I2), leads to reduced accuracy in judging others' mental states, reduced awareness of the pain of others and reduced altruism to others (Moriguchi et al., 2006; 2007; FeldmanHall et al., 2013).

Interpersonal Connection (I2) and Childhood Development

COGNITIVE DEVELOPMENT AND I2

The development of the I2 Intelligence aligns with Piaget's pre-operational stage. During this time the child wishes to be judged by their intentions as well as their behaviour. This aligns with Lawrence Kohlberg's 'good boy, nice girl' stage of moral development. At this stage the individual learns to incorporate their cognition with their persona. This also aligns with Erikson's stage of *intimacy versus isolation*, which sees the individual consider whether they are loved and wanted and who they, in turn, wish to love (Sigelman & Rider, 2006).

DEVELOPING A SOCIAL IDENTITY

During childhood, individuals become aware of relationships between their parents and within the family. The child develops a social identity based on family interactions and their place in it, especially the family's response to their behaviour. They become, for example, a good boy or girl, a clown or perhaps a princess expecting attention (Judith, 1996).

As we have seen in our discussion of P1 and C1, the child also internalises family scripts, which they may play out in later life. For example, they respond to criticism by becoming a 'bad boy' or they become quiet and passive-aggressive. A person's family relationships also impact on their behaviour and who they become.

As the child observes their family, imitates gender roles and adopts family patterns, their persona also becomes part of their social identity. They identify with the 'tough' or problem-solving father or self-sacrificing mother. This is when the child learns how to either access or ignore I2. The little boy might be told not to cry, and the little girl not to be a tomboy. This repressed part of them becomes a further ingredient of their unconscious personality (their Mirror[7]).

Finally, the innate conflict that exists between mother and father is resolved by reconciling the differences and loving both equally. This external reconciliation is matched by an internal reconciliation of the perspectives of their same sex parent (embedded in the child's P1) and their opposite sex parent (embedded in the child's C1).

CHILDHOOD DEVELOPMENT

In healthy development, the individual's identity expands to include all previous Intelligences as it embraces I2 in a balanced way. In this case, the ego or P2 expands as

---

The Role of Parenting in the Development of I2

Children raised in families that discuss people's emotional reactions tend to be more interested in and able to understand others' emotions (Bretherton, 1993; Nelson, 1993). These children also appear to be taught that what they have to say about the contents of their minds is important. Each of these experiences may help to enhance their capacity for emotional regulation (Oppenheim, Nir, Warren & Emde, 1997; Fivush, 1994).

Studies have found significant differences in the manner in which parents help to shape their offspring's narrative processes. Miller & Sperry (1988) suggest that narratives with boys frequently include angry emotions and often reflect autonomy of self and actions. In contrast, girls are guided to create narratives about the self in which their identity is embedded in a social context. They are taught to take responsibility for the feelings of others, which is quintessential I2 development. This may explain why in some *NeuroPower* middle management samples in Australia fewer than 20 percent of the males surveyed have highly functioning I2 compared with 55 percent of the women surveyed.

---

7   For more information about the Mirror, see Principle #3, *NeuroPower* (Burow, 2013).

it learns to love itself and others; the sense of being grounded in P1 acts as a protector for the I2 heart; and the C1 provides a means for emotional release and embraces the pleasure instinct.

For social acceptance the child needs to control their self-centred instincts of C1 and P2. Judith (1996) argues that if the P2 ego is weak, the child may feel the need to deny their instincts entirely and become a 'good child'. What begins as a conscious behaviour to please a parent can become a lifelong unconscious role.

If this compliance becomes continuous and pervasive, the individual will grow up with an under-reliance on P2, an over-reliance on I2, and a dependence on others to keep them grounded and make them feel happy and successful (Judith, 1996).

On the other hand, a highly functioning I2 will give the person the ability to be altruistic and empathetic, cooperative and friendly while maintaining a healthy sense of self. This enables the individual to strike a balance between maintaining autonomy and deferring to others' needs and wishes.

LOVING AND BEING LOVED

Often people report that they feel as if their I2 Intelligence and heart expand when they fall in love. Judith (1996) explains that they lose their egocentricity and rigidity of thought as they encounter and accommodate their beloved's interests, ideas, values and beliefs.

As well as their thoughts, they share with their beloved their bodies and their innermost self. Furthermore, as they are adored by their beloved, they may sense their own beauty. Being beloved is often the basis for self-acceptance and self-esteem, as we know ourselves more deeply, reflected in the eyes of our beloved. It usually follows that we take pride in ourself – our bodies, homes and our actions, all key aspects of self.

Judith (1996) notes that when we fall out of love we return to the vulnerability of the child, and become immersed again in our past identity. As a result of the pain, we are forced to re-examine ourselves in a new light, and in the process our awareness is raised.

I2 AND BALANCE

Some Eastern philosophers suggested that since the physical heart is positioned in the centre of the body, that the essence of the themes of the spiritual (or psychological) heart (I2) is balance. Judith (1996) argues that balance within the person is a prerequisite for developing meaningful and deep relationships with others rather than forming relationships as a subconscious means to completing oneself.

Love Conquers All

A key aspect of intimate love is devotion or surrender without ego (P2)[8]. This

---

8   Discussed in detail in Chapter 4

requires a balance between devotion to the other and to the self. As we explain later, when devotion is excessive, the devoted one can lose their own self, as they follow only the needs and wishes of the other. This is most likely to happen when their own ego strength (their P2) is poorly functioning. In this situation the individual needs to reconnect with their own needs (C1), take action (P2) and re-establish the balance.

True love demands attunement and empathy, but this must not arise from the lover's own need to be needed. When a person shows attunement with another, they are not necessarily expected to fix problems but rather to understand and empathise with the trials of the other. For this to work we must be self-aware enough to know our own needs, open enough to share with the other at a feeling level, and grounded enough to remain centred in self (Judith, 1996).

Grief

If a person is unaware of or denies their grief, they often shut down their capacity for empathy and feel emptiness inside. When acknowledged, grief can be expressed and healing can follow. When this process is completed, we can be filled with hope and life (Worden, 1983).

Briefly, the person needs 'to go inside' themselves to return to their own groundedness, and from there, gain the ego strength to be healed. (For more detail, see *Healing the Heart (I2) as an Adult* later in this chapter.)

Childhood Traumas and Abuse

The most tragic cause of wounding of the heart occurs in childhood when the young person is at their most impressionable. Judith (1996) argues that common traumas and abuses from which many children in our society suffer include rejection, abandonment, loss, shaming, constant criticism, unacknowledged grief (including parents' grief), parental divorce, death of a loved one, a loveless and cold environment, conditional love, sexual or physical abuse, and betrayal. Abuses to the other Intelligences, particularly P1, C1 and P2 can also affect the functioning of I2.

A defenceless child is totally dependent on their family for nurture and love. Yet if a little child is abused it is usually at the hands of their own family. As a result, instead of the child's emerging I2 integrating the self, this child is separated off from the parts of themselves that are rejected by the parents. The child fails to develop some of their capacity to love and connect and may grow up to view relationships as being static rather than a process. Even their primary relationships may be seen as an afterthought, with the individual living their life as if alone. For them, the I2 space hurts and so they learn to rely on the other Intelligences for meaningful interaction (Judith, 1996).

Feeling Worthless

When a young child is abused by those they love, they often lose their love of life and their natural willingness to connect. They withdraw and 'shut down' their I2 function. Further, they grow to believe they are unlovable, with no validity as a human, and see themselves as nothing special. As we have already seen, the quality of parenting determines the way the developing child ends up seeing and relating to the world. They may become responsible or rebellious, they may expect acceptance or rejection, and so on.

Horney (1945) suggests these individuals look to their partner for a sense of value. However, without self-love and self-acceptance, a partnership will not improve the situation.

Projection

Added to their feelings of worthlessness, the abused child will be likely to project the critical, abusing or rejecting parental characteristics onto others. This is particularly difficult when their life partner is the subject of their projections. Instead of seeing the partner as they are, they see only the behaviour of the critical or abusive parent.

For the adult to break these patterns, they need to spend time, with a skilled listener, unravelling the web of childhood experiences and looking again at their current situation. Some abused children grow up to find partners who continue to abuse them. Because as a little child they could not challenge the situation, they may accept the adult relationship without question, never aware that it is unacceptable, because that is how life has always been for them.

Rejection

Rejection is a powerful form of childhood trauma and abuse that impacts the functioning of I2. To a child it is equivalent to death, and results in self-hatred, because the child identifies with the parent and rejects themselves. In adult life it will be just as traumatic when the person is rejected, especially by a partner, because they will relive the original trauma. When this happens, the solution lies in the individual learning to have attunement with themselves. This enables them to love and accept themselves rather than identify with the partner and their rejection (Judith, 1996).

Poorly Functioning Interpersonal Connectedness (I2)

My observation is that a poorly functioning I2 manifests in the person being withdrawn and antisocial, cold-hearted, critical and judgemental, intolerant, isolated, depressed, disconnected and closed, without empathy, and with narcissistic tendencies.

TRAUMA AND AN UNDER-RELIANCE ON I2

When a child experiences trauma such as abuse, they close their heart and their I2 may remain underdeveloped into adulthood. They are afraid of intimacy in any relationship, because they see only the risk of being hurt again. This can happen for all of us, too, after a lover's rejection. Fortuitously, a highly functioning I2 usually recovers after a time of grief.

Unfortunately, for the wounded person, a poorly functioning I2 results in not only a withdrawal of love, but also in the closure of the channel for receiving love. Therefore, the wounded heart is not open to receive the love of friends or family, and the individual becomes lonely and withdrawn. They may function quite well in day-to-day life but cannot connect meaningfully with others.

Knowing Others, Knowing Myself:
When I2 is Impaired

The prefrontal cortex assists in constructing ideas about the beliefs, intentions and perspectives of others (Goel, Grafman, Sadato & Halletta, 1995; Stuss, Gallup & Alexander, 2001). Damage to this area early in childhood, or in later stages of life, results in deficits in the development of empathic abilities (Dolan, 1999). Damage to the orbitofrontal cortex has been correlated with acquired antisocial personality (Meyers, Berman, Scheibel & Hayman, 1992).

Neuroscience has also helped to demonstrate, through functional imaging studies, the important link between understanding our own emotional states and the states of others. Empathy requires conceptual understanding, emotional attunement, and the ability to regulate one's personal emotional state, and early studies with patients suffering brain injuries suggested that damage to either the dorsolateral or orbitofrontal areas (which are linked to these abilities) impairs different aspects of empathic behaviour (Eslinger, 1998).

Since then, research has shown that individuals with a poor ability to be aware of and describe their own emotional states also show poor ability to understand the mental states of others, and reduced activation in the right medial prefrontal cortex (a key area of the brain associated with mentalising). These 'alexithymic' individuals (literally, to be 'without words for emotions') also struggle to recognise when others are experiencing pain and have reduced activity in the DLPFC as well as reduced responses in parts of the brain to do with our threat response (Moriguchi et al., 2006; 2007).

Furthermore, because they received no empathy as a child, the wounded heart feels no empathy for themselves or for others. Thus they can be cold and critical or even cruel in response to their own suffering as well as to the suffering of another. A common characteristic of this person is unforgiveness of themselves and others. The person with little empathy holds on to past hurts and nurses their anger.

For the person with an under-reliance on I2, there is an unconscious but very strong fear of intimacy and with good reason, according to their early experiences and reasoning. As a child, they learned from their parents that they were unlovable. Therefore, the adult resists letting anyone too close for fear of exposing their inner self.

Judith (1996) observes that, from time to time throughout life, many adults display both an over-reliance and under-reliance on I2. After deep hurt they will metaphorically close their heart and withdraw for a time; another time they may become co-dependent and metaphorically open their heart too wide, with no barriers, only to be rejected and close down again. The task for us is to observe and be aware of our behaviour and the deeper intention from which it arises.

OVER-RELIANCE ON I2

My experience concurs with Judith's (1996) when she argues that an over-reliance on I2 causes co-dependency, poor boundaries, excessive demands, a tendency to cling, jealousy and a tendency to be excessively sacrificing.

In particular, an over-reliance on I2 Intelligence often centres around manipulation. This is about using the context of love to ease our own pain or compensate for our own incompleteness; that is, using love for our own needs, using another to do what we will not, or avoiding taking responsibility for our own life in some way.

Over-reliance on I2 can create co-dependency – ignoring our own needs to gain love through our apparent helpfulness and care. There is no real love in co-dependency. Not knowing their own needs, the individual focuses only on the needs of the other, hoping for fulfilment by deserving love in return.

However, with this excessive focus on love comes the flip side of insecurity, which manifests in possessiveness, jealousy and excessive demands. Moreover, so needy is the person that it clouds their own awareness and discrimination. Even an abusive relationship may be explained away by wishful thinking. In the end the craving for intensity of connection can have the opposite effect and drive the beloved away, leaving the individual in total isolation.

Healing the Heart (I2) as an Adult

AWAKENING THE AUTHENTIC SELF

Developing a highly functioning balanced I2 involves knowing our authentic self apart from the dictates of the tribe. Once a person on the I2 journey has entered into this stage of development they may return to the tribe for comfort, but it will no longer be able to fulfil this role. They are now on a different journey within themselves. The questions they ask themselves at this time are related to their own personal desires, strengths, weaknesses, emotions and needs.

Myss (1996) explains that whereas the task during the P2 phase of the journey is for a person to learn to love themselves in relation to the achievement of their own goals (such as the acquisition of material possessions or the climbing of the ladder of success), the I2 journey is about loving themselves in relation to having the courage to listen to their own heart.

Our culture is only recently beginning to embrace I2's needs in marriage. Individuals are beginning to have a strong sense of self when they enter marriage. There is also an emerging expectation that partners will give mutual support not only on a physical level, but also on an emotional, psychological and intellectual level. For many, I2 has resulted in transforming the marriage into a partnership (Myss, 1996).

SELF-LOVE

Before we can form a healthy love relationship with another, we must first love ourselves. Self-love arises from self-awareness, knowing what we need, wish, fear and hope and where our boundaries lie. When we honour ourselves we respect, understand and care for self.

Thomas Moore (1994) advises that an effective method of self-discovery is to neither judge nor change, but simply to witness the self. In so doing, we realise our own sacredness, the divinity in us. This process of self-examination will heal the heart and balance our psyche.

It is through self-reflection that we can do the work of integration of our body, mind and emotions. The I2 stage is the time to heal the heart by working through past hurts, memories and unresolved emotions.

HEALING I2 WITH SELF-ACCEPTANCE

Self-love is the medicine that heals the I2 function. But due to painful events that were supposedly in the context of love, we may be unclear about what true love looks like. So what is love that heals the heart? Acceptance. You must acknowledge all that you are and all that you are not and embrace, honour and respect all of it. To do this thoroughly Judith (1996) suggests the following exercise.

1. Create a four-column table.

2. In the first column, list each part of who you are or the roles you play. For example, you might be the nurturer, parent, friend, protector, critic, carer, inspirer, achiever and hurting child.

3. In the second column add a few words describing how you see that part of yourself. For example, you may see your parent as judgemental, angry and protective, and your achiever as obedient, cute, often lazy but intelligent.

4. Now take some time to consider each specific part listed – to honour, respect and acknowledge that part. Consider how realistic its desires are, how well those desires have been met, and what can be done to make that part whole.

5. Consider which parts relate to other parts. For example, the hurting child may be related to your role in the workplace. Your protector may want to protect the hurting child. Use the third column to draw lines to indicate the relationships and describe them in the fourth column.

6. If you become aware that you would like some of your internal relationships to improve, write a script outlining how you would like the relationship to develop between the two parts of self. Keep going until they come to some resolution.

DEALING WITH GRIEF

We grieve when we lose someone or something dear to us. It is a truism that with the person we lose we also lose some part of ourselves. For example, when we lose a lover, we may temporarily lose the tender part or the playful, sexual part of ourselves. The task is to reclaim and reconnect with the lost part of ourselves rather than fixate on the person lost.

Judith (1996) suggests the following excellent reflection process for healing. To do this reflection, answer the following questions and note the answers in your journal.

Question 1. How was this person special to me?

Question 2. What did this person give that was otherwise missing in me?

Question 3. What parts of me did I especially show to them? What does that part need now? Have I lost contact with that part of myself?

Question 4. What does that part of myself need in order to re-open itself to be healed?

DEALING WITH EMOTIONAL MEMORIES

When we look inside ourselves and listen to our heart, many of us find a 'wounded child'. Many of us also discover this child has had a surprising and unwanted amount of power and influence over our lives. While our heart is unhealed we continue to live in the past. When we are hurt, we close our heart not only to the one who hurt us, but also to everyone else. The same result occurs if we are ashamed of our behaviour and cannot forgive ourselves. Healing can only take place when we can find attunement with the other and ourselves.

Critical to the process of healing is the process of reconsidering our emotional memories, which starts with self-love and forgiveness. We need to open ourselves to the healing power of love and act out the love and attunement of I2.

Many support groups and churches, although intending to help, inadvertently encourage people to see themselves as victims, not responsible for doing anything about their own lives and what has 'happened' to them. The intention of such support groups is to provide a context of unconditional love to work through issues and heal the wounds of abuse, personal violations and injustices. However, to heal the child within's wounds, Myss (1996) points out that the outcome is often that many remain trapped in these warm, caring groups, seeing themselves as needing their wounds in order to receive the love they crave from the group. They then embrace their wound as part of their identity and so do not move on to a new life. Instead of the wound being embraced as a bridge to a new life, it unfortunately becomes an integral part of the new self.

THE POWER OF FORGIVENESS

For self-forgiveness, the victim needs to forgive and embrace the perpetrator, which in some cases includes themselves. Many sensitive individuals beat themselves up long after an event for which they feel ashamed or disappointed. Forgiveness requires heart-felt attunement and empathising with the perpetrator, their intentions, environment, constraints and culture. This requires a separation of the perpetrator's basic essence from their action. Empathising with the perpetrator does not condone their actions, but it does provide the opening for the heart to forgive and heal.

If you want to forgive but you find it is too hard right now, you may find the following exercises recommended by Judith (1996) to be helpful. The first exercise relates to forgiving yourself in order to improve the functioning of your I2 Intelligence.

1. **List the events**
   Identify the events for which you have not been able to forgive yourself.

2. **Recreate the events**
   For each event, recreate what happened that led to the action.

3. **Identify the parts**
   For each event, identify which part of you was acting, for example, the unique child, the unloved spouse, or oppressed teenager.

4. **Understanding**
   Relive the feeling and actions of each event to truly understand what was happening.

5. **Attunement**
   Listen to that part of yourself with attunement. Consider what it needed and what it was looking for. Consider how you would feel if you saw someone else doing what you did – if you can apply attunement with them then you can apply attunement with yourself.

6. **Forgiveness**
   Forgive yourself. Tell that part of yourself, 'I forgive you. I know you were only meaning to ...' If that part of yourself still has not fulfilled what it was looking for at the time, suggest other, more productive, ways of meeting those needs.

FORGIVING OTHERS

This second exercise relates to forgiving others in order to heal the heart.

1. **List the events**
   Identify your wounds, perhaps with the help of a therapist or insightful friend.

2. **Identify your benefits**
   Ask yourself what you gain by keeping the wound open. Rather than say, 'Something's not right in my life,' say, 'Now I have a job to do.' Perhaps you are demanding of others that they make your life go the way you want it to. Perhaps you are letting your wounds fester and giving yourself permission to act negatively to avoid taking

responsibility for your life. Letting the wound fester may mean becoming powerful or avoiding domination. This may take the form of being right, making someone else wrong, and acting as their judge and master. You may be using grumpiness to blackmail another into doing something your way. Perhaps you are being grumpy as a means of communicating what you want without being vulnerable and taking any of the risks involved by asking verbally.

3. **Consider the message**

Access your I2 to ask yourself the question, 'What is the message behind this hurt and unforgiveness?' Sometimes our hearts hurt, prolonging the wound, as a means of carrying a message. Perhaps you have been violated in some way and your heart is merely meaning to emphatically communicate, 'Don't do that!' Letting your heart release its message often helps in letting go. Use this opportunity to really understand the message of your I2 Intelligence.

4. **Empathise**

Empathise with your perpetrator. Imagine the series of events that led up to the wound. Consider the valid needs of your perpetrator. Recreate the event as they would have experienced it.

5. **Identify the cost of keeping the wound open**

Being a victim costs. Look at the costs to your health, energy levels, and your effectiveness. Holding hurt against another is comparable to taking a poisonous pill and expecting someone else to die. Holding hurt hurts you. It affects your health. It consumes your attention. It also impacts your effectiveness in interacting with others. Look at the impact on your ability to express and receive love. Empathise with others about how holding your unforgiveness affects them. You can expect it to be detrimental to others even if they have been too polite to say so. Be clear that you have chosen to be this way by choosing to hold your unforgiveness. It is a reaction from your heart, having a significantly detrimental effect on your own heart and those of others. Identifying the cost provides the fuel for your heart to forgive.

6. **Forgive**

Once you know that your unforgiveness is about you and your benefits, and that it may merely represent a message, that it costs your heart, and costs others' hearts, you may be ready to forgive and let go. If you decide to talk it through with your perpetrator, either face-to-face or by letter, be sure to focus on forgiving rather than blaming. Create a space which completes your spirit, and does not cause yet another message of anger through you being accusational about the issue.

7. **Think love**

Live with gratitude and love and, most importantly, live in the present moment.

UNDERSTAND WHAT LOVE IS

Love is a feeling, but it is sustained by a daily commitment to act in loving and caring ways. Judith (1996) offers the following excellent fantasy to help you be present to what love is. Fantasy helps reprogram the heart through a succession of developmental stages.

> In fantasy, we can imagine our ideal mum, dad or lover. We can imagine how they would speak to us, what they would do for us. In the fantasy, it is important to let the feelings fully permeate the body. [Completely drench your body and your memories in this feeling.] It is often helpful to begin this fantasy imagining ourselves at a young age and gradually growing up with this feeling present. How would it have felt at three years old to have had this kind of support and love? How would it have felt to go to school if you had had this kind of love? How would it have felt going through puberty? Would you walk, talk, or reach out differently? What would college have been like? How would your marriage or your relationship to your children be different?
> (Judith, 1996, p. 291)

I2 is our doorway to love, connection and empathy. The most important thing to remember is always to keep a balance between love and respect for yourself, and love and respect for others.

AFFIRMATIONS

Judith (1996) offers the following affirmations to be used to increase the strength of our I2:

- I love myself and am worthy of my love.

- I love to know that I am worthy of loving myself and others.

- The source of love is unending.

- I live in empathy, forgiveness and acceptance of others.

SUMMARY OF HEALING PRACTICES

According to Myss (1996), the following list identifies some practices which may help to further develop your I2 Intelligence:

- Arm exercises involving reaching out and taking in

- Self-examination and psychotherapy – examine your assumptions about your relationships

- Exercises of emotional release – be complete with others and yourself

- Forgiveness when appropriate

- Inner child work

- Co-dependence work

- Self-acceptance

CREATING A HIGHLY FUNCTIONING I2

Compare your own experience with what you have learned about the I2 Intelligence. Which aspects of I2 are you aware of? Do you focus on one above the other two?

- The I2 somatic element is the physical sensation of being connected with another person or being emotionally responsive to the environment (facilitated by mirror neurons).

- The I2 feeling element is love, generosity and compassion. It involves a sense of attunement and a desire to connect with other people. It also involves feeling what they are feeling within yourself.

- The I2 thinking element involves cognitively understanding what other people are feeling through accurate theory of mind.

Diagram 5.2 shows the three aspects of I2 that require integration so that true Empathy can form.

In integrating this Intelligence the adult needs to align the thinking aspect of Theory of Mind, the feeling aspects of love and compassion, and the somatic aspect of feeling connected to others.

First, focus on awareness of your own emotions and body sensations, be they positive, such as love, attunement and connection, or painful, such as grief, sadness or hurt. To begin, focus on your body. I2 sensations are felt in the chest, around the heart. For some people it is obvious – they place their hands on their heart or they open their arms to open the heart or they may mirror the facial expression of the other person. The task of your conscious self is to observe these somatic sensations, understand them and express them appropriately.

The I2 Intelligence mirrors in you what another person is feeling. This is not your own emotion; it is focused on the other person. This may be attunement (authentic connection) or love, joy or light-heartedness. Above all, there is a sense of connection with the other. If you have well-developed I2, you will be aware of these feelings and will usually express them as appropriate. However, if your I2 is poorly functioning, you will probably not be conscious of this aspect of communication, focusing more on the content of the interaction – the argument or the data. However, you may still pick up

Diagram 5.2 Healthy I2 Intelligence – Noble Quality: Empathy

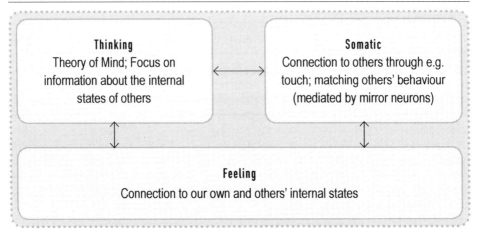

Thinking	Somatic
Theory of Mind; Focus on information about the internal states of others	Connection to others through e.g. touch; matching others' behaviour (mediated by mirror neurons)

Feeling
Connection to our own and others' internal states

For the Neuroscience of Spontaneity see Table 5.3

the feelings and will file the information away into your subconscious mind. Later you may have a 'gut feeling' about the person. It is important to listen to it as it is telling your conscious self what you saw about the person's feelings.

One of the tasks of integrating the three aspects of I2 is to cognitively monitor your feelings and sensations. A person who has highly developed I2 can find themselves overwhelmed by the feelings of others that they 'pick up' from their environment, or they may allow themselves to be controlled by their aesthetic response to their surroundings. The cognitive task is to assess the appropriateness of your response and use 'self talk' to monitor it. Consciously attend to and honour the feelings, then make an executive decision about your response.

I2 is a valuable part of your personality. It can help you connect with others and understand the feelings of both yourself and others. But it is very quiet, maybe unconscious, and so can be ignored when the P1 or P2 Intelligences are busy on a task. The task of integration for your conscious self is to pay attention to the aspect of I2 that 'speaks' to you, however quietly, and integrate it with the other two aspects, so that your responses of feeling, bodily sensation and understanding are unified and whole.

Highly Functioning I2 in Adult Life

The first-order noble quality of Empathy requires integration of the thinking aspect of intuition, the feeling aspect of love, and the somatic aspect of being

Table 5.3 The Neuroscience of Empathy

The table below details the Neuroscience of I2. Refer to Appendix 1 for more details.

Somatic Aspect	Feeling Aspect	Thinking Aspect
• **Maternal Love** (orbitofrontal cortex, periaqueductal gray, anterior insula, dorsal and ventralateral parts of the putamen) • **Attachment** and pair bonding (the medial insula, anterior cingulate, hippocampus and parts of the striatum and nucleus accumbens) • **Mirror Neurons** (prefrontal cortex and Broca's area) give us the ability to have mindsight or empathetic attunement – Fire when another individual is observed engaging in a specific behaviour - their facial expressions and posture are thought to activate similar sensory-motor circuits in the observer – This is thought to generate the emotions that result in a sense of empathy • **Spindle Neurons** (anterior paracingulate cortex and orbitofrontal cortex)	• **Happy, motherly, joyful, warm, love, calm, excited** (areas rich in oxytocin and vasopressin receptors – both produced in the hypothalamus and stored in the pituitary) • **Love and attachment – both romantic and maternal** (neurohypophysical peptides, oxytocin and vasopressin, dopamine also released by the hypothalamus) • **Love** – associated with a deactivation of regions commonly associated with negative emotions and social judgement and a decrease in serotonin levels • Many of these responses are activated by the visual system when we **see the face of a loved one** (cerebral cortex, orbitofrontal cortex, anterior cingulate, cerebellum, insula, posterior hippocampus, caudate nucleus and putamen) • **Generosity** (oxytocin) – treatment with oxytocin leads to greater 'liberality in giving' in tasks that require splitting of money	• **Theory of Mind** – the assessment of other people's intentions and emotions (right temporoparietal junction, left temporoparietal junction, posterior cingulate and the medial prefrontal cortex) • **Romantic love** (activation of the frontal, parietal and middle temporal cortices) anterior cingulate cortex, ventral caudate nucleus, insula, striatum (consisting of putamen, caudate nucleus, globus pallidus), central periaqueductal gray and the hippocampus • When viewing images of loved ones, the amygdala and parts of both the parietal cortex and temporal lobe – **parts of the brain commonly associated with negative emotions** – are **deactivated** (middle temporal cortex, occipital parietal junction, temporal pole and lateral prefrontal cortex) elements not related to the achievement of the identified goal) – enables us to focus on the issue at hand and come up with an appropriate plan of action

emotionally responsive and connective to others.[9] Empathy represents the ability to understand and manage people and to act wisely in human relationships. This noble quality enables the individual to:

1. Accurately empathise with the feelings of other individuals;

2. Interpret the motivations behind the individual behaviours of themselves and others;

3. Understand the likely emotional impact of their own emotional behaviour on others in various situations and actively manage their own behaviour to ensure the best outcome; and

4. Understand emotional concepts and meanings and the links between emotions and relationships.

People with this noble quality enjoy spending quality time with their close friends and are able to monitor the social 'pulse'. They also have the ability to know what to say in difficult, sensitive or emotionally charged moments. Their focus is on building and maintaining honest relationships through authentic connection.

HOW 12 EMPATHY MEETS THE NOBILITY CRITERIA

The first-order noble quality of Empathy answers questions related to the right of the individual to love and be loved. This noble quality enables the individual to discover that they have the right to connect with others and give and receive unconditional love. This noble quality is linked to the desire to authentically connect to others and be 'true' to oneself.

Empathy brings value to the community in three ways. It enables the community to learn to interact in a civilised and sensitive way, and to minimise the amount of needless pain caused by insensitivity. It fosters the idea that community members can be honest and open and form strong ties with other community members based on love rather than simply family or tribal membership. Empathy can also calm another's amygdala, reducing their experience of stress and allowing the space for their more noble qualities to show.

It feels good to empathise. Emotional connection created through the noble quality of Empathy describes a key aspect of well-being marked by the subjective experience of connectivity and love (Ryan & Frederick, 1997). Individuals report that using emotional connection to resolve an internal tension has a paradigm shift impact

---

9   Peterson & Seligman's meta-study of the most widely influential traditions of thought and religion in human history found emotional and social intelligence to be a significant human strength (Peterson & Seligman, 2004).

on their lives.

In high performance teams, Empathy ensures that the team feels connected and listened to. Secure in the knowledge that they are cared for by others in the team, each member is able to bring their own love and passion to the work of the group..

I2 Toolbox

THE IMPORTANCE OF I2 IN BUILDING HIGH PERFORMANCE TEAMS

The emergent cultural impact of I2 is Empathy, which enables the organisation to learn to interact in a civilised and sensitive way, and to minimise the amount of needless pain caused by prejudice and misunderstanding.

When Empathy is absent respect for the individual declines. Behaviours are expressed that cause pain in the workplace, uncaringness, dishonesty and disconnection fragments teams.

However, when there is a highly functioning I2 in the organisation, staff at all levels can be honest and open and form strong ties with other staff members based on understanding.

Leaders looking to improve the function of I2 in their team can increase Empathy by applying the I2 tools.

I2 QUESTIONS FOR PERSONAL DEVELOPMENT AND SELF REFLECTION

The best high performing teams are made up of individuals who have focused on their own personal development. The following questions can be used as a starting point for those leaders looking to improve their I2.

1. Who in life provides you with the opportunity to express your ability to love?

2. Who in life do you provide the opportunity to express their ability to love?

3. How do you show love?

4. How is the way you express your love sometimes mistaken?

5. If there is one aspect of love you can't express what would it be?

6. How well do you connect with others?

7. What is one thing you can do to manage your I2 Intelligence?

8. Who do you know who connects well with others and who demonstrates they understand the world view and motivations of others?

9. Is it possible to have one of these people mentor you so that you can further develop your I2?

I2 TOOL #1:
ENSURE ALL AGREEMENTS ARE WIN-WIN

PROCESS

1. **Familiarise yourself with the concepts outlined by Stephen Covey** in his book, *The 7 Habits of Highly Effective People* (1989), focusing particularly on Habit 4: Think Win/Win: Principles of Mutual Benefit.

2. **Ensure you understand the Six Paradigms of Human Interaction:**
   - **Win.** People who hold a win paradigm think only of getting what they want. Although they don't necessarily want others to lose, they are personally set on winning. They think independently in interdependent situations, without sensitivity or awareness of others. *Characteristics of the paradigm:* Appeals to individuals who are self-centred, think 'me first', don't really care about the outcome for the other person and have a 'Scarcity Mentality'.
   - **Lose-Lose.** People with this paradigm are low on both courage and consideration. They envy and criticise others, put both themselves and others down and are usually highly dependent.

     Characteristics of the paradigm: Ends up with nobody benefiting (i.e. 'no win'). This is the long-term result of win-lose, lose-win or win.
   - **Lose-Win.** People who choose to lose and let others win show high consideration for others, but lack the courage to express and act on their feelings and beliefs. They are easily intimidated and tend to borrow strength from acceptance and popularity.

     Characteristics of the paradigm: Appeals to individuals who voice no standards, no demands and no expectations of others. These people are quick to please or appease and tend to bury their feelings.
   - **Win-Lose.** People with this mindset are concerned with themselves at the expense of others. Like those with a win paradigm, they want to win – but unlike those with a Win approach, they also actively want others to lose. These people see their success as being achieved at the expense or exclusion of another's success. They are driven by comparison, competition, position and power.

     Characteristics of the paradigm: Very common scripting for most people – the authoritarian approach. The individual uses position, power, credentials, possessions or personality to achieve the desired 'win'.
   - **Win-Win.** People with this paradigm choose to win themselves and to ensure that others also practice win-win. They take the time to search for solutions that will satisfy their objectives and simultaneously satisfy others.

Characteristics of the paradigm: Involves seeking mutual benefit – is cooperative, not competitive. Appeals to individuals who listen more, stay in communication longer and communicate with greater courage.

- **Win-Win or No Deal.** This is the highest form of win-win. People who adopt this paradigm seek first for win-win, but if no acceptable solution can be reached, they agree to disagree agreeably.

Characteristics of the paradigm: Allows each party to say no – the highest form of win-win. This is also the most realistic at the beginning of a relationship or business deal.

3. **Do a quick self-audit.** Which paradigm do you adopt in most of your interactions? What does this reflect about your leadership style? How does this mindset affect the achievement of your objectives, both as an individual and for the team?

4. **Explore the four dimensions of Win-Win.** These are: (1) Character; (2) Relationships; (3) Agreements; and (4) Systems and Processes. The Win-Win Exercises on the following page will provide you with a starting point for developing Win-Win Character and Relationships. For more information refer to Stephen Covey's original materials.

5. **Develop an Action Plan for shifting your paradigm to Win-Win.** Based on the outcome of your reflections, develop a three-month Action Plan for developing Win-Win Character and Relationships. Include conducting a workshop with your team to introduce them to the win-win paradigm and foster discussion about how this mindset can be cultivated in the team.

DOS

✓ Do give yourself time to work through enough of your own feelings about the win-win paradigm before introducing it to your team. While you don't need to be a committed convert, it helps if you see value in and benefits of the win-win approach. If you don't, and you try to introduce the concept to your team, they'll pick up on the incongruence between what you're saying and how you really feel.

DON'TS

✗ Don't be disheartened if shifting your mindset seems like a big task. Early in life, we each learn to base our self-worth on comparisons and competition, and tend to think about our success as resulting from someone else's failure. As you work with the exercises, you'll uncover your own personal unconscious script about the nature of power and success in the world. This underpins how you approach life in general. If you can successfully shift your view to win-win, you're therefore likely to find that it impacts more than just your business interactions. So it's well worth persevering!

Win-Win Exercise: Developing Win-Win Character

Your character communicates your deepest beliefs and values. A win-win leader possesses three character traits:

- **Integrity** – The quality of being true to their feelings, values and commitments
- **Maturity** – The ability to express their ideas and feelings with courage and consideration for the ideas and feelings of others
- **Abundance Mentality** – The belief that there is plenty for everyone

The combination of these three traits builds trustworthiness.

Instructions

1. For each of the three characteristics, give yourself a score out of 10 for the extent to which you embody this trait (0 = not at all, 10 = innate to you 100% of the time).

2. Now give yourself a score out of 10 for each for where you would like to shift that to over the next month. Don't automatically assume that the answer will be 10 – make sure that your response both reflects your genuine desire and is realistic.

3. Resolve to focus on bridging the gap over the next month. Start by listing five things that you can action immediately to develop in these three areas.

Our ability to adopt a win-win approach in life reflects our ability to respond to situations with a high degree of both courage and consideration for others. The character traits of integrity, maturity and abundance provide a strong foundation for responding in this way.

1. How would you rate yourself in terms of your courage and consideration of others? Place a dot in the Matrix to show where you think you sit at the moment.

2. Consider the following scenario:

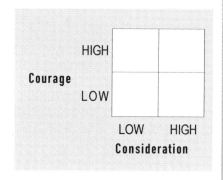

   You're lunching with your boss and a client at a local café. You're pressed for time (you need to be back at the office in 15 minutes) but the place is crowded and service is extremely slow. It's been 15 minutes since the waiter brought your boss's and client's orders, and they've almost finished eating. When the waiter finally brings your meal, it's not the one you ordered.

   For each box in the Matrix above, write a sentence about how a person with that approach (e.g. low courage, low consideration) would respond to the situation.

3. Based on your responses to Question 2, create a name for each box of the Matrix that best describes the approach of someone in the quadrant. For example, you might decide to call those with high courage and low consideration the 'Temper Tantrum' or 'Cause a Scene' group.

Win-Win Relationships

Win-win relationships build high trust between individuals. In the same way that regular deposits in a bank build interest, deposits in the 'Emotional Bank Account' lead to a relationship that flourishes with high interpersonal value.

1. The list below outlines the key skills required to establish win-win relationships. Give yourself a score out of 10 for each according to the frequency with which you demonstrate this capability (0 = never, 10 = all the time).

#	Win-Win Relationship Skill	Score
	How often do I:	
1	Demonstrate consistent actions that convince people I have a well-earned reputation for honesty, integrity and loyalty. My actions are consistent with my behaviour, decisions and position	
2	Believe in the best of other people	
3	Share information to help others understand my position, behaviour and decisions	
4	Communicate clear expectations	
5	Seek others' ideas	
6	Listen with empathy to the ideas of others when they are shared	
7	Provide accurate, timely and honest communications	
8	Treat people with respect and respond to their needs	
9	Respond to the needs of others in my team	
10	Focus on the positive but provide constructive feedback on areas for improvement	

2. Add up your scores and divide by 10 to get your average score for your win-win relationship skills. As a leader, you should be aiming for at least a score of 8, if not higher.

3. Identify the three areas in which you rated yourself as performing most poorly.

4. Reflect on how the absence of these skills is impacting your team, your interpersonal relationships and the effectiveness of your leadership. List some examples of recent instances that are in theme with these skills. What was the outcome of these interactions or events? How might things have ended differently if your win-win relationship skills were more highly developed?

I2 TOOL #2:
COMMUNICATING EFFECTIVELY WITH GROUPS

PROCESS

1. **Schedule your face-to-face communication.** The nature of verbal communications can vary greatly, from large formal team briefings to casual encounters between two or three colleagues from different departments. However, the effectiveness of all communications and the extent to which they build and strengthen relationships is greatly affected by factors that affect the dynamic of the group. In scheduling your face-to-face communication, ensure that you:

   a. **Invite the right people.** Group communication works best when the people present have a legitimate reason for being there, have something to contribute and have an interest in the outcome. This often involves making sure there is P1 clarity about the value people add by being at the meeting (for more information about creating P1, see the P1 Toolbox).

   b. **Invite the right number of people.** For most group discussion, five is recognised as the optimum number for debate and decision-making. In a group of this size, members can adopt different roles and a single member can be in the minority without undue pressure to conform. However, making sure the right people are there always takes priority over number considerations.

   c. **Set a time limit.** Even for informal encounters, this demonstrates sensitivity to the pressures on other people's time. You also need to be realistic about what you can expect to achieve within the group given its representation.

2. **Define the purpose of the communication and facilitate introductions.** These P1 actions are critical to ensuring a stable foundation for the discussion – even the most highly skilled I2 communication and active listening abilities become irrelevant if people are busy wondering why they're even there. Is this a meeting to take decisions, a briefing session to impart information or a brainstorming session to generate new ideas? Who are the people in the room, why are they there and what are they each expected to contribute? Make sure you define your own contributions as well as your authority for making them (either as a function of your position or with vested authority on behalf of someone else). Once you've articulated these things, if your expectations turn out to be unrealistic, allow people to leave or, if appropriate, suggest alternative members to join the group. Make sure you apply good active listening skills in determining that the right people are in the room for the right reasons.

3. **Be rational but open-minded during the session.** Groups work effectively only if participants – including you as leader – are open to listening to new points of view and receiving new information. While it's important that you take up a clear position on issues, be willing to listen to others' positions and be prepared to change your mind. If

you do shift your position, explain why.

4. **Demonstrate good I2 communication skills.** There are many different communication techniques and rules that you may wish to adopt. The following are particularly critical in group discussions:

   a. **Practice active listening.** As you facilitate the group, demonstrate that you've heard what others have been saying by linking your comments to the contributions already made. Where possible, clarify areas of support for the arguments of individual team members or identify potential areas of disagreement or overlap between different points of view.

   b. **Make good use of non-verbal communication.** Make eye contact with each member of the group with a view to connecting with each of them as you do so. Use non-threatening but positive body language and convey an impression of calm and confidence. Use gestures to reinforce your key messages and non-verbal signals to convey attitudes and expressions. Also make sure that you pay attention to other people's non-verbal signals: are you irritating or patronising them?

   c. **Stay calm and don't argue.** Even if you believe the group is taking the 'wrong' decision, stay calm and don't become emotional in defence of your own ideas. Emphasise points of agreement and minimise areas of disagreement with a view to finding a way forward.

   d. **Avoid personal attacks.** The key to effective group communication is mutual respect. If you believe someone is wrong, criticise the idea, not the person. The impact of your criticism can be increased by making it more palatable; preface it with a word of support or agreement on a related topic. Other things to focus on include:

      i. Avoid being too negative, even if someone is deliberately putting forward unhelpful ideas;

      ii. Resist the temptation to allocate blame for previous mistakes or failures – otherwise the group dynamics will break down; and

      iii. Remember that while group members may be competing to present individual positions, you are co-operating to find an overall solution.

5. **Bring the communication to a conclusion.** Review what you were hoping to achieve out of the communication and whether it has been achieved in the session. Articulate the decision and review any action statement so that attendees have the opportunity to express any concern about the final outcome. Make sure you translate this into written form as soon as possible after the meeting and make sure that everyone involved has a copy (including interested parties not present).

DOS

✓ Do be aware of the reference points of other group members: how are they viewing the issue (i.e. apply Theory of Mind to determine what they're thinking and feeling) and what barriers will their views create that impede you achieving your own objectives

✓ Do take part in any discussion with a genuinely open mind. Remember good listening skills are critical

✓ Do be aware of the dangers of unconscious domination. If you as leader always give an opinion first, it is possible the others may: be unduly influenced from the start; be liable to think it's all sewn up and that they are only required to react, not contribute; or get into the habit of not thinking for themselves

DON'TS

✗ Don't dominate the discussion because you are convinced of the merits of your own argument and oblivious to others

✗ Don't bring your own prejudices to the group and assume that certain staff members will react in a certain way

✗ Don't allow 'group think' – the process whereby everyone ends up agreeing by default, usually on what they think the leader wants to hear

✗ Define your contribution in terms of meeting the group's objectives and stick to your position unless you are genuinely convinced by other member's arguments

I2 TOOL #3:
BUILD ACTIVE LISTENING IN YOUR TEAM

PROCESS

1. **Self-assess your own active listening skills.** Complete the Active Listening Exercise on the following page, paying particular attention to the follow up reflection questions.

2. **Ask colleagues to provide you with feedback about your active listening skills.** Identify at least two colleagues who have worked closely with you and whose opinions you value and trust. It's also important that you feel comfortable receiving constructive feedback from the people you choose. Provide each colleague with a copy of Questions 1, 2 and 3 of the Active Listening Exercise. For each skill listed, ask them to rate you (according to the instructions) by asking themselves the question: 'In conversations with others, including me, how often does [your name] ... [insert skill]'.

3. **Compare the assessments.** Look for any discrepancies in scores, particularly any skills for which you gave yourself a high score, while others did not. Have an informal chat with your colleague - show them your self-assessment and ask for further comments about why they scored you as they did. This is your chance to have the benefit of their insights about how you might improve. It is not an opportunity to explain to them why they were wrong/misguided/harsh/foolish in their scoring.

4. **Identify five key skills for improvement over the next month.** Set aside some private time to consider your active listening skills. Consider which skills need to be prioritised first – and make sure you take into account the feedback you received from your colleagues, your own reflections from Questions 4 and 5 of the Active Listening Exercise and the particular circumstances of your position. Identify five key active listening skills that you intend to focus on improving over the next month. Develop an Action Plan for how you intend to achieve this goal.

5. **Take your team through the same process.** Schedule a team-building session and start by explaining the critical importance of empathy to team performance. (You may like to use the introduction to the I2 Toolbox as a thought starter.) Invite each team member to follow the process you've already undertaken – first completing the Active Listening Exercise, getting at least one other colleague to assess them, discussing the results with their colleague, identifying their priority areas for improvement and developing an Active Listening Action Plan. Then bring the group together for a discussion about the insights they gained from the exercise, particularly how the group's listening skills have been affecting team performance. Make sure you link the active listening principles back to any key projects or objectives to 'make it real' for the team. You should be able to cover this in 2-3 hours, depending on the how many colleagues each person asks to assess them (1-2) and the amount of time you want to give to discussion.

DOS

✓ Do give some thought to who you want to ask for feedback. If you can, resist the temptation to invite only people you get along with for comment. Often it's with the people we find challenging that we allow our listening skills to remain unused. This is a great opportunity to challenge yourself to be a good listener even with those you violently disagree with/dislike. If you can master those conversations, your chances of making active listening an innate part of your leadership style will increase dramatically

DON'TS

✗ Don't be devastated if the results show that you're not as good a listener as you thought you were. Most of us aren't. This is a good opportunity to identify areas for improvement so that you can become the excellent listener that you want to be. Also, remember that this is one person's perception, so extract the helpful feedback without taking it too much to heart

Active Listening Exercise

1. The following list details the skills of a good listener. Give yourself a score out of 10 for each according to the frequency with which you demonstrate this capability (0 = never, 10 = always).

#	Good Listening Skill	Score
	In conversations with others, how often do I:	
1	Probe for clarification	
2	Listen for unvoiced emotions (i.e. how the other person is feeling, even if they're not expressing it overtly)	
3	Listen for the story	
4	Summarise what has been said	
5	Empathise	
6	Listen for what's different and new about the narrative, not what's familiar	
7	Take the other person's story seriously (i.e. not say things like, 'You shouldn't worry about that')	
8	Look for hidden assumptions underlying the story	
9	Let the other person 'get it all out of their system'	
10	Ask the other person, 'How do you feel about that?'	
11	Keep asking for more detail to help me understand	
12	Get rid of distractions while listening (e.g. turn off the mobile phone, don't multi-task by reading emails at the same time etc.)	
13	Focus on hearing the other person's version of events first	
14	Let the other person tell their story their way	
15	Try to stand in the other person's shoes, at least while I'm listening	
16	Ask how I might be of help to the other person	
17	Ask the other person what they've thought of before sharing my own thoughts	

#	Good Listening Skill (cont.)	Score
18	Make it seem as if the other person is the only thing that matters and that I have all the time in the world	
19	Look at (not stare at) the other person as they're speaking	
20	Look for congruity (or incongruity) between what the individual says and how he or she gestures and postures	
21	Encourage by nodding my head or giving a small smile	
22	Control my own body movements (i.e. no moving around, shaking legs, fiddling with paper clips, etc.)	

2. The second list below details the skills of a poor listener. Give yourself a score out of 10 for each according to the frequency with which you demonstrate this capability. However, this time 0 = always, 10 = never.

#	Poor Listening Skill	Score
	In conversations with others, how often do I:	
1	Interrupt or respond too soon	
2	Match the other person's points (e.g. 'Oh yes, I had something like that happen to me. It all started when…')	
3	Editorialise while the other person is mid-stream (e.g. 'Well, that option is a non-starter')	
4	Jump to conclusions or judgments	
5	Ask closed-ended questions for no reason	
6	Give my own opinion before asking the other person for their thoughts about the situation	
7	Try to solve the problem too quickly	
8	Take calls or interruptions in the course of client meeting	

3. Add up both sets of scores and divide by 30 to get your average score for your active listening skills. As a leader, you should be aiming for at least a score of 8, if not higher.

4. Identify the lowest five areas in which you rated yourself as performing relatively poorly.

5. Reflect on how these skills are impacting your team, your interpersonal relationships and the effectiveness of your leadership. List some examples of when you can remember yourself doing or not doing these things in conversations (depending on whether you've identified absent good listening skills or the presence of poor listening skills as areas of concern). Then describe the outcome of the interaction and include reflections on how the listening skill may have affected that result.

KEY INTERPERSONAL CONNECTION QUESTIONS FOR BUILDING A HIGH PERFORMANCE TEAM

1. How well do you know each of the other members of the team?

2. In your opinion, how committed are you as a team to ensuring each team member feels heard and understood by other members of the team?

3. How aware are you of the strengths of the other members in your team?

4. How well do you feel your strengths are utilised within the team?

5. As a team, how do you support each other during challenging times?

6. What can you do to facilitate more connection within the team?

Key 12 Questions for High Performance Teams

NeuroPower Case Study

ORGANISATIONAL CASE STUDY #1: STATE HEALTH HAND HYGIENE PROJECT

The Task: To improve compliance by health workers with hand hygiene practice.

Recap:

In 2007, an Australian state health department wanted to address the serious threat that health-associated infections posed to hospital patients. Micro-organisms are readily transmitted on the hands of health care workers. In Australia alone, health officials estimate that up to 7000 people die annually from hand hygiene-related infections in hospitals. The economic burden is also considerable, costing millions each year.

Hand hygiene has been proven to substantially reduce transmission of micro-organisms. However, despite well-established guidelines, compliance throughout the world with hygiene standards is disconcertingly low. International and national health agencies have been grappling with how to deal with the issue for some time, and few interventions have had any impact whatsoever, despite both European and US hospitals and governments spending tens of millions of dollars on communications, incentives, closed circuit TV and education.

Since research demonstrated that the hand hygiene issue centred around human behaviour, one state health department decided on an innovative, behaviour-changing approach using the *NeuroPower* framework to drive the solution. Working with the *NeuroPower* Consulting Team, the department implemented a behaviour change program called Clean Hands are LifeSavers that engaged the health workers and increased compliance from 18% to 60%. A key driver of this behaviour change involved effectively addressing each of the six Intelligences in the correct sequence. How these progressive steps were taken is outlined in the Organisational Toolbox Case Study at the end of each Intelligence chapter.

Having already:

- Created safety and security in the hospital environment by embedding values through a code of conduct
- Empowered spontaneity and self-expression through collaboration and the development of creative promotional materials
- Kick started action and motivation through establishment of goals and the celebration of quick wins

Step 4: Encourage empathy and connection

Most health workers, especially the nursing staff, are very high in empathy (I2). Part of the issue with infectious transmission rests in the fact that many health workers use touch to reassure patients or had a belief that washing hands after each patient made the environment too scientific. Health workers were trained not to rush and to spend time listening to patients and their family and friends, and to engage in other compassionate activity other than touch.

ORGANISATIONAL CASE STUDY #2: MERCHANT BANK EQUITY DERIVATIVES LEADERSHIP TEAM

The Task: Improve employee engagement and tangible business performance

Recap:

In 2006, at the height of the financial boom, one of Australia's leading equity derivatives teams was operating in an environment that was fast-paced, demanding and with a high level of stress. In order to handle large volumes of work in a very volatile market, the team needed to be highly functional and collaborative. Growth was nearly 200 percent over the previous year so the enormous strain was evident. This was mainly caused by a leadership team in crisis.

The Leadership Team was fractured, non-collaborative and driven by their own individual agendas. There was both a lack of respect and a lack of honesty between members which led to highly reactive responses and conflict. The broader team could see this occurring and they felt they were part of a warring tribe with all the insecurities that brought.

NeuroPower consultants devised a program which focused on addressing the splintered leadership team. The intervention involved a series of group structured processes which were embedded by individual coaching sessions.

Having already:

- Created role clarity
- Empowered people's self-expression
- Encouraged healthy egos and passion for work

Step 4: Developing Teamwork and Leadership Capabilities through an expanded I2

A key workshop focused on the Signature Strength or Gift of each team member. The group was introduced to the eight profiles that exist in a healthy and high performing team and what unique qualities and capabilities each profile brought to the group. By the end of the session, the team could see each of their colleagues in a different light, and there was a sense of combined effort and excellence that eased the task ahead. The team displayed an expanded sense of themselves as being leaders that were unified and connected and with the right qualities to lead the whole Equity Team to high performance.

Chapter 6

Our Fifth Social Cognitive Need:
SEEING THE FACTS &
The Objective Learning Function (I1)

SEEING THE FACTS (I1) AT A GLANCE

Seeing the Facts is our Brain's Fifth Social Cognitive Need

The brain looks for constant feedback and needs to have all the information at hand. The brain is a complex, self-regulating machine that adapts constantly to external feedback - much of it visual. Of all the senses, the human brain is heavily invested in perceiving, processing and remembering information, particularly visual information. We need to 'see it to believe it'.

Characteristics of the Seeing the Facts (I1) Functional Network

Data and Facts

STRENGTH	WEAKNESS
Focuses on the detail and works with quantitative information	Can disregard the human element when making decisions

OPPORTUNITY	THREAT
To get comfortable with processing qualitative information	Can be rendered useless when faced with ambiguity

Management Style

- Will want to base all discussions and decisions on data and evidence
- Will assess others on their depth of field-specific knowledge
- May forget to consider the people side of things

LOVE OF LEARNING

I1 THINKING
Pattern Recognition, Explicit Semantic Memory

I1 FEELING
Curiosity, Emotional Connection with Objects

I1 SOMATIC
Withdrawal and Objectification

COMMUNICATION STYLE

- Tends to have an excellent vocabulary
- Tends to listen for interesting or new facts
- Values facts (objectivity) over feelings
- Often oblivious to how people are feeling or to any hidden agendas
- Can talk facts all day and not resolve issues
- Will want to see the evidence for themselves

KEYWORDS INCLUDE

- Evidence
- Data
- Truth
- Facts
- Pattern recognition
- Objectivity

Seeing the Facts (I1) Helps Us to Survive

Seeing the Facts (I1) helps both individuals and the group to survive and thrive by helping them see the world as it is (rather than how they would like it to be), track progress and make detached decisions based on reality.

Seeing the Facts &
The Objective Learning Function (I1)

SEEING THE FACTS: OUR FIFTH SOCIAL NEED EXPLAINED

In Chapter 5, we looked at our need for Interpersonal Connection (I2), which is supported by the brain's sophisticated ability to understand what others are thinking and feel what others are feeling. Our Interpersonal Connection (I2) - sometimes described as our ability to empathise - motivates us to connect with other people, understand them and respond appropriately to this social stream of information[1].

But - as any structural engineer will tell you - **feelings alone can't build a bridge**. Sometimes we need to get the facts right; near enough is not good enough.

Luckily, our brains are exquisitely wired to perceive and respond to the external, physical world, particularly by interpreting and understanding the world through what we see (Seeing the Facts - I1). Sight is extraordinarily difficult. It takes many thousands of calculations for a computer to detect even basic visual shapes, and yet we find it easy. This is because an extraordinary amount - over 50% - of the brain is dedicated to visual processing, pattern recognition and object classification. Over 70% of all your sensory receptors are in your eyes[2], and while most of us hardly think about the millions of visual inputs our brains are piecing together or filtering out every second, a range of findings from neuroscience, social science and communication research have confirmed that the ability to 'see' something is strongly linked to your ability to understand and remember it. For example, simple diagrams on medicine labels increase our ability to understand them by 25% compared to text alone (Dowse & Ehlers, 2005). Being able to see something for yourself increases audience comprehension rates by one third, compared to just hearing it.

---

1   This ability to connect and empathise is hardwired, and at times hard to overcome. In fact, our natural tendency to try to understand the mental states of other living things (whether human or another animal) is so strong that at times we mistakenly attribute mental states and intention to inanimate objects - from computers that 'refuse to cooperate' through to the relationships that some people form with their cars or other precious belongings!

2   Whereas dogs, rats and many other vertebrates have brains with large olfactory bulbs dedicated to discriminating between smells, the human brain has instead invested its resources into visual perception (our ability to see). Interestingly, though, while the human olfactory bulb is a relatively small organ, it has retained its strong and direct links to the amygdala and other parts of the limbic system, which some neuroscientists suggest is why particular odours (like the smell of smoke, for example) have the ability to influence body physiology and evoke strong emotional memories.

Of all the Six Social Needs and their associated systems in the brain, Seeing the Facts (I1) is perhaps the most thoroughly researched. With access to brain imaging technologies, researchers have observed that the data the brain needs about people (Empathy, I2) and the data the brain needs about the physical world (Seeing the Facts, I1) not only belong to two separate systems but also compete for dominance in the brain. Jack et al., (2012) looked at brain activity when people were performing a 'mechanical' reasoning task based on factual knowledge about the physical world (Seeing the Facts, I1) and a 'social' reasoning task based on understanding and predicting what and how people feel (Interpersonal Connection, I2). They found that the network of brain regions activated by the I1 task was suppressed by the I2-related task, and vice versa. This finding was particularly relevant for researchers trying to understand the biological basis of autism, who have similarly found that healthy adult brains have both a tendency to empathise (your empathy quotient, or EQ) and a tendency to think analytically or systemise (your systemising quotient, or SQ) and that the stronger your tendency to systemise (high SQ), the lower your empathy (EQ) (Goldenfeld et al, 2005)[3].

One other insight into our objective learning function (I1) comes from Cambridge University, where researchers have found that people who are good at maintaining precise memories have more folds in specific areas of their frontal lobes; those of us with less pronounced folds seem to be much more likely to confuse things we have experienced with things we have imagined or felt (Simons, 2013).

The I1-driven motivation to 'systemise' (by focusing on observable patterns in the physical world to understand how systems work) is critical to many of the technical fields that are required in modern organisations. Fields built on mathematics and physical sciences rely heavily on people with a high systemising quotient (SQ), and science, engineering and computing faculties have a significant over-representation of 'systemisers' compared to the humanities (Focquaert et al, 2007). Systemisers (high in Seeing the Facts - I1) tend to have more activity in areas of the frontal lobe dedicated to focusing on fine detail and filtering out distractions as well as much more activity in areas dedicated to integrating sensory inputs (Billington, Baron-Cohen & Bor, 2008)[4]. At a structural level, their brains have much more myelinated nerve connections ('white matter') in areas of the brain linked to the external attention system (Takeuchi et al, 2013).

---

3   This line of research has helped contextualise autism by showing that it is the combination of both very high SQ *and* very low EQ that gives rise to a clinical diagnosis of autism; in reality, each of us sits on the SQ spectrum and the EQ spectrum.

4   By contrast, empathisers show more activity in social-processing areas of the brain, including mirror neuron areas such as the left inferior frontal gyrus and inferior parietal lobule, and in temporal areas involved in perspective taking and autobiographical memory (Focquaert, Steven-Wheeler et al, 2010).

Diagram 6.1 Physics vs Friends – The Competition Between Analytical (I1) and Empathic (I2) Systems in the Brain

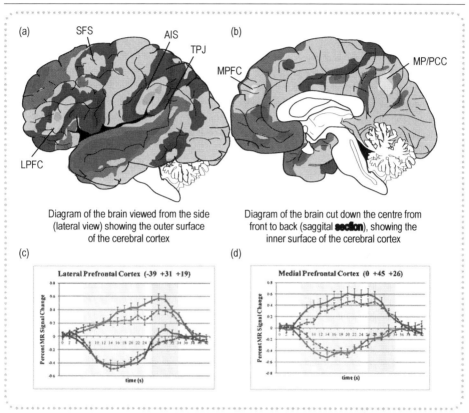

Jack et al., (2013) investigated whether mechanical reasoning (i.e. solving problems based on inanimate physical objects; I1) and social reasoning (i.e. using information about people to understand their thinking and/or predict their behaviour; I2) might recruit different areas in the brain. Their research revealed two distinct patterns of brain activation for these two different types of reasoning and, fascinatingly, showed that the areas involved turn 'on' or 'off' for these two different tasks. What they called the 'mechanical reasoning' areas (I1) increase in activity when we're thinking about the external physical world and then turn off when we start thinking about people's internal states (and vice versa for social areas). *(a,b)* On the diagrams above[1]*, cool colours (purple, blue, cyan, green) activate more for mechanical than social reasoning. Warm colours (pink, red, orange, yellow) activate more for social than mechanical reasoning. Bright colours (orange, yellow, cyan, green) identify areas which were significantly above the rest for one type of task and significantly below the rest for the other. *(c,d)* Tracking the activity of specific areas in the brain reveals activation or deactivation for mechanical (blue lines) and social tasks (red lines). The two examples provided are the lateral prefrontal cortex (LPFC) and medial prefrontal cortex (MPFC), which are more involved during mechanical and social reasoning tasks, respectively. Other activation centres linked to mechanical reasoning (I1) included the superior frontal sulcus (SFS) and anterior intraparietal sulcus (AIS). Activation centres linked to social reasoning (I2) included the temporoparietal junction (TPJ) and medial parietal/posterior cingulate (MP/PC).

---

*   For illustration purposes, the diagram above presents an artist's approximation of reported activation areas from one side only. Detailed, bi-hemispheric maps of brain activation are reported in Jack et al., (2013), (p. 390) Figure 3.

TRACKING PROGRESS: THE BRAIN'S CONSTANT QUEST

The brain is a complex self-regulating machine that adapts constantly to external feedback.[5]

For teams to achieve peak performance each team member's brain needs external, verifiable measures that track the team's progress. These measures need to be simple enough that team members can understand them. Very few teams do this well, because they either fail to keep track of key measures of progress or, alternatively, they measure anything and everything to the point where no one is able to effectively decipher the information in real-time. We call this paralysis by analysis. The simple idea is that tracking progress enables the individual and the team to evaluate the effectiveness of the strategy and tap into the brain's natural ability to respond to feedback in real-time, adapting the strategy with incremental changes along the way. Without an ability to see progress, motivation quickly diminishes.

Within the brain, a diverse range of structures and neuronal networks help us satisfy our need for Seeing the Facts. Within the *NeuroPower* framework, this set of structures is called the 'I1 Objective Learning System' (or sometimes the 'I1 network' or 'I1 function') and gives rise to a particular thinking style referred to as 'I1 Intelligence'. The rest of this chapter explores the I1 Objective System in detail.

THE EVOLUTIONARY SOCIAL BRAIN FUNCTION OF I1

The I1 system enables the individual to survive through:

1. The recognition of objects and recall of information associated with them (Creem and Proffitt, 2001);

2. Communication within the individual internally and externally with others through language;

3. Learning new things about the world and the formation of declarative memory; and

4. The ability to identify patterns in: behaviour (both one's own and others'); the seasons; dangerous situations; and opportunities.

Recognising the Characteristics of Seeing the Facts (I1)

The I1 Intelligence relates to the mind's ability to see patterns and remember facts. I1 involves the psychological ability to stand outside our beliefs and attitudes

---

5   One example of this is apparent in the fascinating clinical discipline of neurofeedback, where your brain trains itself into more constructive patterns through real-time visual feedback.

by focusing on the objective facts and the data of the world. The I1 function enables the mind to process data quickly. The attributes and characteristics of I1 suggest that it is linked strongly with the left hippocampal area and involves the explicit semantic memory system.

The I1 Intelligence loves learning and experiencing life. It gives rise to curiosity that fosters an increased understanding of the external world as it actually is. However, I1 will often be oblivious to hidden agendas and has limited ability to handle ambiguity.

I1 has three elements that require integration. The cognitive thinking aspect focuses on data, learning and pattern recognition. The feeling aspect centres on a sense of curiosity and unique connection with objects, and the somatic behavioural aspect is typified by withdrawal and focusing the eyes.

The factual, data recall aspect of I1 is usually the aspect that is most conscious. This may be because it is this aspect of I1 that is supported, encouraged and developed through formal education. The purpose of I1 is to objectively review our world without judgement or emotional subjectivity. Through these objective perceptions we are able to establish a starting point from which to rechart our next step to help us reach our goals. In the corporate context, this is reflected in the tracking of lead and lag indicators.

Seeing the Facts (I1) has Both Strengths and Weaknesses

Objectivity and a motivation to seek external, validated data are critical to effective decision-making in many fields. Many organisations recognise this and dedicate significant resources to tracking progress using a diverse range of overlapping (and at times contradictory) measures. It is important to recognise that an **overemphasis** on Seeing the Facts, either personally or organisationally, is largely unconstructive for two reasons. The first is that the I1 system alone is not a decision-making system. An overemphasis on I1 manifests as a feeling of 'lacking the data' to make a decision. This leads to an obsession to keep collecting more and more information, instead of synthesising and learning. The second is that the I1 system encourages the brain to focus purely on objective data and largely ignores the human element of most situations. When Seeing the Facts (I1) is overemphasised, many of the positive aspects of Interpersonal Connection (I2) suffer, including the ability to understand other people's thoughts and feelings. This leads to astonishingly bad predictions about what others will do - and when not managed it leads to relationship-damaging decisions.

The Development of a Healthy Objective Perspective (I1)

While a rudimentary I1 circuit develops in most children from as early as two years of age, it only becomes high-functioning as the young person learns to think symbolically and abstractly. In Jean Piaget's developmental model, this occurs during the period of Formal Operations, usually beginning around age twelve. This is when the child begins to think as a scientist, and to reason and philosophise about life. As the child begins to think in abstract concepts and symbols, they start to develop an objective (rather than personal) understanding of the world.

Up until this point in the development journey, the progressive development of the Intelligences has made the following contributions to the individual's identity:

- P1 brings understanding of physical identity as we identify with the body and its needs and abilities, as well as the physical world. It is orientated towards self-preservation.

- C1 develops our emotional identity and life script as the feeling sensations of the physical body are transformed into value-oriented meaning. The drive here is towards self-gratification.

- P2 develops a sense of our autonomous, separate awareness. The primary concern here is with self-definition (ego).

- I2 focuses on our social identity where the ego identity expands to include relationships with others. The quality of this identity is towards self-acceptance, which is essential for acceptance of others.

The I1 Intelligence enables the adolescent to objectively create a sense of personal identity that is separate and removed from the other Intelligences. It can be an aspirational identity based on what the individual likes the look of in others.

COMMUNICATING OUR PERSONAL IDENTITY

Developmentally, the onset of I1 in the teenage years ushers in the idea that we communicate who we are (I2 social identity) with objects (I1) that tell our story for us. In ancient societies this may have been with small, culturally defined objects like earrings, headpieces or bangles. In modern society, we have added thousands of other fashion items and objects to the list. What the teenager wears, the phone they have, the websites they visit, the car they drive, the shoes they wear, the style of haircut etc. are all external symbols of the individual's inner world. They also describe the individual's place in the external world through value-laden objects. This signposting continues through life with the partner you choose (or don't), the holidays you enjoy (snapshots), the suburb you choose to live in and your ever-changing fashion sense.

Regardless of our personal I2/I1 dominance, we all 'believe' the validity of our internal world (I2) once it manifests in external reality (I1). We signpost who we aspire to be, which in turn educates and reinforces this emerging us to ourselves and those we meet. Most recently, the channel of choice in the west is quickly becoming social media options like Facebook that help us clearly encode our sense of ourselves in an I1 reality.

I1 AND EXPLICIT SEMANTIC MEMORY

I1 enables the brain to remember facts. It governs and records the specific, factual and objective memory of an event. This is the library in which we store the images that we link with experience. Unfortunately, these images are not automatically linked with the correct emotional memory of the event centred in I2.

Consider, for example, a memory for a fact, such as the French word for table. Your explicit semantic memory (I1) describes the objective memory of the details. (How is it spelt? Is the noun masculine or feminine?) On the other hand, there may also be an emotive memory such as the memory of sitting at the French table while you were spending last summer at the seaside with Auntie Flo, including how you felt about it (I2). For a memory to be consolidated, I1 and I2 must be consciously reconciled. This is only possible if there is communication between the hippocampus and the outer region of the cortex.

The fact that the emotion (I2) and object (I1) are not linked unless the hippocampus

---

Comparing I1 and I2 Memory Systems

There are two distinct forms of explicit memory. While the explicit autobiographical memory system correlates with I2, it is the semantic memory (or the memory for facts) that relates to I1. I1 is the mind's ability to perceive patterns, focusing on the facts and the data of the world – the semantic memory function of the brain (Wheeler, Stuss and Tulving, 1997). Our memory for facts (I1 semantic memory) is functionally different from our memory of self across time (I2 subjective memory). I1 memory allows for propositional representations – symbols of external or internal facts that can be assessed as 'true' or 'false'. I1 recall has been found to involve a dominance of left over right hippocampal activation. Further, the perceptual, objective representations of the I1 function have been found to involve the visual cortex that processes information on the basis of pattern recognition. This sensory cortex makes links between different patterns and identifies any 'match' with past experiences. For example, when reviewing a document, it links the specific perceptions of a set of angles with the conclusion that they represent a 'table'.

---

is engaged creates a distinct problem. As described earlier in this chapter (e.g. Diagram 6.1), individuals tend to use either I1 or I2 at any one time. Unless we integrate the two, the correlation between our emotional response (I2) and the object (I1) that causes it will remain low. If your I1 Intelligence functions more highly than your I2 Intelligence, you may be aware of an object but not the emotion it causes within you. If your I1 is not functioning as well, you will probably be aware of your emotions, but not the object in your environment that is causing them. When the image or memory of an event is disconnected from the rest of the experience, the energy that is split off from it becomes a false image and we become sincerely confused.

Poorly Functioning (I1)

The strength of I1 is to recognise patterns. The process of learning occurs as patterns reveal the identity of a thing, what it is, what it is for, and how to relate to it. But too often we look at something only until we recognise the pattern and then we stop. This point is often when the amygdala makes an inaccurate and often irrelevant emotive connection to the pattern.[6]

Since visual memory is strongly linked with our somatic, or physical experience, it follows that abuses to any of the Intelligences – to the body, the emotions, one's autonomy, one's heart, or freedom of expression – will affect I1. Any abuses to P1, C1, P2 and I2 will therefore become embedded within the body's defensive mechanism – the limbic system, particularly the amygdala. Part of our more primitive centre for interpreting our environmental stimuli, the amygdala's primary function is to scan the environment for potentially hostile inputs and to arrive at an immediate response. This is a role that it plays in all animals. In humans it performs the same function of interpreting hostile events and determining whether to fight (engage P2), to comply (engage P1) with the threat, or to withdraw completely from the situation (engage I1).

The amygdala prompts us to action by chemically inducing emotion. It effectively mediates our library of emotional memories. As the 'librarian' for emotional memory, the amygdala scans experience, comparing what is happening now with what happened in the past.[7] Its method of comparison is associative: when a key element of a present situation is similar to the past, it identifies a 'match' and responds accordingly. Therefore, what something reminds us of will be more important than

---

6   Often the first step of therapy is to challenge unconscious associations that have formed between the object and the emotion. The realignment of these is an important first step of awareness.

7   In reality, the amygdala is much closer to a guerilla leader, military general and arms trader all rolled into one. It is constantly scanning for risk and rapidly marshalling the troops to head off any threat (however small).

The Impact of Priming on Memory

The divided attention phenomenon reveals an important aspect of memory priming. Experiences must be concentrated on and be a focal point of awareness for them to be consciously recalled in the laboratory. This phenomenon can be tested when a subject is asked to pay attention to only one ear while listening to two auditory lists on a set of headphones. (An example of the two lists may be that one discusses a list of politicians while the other is a list of zoo animals.) When the subject is asked to repeat what it was that they heard in the focally attended ear (say, the right) then they will have excellent recall about the zoo animals. When they are then asked what they heard in the left ear, subjects typically state that they have little recall. When the subjects are then asked to fill in the blank spaces on partially spelled words from the list of words spoken into the left ear, they are statistically more likely to fill in the correct word over subjects who were given a different list. This is a clear example of indirect recall, a measure of implicit memory. The subject's brain has encoded the politicians' names implicitly and so their brain is 'primed' to bring up a politician's name when given a cue. Subjects may have no conscious recall of what they heard, or even a sense that what they are writing is a reflection of a list that they heard or something that they have experienced. While implicit memory is intact, without focal attention, experience does not become encoded explicitly (Schachter, 1992).

what it actually 'is', and only one part of an identity is needed to evoke the whole memory. So the amygdala will make connections between things that merely have similar striking features (Epstein, 1994). These associations will represent inaccurate linkages, as they will be based on partial matches and incomplete assessments. We therefore need high functioning I1 to see the entirety of a situation or event, and identify a more complete reality.

ILLUSIONS

When we suffer from an illusion, our attention is fixated on a specific image or outcome we desire. We do not focus on reality, but instead on how we think the present situation should be.

These incorrect associations could be referred to as illusions. An illusion is bound up in the static nature of the amygdala's emotional associations with objects. The more we are attached to an illusion, the more energy we need to invest.

The Trick to Selective Attention

People tend to engage in what psychologists call *belief perseverance*, which is our tendency to see only facts that support our beliefs and ignore those that contradict them (Lord, Ross & Lepper, 1979). This tendency helps us hold on to a world that has, thus far, led to our personal survival (Janoff-Bulman, 1992). However, this confirmation bias can also justify maintaining the status quo long after it has ceased to be constructive. The development of a well-functioning I1 allows for the perception and acceptance of objective truth – even if these facts do not support our beliefs.

The illusion can become either an obsession or a delusion. When they become obsessions, our perceptions fixate on obtaining a desired outcome. We focus an unusual amount of energy on one particular issue, often to the exclusion of others that are more important.

A delusion is a total misconception of a situation. I once worked with a chairman of a large public company whose father had been a much liked and enthusiastic Presbyterian minister. The chairman lived under the illusion that he was a charismatic preacher just like his father had been. Suffering under this delusion, he was unable to see the reality of his situation, which was really quite the opposite. Despite the best efforts of those around him to help him see things as they were, his perception kept him imprisoned in repetitive cycles of appalling speeches which ultimately led him to losing his appointment as chairman.

TRAUMA AND ABUSE

As we have seen in previous chapters, childhood traumas can affect the development of well-functioning Intelligences. When the child is laying down their memories of family, traumatic memories can impair the developing I1. Judith (1996) argues that this results in adult repression or dissociation. In an effort to shut out the unhappy feelings associated with a memory, we can repress it, close down our perception and limit what we see. This reflects an under-reliance on I1. An alternative is to dissociate from it; in other words, shut down our feelings about the experience and so limit our ability to make sense of it. This results in an over-reliance on I1, at the expense of I2 feelings.

Judith (1996) relays the story of Tom who could recall many incidents of abuse from his childhood, but he completely dissociated himself (and his feelings) from them. In his successive unhappy relationships, he could not 'see' the impact his words and actions had on his partners because he could not feel them. Judith (1996) reports that although a talented, elegant man, 'he had a streak of coldness in his relationships that made one shudder'. He had developed total reliance on I1 and his I2 had atrophied.

An individual's ability to see what they do not want to see can also be impacted if, as a child, they saw something and were told the situation was not as they saw it. For example, if a child sees parents being abusive and is told they come from a family who love one another dearly, this creates a contradiction which may end in illusion. The child does not trust their observations and so their I1 does not develop.

Judith (1996) cites another cause of psychological blindness – childhood shaming. This causes the young child to turn their eyes inward, to ensure there are no more faults to be accused of. Hence, the child does not learn to look outward to see how others are feeling.

DETACHMENT AND I1

The I1 Intelligence enables us to detach from subjective perceptions and see the truth in a situation. Detachment involves stilling your internal fear-driven voices until no external influences have authority over your sense of objectivity. In a healthy sense, this is the realisation that no one person or group of people can dictate reality.

The capacity for detachment is linked to the pattern recognition capacity of I1. With detachment comes the awareness that all things end at the appropriate time and all things begin at the appropriate time. This means that the individual does not hold on to emotional bonds past the point where they are constructive. Detachment also prevents others from having emotional power over you.

Detachment is vital in order to appreciate the truth of revealed patterns removed from their social or cultural form. But if taken too far, and if the entire personality is built around the behaviour of I1, neurosis can occur.

OVER-RELIANCE ON I1

Karen Horney (1945) describes the thinking and behaviour of the adult whose excessive I1 has made them neurotic. She suggests that life, for those over-reliant on I1, is lived like the zombies of Haitian lore. Revived from death through witchcraft, they function like live people, but there is no real life in them. What all detached (excessively I1) minds have in common is their capacity to look at themselves with an objective view. They have an 'on-looker's' attitude towards themselves and towards life in general. They effectively 'move away' from people. This contrasts with the other types identified by Horney: the aggressive (P2) types 'move against', while the compliant (P1) types 'move towards' people.

The goals of the detached person are negative: they want to remain uninvolved, not to need anybody, not to allow others to intrude on or influence them. The underlying and driving end of the detached person is a need for utter independence. From this comes a drive towards self-sufficiency and a withdrawing from people to gain privacy.

Privacy

I1-dominated individuals have an inner need to put emotional distance between themselves and others. They do not want to get emotionally involved with others in any way, whether in love, fight, cooperation or competition. They draw around themselves a kind of magic circle, which no one may penetrate. While they may appear to get along with people at a superficial level, this is only because they are not really relating to others at all. The compulsive character of the need shows up in their reaction of anxiety when the world intrudes on them. They may dislike sharing any experience because the other person may disturb them. Even when they interact with others, their real enjoyment only comes later, in retrospect as they privately review the experience.

Self-Sufficiency

For the mind with an over-reliance on I1, all needs and qualities are applied to support their desire to not get involved. Among the most striking is a need for self-sufficiency. A more precarious way to maintain self-sufficiency is by consciously or unconsciously restricting one's needs. The underlying principle is never to become so attached to anybody or anything that that person or thing becomes indispensable.

Neurotically detached people avoid competition, prestige and success. They are inclined to restrict their eating, drinking and living habits and keep them on a scale that will not require them to spend too much time or energy earning the money to pay for them. They may insist on acquiring their knowledge first hand; rather than take what others have said, they will want to see or hear for themselves.

Neurotic Superiority

All neurotic tendencies have a need for superiority as a motivating factor and are umbilically linked to the maintenance of the neurosis. Detached people want the uniqueness within themselves to be recognised without any effort on their part. Their hidden greatness should be felt without them having to make a move. A sense of their own uniqueness is an outgrowth of their desire to feel separate and distinct from others.

Emotions

For the neurotic person controlled by I1, there is a general tendency to suppress all feeling, even to deny its existence. This pertains primarily to feelings towards others and applies to both love and hate. Any strong emotion would bring them either closer to others or into conflict with them.

This can even extend beyond the sphere of human relationships, motivated by the desire to maintain self-sufficiency. Any desire, interest or enjoyment that might make the detached person dependent upon others is viewed as treachery from within and may be checked on that account. Any threat of dependence will cause them to withdraw emotionally.

The more the emotions are checked, the more likely it is that emphasis will be placed upon intelligence. The expectation then will be that everything can be solved by sheer power of intellect, as if mere knowledge of one's own problems is sufficient to cure them, or as if information alone could cure all the troubles of the world (Horney, 1945).

Judith (1996) argues that an over-reliance on I1 can induce the following additional issues:

- Hallucinations;
- Illusions;
- Difficulty concentrating; and
- Nightmares.

When there is an over-reliance on I1, the individual is likely to have poor discernment as they are overly bombarded with data input. As they focus on everything, they focus on nothing in particular. This happens when energy is withdrawn from the P1, C1, P2 or I2, and the individual is left without the capacity to discern and sort through the images they perceive. The effect can range from 'mild neurotic annoyance to full-blown psychosis' (Judith, 1996).

An over-reliance on I1 somatic, feelings or thinking will result in the following[8]:

Somatic over-reliance on I1: An over-reliance on the I1 somatic aspect fosters an individual's love of exploring things kinesthetically, taking things apart with their hands to see how they work, understanding complex things but only through physical interaction.

---

8   Each of these three situations reflects a particular Neuro-Limbic Type; the Nine, Four and Five respectively. The Neuro-Limbic Types relate to *NeuroPower* Principle #2, *NeuroPower* (Burow, 2013).

Feeling over-reliance on I1: An individual with an over-reliance on the I1 feeling aspect of the Intelligence emotionally connects with objects of perceived beauty or significance.

Thinking over-reliance on I1: An over-reliance on the I1 thinking aspect of the Intelligence creates compulsive observers who get easily overwhelmed, who want to watch and analyse rather than play in the game of life.

All of these reactions are different from the problems that occur if the I1 function is not sufficiently developed.

UNDER-RELIANCE ON I1

An under-reliance on I1 Intelligence prohibits people from following through on the ideas that they have. They appear to be surrounded by plans that never quite come to completion. Physically, the area most affected by poorly functioning I1 is eyesight and the person may suffer from eyestrain, conjunctivitis, poor sight or even blindness. Headaches and migraines may occur and there may be difficulties with memory (Judith, 1996).

The following issues may also result from an under-reliance on I1:

- Insensitivity to self and others;
- Believing there is only one true way/reality;
- Poor memory (because the mind is busy with repressed memory);
- Denial (cannot see what is really going on);
- An inability to learn from life's lessons; and
- An inability to link cause and effect.

CLARITY

As the objective and pattern recognition capacity of I1 is developed, we can see more of ourselves and more deeply into the behavioural patterns of the people around us. As we expand our internal picture into a larger, more comprehensive world view, we inevitably begin to create a clear picture of what is happening. This is the counterpart to illusion.

Clarity arises when we extricate ourselves from the social and cultural patterns of behaviour which we have adopted and develop a plan and purpose for ourselves. With a well-functioning I1 we can be clear about the patterns of our life.

Diagram 6.2 Healthy I1 Intelligence — Noble Quality: Love of Learning

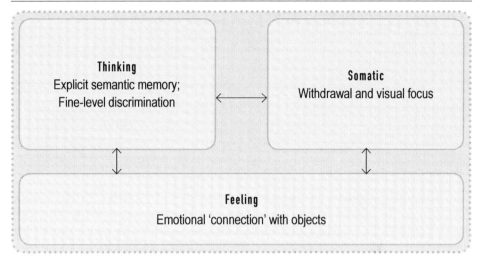

For the Neuroscience of the Love of Learning see Table 6.3

Developing Healthy Objectivity (I1)

The following exercise can help develop your I1.

Look up from this page and closely scrutinise the room that you are in. Look at the walls, look at the furnishings of the room and see them as they actually are - not just as a 'wall' or 'desk'. Now try sketching an object that caught your attention. Notice the difference between what you think the object looks like and what it really looks like. This is the gap between your I1 representation of the object and the object itself.

CREATING A HIGHLY FUNCTIONING I1

Compare your own experience with what you have learned about the I1 Intelligence. Which aspects of I1 are you aware of? Is there one aspect (thinking, feeling or somatic) that you tend to focus on above the other two?

Diagram 6.1 shows the three aspects of I1 that require integration so that true Love of Learning can emerge.

- The I1 somatic element is withdrawal and visual focus.

- The I1 feeling element involves forming our emotional link with objects.

Table 6.3 The Neuroscience of the Love of Learning

The table below details the Neuroscience of I1. Refer to Appendix 1 for more details.

Thinking	Feeling	Somatic
• **Object discrimination** (inferior temporal lobe) • Initial **processing of visual information** and distribution to specialised cortical areas for further processing (visual cortex and hippocampus) • **Semantic, phonological and syntactic verbal fluency** (Broca's areas etc.) • Other relevant structures: posterior parietal lobe, medial temporal cortex, prefrontal cortex (including the hippocampus and parahippocampal cortex), parietal cortex, middle temporal area, medial superior temporal area and posterior parietal cortex)	• **Fascination** – intense interest and a love of learning (midbrain dopaminergic regions) • **Withdrawal – wanting to move back to get perspective and look or watch from a safe place** (amygdala fear response) • **Feelings of either fascination and interest or boredom** (associated respectively with increases and decreases in activity in the prefrontal cortex – monitored by the singular cortices, hypothalamus, tegmentum and interpreted by lateral and polar parts of the cortex in the frontal lobe)	• **Working memory** (prefrontal cortex) • **Medium-term memories (i.e. less than a few years old)** (hippocampus) • **Long-term memories** (frontal lobe)

- The I1 thinking element involves consciously perceiving patterns, as well as short term and working memory.

If you tend to prefer the I2 to the I1 Intelligence, you are still likely to feel curious and be able to work with data. However, there is always the risk that you will ignore objective data in favour of paying attention to the people and environment around you. In this case, to develop your I1 ask yourself, 'What are the facts of the situation?' 'What is the objective reality here?' Accept the validity of the insight provided by the I1 Intelligence. Nurture your curiosity, recall facts and look for repeated patterns in your life. Being able to detach, withdraw and focus is a valuable quality. Encourage this part of you to grow, honour it and integrate it into your personality.

AFFIRMATIONS

The following affirmations can help to build the power of your I1:

- I am clear.

- I am open to my own wisdom and clarity.

- I see things as they actually are.

- I see the repeating patterns in my life.

- I can see.

Highly Functioning I1 in Adult Life

The first-order noble quality of a Love of Learning requires integration of the thinking aspect of pattern recognition and a focus on data, the feeling aspect, and the somatic aspect of withdrawal.[9] This noble quality includes the process of finding content that may or may not result in immediate achievement or any immediate benefit. Instead, the purpose is the discovery of information and knowledge for its own sake (Harackiewicz, Barron & Elliot, 1998). Over time, an individual with this noble quality will develop a deeper or wider knowledge of their subject matter and will be in an ideal position to coach, train or mentor others on the subject. The noble quality of a Love of Learning, strongly correlates with being open-minded to new or confronting data, which means that teams are able to operate with a much broader knowledge base. This noble quality seeks to find, store, retrieve and understand data. It will enjoy categorising information and cross-referencing it with data from other sources.

Experimental studies have found that acquiring specific knowledge evokes curiosity, which is the desire for further information (Loewenstein, 1994). It can also be an orientation towards investigating specific objects, events and problems to understand them better. A Love of Learning improves the individual's ability to recognise patterns of behaviour, seasonal patterns, social patterns – in fact, the patterns in any set of data.

HOW I1 LOVE OF LEARNING MEETS THE NOBILITY CRITERIA

The noble quality of the Love of Learning can answer the individual's current questions of existence in two ways. It answers the questions we all have about understanding how the world works and the true nature of cause and effect. It is also central to answering

---

9   Peterson & Seligman's meta-study of the most widely influential traditions of thought and religion in human history described Love of Learning as a general disposition towards new information and the search for more content on any particular topic. This was found to be a significant human strength (Peterson & Seligman, 2004).

questions about the true nature of the natural, emotional, material, spiritual and metaphysical worlds.

The Love of Learning brings value to the community. A Love of Learning enables the community to develop the ability to see the patterns in the data, to then understand the natural cycles of trading, wealth creation, war strategy, farming, technology and patterns of individual and group behaviour. A Love of Learning also fosters the idea that community members can learn how the world works and maximise their strengths, minimise their weaknesses, and predict future patterns and prepare for them. This noble quality allows for the passing of hard-won knowledge from generation to generation.

The Love of Learning evokes highly positive feelings in the process of acquiring new knowledge, satisfying curiosity, building on existing knowledge and/or learning something completely new (Krapp & Fink, 1992). Individuals report that experiencing a Love of Learning to resolve an internal tension has a paradigm shift impact on their lives.

In teams, a Love of Learning ensures that the team is constantly acquiring new knowledge and can continue to refine its approach based on these insights. This ensures that the high performance team remains competitive in a fast-paced, constantly changing market.

I1 Toolbox

THE IMPORTANCE OF I1 IN BUILDING HIGH PERFORMANCE TEAMS

The emergent cultural impact of I1 is A Love of Learning, which enables the organisation to develop the ability to see the patterns in the data of everyday business.

When A Love of Learning is absent the organisation fails to assess the meaning of information being generated daily, ignorance about the business escalates and denial of the organisation's true status grows.

However, when there is a culture with an effective I1, the organisation can learn how the business works and maximise its strengths, minimise its weaknesses, predict future patterns and prepare for them.

Leaders looking to increase the functioning of I1 in their teams can apply these I1 tools.

I1 QUESTIONS FOR PERSONAL DEVELOPMENT

The best high performing teams are made up of individuals who have focused on their own personal development. The following questions can be used as a starting point for those leaders looking to improve their I1 function.

1. What attitudes do you have that disempower you that may need to be updated?

2. What beliefs do you continue to accept that you know are not true?

3. What negative behavioural patterns continually surface in your relationships with others?

4. Are you judgemental? If so, what situations or relationships tend to bring out that tendency in you? Re-examine the information on which you have based these judgements to ensure their accuracy.

5. Do you give yourself excuses for behaving in unproductive ways? On what data are your excuses based?

6. What new topic areas do you need to learn about to realise your life goals?

7. How would you describe your learning style?

8. If there was one topic that you could learn more about that would have a positive impact on the quality of your life, what would it be?

9. Are you comfortable thinking about your life in impersonal terms?

10. What beliefs and attitudes would you like to change in yourself? Are you willing to make a commitment to making those changes? Are you frightened of the changes that might occur in your life should you openly embrace a conscious lifestyle?

11. Is curiosity a driver for your acquisition of data? Are there occasions when this has driven you to actions which did not honour you or another person? Do you manage this curiosity in a conscious, noble way?

12. When you think about it, have there been occasions when you have allowed avarice to control your behaviour? Could you have used the cognitive part of your I1 to assess the reality of the situation and advise the feeling part of yourself so that your behaviour became integrated with the reality you saw?

13. Do you recall feeling a sense of detachment at times during your life? Let the thinking aspect of your I1 re-examine the situational patterns to see the reality – were there times when this was entirely appropriate? Were there times when this was a reaction to something negative in your environment? Was this a way of collapsing into the tension instead of dealing creatively with the situation?

I1 TOOL #1:
CREATE A 'LEARNING LAB' TEAM CULTURE BY EMBRACING DOUBLE-LOOP LEARNING

PROCESS

1. **Assess the current learning culture** in your team by deciding which of the following the current culture is based on:

   a. **Single-loop learning** (i.e. the detection and correction of organisational error that permits the organisation to carry on its present policies and achieve its current objectives); or

   b. **Double-loop learning** (i.e. where organisational error is detected and corrected in ways that involve the modification of underlying norms, policies and objectives).

2. **Review the literature on organisational learning models,** including Argyris & Schön's seminal text, Organisational Learning (1995). Make sure you're aware of current thinking about different learning models, and if possible find case studies and examples that are relevant to your industry. You need to be able to demonstrate the benefits of double-loop learning.

3. **Schedule a series of workshops** with key thought leaders in your organisation. Introduce them to the concept of different learning models and present the case for the importance of double-loop learning for the organisation to achieve its strategic objectives. Facilitate discussion about the organisation's current position, desired position and what needs to be done to bridge the gap.

4. **Create an action list for creating a learning lab culture.** Make sure that by the conclusion of the workshop sessions there is clarity about steps that need to be taken moving forward. Examples may include developing new systems for obtaining information, scheduling regular sessions for reviewing systems, policies and practices in light of new data or creating opportunities for learning to be shared and embedded within the team. The 'Keep, Stop, Start' technique may be a useful strategy to conclude the workshop. Have the team agree on a list of things that they need to keep doing, stop doing and start doing in order to create a learning lab culture.

5. **Follow through on the action list.**

DOS

✓ Do continue to explore ways in which you can embed a learning culture within your team

✓ Do encourage the team to think laterally about how the systems could be improved to encourage double-loop learning. This may involve wider reform than you first anticipate. At this point, it's helpful to remind the team that, as Gary Hamel (described by *Fortune* as the world's leading expert on business strategy) notes, *"If your organisation has not yet mastered double-loop learning, it is already a dinosaur. No one can doubt that organisational learning is the ultimate competitive advantage."*

DON'TS

✗ Don't be disheartened if the team finds the exercise challenging. Deutero-learning (the process of inquiring into a learning system by which an organisation detects and corrects its errors) offers even greater challenges than mastering double-loop learning. While it can be tricky for the team to get its head around, it's central to the contemporary concept of the learning organisation, and well worth the effort

I1 TOOL #2:
MAKE, IDENTIFY AND TRACK YOUR LAG AND LEAD INDICATORS AND USE THIS TO DRIVE STRATEGY (KAPLAN & NORTON'S BALANCED SCORECARD)

PROCESS

1. **Prepare** for the development of your organisation's Balanced Scorecard by:

    a. ***Making the team/organisation aware of the scorecard initiative.*** Ensure that the purpose of the balanced scorecard is clear (i.e. to provide a balanced view of the organisation's performance with a view to continual improvement). Highlight that the process should not affect the ability of the team to get on with its work; and

    b. ***Clearly defining the corporate strategy*** and ensuring that the team is familiar with the key issues. Make sure there is clarity about:

        i. the strategy;

        ii. the key objectives or goals to achieve the strategy; and

        iii. the three or four critical success factors fundamental to achieving each major objective or goal.

2. **Identify the key measures of successful goal attainment.** These should be linked to specific strategic goals, and there should be no more than 15-20 key measures in total – significantly fewer may not result in a balanced view, significantly more may result in an unwieldy process that includes non-critical issues. Suggestions from Robert Kaplan & David Norton (who developed the Balanced Scorecard approach) appear below (Kaplan and Norton, 1996), but it's important that your organisation determines its own strategic goals and activities to be measured.

Goals	Measures
Financial (Shareholder) perspective Increased profitability, growth, increased returns on assets	Cash-flows, cost reduction, economic value added, gross margins, profitability, return on capital/equity/ investment/sales, revenue growth, working capital, turnover
Customer perspective New customer acquisition, retention satisfaction	Market share, customer service, customer satisfaction, number of new/retained/lost customers, customer profitability, number of complaints, delivery time, quality performance, response time
Internal perspective Improved core competencies, improved critical technologies, streamlined processes, better employee morale	Efficiency improvements, development of leads/cycle times, reduced unit costs, reduced waste, amount of recycled waste, improved sourcing/supplier delivery, employee morale and satisfaction, internal audit standards, number of employee suggestions, sales per employee

I1 Tool #2

Goals (cont.)	Measures (cont.)
Innovation and learning perspective New product development, continuous improvement, training of employees	Number of new products and percentage of sales from these, number of employees receiving training, training hours per employee, number of strategic skills learned, alignment of personal goals with the scorecard

In order to finalise your organisation's objectives and measures, you may need to conduct further discussions, interviews or workshops throughout the wider business. Ensure that the finalised implementation plan includes setting targets, rates or other criteria for each of the measures, as well as defining how, when and where they should be recorded.

3. **Implement the system and track the results.** Produce an implementation plan and communicate it to the staff. Ensure that employees have a clear line of sight between their individual Key Performance Indicators (KPIs) and the organisation's KPIs.

4. **Identify the key lead and lag indicators.** This is the step that is often overlooked. As a team, identify the lead indicators that result in the lag indicators. Often, as unlikely as it sounds, teams have no real understanding of how these two align. These interdependencies must drive the corporate strategy and are the true, proprietary I1 insights.

5. **Publish the results.** Decide in advance:
   a. Who will receive the specifics of the data (e.g. senior management, divisional/departmental heads/all staff);
   b. How much information to make available (i.e. the complete body of data available or whether to circulate partial information on a need-to-know basis); and
   c. How the results can be best publicised (e.g. through meetings, newsletters, organisation's intranet etc).

6. **Use the results to drive improvements.** Measurement is not an end in itself it simply highlights areas (e.g. management, operations, procedures, processes) that need strengthening. Taking action on the information you obtain is as important as the data itself.

DOS

✓ Do define your goals clearly
✓ Do select measures that focus on the critical success factors of each goal
✓ Do limit yourself to a manageable number of measures
✓ Do reassure staff about the purpose of the scorecard
✓ Do review the system at the end of the first cycle, taking care to assess the quality of information gathered and the success of subsequent actions. Modify the system if required

DON'TS

✗ Don't simply use the Kaplan & Norton approach suggested as your measures - take the time to reflect on what will be most appropriate for your organisation
✗ Don't over-measure your organisation
✗ Don't allow the measurement process to interfere with employees' ability to get on with the job

I1 TOOL #3:
LEVERAGE FROM YOUR TEAM'S INTELLECTUAL CAPITAL

PROCESS

1. **Schedule a workshop** with key thought leaders in your organisation to focus on how the business can optimise its intellectual capital. Make sure the room has a whiteboard, flip charts (for smaller group working) and enough space for the people attending.

2. **Prepare for the workshop** by reviewing and collating information about the current use of intellectual capital within the organisation. Use any statistics or data available to you to achieve a good understanding of the organisation's current performance across the three areas that comprise intellectual capital:

   a. **Human capital:** The knowledge residing in the heads of employees that is relevant to the purpose of the organisation. Human capital is formed and deployed when more of the time and talent of employees is devoted to activities that result in innovation that drives strategic performance. This occurs either when the organisation uses more of what people know, or when people know more that is useful to the organisation. Unleashing human capital requires the organisation to minimise mindless tasks, meaningless paperwork and unproductive infighting.

   b. **Customer capital:** The value of a business' ongoing relationship with its clients/customers. Indicators of customer capital include market share, customer retention, defection rates and profit per customer. This is often the worst managed intangible asset—many organisations don't even have clarity about who their customers are.

   c. **Structural capital:** The knowledge retained by the organisation. It belongs to the business as a whole and can be reproduced or shared—this includes technologies, inventions, publications and business processes.

Prepare a briefing sheet/brief presentation if needed.

3. **Introduce the concept of leveraging from intellectual capital.** At the start of the workshop, explain the reason for the workshop, the benefit of reviewing how the team uses its intellectual capital and the story behind your interest in the exercise. Introduce the different types of intellectual capital (see above) to the team and acquaint them with the nine principles for managing intellectual capital:

   a. Companies don't own human and customer capital. Only by recognising the shared nature of these assets can a company manage and profit from them.

   b. To create usable human capital, a company needs to foster teamwork, communities of practice and other social forms of learning.

   c. Organisational wealth is created around skills and talents that are proprietary and scarce. Companies must recognise that people with these talents are assets to invest in.

d. Structural assets are the easiest to manage but those that customers care least about.

e. Organisations need to move from amassing knowledge 'just in case' to having information that customers need ready to hand.

f. Information and knowledge can and should substitute for expensive physical and financial assets.

g. Every company should re-analyse its own industry to see what information is most crucial.

h. Organisations should focus on the flow of information, not the flow of materials.

i. Human, structural and customer capital work together. It is not enough to invest in people, systems and customers separately.

4. Get the group to assess the organisation's use of intellectual capital by:

a. Conducting a SWOT analysis (strengths, weaknesses, opportunities, threats) regarding the organisation's intellectual capital;

b. Identifying the key existing sources of human, customer and structural capital;

c. Scoring the organisation's current utilisation of these resources;

d. Setting a target for desired usage; and

e. Identifying key actions to bridge the gap.

Operationalise the action plan that emerges from the workshop.

DOS

✓ Do use the information you gathered in preparation for the workshop to guide the discussion. However, make sure that you build on the reflections of the group about the organisation's ability to leverage from its intellectual capital

DON'TS

✗ Don't forget to consult widely across the organisation in your preparations. This will ensure that you bring comprehensive and valid data to the workshop

KEY SEEING THE FACTS QUESTIONS FOR BUILDING A HIGH PERFORMANCE TEAM

1. How good are you as a team at taking the learnings from results and using them to update your strategy and approach?

2. How well do you as a team use information and data to track trends and anticipate changes to the way the strategy needs to be executed?

3. How well does the team share knowledge between team members?

4. How effectively does the team document decisions and make sure that they are implemented?

5. Are there information silos within the team and how could they be broken down?

6. Are there any skills you need to learn that would allow you to better work as a team to deliver on your strategy?

Key 11 Questions for High Performance Teams

NeuroPower Case Study

ORGANISATIONAL CASE STUDY #1: STATE HEALTH HAND HYGIENE PROJECT

The Task: To improve compliance by health workers with hand hygiene practice.

Recap:

In 2007, an Australian state health department wanted to address the serious threat that health-associated infections posed to hospital patients. Micro-organisms are readily transmitted on the hands of health care workers. In Australia alone, health officials estimate that up to 7000 people die annually from hand hygiene-related infections in hospitals. The economic burden is also considerable, costing millions each year.

Hand hygiene has been proven to substantially reduce transmission of micro-organisms. However, despite well-established guidelines, compliance throughout the world with hygiene standards is disconcertingly low. International and national health agencies have been grappling with how to deal with the issue for some time, and few interventions have had any impact whatsoever, despite both European and US hospitals and governments spending tens of millions of dollars on communications, incentives, closed circuit TV and education.

Since research demonstrated that the hand hygiene issue centred around human behaviour, one state health department decided on an innovative, behaviour-changing approach using the *NeuroPower* framework to drive the solution. Working with the *NeuroPower* Consulting Team, the department implemented a behaviour change program called Clean Hands are LifeSavers that engaged the health workers and increased compliance from 18% to 60%. A key driver of this behaviour change involved effectively addressing each of the six Intelligences in the correct sequence. How these progressive steps were taken is outlined in the Organisational Toolbox Case Study at the end of each Intelligence chapter.

Having already
- Created safety and security in the hospital environment by embedding values through a code of conduct
- Empowered spontaneity and self-expression through collaboration and the development of creative promotional materials
- Kick started action and motivation through establishment of goals and the celebration of quick wins
- Encouraged empathy and connection through active listening and team building

Step 5: Maintain the flow of information

Hand-held recording devices, which observers used to gather factual data about hand hygiene, were implemented to track the results of the each ward's progress. These results were communicated throughout each hospital and throughout the state, thereby providing everyone with up-to-date information about progress, maintaining interest in compliance and embedding the behaviour.

ORGANISATIONAL CASE STUDY #2: MERCHANT BANK EQUITY DERIVATIVES LEADERSHIP TEAM

The Task: Improve employee engagement and tangible business performance

Recap:

In 2006, at the height of the financial boom, one of Australia's leading equity derivatives teams was operating in an environment that was fast-paced, demanding and with a high level of stress. In order to handle large volumes of work in a very volatile market, the team needed to be highly functional and collaborative. Growth was nearly 200 per cent over the previous year so the enormous strain was evident. This was mainly caused by a leadership team in crisis.

The Leadership Team was fractured, non-collaborative and driven by their own individual agendas. There was both a lack of respect and a lack of honesty between members which led to highly reactive responses and conflict. The broader team could see this occurring and they felt they were part of a warring tribe with all the insecurities that brought.

NeuroPower consultants devised a program which focused on addressing the splintered leadership team. The intervention involved a series of group structured processes which were embedded by individual coaching sessions.

Having already:
- Created role clarity
- Empowered people's self-expression
- Encouraged healthy egos and passion for work
- Developed teamwork and leadership capabilities through an expanded I2

Step 5: Create a Learning Lab Culture through Driving Excellence in I1

The Equity Derivatives Team operated in a fast-paced and volatile market where speed of response was based on the power of the information received. The right information at the right time was key to their success on a daily basis. During this part of the intervention, more emphasis was placed on maintaining a good flow of information and sharing results. Before the intervention began, the Back Office – the technical engine of the group – had felt under-valued and under pressure. Now their expertise and importance was brought to the fore, as the Team learned the power of the Learning Lab Culture where every team member has crucial information and insight that can be shared with the group. This was achieved by conducting a series of three intellectual capital workshops and coaching sessions where double-loop learning was culturally embedded in the team's approach.

NeuroPower Case Study

Chapter 7

Our Sixth Social Cognitive Need:
HOPE FOR THE FUTURE &
The Open Function (C2)

HOPE FOR THE FUTURE (C2) AT A GLANCE

Hope for the Future is our Brain's Sixth Social Cognitive Need

The brain loves moving forward based on hope for the future. The brain is an anticipation machine - constantly projecting into the future the consequences of staying on its current path. Importantly, our level of hope is directly linked to our sense of whether our current path will lead to a positive future, which is highly influenced by how well the first six needs are being met.

Characteristics of the Hope for the Future (C2) Functional Network

Future Vision

STRENGTH	WEAKNESS
Able to see the future and take a long-term perspective	Attachment to particular future

OPPORTUNITY	THREAT
Being present and expressing emotions instead of focusing on abstract principles	Can be too abstract to the point where others struggle to understand

Management Style

- Great at painting a new vision
- Motivates by drawing others into the vision
- Sensitive and often reluctant to share
- Can accurately anticipate difficulties further down the track

WONDER

C2 THINKING
Paradigm-shifting visions

C2 FEELING
Appreciation and Awe

C2 SOMATIC
Daydreaming, meditation and/or prayer

COMMUNICATION STYLE
- Has creativity that is visionary and has a clear sense of the future
- Describes future events
- Conceptualises things

KEYWORDS INCLUDE
- Imagine
- Vision
- Future
- Possibility
- What could be

Hope for the Future (C2) Helps Us to Survive

Hope for the Future (C2) helps both individuals and the group to survive and thrive by helping us look past the immediate reality and envisage a different future. It draws on our ability to completely re-imagine a situation - almost like downloading a whole new vision.

Hope for the Future &
The Open Function (C2)

HOPE FOR THE FUTURE: OUR BRAIN'S SIXTH SOCIAL NEED EXPLAINED

The brain is an anticipation machine - constantly projecting into the future the consequences of staying on its current path. Our brain actively creates a future image of what our current actions or trends are leading towards. In this way, our level of hope is directly linked to our sense of whether our current path will lead to a positive future. Vision is the end result of a current trajectory. We call vision a lag indicator rather than a lead indicator. If, as a leader, you have been able to effectively implement the previous five steps then your team will naturally be more optimistic and hopeful about their future and being a part of your team.

Whether from a community or organisational perspective, in order for a team to have vision for the future, leaders must effectively implement the previous five steps and show their team that by continuing along their current trajectory, a positive future state exists.

EVOLUTIONARY FUNCTION OF C2

The neurocircuitry of C2 is not yet well understood, but we see that **the C2 intelligence enables the individual to 'download' new ideas, paradigms or concepts.** These reflect a fundamentally changing world that requires a new map of understanding. C2 is a difficult system to chart and neuroscience is still not clear about exactly how the C2 Intelligence works. fMRI research on the neural pathways linked to meditation, as well as some research in 'mystical experiences' (MEs) provide useful first steps of insight into how the C2 system may function.

Recognising the Characteristics of
Hope for the Future (C2)

Joseph Conrad once said, 'Only in men's imagination does every truth find an effective and undeniable existence. Imagination, not invention, is the supreme master of art as life.'

The C2 function also enables the brain to connect our spiritual nature with our physical experience. This often manifests as the human drive to experience an intimate relationship with a 'greater, other or the divine'. To the secular mind, C2 gives access to a sense of awe and wonder at the physical world, from the immensity of the cosmos to the interdependencies of the physical world that at times seem too complex for any one mind to comprehend and almost too perfectly balanced to be plausible.

The Neural Correlates of Mystical Experiences (MEs)

Researchers in the field of neurotheology, or spiritual neuroscience, have undertaken studies revealing that MEs (involving altered states of consciousness such as a sense of timelessness and spacelessness, a dissolution of fear and self-consciousness, or feelings of oneness with the universe) are associated with complex patterns of activity in the brain. These studies are beginning to give us insight into the workings of the C2 system.

One particularly influential researcher in this area, Mario Beauregard, worked with a group of Carmelite nuns who had altogether spent over 210,000 hours in prayer and who reported having an 'intense union with God'. As they relived their most intense ME in an MRI scanner, Beauregard observed a complex network of regions being activated, including the right middle temporal cortex (giving the subjective impression of contacting a spiritual reality), the insula (integrating representations of external sensory experience and internal somatic state), the caudate nucleus (facilitating feelings of joy and unconditional love) and the left medial prefrontal cortex (gaining conscious metacognitions of one's emotions).

This pattern of activity seems consistent with the complex and multidimensional nature of MEs as described by those who experience them - with potential neural correlates for reports of changes in perception (e.g. visual mental imagery), cognition (e.g. representations about the self) and emotion (e.g. peace, joy, unconditional love). Interestingly, they also align broadly with some of the findings of other researchers such as Nataraja, who have looked at the impact of certain forms of meditation practice on the brain (explored in detail in Appendix 1).

Studies like these inevitably lead to questions about the nature of the universe itself. For example, when an individual reports a sense of 'spacelessness', is that directly caused by reduced activity in areas of the brain linked to the physical body? Or is the reduced activity a product of a transcendent metaphysical experience? Unfortunately, as with many brain imaging studies, the causal relationship is very difficult to establish and so it may be sometime before neuroscience - or any other discipline - can give us a clear answer to satisfy our I1 system (Seeing the Facts).

Fortunately, however, the strong positive benefits associated with more 'transcendent' forms of meditation - independent of spiritual belief - confirm that the C2 system is accessible for both those who believe in a higher power and those who don't.

A mind with an over-reliance on C2 can be interpreted as 'dreamy'. The person can appear as though they are 'on another planet', or they are constantly distracted. In fact, if an individual relies heavily on C2, their personal reality may well be somewhere completely different from the existing reality.

C2 has three elements that require integration. The visionary (cognitive) aspect focuses on finding entirely new possibilities and creatively bringing about a whole new paradigm. This is the creative function we use when we visualise new and abstract ideas. The emotional aspect centres around a sense of inspiration, transcendence, nirvana or awe. The somatic aspect is typified by a melancholic lamenting of the world that is, since it cannot match the world that could be, almost like a wistful wondering.

Of all the Intelligences, C2 is the one that is least understood from a functional perspective; even with recent advances in neuroscience, we are still not quite sure how it works. Our best current insights about C2 come from studies of meditation. In Appendix 2, *NeuroPower* (Burow, 2013) you'll find excerpts from Dr Nataraja's book *A Blissful Brain* (2009), which explores the experience of meditation from both subjective and objective perspectives (i.e. from the point of view of both the meditator and a neuroscientist observing the activity in the meditator's brain. If C2 and meditation are

C2 Activity and its Possible Link to the Parietal Lobes

Albert Einstein, the quintessential absent-minded professor who did poorly in maths classes during his adolescence, became renowned for solving complex problems of mathematics and physics using visual imagery. Many of his intuitive theories have been proven to be accurate with the development of more sophisticated technology and space exploration. In a post mortem examination of his brain, it was revealed that there were differences in the inferior parietal area in the ratio of neurons to glia cells when compared to other areas of his brain and two control subjects (Diamond, Scheibel, Murphy & Harvey, 1985). Diamond and her compatriots (Diamond, Krech & Rosenweig, 1966) suggested that these lower ratios represented the capacity for higher levels of neuronal activity. Another research group concluded that Einstein's brain differed from ninety-one other brains only in the size of the inferior parietal lobe (Witelson, Kigar & Harvey, 1999). This is particularly interesting given that Einstein often reported that he arrived at the answers to complex mathematical questions based on vague mental images and bodily sensations rather than empirical logic, suggesting that the parietal lobes may play a key role in the C2 Intelligence.

C2 and Out-of-Body Experiences

Dr Olaf Blanke and colleagues observed that stimulating a patient's angular gyrus of the right cortex resulted in an out-of-body experience. Their patient described the experience thus: 'I see myself lying in bed, from above.' Blanke interpreted this as being the region in the brain where the visual system and the self-awareness system overlap (Blanke, Ortigue, Landix & Seeck, 2002, pp. 269-280, 419).

This suggests that an individual can perceive two realities simultaneously and that this ability can be deliberately switched on in the brain.

of interest to you, Dr Nataraja's book is fascinating and well worth a read.

The purpose of this Intelligence is to provide direction through future-centred visioning. What blocks the use of C2 is an attachment or fixed insistence on one idea, concept, notion or vision. Judith (1996) argues that physical problems arising from an unbalanced C2 include comas, migraines, brain tumours, amnesia and cognitive delusions. The developmental task of the individual at this stage is to assimilate knowledge and to develop wisdom (Judith, 1996).

The primary fears of C2 are related to spiritual issues such as the 'dark night of the soul', spiritual abandonment, loss of identity, or loss of connection (Myss, 1996).

C2 ACTS AS THE BRAIN'S 'WIFI' – READY TO DOWNLOAD NEW IDEAS OR PARADIGMS

One fascinating idea posited by Dr David Hawkins, author of *Power versus Force* (2005), is the proposition that there exists a unified consciousness that is external to time and space and encapsulates all the knowledge and experience of life. Chaos theory suggests that the universe does not follow a linear, cause and effect Newtonian model. Rather, all elements of the universe are interrelated and in a fashion independent of time and space.

Hawkins refers to physicist David Bohm's description of the universe as being holographic with an invisible *implicit* ('enfolded') and a manifest *explicit* ('unfolded') order. **This means that while the universe appears to be unfolding in a linear manner from our perspective in time, this may not be the case.** Time is the manner in which the implicit reality becomes explicit reality. For example, a person driving through a forest can see only the road ahead of them. But the satellite in space beaming to their GPS receiver has a view of the terrain. C2 is like every individual's personal GPS unit. Hawkins' field of consciousness stands external to time and is accessible through the C2 function of the mind.

Our capacity to download information from this storehouse of knowledge is dependent upon the effective functioning of our C2. Using Hawkins' language, it acts as the bridge between this universal field of consciousness and our own personal consciousness. In the commercial context, this is the part of the brain that enables us to envision revolutionary new ideas that provide a giant leap forward (e.g. the shift from typewriter to computers). Without highly functioning C2, teams have no sense of what lies ahead and no appreciation of non-linear inter-dependencies. This means that they are constantly forced to be tactical, rather than strategic, and are always one step behind the competition. Judith (1996) describes C2 as a doorway between the individual consciousness and the universal consciousness.

Using C2 Intelligence feels a bit like the wireless connection (WIFI) on your laptop or mobile phone that allows you to download the information available on the internet. Accessing C2 is about expanding our personal perspective so that it can embrace a much larger truth. The work to be done with C2 is to examine our belief systems, for they are the windows through which we see the world and this view informs and ultimately determines our view of reality. The awakened C2 can act to constantly reprogram and upgrade the 'map room' that runs our life.[1]

Christian theology argues that, with God's help, man is able to see 'dreams and visions'. Eric Jantsch's (1975) theory of the evolution of human consciousness argues that as we evolve we have a greater awareness of and reliance on C2. He outlined three distinct systems of human consciousness: the *rational*, the *mythical*, and the *evolutionary*.

The *rational system* is where knowledge comes through science and other logical, empirical means. This mode of thinking focuses on observation and acting upon the observations. The method of inquiry that dominates is characterised by *I-it* relationships —subject to object. We do things to *it* and observe *its* reaction. (This relates to the I1 thinking function.)

The *mythical system* moves from observation to experience. The collection of data gathered at the rational level now assembles itself into an intuitive whole, a complete gestalt that involves mind and body simultaneously. Inquiry moves to *I* and *You* as subject embraces subject. This type of inquiry gives us what Jantsch terms as 'a sense of systemic existence'.

The *evolutionary system* is an expansion into the universal mind, the union with the divine and the all-inclusive state of being where system boundaries have dissolved and re-formed to a greater and deeper whole. Inquiry moves to *I* and *We* as the *I* now

---

1   The term 'map room' was first introduced to me by Dr Moishe Perl, an internationally recognised authority in the field of clinical neurofeedback. Neurofeedback techniques that work with C2 put the individual in a highly suggestible state by taking the brain down to the alpha-theta state (8-10Hz). They call this the map room because in this semi-conscious state the individual can reprogram many of their unconstructive beliefs about themselves and their world.

C2, Psilocybin and Mystical Experiences

Individuals with high C2 system sometimes describe themselves as having feelings of no boundaries between self and others, belonging to a larger state of consciousness, unity to all things, and feelings of peace and intense happiness. Interestingly, these feelings are exactly what individuals using specific cognition-altering psychotropic drugs have reported. In fact, these substances have been used in religions throughout history and across the world to initiate C2 experiences such as mystical states of consciousness and communication with the spirit world. The Aztecs, Rig Veda and Native American cultures each used plants such as the morning glory vine, magic mushrooms, and the peyote cactus for their active compounds (e.g. mescaline, psilocybin and psilocin).

In the last few decades, despite the strong negative connotations also associated with western drug-users (many of which were established with US President Richard Nixon's war on drugs), some published research suggests these substances can provide users with both mystical experiences (MEs) and long-term improvements in well-being.

In one Harvard study, participants received either the psychedelic substance psilocybin or a placebo prior to a Good Friday church service. Nearly all the participants in the psilocybin group reported ME experiences, whereas those in the control group experienced nothing unusual. In a similar experiment, conducted at John Hopkins University, participants were given either psilocybin or a placebo and told to close their eyes and direct their attention inward. Two thirds of participants in the psilocybin group experienced feelings of enhanced well-being and satisfaction and rated it as either the best experience in their life or in the top five. What is astounding is these feelings were ongoing and still apparent at two months and fourteen months after the experiment was conducted. Although these substances are often thought of as mind expanding, they in fact cause brain activity to decrease in the brain's most dense areas. These dense hubs are what constrain our experience and filter out information that's irrelevant to our biological survival. It is through deactivation of these areas that people can experience the mind at large.

So while *NeuroPower* is not actively encouraging its readers to engage in psychedelic use, it is important to note that access to the C2 system, even for a short period of time, can have a substantial and profound positive impact on people's well-being.

includes all that is encompassed in the universal consciousness. There is no *We* without an *I*. Consequently, to the spiritually inclined, embracing the use of C2 is not to abandon the sense of personal awareness, but to realise that divine consciousness is part of that personal awareness (Judith, 1996).

They would argue that to connect with the divine, we need to give up our attachment to the rational system of thought when it is unable to give us a deeper meaning to life's themes. Evolutionary inquiry gives us a sense of direction.

C2 AND INSPIRATION

Some Eastern traditions suggest that C2 operates as a two-way channel of inspiration from the universe. It is the source of creativity and vision. This in turn inspires ideas and plans from which come actions and experiences. The C2 Intelligence provides us with an opportunity for transcendence, for expansion of consciousness to awakening (Judith, 1996).

For Christians, Jews and Muslims, the purpose of C2 is to merge with divine consciousness and realise our individual true nature – that we are children of the divine seeking our way home. Not only is the purpose to contact the divine, but also to manifest divinity in our bodies and actions on a daily basis and so transform the world as a consequence of our relationship with God (Myss, 1996, p. 267).

The Development of Hope for the Future (C2)

The development of the C2 Intelligence for an individual is not age specific since it develops in different ways from the moment of birth until the day we die. The development of C2 is primarily about learning, building on and adding meaning and wisdom to our previous understandings and beliefs, and our ability to think independently (Judith, 1996).

Though this is a process that occurs throughout our life, it is well known that it is in late adolescence that we start asking questions about the meaning of life. This is the dawning of idealism and spirituality for many young people.

C2 AND I1 DIFFERENCES

The development of C2 moves from the search for knowledge in I1 ('This is who I am in the greater scheme of things') to a shift beyond the ego, with a search for meaning that asks the bigger questions about life, such as 'What does it all mean?'

C2 gives meaning to the images already in the memory and incorporates them into an ever-growing body of understanding about why the world works the way it does.

BEWARE OF ATTACHMENT

Judith (1996) makes the interesting point that one downside of an underactive C2 network is the kind of unhelpful 'attachment' referred to in Buddhist teachings. Development through the first five Intelligences demands a degree of attachment to outcome as we navigate increasing responsibilities to the people we love, our own goals and our commitments. And we should honour our attachment to these things; they are necessary for a balanced life.

However, we can become so attached to certain relationships, desires, outcomes or belief systems that we shut down our C2 in a desire to control our life circumstances. This denies the belief that the universe is conspiring to help us, and closes us to new possibilities.

Another form of attachment is avoidance, which is really attachment to *not* having something, in order to avoid facing some issue which makes us feel inadequate.

By focusing outward on the attachment and closing down our use of C2, we lose the chance to grow. Judith suggests we need to turn our attention inward and examine ourselves to identify both the reason for our attachment and our underlying needs, and then meet those needs. This is usually about facing something or letting something go, and it is usually an issue of our ego (our P2). We need to let go and trust the universe if we wish to awaken our C2 and live at a higher level of consciousness. If you rarely access your C2, it is as if you don't get updates to your operating system, and thus live on old paradigms.

TRAUMAS AND ABUSES

Abuses to C2 tend to be subtle, but with profound impacts. They can occur at any age and in many different ways.

The inquisitive nature of children, with their burning desire to understand the world that surrounds them, sets the development of their personal belief systems. If the curiosity of a child is stifled, the child may either make up the information or they stop asking questions. In either case the searching stops and their C2 ceases to draw in new ideas, visions and future possibilities so it shuts down. But in the busy modern world of today's children, bombarded as they are by technology and a focus on outcomes like maths and reading scores, there is little time for simple daydreaming and letting the mind imagine.

In a similar manner, poor education can damage the development of C2. C2 needs encouragement, time, a stress-free environment, and a chance to be expressed. When this is not provided, the functioning of the C2 Intelligence can be affected.

Judith (1996) also strongly argues that unpleasant spiritual experiences in Christian churches which focus more on sin and shaming than on love and respect of the individual developing young person, will also shut down a child's C2, and so, ironically, therefore,

The Power of Visualisation

Neuroscience has shown that visualising an activity is almost as powerful as actually doing it when it comes to the formation of new neural networks. In a neuroplasticity experiment involving piano playing, those who mentally rehearsed a five-fingered keyboard exercise demonstrated similar reorganisation of their motor outputs as those who physically practiced the movements (Pascual-Leone, 1995). This suggests that visualisation of motor activities changes neural circuitry and may be used to acquire skills more rapidly with reduced physical practice. This technique is now commonly used by athletes looking to enhance their performance.

blocking their access to the divine.

Poorly Functioning C2

OVER-RELIANCE ON C2

Having an over-reliance on C2 is quite common as individuals withdraw into their heads to avoid feelings and to distance themselves from worldly demands, or to avoid emotions or the sensations of the body. Judith (1996) notes that, in general, excessive C2 leads to a loss of discrimination. This reliance tends to have a number of manifestations:

- Intellectualisation;
- Spiritual obsession;
- Confusion;
- Dissociation from the body; and
- Fixation on one paradigm or vision.

Intellectualisation is a particularly common result, with constant thinking and analysing typifying this type of individual. Such individuals overdevelop their intellect at the cost of their other aspects of self, in order to escape the more difficult issues of life. However, knowledge for its own sake is useless without wisdom and insight that the C2 Intelligence brings.

Spirituality can also be used as an escape route from the demands of the other Intelligences, and spiritual obsession is another common consequence of an over-reliance on C2. This may be expressed as 'Bible bashing', 'guru chasing' or through vows

Diagram 7.1 Healthy C2 Intelligence — Noble Quality: Wonder

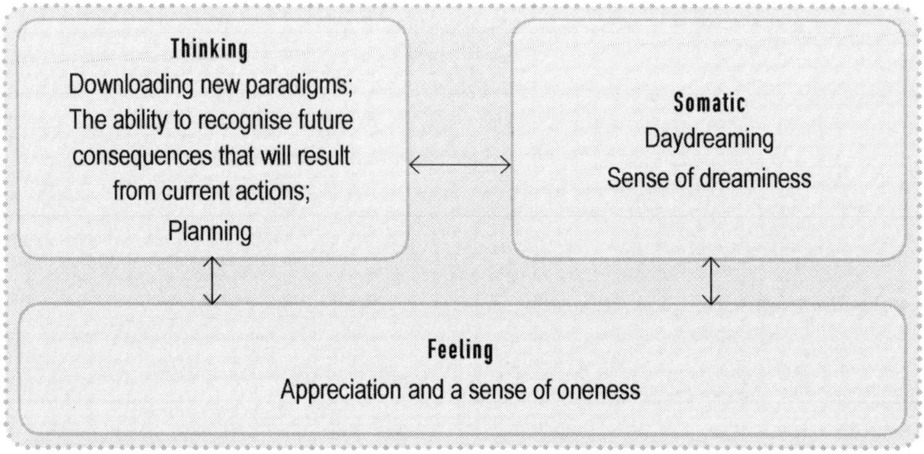

of poverty, chastity and obedience. Whatever the form, this is often merely another attachment that prevents the growth of the individual (except, of course, if it is sensibly applied in ways which help the person evolve).

Another result of excessive use of C2 can be psychosis. Psychotic disturbances are characterised by a break from reality and from the grounded aspects of the other Intelligences. They are manifested as a lack of predictable patterns, with voices, hallucinations and delusional beliefs (Judith, 1996).

UNDER-RELIANCE ON C2

According to Judith (1996), poorly functioning C2 can manifest in the following patterns:

Fixation: The opposite of infinite knowledge is fixation, where only one point of view is accepted. As their mind is closed to new information, the person may become a sceptical 'know it all'.

A need to be right: Being right supports the sense that we know everything and bolsters our ego as it provides a (delusional) sense of superiority.

Belief in limitations: Being convinced that there is no possibility of a situation being remedied is a form of C2 deficiency. These beliefs will then become a self-fulfilling prophecy.

The general characteristics of an individual with poorly functioning C2 are:

- Spiritual scepticism;

- An inability to take on new concepts that fall outside the current paradigm;

- Out-of-date belief systems;

- An over-reliance on other Intelligences in life without the mediating and conceptualising function of C2; and

- An inability to imagine the future or how reality could be different.

C2 AND PARADIGMS

As we have seen, C2 assigns ultimate meaning to all areas of our life and the meanings we give to our experiences in life eventually construct for us a coherent belief system. In turn, this belief system, based on the past, impacts how we interpret all future experiences and the decisions we make. The world in which we live, therefore, both causes our reality and is caused by it[2].

We can easily identify our level of consciousness by looking at the world we have created for ourselves. There is no point trying to help people change their life if they do not also change their belief system. In order to awaken our consciousness, we need to examine every belief system in our life.

If our C2 is poorly functioning, we will be guided by our Dionysian needs (C1) to move towards pleasure and away from pain, by our P1 family rules, our P2 ego or our I2 desire to connect. There is no unifying Apollonian paradigm. When we are trying to solve a problem, if we use first-order thinking, we stay within the paradigm without being aware the paradigm exists. If we use second-order thinking, we are aware and see that we are working to a paradigm (that is, we see closer to the reality of our life). When we are using third-order thinking, not only do we understand our paradigm, we also develop our awareness and change our paradigm, and so transform it into more productive action. The C2 Intelligence gives us access to second- and third-order thinking.

Reintegrating Wonder (C2) as an Adult

EXERCISE ONE[3]

Imagine you are an eagle flying through your own life. What does it look like from above? How does it appear from the removed perspective? What issues do you see in the horizon of your life? When I was working with accountants I would instruct them to visualise themselves flying through the city and looking into the windows of

---

2   This concept, which is based on insights emerging from quantum physics paradigms, is explored in more detail in Principle 3.

3   I have used this simple exercise to improve the C2 function of accounting directors in one of Australia's largest accounting and management practices. It had dramatic and profitable results.

their potential clients to see if they could see any new work opportunities – this system yielded millions of dollars worth of new work for them. In the same way you can look at your life through the C2 function for new opportunities and options.

EXERCISE TWO

This exercise is suggested by author Brian Tracy. According to Tracy (2004), the development of C2 is about creating a future orientation and forming a habit of idealisation. Idealisation involves taking your thoughts off the present situation and imagining a perfect future for yourself, your business, your finances or your relationships. It involves practising 'back from the future' thinking. This is about projecting forward into the future the ideal results that you desire and imagining what it would look like in every way. You then look back to the present and ask yourself, 'What would I have to do, starting today, to create the ideal future that I desire?' This process is articulated in a more structured way in C2 Tools #1 and #3.

CREATING A HIGHLY FUNCTIONING C2

Consider your own experience in light of what you have learned about the C2 Intelligence. Are you aware of C2 thinking, feeling and somatic in your life? Is there one that you tend to focus on above the other two?

- The C2 somatic behaviours include dreaminess, light-headedness and having a straight back.

- The C2 feeling element involves a sense of appreciation and oneness with the universe.

- The C2 thinking element involves a strong capacity to visualise images and events.

Diagram 7.1 shows the three aspects of C2 that require integration so that a unified Intelligence can form.

The task of integration of C2 is to relax the body, quieten the mind's visioning of egocentric plans and strategies, and tune into a sense of Wonder and appreciation of the mystery and miracles of life. This allows you to 'let go and let God', trusting that the universe is conspiring to bless you.

While every individual is different, the majority of the population is most familiar with the feeling aspect of C2.

AFFIRMATIONS

Judith (1996) suggests the following affirmations can help you increase the functioning of your C2:

- Divinity resides within.

- I am open to new ideas.

- Information I need comes to me.

- The world is my teacher.

- I am guided by a higher power.

- I am guided by inner wisdom.

- I am open to God's wisdom.

Highly Functioning C2 in Adult Life

The first-order noble quality of Wonder requires the thinking aspect of creative vision, the feeling aspect of appreciation, and the somatic aspect of daydreaming, meditation or prayer[4]. This noble quality is described by Plotinus (205-270 AD), the founder of Neoplatonism, as when 'the soul finds joy in contemplating beauty, for it sees in works of art a hint of the divinity that it (the soul) shares'.

The behavioural manifestations of Wonder are subtle, because appreciation, awe, and responses to beauty and excellence often involve passive receptivity and stillness (Frijda, 1986). This appreciation is likely to be associated with certain physiological symptoms such as goose bumps, tears or even a lump in the throat. This noble quality of Wonder fosters a desire to improve the self and strive for the greater good (Keltner & Haidt, 2003). Abraham Maslow (1964) focused on the importance of this noble quality and identified character traits that are commonly associated with it. When this first-tier noble quality is manifested:

1. Perception is relatively ego transcending, self-forgetful, unselfish and more object-centred than ego-centred;

2. The world is seen as beautiful, good, desirable and worthwhile, even as evil and suffering are recognised and accepted as part of the world; and

3. Cognition is much more passive, receptive and humble. The person is more ready to listen and much more able to hear.

---

4   Peterson & Seligman's meta-study of the most widely influential traditions of thought and religion in human history found that appreciation represented a consistent aspiration across cultures and through time. They identified appreciation as a strength because it enables self-transcendence (and its associated loss of ego, and increased openness to others) (Peterson & Seligman, 2004).

It is from this noble quality that the Greek idea of divine creativity arises. The Greeks believed that muses (of poetry, tragedy, comedy, music, dance, astrology and history) bestowed creativity upon certain individuals. This creativity is able to flow through the noble quality of Wonder. Plato referred to this style of thinking as Apollonian transcendence. Jung refers to this noble quality as the Transcendent function.

HOW C2 WONDER MEETS THE NOBILITY CRITERIA

The noble quality of Wonder provides the individual with a sense of perspective about where they fit into the world. This noble quality is central to answering questions about how the individual communicates with their Maker and future paces[5] to anticipate what lies ahead.

Wonder brings value to the community. It enables the community to join together to appreciate the world in which they live and work. Wonder fosters the idea that community members can celebrate their involvement in a world that is beyond the control of their ego.

There is a yearning to act in accordance with the noble quality of Wonder. When it is expressed it is often associated with a paradigm shift. Being in awe or experiencing Wonder creates a space of perceiving a world that is beautiful, good, desirable and worthwhile. When in Wonder, the individual transcends ego, is self-forgetting, unselfish, and enters a state of flow. Individuals report that using Wonder to resolve an internal tension has a paradigm shift impact on their lives because cognitive resistance is reduced, and individuals are more ready to listen and much more able to hear.

In teams, Wonder enables us to look beyond the status quo and create a new reality that fundamentally improves the position of the business.

---

5   Future pacing is an NLP methodology which comes naturally to those high in C2.

C2 Toolbox

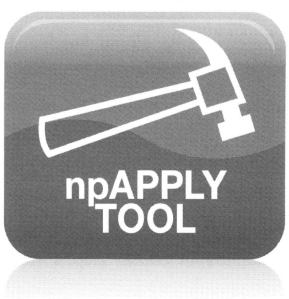

THE IMPORTANCE OF C2 IN BUILDING HIGH PERFORMANCE TEAMS

The emergent cultural impact of C2 is Wonder, which enables the organisation to join together to appreciate the world in which they live and work.

When Wonder is absent from an organisation, its existence and activity is mundane, perfunctionary and without true appreciation.

However, when there is highly functioning C2 in the organisation, staff members can celebrate their involvement in a world that is beyond the control of their ego.

Leaders looking to improve the effectiveness of C2 in their team can increase Wonder by applying the C2 tools.

C2 Intelligence Questions

C2 QUESTIONS FOR PERSONAL DEVELOPMENT

The best high performing teams are made up of individuals who have focused on their own personal development. The following questions can be used as a starting point for those leaders looking to improve their C2.

1. How and from where do you seek guidance when all your solutions have failed?

2. If that source of guidance were to respond, what answers to your questions would you most fear?

3. What is your concept of God (Grand Organising Design)? Is there such a thing?

4. Do you complain to others more than you express your gratitude? Explain.

5. Do you tend to wish for specific things rather than show appreciation? Explain.

6. Are you devoted to a particular spiritual path? If not, what spiritual path best reflects your world view?

7. Are you waiting for life, your parents, friends or family to send you an explanation for your painful experiences? If so, list those experiences.

8. How would your life change if suddenly all your questions were answered?

9. How would your life change if you spoke to God and the answer you received was, "I have no intention of giving you insight into your questions at this point in your life"?

10. How do you explain sudden flashes of insight? What are they?

11. Have you started and stopped a meditation or spiritual practice? If so, what were the reasons that you failed to maintain it?

12. What spiritual truths are you aware of that you do not live by? List them.

13. Are you afraid of a closer spiritual connection to something greater because of the change that it might trigger in your life?

C2 TOOL #1:
CREATE THE FUTURE YOU WANT

C2 VISIONING

The C2 Intelligence is accessed when the brain settles into an Alpha-Theta state. The below experience enables you to achieve this relaxed state.

PROCESS

1. **Set aside the time** for a personal planning session an hour is a good start. The ideal time from a physiological perspective is during the evening at a time when you usually feel relaxed but not yet sleepy this is a good indication that your brain is in a state that will support the C2 exercise. If that's not possible, and you need to take time during the day, arrange things so that you don't have to go rushing off to another meeting or event straight away.

2. **Choose your venue.** Environment can have a big impact on how our brain functions, and certain environmental cues make it easier to access the different intelligence circuits. If you've scheduled your session during the day, the ideal location for C2 planning is outside, in an open expanse with a view (preferably on top of a hill). At night time, when you're likely to be inside, it's better to have soft ambient light rather than bright fluorescent lights overhead. Of course, it may not be possible for you to coordinate this. Even so, it's still a good idea to introduce a change of scenery – you'll find it easier to think outside the square if you take yourself out of your usual environment.

3. **Prepare** for your session by making sure you won't be interrupted. This includes turning off phones and letting family and others know that you won't be available during the hour. Also make sure that you have supplies of water, paper, pencil etc. Once that's all taken care of, take a few minutes to settle into wherever you've decided to conduct your session. Sometimes it takes a while to switch from 'go-go-go' mode to a more reflective, relaxed space. Make sure you've changed gear before you start the actual exercise.

4. **Visualise your ideal future.** The focus of the exercise is on projecting forward into the future the results that you desire and imagining what it would look like in every way. Where do you want to be in five, ten, twenty years? What are you doing? What are you focusing on? How are you feeling? What do you notice about this future reality?

5. **Work your way backwards to the present.** As you imagine every detail of that future, look back to the present and ask yourself, 'What would I have to do, starting today, to create the ideal future that I desire?' Use the insights that arrive to create an action list and begin working towards that future reality.

DOS

✓ Do allow your mind to wander, provided it's broadly on track. While there's certainly a fine line between getting distracted and thinking freely, it's often by following seemingly unrelated tangents when contemplating the future that brainwaves about how to create a radically different future reality will arrive.

DON'TS

✗ Don't forget to write down the important things! The C2 space feels quite dreamy, and much like dreams – people often forget the insights they've gained as they 'wake up again' and their brain shifts back into 'normal operating mode'.

C2 TOOL #2:
UNDERTAKE SCENARIO PLANNING TO CREATE A NEW FUTURE

PROCESS

1. **Schedule a two-day scenario planning workshop.** It is important to hold the workshop offsite to signal the difference from routine work. A two-day residential format allows optimum reflection and absorption time. Make sure that the venue is a light and airy environment, preferably in a location that is elevated and surrounded by greenery. (These environmental factors will affect the capacity of the brain to access C2.)

   In positioning the event and its purpose for your people, prepare a briefing sheet about the concept of scenario planning: imagining potential qualitatively different futures and using these forecasts to improve the quality of decision-making. Explain the importance of scenario planning to your business, and how it can be invaluably used to:
   - Stimulate debate about the organisation's options moving forward;
   - Develop a strategy that is resilient against several futures;
   - Test existing business plans against potential futures; and
   - Anticipate futures as an aid to decision-making.

2. **Identify future scenarios.** Many organisations are shifting focus from developing new scenarios towards using and tailoring existing scenarios. Explore whether your organisation has existing scenarios that may be appropriately modified. If not, your leadership team will need to take one to two days to develop scenarios based on existing information. This can also be a valuable exercise in exploring shared perceptions. You may wish to research current trends more quantitatively to provide a platform for developing your scenarios. Alternatively, consultants may be employed to fulfil this role.

3. **Develop the agenda for the two-day scenario workshop.** This is likely to be specific to your industry, organisation and your people's familiarity with the exercise of scenario planning. However, a broad template (involving both plenary sessions, workshops and break out sessions into smaller working groups) might look like:

Day One	
Plenary	Purpose of the workshop. Briefing on current trends – positive and negative
Groups	Discuss effect of positive and negative trends on the organisation. Report findings back to group. Identification of which trends are certain and which uncertain, and the degree to which they would impact the organisation.
Workshop	Articulation of key scenarios taking each of the most likely/high impact positive and negative trends and chart the impact on the organisation. From this identify the top six scenarios.
Groups	Explore strategies and tactics to make the most of the positive trends and turn the negative trends into the organisation's advantage.
Groups	Report back and discuss strategies.

C2 Tool # 2

Day Two	
Groups	Explore non-linear dependencies and ways that each strategy/tactic can be refined.
Workshop	Explore what the organisation needs to focus on short/medium/long-term.
Groups	Develop timeline for action.
Workshop	Report back to group. Plan actions moving forward.

4. **Conduct the workshop.** Make sure there's plenty of time for debate and discussion, and allow the groups lots of breaks to have unrestricted discussion time. Remember, part of the purpose of scenario planning is to enable your people to think beyond the current status quo. You need to be prepared for them to think outside the square and supportive of them when it happens.

5. **Make the most of the scenario planning.** Most people who work with scenarios find it to be stimulating and enjoyable, and are keen to incorporate the insights when they return to work. The success of the next stage will depend on:

   a. Deciding what problem the scenarios are intended to help solve. You need to ask: *What are the crucial questions facing the organisation, the ones that, seven years in the future, we'll wish we'd know the answer to seven years ago (i.e. now)?*

   b. Exploiting the scenarios that explore areas of uncertainty, rather than falling into the trap of focusing only on close-to-home and internal problems.

   c. Incorporating the scenarios into BAU decision-making by using them to stimulate project-based debate, developing strategies, testing business plans and anticipating future developments.

DOS

✓ Do make sure that the timescale for the scenarios is longer than the budget or planning cycle of the organisation – a longer time-scale is easier to work to as many defining trends will have run their course and be largely resolved at that future time, whereas in the medium-term current complexities are often still unresolved and confusing

✓ Do make sure that the scenario effort is given high enough status by making sure the workshop is offsite and ensuring high level sponsors and management feedback

DON'TS

✗ Don't simply adopt the budget or planning cycle of the organisation as the time frame for the scenarios, it needs to be longer. There are two reasons for this:
(1) A longer time-scale is easier to work with than medium-term, as many defining trends will already be clear and current complexities are often still confusing in the medium-term; and
(2) Many of the people at the session are unlikely to be in their current position at the end of this longer time frame. This gives them the freedom to think outside the square without feeling hampered by personal interest/implications

C2 TOOL #3:
VISUALISE IDEAL OUTCOMES

PROCESS

1. **Identify the event or activity.** It may be a big upcoming presentation, a team meeting where you need to introduce a new concept or a challenging one-on-one meeting that you need to have with a subordinate or peer.

2. **Set aside uninterrupted time in a quiet environment.** Environment can have a big impact on how our brain functions, and certain environmental cues make it easier to access the different intelligence circuits (see point # 2 in C2 Tool #2). In order to make the most of your time, make sure others know not to interrupt you.

3. **Visualise the setting for the future event.** The focus here is to imagine the event if it were to go absolutely perfectly from your perspective. The more detail you can see as you're visualising the event, the better. What does the room look like? Who else is there? How do they seem? What can you hear? Most people find it easiest to do this (and the rest of the process) with their eyes closed – simply closing your eyes slows the pace of your brainwaves, making it easier to access a brain state that is conducive to the slower C2 space.

4. **Focus on visualising yourself as the event proceeds.** Once you can see the setting clearly in your mind, visualise the event as it proceeds – again focusing on things going according to your ideal plan. Make sure you focus on how you're feeling and what you're thinking, as much as on what you're actually doing. For example, if you were to apply this technique to a presentation, you might visualise yourself arriving on time, feeling calm, collected and prepared. You see yourself conversing easily with other attendees, comfortable in the knowledge that you're ready for the show to start. As it gets closer to the time to present, you're feeling excited and enthusiastic about being there. The technology all runs smoothly and you visualise yourself presenting at your very best – 10 out of 10. When people ask questions, you see yourself giving great answers that both give them the information they need and enable you to weave in your message and support your argument. At the end, people congratulate and thank you for a fantastic presentation, and the key business objectives of the event are achieved. This is very different from imagining – or fearing (which often has much the same effect emotionally and physically) – yourself arriving late, frantic, unprepared, anxious and nervous about the presentation, grappling with technology that doesn't work, not having answers to questions people ask and, at the end of all that, not achieving the outcomes you need to with the presentation! By focusing

on the former, you set up a different expectation in your mind and cue your body to respond differently to the same stimulus. For example, a question from the audience is an opportunity to reinforce and embed your argument, not an interruption to be feared. This sets up a fundamentally different self-created expectation about the future event.

5. **Repeat the visualisation process.** Once you've imagined the event in its entirety, visualise it again... and again... and again. As you repeat the process, more and more neural networks are created around that particular activity, thus fundamentally changing the structure of your brain. The more you are able to see yourself performing successfully, the more likely it is that your brain will get on board and help you along the way – all because you've created a superhighway in your brain that's leading the way towards a successful outcome.

DOS

✓ Do give yourself the space to imagine things going perfectly. While realistically there may be hiccups in the plan, the focus of this exercise is to concentrate on the positive to influence how you feel about the event. If you find it particularly challenging to imagine an event with any difficulties, you may like to focus instead on how you respond to these problems – taking them all in your stride, working calmly to find solutions and not letting them upset your equilibrium.

DON'TS

✗ Don't underestimate the power of this exercise. Visualisation is a common technique used by top athletes to improve their performance, and has been shown to affect the neural networks in the brain. It's powerful stuff and definitely has applications in the commercial world.

KEY HOPE FOR THE FUTURE QUESTIONS FOR BUILDING A HIGH PERFORMANCE TEAM

The C2 system runs at a much slower pace than the other circuits and involves the brain downloading an entirely new paradigm/operating system. This really involves the brain stopping searching frantically for answers to questions and instead creating the space so that they can arrive.

Therefore, rather than focusing on a lot of different questions, it's better for teams looking to enhance their C2 functioning to ponder just a few key questions and see where the answers naturally take them.

If the team successfully delivers on its value proposition over the next few years, consider the ideal future outcomes in the following areas:

1. What will the style and quality of teamwork be like?

2. What will the team have achieved?

3. What will internal and external stakeholders have to say about the team?

4. What will the team be doing differently?

NeuroPower Case Study

ORGANISATIONAL CASE STUDY #1: STATE HEALTH HAND HYGIENE PROJECT

The Task: To improve compliance by health workers with hand hygiene practice.

Recap:

In 2007, an Australian state health department wanted to address the serious threat that health-associated infections posed to hospital patients. Micro-organisms are readily transmitted on the hands of health care workers. In Australia alone, health officials estimate that up to 7000 people die annually from hand hygiene-related infections in hospitals. The economic burden is also considerable, costing millions each year.

Hand hygiene has been proven to substantially reduce transmission of micro-organisms. However, despite well-established guidelines, compliance throughout the world with hygiene standards is disconcertingly low. International and national health agencies have been grappling with how to deal with the issue for some time, and few interventions have had any impact whatsoever, despite both European and US hospitals and governments spending tens of millions of dollars on communications, incentives, closed circuit TV and education.

Since research demonstrated that the hand hygiene issue centred around human behaviour, one state health department decided on an innovative, behaviour-changing approach using the *NeuroPower* framework to drive the solution. Working with the *NeuroPower* Consulting Team, the department implemented a behaviour change program called Clean Hands are LifeSavers that engaged the health workers and increased compliance from 18% to 60%. A key driver of this behaviour change involved effectively addressing each of the six Intelligences in the correct sequence. How these progressive steps were taken is outlined in the Organisational Toolbox Case Study at the end of each Intelligence chapter.

Having already:

- Created safety and security in the hospital environment by embedding values through a code of conduct
- Empowered spontaneity and self-expression through collaboration and the development of creative promotional materials
- Kick started action and motivation through establishment of goals and the celebration of quick wins
- Encouraged empathy and connection through active listening and team building
- Maintained the flow of information through data tracking and communication

Step 6: Create hope for the future and a new vision of success

With the advent of more infectious diseases entering the community as a result of global travel, *NeuroPower* ensured that the LifeSavers encourage health workers to keep the future in mind at all times so the community does not get ravaged by outbreaks. Hand hygiene has become more urgent than ever and has to be kept top of mind with new programs and a fresh approach being implemented on a regular basis.

ORGANISATIONAL CASE STUDY #2: MERCHANT BANK EQUITY DERIVATIVES LEADERSHIP TEAM

The Task: Improve employee engagement and tangible business performance

Recap:

In 2006, at the height of the financial boom, one of Australia's leading equity derivatives teams was operating in an environment that was fast-paced, demanding and with a high level of stress. In order to handle large volumes of work in a very volatile market, the team needed to be highly functional and collaborative. Growth was nearly 200 per cent over the previous year so the enormous strain was evident. This was mainly caused by a leadership team in crisis.

The Leadership Team was fractured, non-collaborative and driven by their own individual agendas. There was both a lack of respect and a lack of honesty between members which led to highly reactive responses and conflict. The broader team could see this occurring and they felt they were part of a warring tribe with all the insecurities that brought.

NeuroPower consultants devised a program which focused on addressing the splintered leadership team. The intervention involved a series of group structured processes which were embedded by individual coaching sessions.

Having already:

- Created role clarity
- Empowered people's self-expression
- Encouraged healthy egos and passion for work
- Developed teamwork and leadership capabilities through an expanded I2
- Created a learning lab culture through driving excellence in I1

NeuroPower Case Study

Step 6: Celebrate Success and Scenario Plan for a new Future using C2

As the end of the financial year loomed, the Team was now well on track to reach their financial goals and reap the rewards in terms of bonuses which were linked to their performance. The Team held a celebratory event and invited the Bank's top executives to witness the fast turnaround which had unleashed enormous energy and passion and had tangible business performance results. Employee satisfaction had been raised from 54 to 94 percent in just four months. The head of the Team saw they had a new vision for success and began scenario planning for the coming year with his leadership group.

Chapter 8

Leading From the Front with the Six Intelligences

For those of you who are business leaders, your world is complex. There are always time-critical problems to solve, budgets to achieve, stakeholders to manage and external market dynamics to anticipate. And amidst all of this, there's a team of people–your team–looking to you to guide, lead and help them succeed. From my work with leaders at all levels, I've observed a consistent pattern. Effective leaders are able to focus simultaneously on two fronts: firstly on how they, as leaders, can manage themselves –their own energy levels, enthusiasm and sanity; and secondly on empowering and motivating their teams by creating the conditions required to enable them to perform at exceptionally high levels.

The key to these two seemingly distinct tasks is essentially the same. Both require that the six Intelligences are functioning at a high level, modelled by you as a leader and within your team. To recap in a nutshell, we know from neuroscience that each of the Intelligences represents a distinct human need that exists regardless of the external environment. Interestingly, when times are good and there is plenty of money, these needs tend to get met easily (or at least the fact that the Intelligences aren't functioning well seems on the surface to be less of an issue). When times are tough and stress levels increase, however, these needs become much harder to satisfy, and the poor functioning Intelligences within the teams have a much more obvious impact on team output. The reassuring news is that when these needs are met, and the unconscious preoccupation with satisfying something that we can't always put our finger on is resolved, team members and teams are able to perform at exceptionally high levels. By accessing the six noble qualities that we've looked at (Tribal Loyalty, Spontaneity, Vitality, Empathy, Love of Learning and Wonder), they become secure, innovative, motivated, passionate, realistic and optimistic–the six foundational characteristics of High Performance Teams.

In this chapter, we review how to apply the six Intelligences in teams. If you want to be a successful leader you will need to learn how to meet these six needs and create these characteristics in your team, regardless of the external circumstances and dynamics. How you do this will vary according to your situation, but somehow—if you are going to create a High Performance Team— you will need to develop these very specific capabilities. You also need to know which of the Intelligences are foundational to the others. In other words, these needs present in a definite order—address the right needs in the wrong order and you will still fail. The previous chapters have provided you with a lot of detail about each of the Intelligences, including their evolutionary social function, their characteristics, how they form, what we know about the brain activity that enables them to function and the implications of different levels of functioning, both for individuals and for the team. The Toolboxes have provided you with practical insights about how to strengthen each of the Intelligences for personal, career and organisational development. Let's recap the order and the themes of each Intelligence at a topline level to ensure that you understand the entire process of creating High Performance Teams in a nutshell. We'll do this by recapping each of the Intelligences as a key leadership capability that you need to master.

The Six Capabilities you need to learn how to address as a leader if you are going to lead effectively and drive team performance

CAPABILITY #1: LEARN HOW TO CREATE SAFETY AND SECURITY

Your first task is to create a sense of security. If you don't do this, you and your team will constantly be in 'emergency mode'. When you feel insecure your brain activity moves from your cerebral cortex (the big modern brain) to your limbic system (your primitive survival brain). In this mode, everyone else is considered to be competition or food. You cannot build teams when all team members are competing with everyone else to survive. You need to learn how to help your people feel safe and know that the environment around them is secure—regardless of whatever external factors may be at play. Focus on encouraging a collaborative and unified team effort—very much in the theme of 'One for All and All for One'. This is the noble quality of Tribal Loyalty. For example, remind your team that making budget is not just an issue for the sales people; it's a 'whole of organisation problem' that needs to be tackled together requiring input from all levels. Give your people ownership of the key problems the organisation is facing and allow them to develop solutions together. Because you're looking to create calm and balance, this phase needs to be done at a slow, 'one step at a time' pace for the group, so the team has time to consider the ideas fully.

In Chapter 2, we looked at the themes that underlie the functioning of the P1 Intelligence, and provided you with tools to enable you as a leader to:

1. Clarify each team member's role and give feedback about how they are going;

2. Develop you team's Value Proposition; and

3. Develop leadership Codes of Conduct, both for yourself as an individual and for your team.

CAPABILITY #2: LEARN HOW TO EMPOWER YOUR PEOPLE TO EXPRESS THEMSELVES BY TURNING EMOTIONS INTO WORDS

It may sound counter-intuitive to **encourage moaning from your team**, but the rationale is deeply rooted in brain science. In Chapter 3, we looked at the importance of self-expression in enabling individuals to take in new ideas, to think conceptually and to work collaboratively. All these abilities are facilitated by the right side of the brain, which easily becomes 'full' of emotion when we're emotionally charged. This prevents the full functioning of this Intelligence. So, as a leader, you need to help your team unblock or empty their system by turning emotions into words.

At the first step you have already enabled your team to feel safe and secure and to understand, respect and value each individual's role within the group. With this in place they will begin to take on a more collaborative approach to solving the problems at hand and access the innovation that is characteristic of High Performance Teams. It is at this point you will need to learn how to encourage them to express how they are feeling about everything—their role, their KPIs, the role of the team in the organisation, even the stresses and disappointments they're facing. It is only by allowing your team to fully articulate how they're feeling that a truly resourceful space will arise and make way for effective solutions to emerge from their problem solving. This engenders creative spontaneity. But remember, as people express themselves, conflict increases. This means that as a leader you will need to upskill your team members on how to effectively manage this conflict.

In Chapter 3, we looked at the themes that underlie the functioning of the C1 Intelligence, and provided you with tools to enable you as a leader to:

1. Actively foster creativity;

2. Make conflict a business-as-usual activity (by using the Pinch Crunch model to establish a way to manage emotional expression); and

3. Use brainstorming to drive innovation.

CAPABILITY #3: LEARN HOW TO MOTIVATE BY IDENTIFYING, DELIVERING AND CELEBRATING QUICK WINS

With clear roles, lively discussion and enthusiasm starting to build, the team is now ready for some focus. Here, your role as a leader is to take your team through a process of identifying the three or four key objectives it can achieve that are on strategy. You need to **create urgency and focus resources on kicking a few high profile goals**. The key is to ensure that each individual's ego, drive, motivation and sense of competition are focused on achieving for the team, rather than for themselves as an individual at the expense of the team. Once the team starts to feel that by working together it can achieve whatever it focuses on, you will have mastered the capability of motivation and invoked the noble quality of Vitality in the team.

In Chapter 4, we looked at the themes that underlie the functioning of the P2 Intelligence, and provided you with tools to enable you as a leader to:

1. Develop a competitive strategy for your team;

2. Dynamise the group; and

3. Effectively manage any plateaued performers.

CAPABILITY #4: LEARN HOW TO FACILITATE EMPATHY THROUGH ACTIVE LISTENING

We all have a need to feel heard and understood. It may sound fluffy, but feeling emotionally connected to those with whom we work not only has a significant impact on our enjoyment of daily life, it can also be a pivotal factor in performance—both our own and the team's. In the face of major challenges, both internal and external, bonds between individuals can be critical in determining the resilience and responsiveness of a group. When team members enjoy strong interpersonal connections, they're able to support each other through tough times and together find the heart to persevere. This is the noble quality of Empathy. In the absence of these bonds, teams often become fractured and performance drops.

The key for you as a leader is to **learn and model the noble art of active listening to drive win-win outcomes**. When you encourage team members to listen to each other and try to see situations from another's point of view, you promote the development of Empathy within the team. Even when it's all smooth sailing, this can mean the difference between a team that merely performs and one that excels. Leaders that have mastered the capability of empathy create teams that are cohesive, connected and have a culture of empowerment and support (rather than politics and white-anting).

These characteristics enable team members to work seamlessly together to achieve exceptional win-win outcomes.

In Chapter 5, we looked at the themes that underlie the functioning of the I2 Intelligence, and provided you with tools to enable you as a leader to:

1. Build active listening in your team;

2. Communicate effectively with groups; and

3. Ensure all agreements are win-win.

CAPABILITY #5: LEARN HOW TO GET INFORMATION FLOWING—LEAD AND LAG INDICATORS

Your role as a leader is now to **ensure everyone is working from accurate data** about how they are performing, both individually and as a team. This involves invoking the noble quality of Love of Learning, so that data and information is valued and used to drive team performance. To master this capability you as a leader need to understand the difference between lead and lag indicators and their impact on strategy development. As we explored in Chapter 6, lead indicators are inputs, lag indicators are outputs and both are needed to ensure team strategies are effective. As a leader, you need to understand how to identify and then share lead and lag information so that the team is a living, learning group—not a collection of automatons following an inaccurate strategy.

In Chapter 6, we looked at the themes that underlie the functioning of the I1 Intelligence, and provided you with tools to enable you as a leader to:

1. Create a 'learning lab' team culture;

2. Identify and track your lead and lag indicators and use this to drive strategy; and

3. Leverage from your team's intellectual capital.

CAPABILITY #6: LEARN HOW TO CREATE HOPE FOR THE FUTURE

In the brain, there is no chemical difference between anticipation and anxiety. The only difference between these profoundly different emotions is our perception of what is going to happen in the future. Anxiety is a feeling of future dread. Anticipation is an expectation of something positive happening in the future. Your job as a leader is to **transform anxiety into anticipation by creating a sense that somehow something positive is coming up**. This is a capability that all the great leaders have mastered. It encourages the team to access their own C2 Intelligence to vision how a different future for the team could be created, through revolutionary ideas, paradigm shifts and strategic thinking. At this stage, your role as a leader is critical, because your ability to create a sense of anticipation (rather than anxiety) about the future will determine whether your team is forward-thinking, optimistic and eager to face the challenges that the future brings or is quietly dreading the next meeting.

In Chapter 7, we looked at the themes that underlie the functioning of the C2 Intelligence, and provided you with tools to enable you as a leader to:

1. Create the future you want through visualisation;

2. Undertake scenario planning to create a new future for the team; and

3. Visualise and focus on ideal outcomes.

When these six capabilities are mastered by leaders and the six Intelligences are fully functioning in teams, the results are breathtaking. Team members work seamlessly together to achieve outstanding results and the success and impact of the team, as a whole, far exceeds anything that could have been achieved by just one or two of the team members working in isolation.

Creating high performance teams is not a simple task. It takes commitment, time, energy and internal fortitude from you as a leader and commitment from the team members. However, it's well worth the effort. Your team will achieve exceptional outcomes, your people will feel engaged, motivated, fulfilled, self-actualised and optimistic about the future. And, of course, so will you.

APPENDIX 1

The Neuroscience of the Six Intelligences

R E L I S H

| Relatedness | Expression | Leading the Pack | Interpersonal Connection | Seeing the Facts | Hope for the Future |

SUMMARY OF THE KEY NEUROBIOLOGICAL SYSTEMS OF P1 (RELATEDNESS)

THE EVOLUTIONARY SOCIAL BRAIN FUNCTION OF P1

The P1 system enables survival through:

- Membership of a community (kinship) through compliance with a specific social role and understood social rules, socially known as moral behaviour (Ciaramelli et al, 2007)

- Movement of behaviour from a conscious action to a habitual response, freeing up mental energy for novel situations requiring creative thought (Saling & Phillips, 2007)

- Control of behaviour in terms of thoughts and physical reactions (Lieberman & Eisenberger, 2004)

- Sequencing events and behaviours (Ratey, 2002)

- The sense that we are the author and controller of our actions (Frith, 2002)

THE P1 SOMATIC ASPECT

Key neurobiological components in the P1 system:

1. The anterior cingulate cortex (ACC), a highly heterogenous substructure of the brain located between the superior surface of the corpus callosum and the cortex, contains several sub-regions implicated in the control of attention, particularly in tasks involving a conflict between learned automatic behaviour and task requirements (Frackowiak, 2004). Increased activity in the dorsal ACC has also been strongly associated with social distress resulting from social ostracism or exclusion (Eisenberger & Lieberman, 2004).

2. The primary motor cortex (M1), in association with the pre-motor area, is involved in the planning and execution of muscle movement (e.g. movement of the legs, abdomen, shoulder, arm, fingers, tongue etc). The M1 initiates movements "...from pressing an elevator button to performing a gymnastic exercise or tying a shoe it provides the organisation of smooth, timed and rhythmic movements among the many brain structures and the spinal chord" (Ratey, 2002, pp. 163-164).

3. Descending signals from the primary motor cortex are subject to modification by the cerebellum. The cerebellum, a distinct, cauliflower-shaped structure

at the back of the brain where the spinal chord merges with the brain stem, integrates feedback from the body's sensory systems following a movement and adjusts output signals from the primary motor cortex (Jueptner & Weiller, 1998). Damage to the cerebellum often results in poor coordination, clumsiness or ataxia (Greenfield, 2000). The cerebellum has also recently been implicated in the normal functioning of social behaviour (Ratey, 2002), and is equally important in mediating learned automatic responses to physical stimuli. For example, lesions to the cerebellum prevent the acquirement of classically conditioned responses (such as an eyeblink response created by pairing an auditory cue with a tap on the forehead; Bracha et al., 1997).

4. The basal ganglia, a diverse group of structures that sit below the cortex (including, amongst others, the striatum), are important for the execution of sustained movement; progressive degeneration of the basal ganglia is a hallmark feature of movement disorders including Parkinson's Disease and Huntington's Chorea (Greenfield, 2000). The basal ganglia are also involved in the selection of behaviours from a previously learned repertoire, introducing flexibility into learned automatic processes (Saling & Philips, 2007). While well-learned motor processes can be executed without activity in the pre-frontal cortex ('cognition'), subsequent adjustments to these actions will recruit the basal ganglia again (Saling & Philips, 2007).

5. The anterior insula (required for interoception/physical self-awareness; Craig, 2002) in concert with the orbito-frontal cortex (involved in reward and punishment processing; Amodio & Frith, 2006) help us make associations based on experiences of objects, that guide future decisions and may promote our survival (Ratey, 2002).

P1 SOMATIC MARKERS[1]: CHOOSING ACTION TO PROMOTE BELONGING

Somatic markers give the individual access to information about the likely best way forward based on past experience, by using current physiological body states to cue information from previous experiences involving similar states. "When circuits in posterior sensory cortices and in temporal and parietal regions process a situation that belongs to a given conceptual category, the pre-frontal circuits that hold records pertinent to that category become active. Next comes activation of regions that trigger

---

1   Damasio's somatic marker theory has recently been the subject of much debate. While it hasn't been discredited, it will be interesting to see where these ongoing directions take us.

appropriate emotional signals such as the ventromedial pre-frontal cortices, courtesy of an acquired [that is, learned] link between that category of event and past emotional-feeling responses" (Damasio, 2003, p. 147). This 'feeling'-based activation of behaviour shortens the window of time required to choose a response that has previously proved successful in similar situations.

For P1, somatic markers prompt decision-making focused on safety.

P1 EMOTION/FEELING ASPECT

> *Because of the ascending interactions with higher brain areas, there is no emotion without a thought, and many thoughts can evoke emotions. Because of the lower interactions, there is no emotion without a physiological or behavioural consequence, and many of the resulting bodily changes can also regulate the tone of emotional systems in a feedback manner.*

(Panksepp, 1998, p. 27)

In addition to areas that directly receive sensory input, parts of the brain are dedicated to representational maps of the body's condition, giving rise to our senses of proprioception and interoception (the awareness of 'how you feel'). What we experience as emotions are strongly related to the physiological state of our bodies, as represented in these areas and interpreted by the frontal lobe. These maps are located in parts of the somatosensory cortex (specifically the insular cortex and secondary somatosensory cortex/SII), the hypothalamus and nuclei in the brain stem tegmentum (Damasio, 2003) and, in particular, the anterior insular and cingulate cortices (Craig, 2009). "Almost all recent imaging studies of emotion report joint activation of the AIC [anterior insular cortex] and the ACC [anterior cingulate cortex] in subjects experiencing emotional feelings, including [P1 emotions]… disgust, aversion, inequity, social exclusion, trust" (Craig, 2009, p. 60).

Damasio (2003) reports that positive feelings (i.e. 'happiness') give rise to significant increases in activity of the pre-frontal cortex, while negative feelings ('sadness') give rise to marked deactivation in pre-frontal cortices, consistent with a loss of cognitive fluency in those who are distressed. In the P1 emotional circuit, this includes positive feelings of acceptance and safety, and negative feelings of rejection and ostracism.

The P1 emotional system is characterised by:

1. Feelings of loneliness or panic if isolated from the group or feeling lonely. Studies

with mammals suggest brain areas involved in driving tribal belonging include areas of the diencephalon, including the thalamus and preoptic area, with stimulation of these structures eliciting panic and distress vocalisations (Klein, 2006). Corticotrophin-releasing hormone (CRH) is released into the blood by the hypothalamus in response to stress, including social isolation and promotes cortisol release from the adrenal cortex. While this response mobilises the body's energy stores and reduces inflammation [the 'fight or flight' response], prolonged activation is associated with many illnesses, and CRH has also been associated with a sense of loneliness and even panic (Klein, 2006). Prolonged administration of exogenous CRH can promote depressive responses (Panksepp, 1998).

2. Neutrality/Homeostasis. Serotonin modulators and anxiolytics (including the benzodiazepines, e.g. Valium) increase the ability of GABA inhibitory neurons to reduce excitatory transmission, particularly within the amygdala (Panksepp, 1998). "...drugs such as morphine that powerfully reduce [separation-induced] anxiety are also powerful alleviators of grief and loneliness in humans" (Panksepp, 1998, p. 263). Genetic abnormalities in serotonin transporters (and consequent changes to brain anatomy and physiology) are associated with higher levels of trait anxiety, particularly 'neuroticism' and 'harm avoidance' (Hariri & Holmes, 2006).

3. Positive emotions associated with social acceptance and belonging. Endorphins, naturally occurring opium-like compounds that stimulate well-being, are released in the brain in positive social situations. Lowered endorphin levels resulting from lack of stimulation can be compensated with alcohol, sweets and recreational drugs (Klein, 2006).

P1 THINKING ASPECT

1. Frontal cortex and left pre-frontal cortex (LPFC) are linked to three kinds of self control:

   - Suppressing/disrupting unwanted cognitive, affective or behavioural responses.

   - Involved in boosting the strength of weaker, but contextually appropriate, representations and action plans

   - The LPFC, along with the frontopolar region of the pre-frontal cortex (PFC), can flexibly combine symbolic representations using propositional rules to consider novel courses of action and, ultimately, set one in motion. (Eisenberger & Lieberman, 2009)

2. Ventromedial pre-frontal cortex (VMPFC). Linked with ensuring pro-social

behaviour by enabling the individual to 'fast forward' and play scenario options in a given social situation and then choose an appropriate one based on past similar situations and the best and worst emotional outcomes that have been experienced in the past (Damasio, 1999).

3. VMPFC also correlates well with several studies investigating moral reasoning. This area shows increased activity when healthy individuals are engaged in moral reasoning, and those with lesions in this area are more willing and faster to judge personal moral violations as acceptable behaviour. Lesions to the VMPFC in childhood impair the development of moral knowledge and the ability to make ethical judgements (Ciaramelli, 2007).

4. The striatum, cerebellum and brain stem are important in implicit and procedural learning, including priming, conditioning and skill-learning tasks (Richmond & Nelson, 2007).

5. Rapid eye movement (REM) sleep has been shown to be critical to consolidating episodic and declarative memories (linked to I1 and I2), but not procedural memory. Rasch et al., (2009) reported that preventing the REM phase during sleep (using selective serotonin reuptake inhibitors) improved, rather than inhibited, the consolidation of simple motor tasks.

Slow Ritualised Behaviour of P1

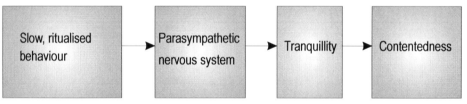

Adapted from Nataraja (2008)

Summary of the Key Neurobiological Systems of C1 (Expression)

THE EVOLUTIONARY SOCIAL BRAIN FUNCTION OF C1

The C1 system enables:

- Adaptation to novel situations by thinking laterally or creatively, using creativity to problem-solve and resolve conflict with others.

- Maintaining positive expectations for the future (Klein, 2006).

- Motivation to repeat constructive activities. Natural rewarding activities are necessary for survival and appetitive motivation ('pleasure'), usually governing beneficial biological behaviours like eating, sex, and reproduction and behaviour directed towards hedonic or pleasurable processes. Social contacts can further facilitate the positive effects exerted by pleasurable experiences (Esch and Stefano, 2004).

- Aversive motivation (pain) or getting away from hedonically unpleasant experiences of food, recreational drugs, sex and the like (Esch & Stefano, 2004).

- The experience of pleasure, the state of feeling happiness and satisfaction resulting from an experience that one enjoys (Esch & Stefano, 2004).

- The experience of extraversion and subjective well-being (Pavot et al., 1990).

- Satisfaction of the body returning to homeostatic conditions ('sensory alliesthesia'; Burgdorf & Panksepp, 2006).

DISTINGUISHING 'PLEASURE' (C1) FROM 'REWARD' (P2)

While much of neuroscientific research has historically blurred the distinction between external and internal rewards, each of these components is distinct. Where P2 relates to external rewards, goals and motivations, C1 involves the pursuit of pleasure resulting in internal neurochemical rewards arising from activation of dopaminergic pathways.

As Burgdorf & Panksepp (2006, p. 184) surmise:

> There appear to be at least two distinct classes of positive affect (PA) states represented in the brain, with separate but overlapping neuroanatomical substrates. An appetitive PA system, devoted to foraging and reward-

seeking, associated in part with the effects of psychostimulants such as cocaine and amphetamine is dependent in part on the ventral striatal dopamine system. [This is the P2 goal- and reward-oriented system.] A nearby PA system involved in processing sensory pleasure such as pleasurable touch and hedonic tastes, involves the opiate and GABA system in the ventral striatum and orbital frontal cortex. [This is the C1 pleasure-oriented system.] These classical distinctions between appetitive and consummatory processes have been encapsulated in motivational theories which distinguish the brain substrates of expectancy type processes, such as seeking and wanting, from consummatory reward processes... and are well illustrated by the work of Jurgens (1976), in which electrical brain stimulation revealed two distinct brain rewarding brain circuits that elicited two separate call types.

C1 SOMATIC ASPECT

Key neurobiological components in the C1 system:

1. [When C1 is engaged] the blood pulses faster (three to five heartbeats a minute faster than their normal state) skin temperature rises by about a tenth of a degree centigrade. This stimulation causes the skin to become somewhat damper, and skin conductance drops. Even the fingers tremble, though not in a jerky way (Klein, 2006).

2. When you feel good, the muscles relax and become more flexible. In addition, since happiness also shifts our hormonal balance, changes take place that we don't feel directly. The zygomatic muscle, which pulls the mouth upward, tenses slightly. The orbicularis oculi muscle with its crow's feet has also contracted slightly. By contrast, the corrugator supercilii muscle, which creates expressions of disgust, sadness and fear by pulling up the eyebrows, is relaxed (Klein, 2006).

3. Every feeling has its own corresponding pattern of brain activity, including both limbic and cortical components, and some parts of the brain are activated in both positive ('happy') and negative ('sad') feelings. Data arrives from the body through the brainstem, activating many regions of the mid-brain. The cerebellum processes impulses from the brainstem and gives orders to the muscles (e.g. the command to laugh when we are amused). Above the cerebellum, the diencephalon is activated to release emotional excitement. In the cerebrum, the pre-frontal cortex is especially active, converting emotions to plans and actions (Klein, 2006; Damasio, 2003).

4. The pleasure and pain centre in the brain is linked to the limbic system, which is made up of the limbic lobe and certain additional structures. The limbic lobe surrounds the corpus callosum and consists of the cingulate gyrus and the parahippocampal gyrus. The hippocampus, which is in the floor of the temporal horn of the lateral ventricle and is closely linked to memory processing, is also included in the limbic lobe. Additional structures incorporated in the limbic system are the dentate gyrus, amygdala, hypothalamus (especially the mamillary bodies), septal area (in the basal forebrain) and thalamus (anterior and some other nuclei). "Functionally, the 'hippocampal formation' consists of the hippocampus, the dentate gyrus and most of the parahippocampal gyrus. Neurobiologists have long known that the euphoria induced by drugs or abuse, sex or other things we enjoy arises because all these factors ultimately boost the activity of the brain's pleasure and reward systems" (Esch & Stefano, 2004, p. 236).

5. Reward pathways are evolutionarily ancient, like limbic structures, and the two share common mechanisms and morphologies. In fact, integral central nervous system (CNS) components involving reward and motivational processes are of limbic origin. Pre-frontal or orbito-frontal cortices, cingulate gyrus, amygdala, hippocampus and nucleus accumbens all participate in reward physiology. Thus pleasure, the limbic system and reward circuitry seem to be biologically connected. Memories of the pleasure of wellness, i.e. 'remembered wellness', are accessible to this circuitry through hippocampal mechanisms (Esch & Stefano, 2004).

6. Natural rewards can be modulated by the activity of the brain's reward and motivation circuitry. Feeding, sexual activity or maternal behaviour can be facilitated by opiate activation of the reward system. The origin of the ventral tegmental dopamine system (including the ventral tegmental area/VTA) seems to provide an important neurochemical interface where exogenous opiates and endogenous opioid peptides can activate a CNS mechanism involved in appetitive motivation and [internal neurochemical] reward... the VTA serves as an appetitive motivation system for diverse behaviours, since it controls both normal and pathological behaviours (Esch & Stefano, 2004).

C1 EMOTION/FEELING ASPECT

Because of the ascending interactions with higher brain areas, there is no emotion without a thought, and many thoughts can evoke emotions. Because of the lower interactions, there is no emotion without a physiological or behavioural consequence, and many of the resulting bodily changes can also regulate the tone of emotional systems in a feedback manner.

(Pankscpp, 1998, p. 27)

In addition to areas that directly receive sensory input, parts of the brain are dedicated to representational maps of the body's condition, giving rise to our senses of proprioception and interoception (the awareness of 'how you feel'). What we experience as emotions are strongly related to the physiological state of our bodies, as represented in these areas and interpreted by the frontal lobe. These maps are located in parts of the somatosensory cortex (specifically the insular cortex and SII), the hypothalamus and nuclei in the brain stem tegmentum (Damasio, 2003) and, in particular, the anterior insular and cingulate cortices (Craig, 2009). "Almost all recent imaging studies of emotion report joint activation of the AIC [anterior insular cortex] and the ACC [anterior cingulate cortex] in subjects experiencing emotional feelings, including [C1 emotions]... happiness and sexual arousal" (Craig, 2009, p. 60).

Damasio (2003) reports that positive feelings (i.e. 'happiness') give rise to significant increases in activity of the pre-frontal cortex, while negative feelings 'sadness') give rise to marked deactivation in pre-frontal cortices, consistent with a loss of cognitive fluency in those who are distressed. In the C1 emotional circuit, this includes positive feelings of excitement, happiness and the anticipation of pleasure.

The C1 emotional system can be characterised by:

1. **Dopamine:** While oxytocin, vasopressin and beta-endorphin play important roles in desire, contentment and sexual attraction, however, the C1 system is dominated by dopamine (Klein, 2006).

2. **The Pleasure Pathway:** Amphetamines are one of many ruinously addictive drugs available throughout the world, including cocaine, crack, heroin, opium, etc. They all work by supplying dopamine to the tegmentum-nucleus accumbens (or 'pleasure pathway'), similar to the effects shown in sensation seekers. The mechanism of addiction is the activation and high reactivation potential of the neural pathways that cause a person to find a particular drug pleasurable. This makes sense: you anticipate how pleasurable it will be and come back for more (Department of Psychology, Florida State University, 2007).

3. Neuroscientist Bejjani triggered the sudden onset of mirth in 1999 by stimulating the **nucleus accumbens**. Until recently the dopamine pathway to the nucleus

accumbens was largely considered to be the key brain substrate for pleasure (Burgdorf and Panksepp, 2006).

4. In humans, the anticipation of an **imminent and highly predictable reward** elicits positive affect (Burgdorf & Panksepp, 2006).

5. Berridge (2003) suggests that the areas linked with positive affective reactions in the brain are **pre-frontal and cingulate cortex, the nucleus accumbens and its mesolimbic projection, lateral hypothalamus** and other structures associated with brain stimulation reward, **the ventral pallidum, and the brain stem** (especially the parabrachial nucleus).

C1 THINKING ASPECT

1. The left pre-frontal cortex (LPFC) is linked to cheerfulness and optimism (Klein, 2006).

2. The orbital frontal cortex (OFC) has been found to be activated in fMRI brain imaging of positive emotional states related to taste-induced positive arousal, olfactory-induced positive arousal, as well as somatosensory-induced positive arousal. Positive arousal states induced by music as well as mothers viewing pictures of newborn babies have also been shown to increase orbital frontal activity. In non-human primates, a subset of orbital frontal cortex neurons are activated specifically by taste stimuli that are palatable to the species (Burgdorf & Panksepp, 2006).

3. Divergent or creative thinking, the "...general process underlying the fluent production of alternative ideas during creative problem-solving", is characterised by strong increases in the complexity of EEG recordings within the frontal cortex, "...reflecting higher degrees of freedom in the competitive interactions among cortical neuron assemblies" (Molle et al, 1996).

Summary of the Key Neurobiological Systems of P2 (Leading the Pack)

THE EVOLUTIONARY SOCIAL BRAIN FUNCTION OF P2

The P2 system enables:

1. Survival through goal directed behaviour and independent action (Berkman & Lieberman, 2009).

2. Motivation and drive to push the mind and behaviour to stay on track for the achievement of purposeful goals that may involve competition with other members of the group for individual reward. Specifically, this involves attention, motor control, response inhibition and progress monitoring (Decety et al., 2004).

3. Prioritisation of options so that the individual can achieve the greatest benefit with minimum cognitive, somatic or emotional effort.

4. A sense of urgency and independence; a sense of willpower and ego.

DISTINGUISHING 'PLEASURE' (C1) FROM 'REWARD' (P2)

While much of neuroscientific research has historically blurred the distinction between external and internal rewards, each of these components is distinct. Where P2 relates to external rewards, goals and motivations, C1 involves the pursuit of pleasure resulting in internal neurochemical rewards arising from activation of dopaminergic pathways.

As Burgdorf & Panksepp (2006, p. 184) surmise:

There appear to be at least two distinct classes of positive affect (PA) states represented in the brain, with separate but overlapping neuroanatomical substrates. An appetitive PA system, devoted to foraging and reward-seeking, associated in part with the effects of psychostimulants such as cocaine and amphetamine is dependent in part on the ventral striatal dopamine system. [This is the P2 goal- and reward-oriented system.] A nearby PA system involved in processing sensory pleasure such as pleasurable touch and hedonic tastes, involves the opiate and GABA system in the ventral striatum and orbital frontal cortex. [This is the C1 pleasure-oriented system.] These classical distinctions between appetitive and consummatory processes have been encapsulated in motivational theories which distinguish the brain substrates of expectancy type processes, such as seeking and wanting, from consummatory reward processes... and are well illustrated by the work of Jurgens (1976), in which electrical brain stimulation revealed two distinct brain rewarding brain circuits that elicited two separate call types.

P2 SOMATIC ASPECT

Key neurobiological components in the P2 system:

1. **Motor Control.** Literature on the neural bases of goal pursuit observes the importance of brain regions related to motor control, including primary motor cortex, supplementary motor area, premotor cortex, cerebellum and basal ganglia (Berkman & Lieberman, 2009). This reflects recruitment of P1 motor circuits to enable execution of behaviours to achieve a set goal (P2).

2. **The orientation association area.** This area in the parietal lobe establishes a three-dimensional sense of 'self', creating a boundary between 'self' and 'non-self' that orientates us in physical space and time. The construction of an arbitrary boundary line between 'self' and 'non-self' is clearly essential to our ability to interact with our physical world. Our ability to move around without bumping into things, for example, requires the formation of a mental map that contains details about the environment in terms of how far away objects are and what relevance they have. In many ways, therefore, the sense of 'self' can be viewed as an artefact of our interaction with the physical world (Nataraja, 2008, pp. 82-83).

P2 SOMATIC MARKERS[2]: CHOOSING ACTION TO PROMOTE SUCCESS

Somatic markers give the individual access to information about the likely best way forward based on past experience. "When circuits in posterior sensory cortices and in temporal and parietal regions process a situation that belongs to a given conceptual category, the pre-frontal circuits that hold records pertinent to that category become active. Next comes activation of regions that trigger appropriate emotional signals such as the ventromedial pre-frontal cortices, courtesy of an acquired [that is, learned] link between that category of event and

---

2   Damasio's somatic marker theory has recently been the subject of much debate. While it hasn't been discredited, it will be interesting to see the direction in which these ongoing directions take us.

past emotional-feeling responses" (Damasio, 2003, p. 147). This 'feeling'-based activation of behaviour shortens the window of time required to choose a response that has previously proved successful in similar situations.

For P2, somatic markers prompt decision-making focused on previous experiences where there has been success or achievement. Actions are selected that give the greatest chance of achieving success.

P2 EMOTION/FEELING ASPECT

> *Because of the ascending interactions with higher brain areas, there is no emotion without a thought, and many thoughts can evoke emotions. Because of the lower interactions, there is no emotion without a physiological or behavioural consequence, and many of the resulting bodily changes can also regulate the tone of emotional systems in a feedback manner.*
>
> (Panksepp, 1998, p. 27)

In addition to areas that directly receive sensory input, parts of the brain are dedicated to representational maps of the body's condition, giving rise to our senses of proprioception and interoception (the awareness of 'how you feel'). What we experience as emotions are strongly related to the physiological state of our bodies, as represented in these areas and interpreted by the frontal lobe. These maps are located in parts of the somatosensory cortex (specifically the insular cortex and SII), the hypothalamus and nuclei in the brain stem tegmentum (Damasio, 2003) and, in particular, the anterior insular and cingulate cortices (Craig, 2009). "Almost all recent imaging studies of emotion report joint activation of the AIC [anterior insular cortex] and the ACC [anterior cingulate cortex] in subjects experiencing emotional feelings, including [P2 emotions]... anger, fear and indignation" (Craig, 2009, p. 60).

Damasio (2003) reports that positive feelings (i.e. 'happiness') give rise to significant increases in activity of the pre-frontal cortex, while negative feelings ('sadness') give rise to marked deactivation in pre-frontal cortices, consistent with a loss of cognitive fluency in those who are distressed. In the P2 emotional circuit, this includes positive feelings of success, and negative feelings of failure or frustration arising from external constraint.

P2 goal-oriented feelings include:

1. **High motivation to succeed.**

2. **Anger and frustration.** Anger is associated with activation of the left orbital frontal cortex, right anterior cingulate cortex, and bilateral anterior temporal poles (Dougherty et al., 1999).

3. **Power and perception of strength and dominating behaviour.** Testosterone is linked to aggressive behaviour in animals, and engaging in competitive tasks increases blood testosterone levels in human males (Nelson & Trainor, 2007). Cortisol, released during the fight or flight response, mobilises energy reserves and suppresses the immune system, contributing to increased short-term performance.

4. **Urgency or impatience.** Adrenaline and testosterone. Recent studies have suggested considerable overlap in the neural circuitry activated by rewards in the social (e.g. praise and status) and economic (e.g. money) domains (Saxe & Haushofer, 2008).

P2 THINKING ASPECT

1. **The attention association area.** "Across the different contemplative disciplines, various techniques are used to focus the mind to single-pointed attention, including mantras, chanting, images and repetitive movement. All these techniques trigger activity in the attention association area in the pre-frontal cortex. The neurons in this area of the brain are associated with goal-directed behaviour; both physical and psychological. Navigation through a crowded train station, for example, requires activity in this part of the brain, as we filter out redundant sensory information and focus only on those elements that can guide our path through the station. Similarly, in order to examine a thought properly or come up with a plan of action, we need to focus on the issue at hand and filter out redundant thoughts" (Nataraja, 2008, pp. 82-83).

2. **Pre-frontal cortex.** Areas of the pre-frontal cortex (PFC) are involved in the generation and maintenance of goal representation, as well as response inhibition in the service of maintaining action towards those goals. "Many forces pull us away from or against our goals, and a major role of the PFC is to guide our attention and behaviour through this gauntlet in a 'top-down' or executive manner, in a process that is known as Top-Down Excitatory Biasing (TEB). Within a goal

pursuit context, TEB can be thought of as a form of attentional control that serves to focus our cognitive resources on a goal or goal-relevant behaviour to the exclusion of other temptations or distractions. The PFC is involved in top-down regulation of both motor and non-motor responses such as cognitions and emotions" (Berkman & Lieberman, 2009).

Rapid Ritualised Behaviour Fosters P2

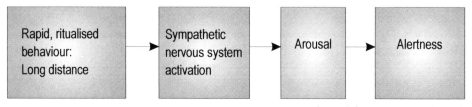

Adapted from Nataraja (2008)

Summary of the Key Neurobiological Systems of I2 (Interpersonal Connection)

THE EVOLUTIONARY SOCIAL BRAIN FUNCTION OF I2

The I2 system enables an individual to:

1. Survive through understanding and empathising with others, and through connection and loving friends and family.

2. Empathise with others and provide support and comfort during both good and bad times (attachment).

3. Best guess how others will react through Theory of Mind being able to guess what somebody else is thinking about you and others. This can be described as a process by which most healthy human adults:

    a. attribute unobservable mental states to others (and under certain circumstances, to the self); and

    b. integrate these attributed states into a single coherent model that can be used to explain and predict the target's behaviour and experiences (Saxe & Wexler, 2005).

4. Form lasting and meaningful relationships through romantic (pair bonding) and maternal love (Dêbiec, 2007).

I2 SOMATIC ASPECT

Key neurobiological components in the I2 system:

1. **Maternal Love:** Mothers viewing their own child showed increased activation of the orbital frontal cortex (OFC), periaqueductal grey, anterior insular cortex, and dorsal and ventrolateral parts of the putamen (Noriuchi, Kikuchi & Senoo, 2008).

2. **Attachment and Pair Bonding** recruit the medial insular cortex, anterior cingulate cortex and hippocampus and, in the subcortex, parts of the striatum and nucleus accumbens which together constitute core regions of the reward system (Zeki, 2007).

3. **Mirror Neurons** give us the ability to have mindsight or empathetic attunement.

These neurons are found within the pre-frontal cortex and Broca's area and fire when another individual is observed engaging in a specific behaviour. Empathy is thought to emerge when the facial expressions and posture of another individual activate similar sensory-motor circuits in an observer. These motor systems, in turn, are assumed to activate networks of emotion in the observer associated with such actions (Rizzolatti & Craighero, 2004; Wolf, Gales, Shane & Shane, 2000; 2001).

4. **Spindle Neurons** (also known as Von Economo Neurons) that are shared by humans with only a few species of higher primates, whales and elephants, are located in layer V of both the anterior paracingulate cortex (Gallagher & Frith, 2003) an orbito-frontal cortex (particularly the fronto-insular cortex, FI; Phillips, 2004). These large, high velocity neurons are currently the focus of intense research for their role in social cognition and emotions. John Allman from the California Institute of Technology has argued for the place of spindle neurons in distinguishing between two (of several) behavioural circuits in the brain:

> One is more deliberating, thinking about issues of fairness, punishment, moral judgements and the like. [This is the logical and moral reasoning encompassed in the P1 thinking style.] The second, faster system mediated by spindle cells controls more intuitive behaviour during social interactions. If you love someone, you know instantly how to react to them. You don't have to think. This is where spindle cells are important, Allman believes. "The main thing [spindle cells] do is to adjust your behaviour in a rapid real-time interaction in a complex social environment," he says.

(Cited in Phillips, 2004)

5. **Visual system** – for when we see the face of someone we love, namely the cerebral cortex, orbital frontal cortex, anterior cingulate, cerebellum, insula, posterior hippocampus, caudate nucleus and putamen (Zeki, 2007).

6. **Romantic love.** Includes the activation of the frontal, parietal and middle temporal cortex as well as a large nucleus located at the apex of the temporal lobe, known as the amygdala (Zeki, 2007).

7. **Regions of the brain linked to either maternal or romantic love.** The anterior cingulate cortex, the ventral, caudate nucleus, insula, striatum, (consisting of putamen, cordate nucleus and globus pallidus) periaqueductal (central) grey and hippocampus (Zeki, 2007).

I2 EMOTION/FEELING ASPECT

Because of the ascending interactions with higher brain areas, there is no emotion without a thought, and many thoughts can evoke emotions. Because of the lower interactions, there is no emotion without a physiological or behavioural consequence, and many of the resulting bodily changes can also regulate the tone of emotional systems in a feedback manner.

(Panksepp, 1998, p. 27)

In addition to areas that directly receive sensory input, parts of the brain are dedicated to representational maps of the body's condition, giving rise to our senses of proprioception and interoception (the awareness of 'how you feel'). What we experience as emotions are strongly related to the physiological state of our bodies, as represented in these areas and interpreted by the frontal lobe. These maps are located in parts of the somatosensory cortex (specifically the insular cortex and SII), the hypothalamus and nuclei in the brain stem tegmentum (Damasio, 2003) and, in particular, the anterior insular and cingulate cortices (Craig, 2009). "Almost all recent imaging studies of emotion report joint activation of the AIC [anterior insular cortex] and the ACC [anterior cingulate cortex] in subjects experiencing emotional feelings, including [I2 emotions]... maternal and romantic love... and empathy" (Craig, 2009, p. 60).

Damasio (2003) reports that positive feelings (i.e. 'happiness') give rise to significant increases in activity of the pre-frontal cortex, while negative feelings 'sadness') give rise to marked deactivation in pre-frontal cortices, consistent with a loss of cognitive fluency in those who are distressed. In the I2 emotional circuit, this includes positive feelings of love and compassion and negative feelings of disconnection, disassociation and lack of generosity.

Emotional components of the I2 system include:

1. **Happiness, motherliness, joy, warmth, love, calmness, excitement** (Noriuchi et al., 2008). These feelings are made possible through areas of the brain that are rich in oxytocin and vasopressin receptors. Both are produced in the hypothalamus and released from the pituitary (Zeki, 2007).

2. **Love and attachment** are made possible through neuro-hypophyseal peptides oxytocin and vasopressin (Dêbiec, 2007; Zak, Stanton and Ahmadi, 2007). The receptors for both are distributed in many parts of the brain stem and are activated during both romantic and maternal love. Dopamine is released by the hypothalamus,

which is deep within the brain and functions as a link between the nervous and endocrine systems (Zeki, 2007).

3. **Love is associated with the deactivation of a common set of regions associated with negative emotions, social judgement and 'mentalising'** that is the assessment of other people's intentions and emotions (Zeki, 2007). This coincides with decreased levels of serotonin (Zeki, 2007).

4. **Generosity.** Treating individuals with oxytocin leads to greater demonstrated generosity, or 'liberality in giving', in tasks that require splitting of money with a stranger (Zak et al., 2007).

I2 THINKING ASPECT

1. **Theory of Mind (TOM) or mentalising.** The four generally accepted brain regions that make TOM possible are the right tempo-parietal junction for the attribution of mental states, the left temporo-parietal junction posterior cingulate and medial pre-frontal cortex (Saxe & Wexler, 2005).

2. **Deactivated parts of the brain when in love.** The amygdala, related to fear, areas of the frontal and parietal cortices and parts of the temporal lobe are all commonly involved with negative emotions and cognitions. These areas are deactivated when faced with pictures of loved ones. Specifically this includes: the middle temporal cortex, occipital parietal junction, temporal pole, lateral pre-frontal cortex. "States of 'romantic love' involve 'a suspension of judgement or a relaxation of judgemental criteria by which we assess other people" (Zeki, 2007).

Summary of the Key Neurobiological Systems of I1 (Seeing the Facts)

THE EVOLUTIONARY SOCIAL BRAIN FUNCTION OF I1

The I1 system enables:

1. Survival through the recognition of objects and recall of information associated with them (Creem & Proffitt, 2001).

2. Communication with themselves internally and externally and with others through language.

3. Learning new things about the world and the formation of declarative memory.

4. The ability to identify patterns: in behaviour (both one's own and others'); the seasons; and dangerous situations.

I1 SOMATIC ASPECT

Key neurobiological components in the I1 system:

1. **Visual information** that is received by the visual cortex is distributed to cortical areas that perform specialised visual processing functions. This system includes: the posterior parietal lobe, temporal cortex, parietal cortex, V1 through V2, V3, the middle temporal area, medial superior temporal area, and posterior parietal cortex (Creem & Proffitt, 2001).

2. **Two visual processing streams** are classically defined, responsible for 'what' (ventral stream) and 'where' (dorsal stream) processing, respectively (Creem & Proffitt, 2001).

3. **The ventral stream**, projecting from V1 to the inferior temporal lobe, is responsible for object discrimination; the dorsal stream is responsible for object localisation in space (Creem & Proffitt, 2001).

4. **Information from the visual processing pathways** provides inputs to the pre-frontal cortex, which plays a critical role in working memory (LeDoux, 1998).

5. **The hippocampus** is involved in the creation and retrieval of declarative (factual) memories (Creem & Proffitt, 2001).

6. **The medial temporal lobe and the pre-frontal cortex** (Bontempi & Durkin, 2007) including the hippocampus and parahippocampal cortex (Richmond & Nelson, 2007).

7. **Language-based communication** depends on healthy functioning of **Broca's region**, including BA44, BA45, and other areas involved in semantic, phonological, and syntactic verbal fluency (Heim, Eickhoft & Amunts, 2008; Davis et al., 2006; Cozolina, 2002).

I1 EMOTION/FEELING ASPECT

Because of the ascending interactions with higher brain areas, there is no emotion without a thought, and many thoughts can evoke emotions. Because of the lower interactions, there is no emotion without a physiological or behavioural consequence, and many of the resulting bodily changes can also regulate the tone of emotional systems in a feedback manner.

(Panksepp, 1998, p. 27)

In addition to areas that directly receive sensory input, parts of the brain are dedicated to representational maps of the body's condition, giving rise to our senses of proprioception and interoception (the awareness of 'how you feel'). What we experience as emotions are strongly related to the physiological state of our bodies, as represented in these areas and interpreted by the frontal lobe. These maps are located in parts of the somatosensory cortex (specifically the insular cortex and SII), the hypothalamus and nuclei in the brain stem tegmentum (Damasio, 2003) and, in particular, the anterior insular and cingulate cortices (Craig, 2009). "Almost all recent imaging studies of emotion report joint activation of the AIC [anterior insular cortex] and the ACC [anterior cingulate cortex] in subjects experiencing emotional feelings, including [I1 emotions]... sadness... and aversion." (Craig, 2009, p. 60)

Damasio (2003) reports that positive feelings (i.e. 'happiness') give rise to significant increases in activity of the pre-frontal cortex, while negative feelings 'sadness') give rise to marked deactivation in pre-frontal cortices, consistent with a loss of cognitive fluency in those who are distressed. In the I1 emotional circuit, this includes positive feelings of curiosity and fascination.

I1 emotions include:

1. **Fascination:** Intense interest, a love of learning (if turned up too high this can

lead to greed or addiction). This fascination is driven by mid-brain dopaminergic regions that are engaged during learning (Poldrack & Foerde, 2008). If turned up too high this can lead to greed or addiction.

2. **Withdrawal:** Wanting to move back to get perspective and look or watch from a safe place (Damasio, 2003).

THINKING ASPECT OF I1 — CREATING SHORT- AND LONG-TERM MEMORIES

1. **The process of creating a memory:** After the information is perceived by the posterior cortex, the pre-frontal cortex captures and stores it in working memory for a while. "After a few minutes the frontal lobe washes its hands of the memory, and the hippocampus has to be recruited in order to retrieve it. When a memory is recalled with the help of the hippocampus, it is placed back in working memory in the frontal lobe. [In many ways, working memory is analogous to computer random-access memory (RAM)]. This is crucial for holding and manipulating words and our special representation. These functions fit roughly into the two components proposed by Allan Baddely, the phonological loop and the visuospatial sketchpad. A few years after the memory is acquired, the frontal lobe can access it directly without help from the hippocampus" (Ratey, 2002, p. 197).

2. **The process of long-term potentiation (LTP):** Memory is a set of distributed pieces that are pulled together on demand – they are literally created in the moment. Each new experience causes the neuronal firing across some synapses to strengthen and others to weaken. The pattern of change represents an initial memory of the experience. The memory will weaken and even disappear unless made stronger by LTP, which at a cellular level causes synapses to strengthen their connection to each other, coding the data as a series of connections. When such a memory is made, LTP blazes a trail along a series of neurons making it easier for subsequent messages along the same path.

3. **CREB** (cAMP Responsiveness Element Binding protein), an enzyme that regulates DNA transcription in neurons, enables the brain to produce proteins that are critical to synapse formation and the ability to move memories from short-term to long-term stores (Ratey, 2002).

Summary of the Key Neurobiological Systems of C2 (Hope for the Future)

C2 INTRODUCTION — THE MIND'S WIFI

The C2 system enables the individual to 'download' new ideas, paradigms or concepts that reflect a fundamentally changing world requiring a new map of understanding. C2 is a difficult system of the mind to chart and neuroscience is still not clear about exactly how the C2 Intelligence works. fMRI research on the neural pathways linked to meditation gives us the best current insight into how C2 may function.

> *Human characteristics such as inspiration and creativity are not determined by activity in a distinct and identifiable region of the brain; they emerge through the coordinated behaviour of large collections of neurons, spread over different regions of the human brain.*
>
> *If we are to gain a better understanding of some of our more elusive cognitive skills, our brain's emergent properties, we must examine them at the level of the whole brain.*
>
> *With the advent of non-invasive imaging techniques, such as Magnetic Resonance Imaging (MRI), we can study and measure activity across groups of neurons, even across the whole brain, and watch it in real time...*
>
> *This has revealed the different areas of the brain involved in specific tasks, the sequence in which activity in different brain regions changes during a particular task, and the impact of lifestyle factors and disease on brain function.*
>
> *Combining this new knowledge with detailed studies of individual neurons, their connections and their chemical signals, offers a more complete picture of how the brain works and responds, and is allowing us slowly to unravel the neural basis of human experience.*
>
> (Nataraja, 2008, pp. 72-73).

One controversial line of research into C2 states by Persigner attempted to use transcranial magnetic stimulation to induce mystical experiences by activating areas in the right parietal and temporal lobes (Khamsi, 2004).

"In John Horgan's book, Rational Mysticism, Persinger states that his helmet –

sensationally named the 'God machine' by the media – has, as yet, not been able to induce a religious or mystical experience in its creator. Persinger attributes this lack of effect to his generally sceptical and scientific state of mind. As higher levels of temporal lobe lability are associated with right-brained thinking, individuals who are predominantly left-brained thinkers can be assumed to have lower levels of temporal lobe lability and therefore a reduced likelihood of a religious or mystical experience on temporal lobe stimulation" (Nataraja, 2008, p. 79).

"Interestingly, people with higher temporal lability were also found to be associated with predominately right-brained – intuitive rather than rational – thinking. Stimulation of the right temporal lobe was reported to produce more pleasant experiences than those evoked by stimulation of the left temporal lobe" (Nataraja, 2008).

"Through their research, Newberg and d'Aquili have shown that mystical experiences are associated with specific patterns of brain activity not limited to the temporal lobes. Whereas spontaneously evoked religious experiences appear to

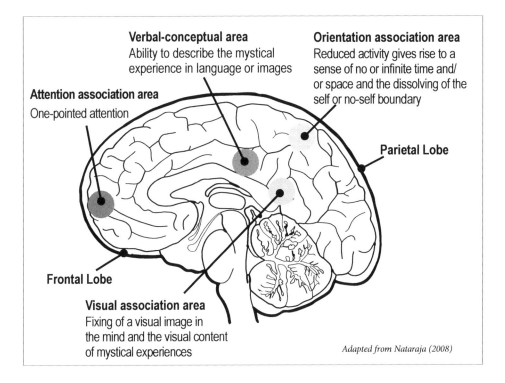

Verbal-conceptual area
Ability to describe the mystical experience in language or images

Orientation association area
Reduced activity gives rise to a sense of no or infinite time and/ or space and the dissolving of the self or no-self boundary

Attention association area
One-pointed attention

Parietal Lobe

Frontal Lobe

Visual association area
Fixing of a visual image in the mind and the visual content of mystical experiences

Adapted from Nataraja (2008)

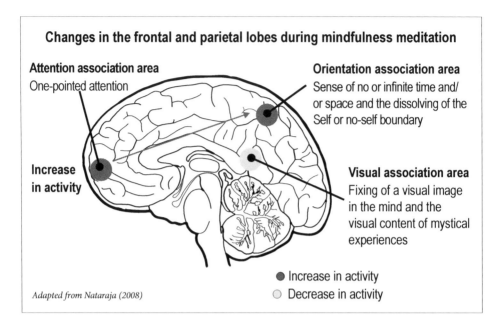

Changes in the frontal and parietal lobes during mindfulness meditation

Attention association area
One-pointed attention

Increase in activity

Orientation association area
Sense of no or infinite time and/ or space and the dissolving of the Self or no-self boundary

Visual association area
Fixing of a visual image in the mind and the visual content of mystical experiences

● Increase in activity
○ Decrease in activity

Adapted from Nataraja (2008)

involve circuitry that lies within the temporal lobe, mystical experiences evoked by meditation appear to involve circuitry throughout the entire brain" (Nataraja, 2008, p. 81).

CHANGES IN THE FRONTAL AND PARIETAL LOBES DURING PASSIVE MEDITATION

Meditator: "Periodically, throughout the day, I become consciously aware of the fact that my mind is not focused on the now - instead, I'm fretting about some potential experience in the future. As I become aware of this, I bring my mind to focus on whatever I'm doing. This might be writing a letter or something as mundane as doing the washing up. With this intention my body relaxes and there is a conscious decision to focus my attention on experiencing the moment. Thoughts spontaneously pop into my head -something I forgot during a recent trip to the supermarket, a comment from a work colleague earlier in the day - but after acknowledging them I just return to the present-now. Slowly, over time, the gap between these interrupting thoughts gets longer and it takes no effort to focus my attention on the task at hand".

Neuroscientist: "At this point, there is an increase in activity in the attention association area and a decrease in activity in the surrounding areas of the frontal cortex and, from time to time, there are short bursts of activity in neurons in the frontal cortex. This reflects random thoughts arising and then dissipating. As the

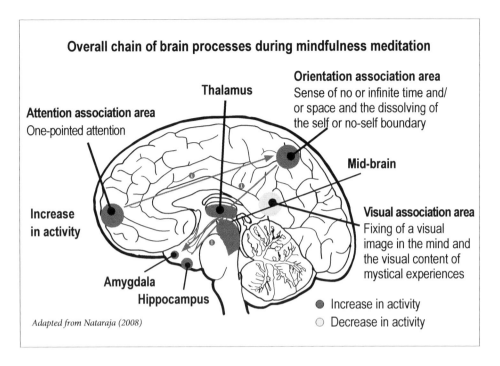

Overall chain of brain processes during mindfulness meditation

Thalamus

Orientation association area
Sense of no or infinite time and/ or space and the dissolving of the self or no-self boundary

Attention association area
One-pointed attention

Mid-brain

Increase in activity

Visual association area
Fixing of a visual image in the mind and the visual content of mystical experiences

Amygdala
Hippocampus

● Increase in activity
○ Decrease in activity

Adapted from Nataraja (2008)

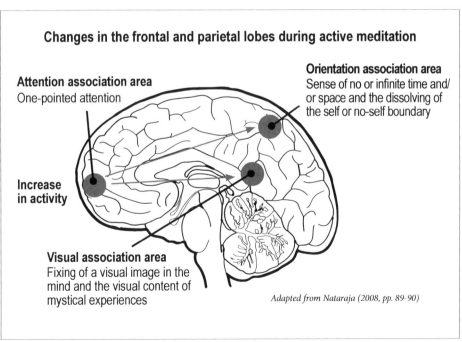

Changes in the frontal and parietal lobes during active meditation

Attention association area
One-pointed attention

Orientation association area
Sense of no or infinite time and/ or space and the dissolving of the self or no-self boundary

Increase in activity

Visual association area
Fixing of a visual image in the mind and the visual content of mystical experiences

Adapted from Nataraja (2008, pp. 89-90)

activity in the attention association area increases even further, with persistent one-focused attention, the short bursts of activity are eventually dampened and thoughts become more infrequent and less interrupting" (Nataraja, 2008, pp. 85-94).

Meditator: "My awareness of my surroundings recedes into the background. At times I lose myself in the present-now, and time passes during which I'm not aware of my surroundings, not aware of my body or the ache in my back that was troubling me earlier, not really aware of where I begin and where I end. I feel a union with something much greater than myself, something much more expansive than my restricted and rigid sense of self."

Neuroscientist: "A decrease in activity in the orientation association area has occurred. Through one-pointed focus, the individual effectively filters out any so-called redundant information, including information from the sensory elements that build up an internal body image. As a result, the body image becomes blurred, and the boundary between body and everything else also becomes blurred. This gives rise to the sensation of unity with something that is greater than 'self'" (Nataraja, 2008, pp. 85-94).

Meditator: "As my awareness of the unity that lies beyond my restricted sense of self grows, my whole body appears to respond. A wave of bliss washes over me, like the sun emerging from a cloud and bathing me in light. I feel tremendous peace and union with

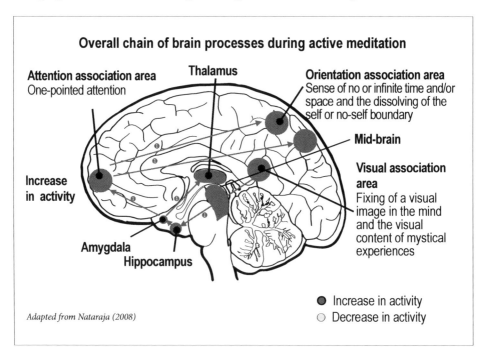

Overall chain of brain processes during active meditation

Attention association area — One-pointed attention

Thalamus

Orientation association area — Sense of no or infinite time and/or space and the dissolving of the self or no-self boundary

Mid-brain

Visual association area — Fixing of a visual image in the mind and the visual content of mystical experiences

Increase in activity

Amygdala

Hippocampus

● Increase in activity
○ Decrease in activity

Adapted from Nataraja (2008)

all. Sometimes, at this point, an image or memory might appear and, with it, strong emotions. This can be enough to pull me back to myself as I delight in the image or replay the memory. But sometimes I manage to merely acknowledge the image or memory, storing it away for future examination, and then return to the present-now experience. Other times, I remain in this peaceful state for an indeterminable amount of time before emerging from my meditation. Sometimes, I become aware of a clarity of mind I don't normally experience in everyday life. From time to time, this clarity provides me with an insight or the answer to a question I'd been thinking about earlier in the day. I just seem to know the answer without being sure of the source. It's hard to explain. It appears to defy logic." (Nataraja, 2008, pp. 85-94)

Neuroscientist: "The decrease in activity in the orientation association area produces an autonomic nervous system response. This gives rise to the feelings of bliss that accompany the dampening of activity in both the right and left parietal lobe. The right-brain function stemming from meditation gives the individual access to right-brained 'big picture' thinking and right-brain vivid and accurate memories. The lack of activity in the left parietal lobe explains why knowledge gained during meditation is seen to stem from something greater than self." (Nataraja, 2008, pp. 85-94)

Meditator: "I settle down for meditation in a relaxed, upright position, and slowly relax my body, from the toes of my feet to the top of my head. At the same time I focus my attention on an image of the Virgin Mary. Thoughts appear, interrupting and demanding attention. However, I just return to the image and these thoughts disappear. I try to build up the image in my mind, seeing every single detail, and slowly it becomes clearer and it becomes easy to hold the image in the stillness. The Virgin Mary is fixed in my mind."

Neuroscientist: "At this point, there is an increase in activity in the attention association area and a decrease in activity in the surrounding areas of the frontal cortex. This is accompanied by an increase in activity in both the visual and orientation association areas. These areas are necessary to fix an object in the mind. As activity in the parietal lobe decreases, the individual's ability to see the boundary between 'self' and 'object' also decreases. This accounts for the sense of absorption into the object" (Nataraja, 2008, pp. 85-94).

CHANGES IN THE FRONTAL AND PARIETAL LOBES DURING PASSIVE MEDITATION

Meditator: "After a while the boundary between myself and the image slowly seems to dissolve. It's a strange feeling; losing my sense of self and being in the embrace of something boundlessly infinite. I'm absorbed into the image; the distinction between it and me becomes blurred, irrelevant. A wave of blissful peace washes me from head to foot in light and love (later I interpret this to be an overwhelming sense of the Virgin Mary's love for us all). As I emerge from meditation, I'm often struck by a clarity and presence of mind I don't associate with my normal waking life. In these moments sometimes images, vivid memories, or even profound insights, surface, along with strong emotions."

Neuroscientist: "At this point, the decrease in activity in the orientation association area in the parietal lobe produces an autonomic nervous system response. As before, this accounts for the wave of peaceful bliss passing through the individual's body. The autonomic nervous system also triggers the clarity of mind, however, as it is accompanied by a dampening of activity in both the right and left parietal lobes, there is a corresponding decreased awareness of 'self' during this meditative experience, so the individual is unlikely to become aware of this clarity until after the meditative session" (Nataraja, 2008, pp. 85-94).

BEGINNER'S MIND AND THE BENEFITS OF MEDITATION PRACTICE

The term 'beginners mind' refers to a receptive and open attitude, a willingness to see things as they are rather than how we think they are.

By the time we reach adulthood, many of us have developed fairly firm ideas about life, the universe and everything. This can leave us closed off to the new experiences, thoughts and behaviour that are so essential to our personal development.

Mindfulness-based Stress Reduction encourages the cultivation of 'an open mind', experiencing everything as if it were occurring for the very first time with no preconceptions or expectations. In this open mind there is space for new ideas, new ways of thinking and behaving; a readiness to see things from a different, less restrictive perspective.

(Nataraja, 2008, p. 196)

Bibliography

Abrahamson, E. (2000). Change without pain. *Harvard Business Review, July-August.*

Adams, R.D., Victor, M., & Ropper, A.H. (1997). *Principles of neurology.* New York: McGraw-Hill.

Ader, R., Felton, D., & Cohen, N. (1991). *Psychoneuroimmunology, 2nd edition.* San Diego: Academic Press.

Ahern, G. L., Schomer, D. L., Kleefield, J., Blume, H., Rees Cosgrove, G., Weintraub, S. et al. (1991). Right hemisphere advantage for evaluating emotional facial expressions. *Cortex, 27,* 193-202.

Ainsworth, M. D. S., Blehar, M. C., Waters, E., & Walls, S. (1978). *Patterns of attachment: A psychological study of the strange situation.* Hillsdale: NJ: Erlbaum.

Alexander, C., Harung, H. S., & Heaton, D. P. (1999). *Evolution of organizations in the new millennium, 20* (4). MCB University Press: The Leadership and Organization Development Journal.

Amodio, D.M., & Frith, C.D. (2006). Meeting of minds: The medial frontal cortex and social cognition. *Nature Reviews Neuroscience, 7,* 268-277.

Amodio, D., Shah, J., Sigelman, J., Brazy, P., and Harmon-Jones, E (2004). Implicity regulatory focus associated with frontal cortical activity, J. Exp. Soc. Psychol 40, 225-232.

Anik, L. Aknin, L.B., Norton, M.I., & Dunn, E.W (2009). Feeling Good about Giving: The Benefits (and Costs) of Self-Interested Charitable Behavior. *Harvard Business School. Working Paper 10-012.*

Anticevic, A., Repovs, G., & Barch, D.M. (2010). Resisting emotional interference: Brain regions facilitating working memory performance during negative distraction. *Cognitive, Affective, & Behavioral Neuroscience, 10 (2), 159-173.*

Argyris, C., & Schön, D. (1995). *Organisational Learning* (2nd edition). Harlow: Addison-Wesley.

Aristotle, translated by Ernest Barker, revised by R.F. Stalley. (1995). *The Politics.* Oxford: Oxford.

Ashkanasy, N.M., Härtel, C.E.J., & Zerbe, W.J. (Eds.) (2000). *Emotions in the work place: Theory, research, and practice.* Westport, CT: Quorum Books.

Aspinwall, L.G. (1998). Rethinking the role of positive affect in self-regulation. Motivation and Emotion, 22, 1-32.

Astin, J.A., & Forys K. (2004). *Psychosocial Determinants of Health and Illness: Integrating Mind, Body and Spirit.* Advances.

Badaracco, J.L. (1998). The discipline of building character. *Harvard Business Review, March-April.*

Baird, A., Scheffer, I.E., & Wilson, S.J. (2011). Mirror neuron system involvement in empathy: A critical look at the evidence. *Social Neuroscience, 6 (4), 327–335.*

Baltes, P.B., & Staudinger, U.M. (2000). *Berlin Wisdom Paradigm.*

Bakermans-Kranenburg, M.J. et al., (2012). Oxytocin decreases handgrip force in reaction to infant crying in females without harsh parenting experiences. *Social Cognitive and Affective Neuroscience, 7 (8), 951-957.*

Bandura, A. (1982). Self-efficacy mechanism in human agency. *The American Psychologist, 37*(2), 122 - 147. Baron, 1988.

Baron-Cohen, S. (1995). *Mindblindness: An essay on autism and theory of mind.* Cambridge, MA: MIT Press.

Bartz, J.A. et al., (2010). Effects of oxytocin on recollections of maternal care and closeness. *PNAS 107 (50) 21371–21375.*

Bartz, J.A. et al., (2010). Oxytocin Selectively Improves Empathic Accuracy. *Psychological Science, 21(10) 1426–1428.*

Bartz, J.A., Zaki, J., Bolger, N., Oschsner, K.N. (2011). Social effects of oxytocin in humans: context and person matter. *Trends in Cognitive Sciences, 15 (7), 301-309.*

Bateson, M.C. (1979). The epigenesis of conversational interaction: A personal account of research development. In M. Bullowa (Ed.), *Before speech: The beginning of human communication* (pp. 63-77). Cambridge, UK: Cambridge University Press.

Bauer, P. J. (1996). What do infants recall of their lives?: Memory for specific events by one- to two-year-olds. *American Psychologist, 51,* 29-41.

Baxter, L.R., Schwartz, J.M., Bergman, K.S., Szuba, M.P., Guze, B.H., Mazziotta, J.C. et al. (1985). Caudate glucose metabolic rate changes with both drug and behaviour therapy for obsessive-compulsive disorder. *Archives of General Psychiatry, 40,* 681-689.

Baxter, L.R., Schwartz, J.M., Phelps, M.E., Mazziotta, J.C., Guze, B.H., Selin, C.E. et al. (1989). Reduction of prefrontal cortex glucose metabolism common to three types of depression. *Archives of General Psychiatry, 46,* 243-350.

Bear, M.F., Connors, B.W., & Paradiso, M.A. (2001). *Neuroscience: Exploring the Brain.* Baltimore: Lippincott.

Beauregard, M., Paquette, V. (2006). Neural correlates of a mystical experience in Carmelite nuns. *Neuroscience Letters 405, 186–190.*

Bechara, A., Damasio, H., Tranel, D., & Damasio, A. (1997). Deciding advantageously before knowing the advantageous strategy. *Science, 275,* 1293-1295.

Beck, D.E., & Cowan, C.C. (1996). *Spiral Dynamics.* Oxford: Blackwell Publishing.

Beer, J. S., John, O. P., Scabini, D., & Knight, R. T. (June 2006). Orbitofrontal Cortex and Social Behavior: Integrating Self-monitoring and Emotion-Cognition Interactions. *Journal of Cognitive Neuroscience, 18* (6) , 871-879.

Benoit, D., & Parker, K. C. H. (1994). Stability and transmission of attachment across three generations. *Child Development, 65,* 1444-1456.

Benson, F. D. (1994). *The Neurology of Thinking.* New York: Oxford University Press.

Berkman, E., & Lieberman, M. D. (2009). The neuroscience of goal pursuit: Bridging gaps between theory and data. In G. Moskowitz & H. Grant (Eds.) *The Psychology of Goals* (98-126). New York, NY: Guilford Press.

Berkowitz, L., & Lutterman, K. (1968). The traditionally socially responsible personality. Public Opinion Quarterly, 32, 169-185.

Berne, E. (1975). *Games People Play: The basic handbook of transactional analysis.* Ballantine Books.

Berne, E. (1970). *Sex in Human Loving.* Simon & Schuster.

Berne, E. (1986). *Transactional Analysis in Psychotherapy.* Ballantine Books; Reissue edition.

Berne, E. (1975). *What do you do after you say hello?* London: Corgi Books.

Bernick, C. (2001). When your Culture Needs a Makeover. *Harvard Business Review, June.*

Berridge, K.C. (2003). Pleasures of the brain. *Brain and Cognition, 52,* 106-128.

Billington, J., Baron-Cohen, S., & Bor, D. (2008). Systemizing influences attentional processes during the Navon task: An fMRI study. *Neuropsychologia 46, 511–520.*

Bittel, L. R. (1989). *The McGraw-Hill 36-hour management course.* McGraw-Hill.

Blanchard, K. & Johnson, S. (1996). *The One Minute Manager.* Harper Collins Business.

Blanke, O., Ortigue, S., Landis, T., & Seeck, H. (2002). Stimulating Illusory Own-Body Perceptions. *Nature,* 419 (6904), 269-270.

Blonder, L. X., Bowers, D., & Heilman, K. M. (1991). The role of right hemisphere in emotional communication. *Brain, 114,* 1115-1127.

Bonda, E., Petrides, M., Frey, S., & Evans, A. C. (1994). Frontal cortex involvement in organised sequences of hand movements: Evidence from a positron emission tomography study. *Social Neuroscience Abstracts, 20* (7353).

Bontempi, B., & Durkin, T.P. (2007). *Dynamics of hippocampal-cortical interactions during memory consolidation: Insight from functional brain imaging.* Heidelberg: Springer-Verlag.

Bowlby, J. (1969). *Attachment.* New York: Basic Books.

Bowlby, J. (1988). *A secure base: Parent-child attachment and healthy human development*. New York: Basic Books.

Bracha, V., Zhao, D.A., Wunderlich, S.J., Morrissy, S.J. & Bloedel, J.R. (1997). Patients with cerebellar lesions cannot acquire but are able to retain conditioned eyeblink reflexes. *Brain, 120,* 1401-1413.

Bradshaw, J. (1990). *Homecoming: Reclaiming and championing your inner child.* New York: Bantam.

Brannon, L. & Feist, J. (2004). *Health Psychology* (5th ed). Thomson Wadsworth.

Bretherton, I. (1992). Social referencing, international communication, and the interfacing of minds in infancy. In S. Feinman (Ed.), *Social referencing and the social construction of reality in infancy* (pp. 57-77). New York: Plenum Press.

Bretherton, I. (1993). From dialogue to internal working models: The co-construction of self in relationships. In C. A. Nelson (Ed.), *Minnesota Symposia on Child Psychology: Vol. 26. Memory and affect in development* (pp. 237-264). Hillsdale, NJ: Erlbaum.

Brodsky, M., & Lombroso, P. J. (1998). Molecular mechanisms of developmental disorders. *Development and Pschopathology, 10.*

Bromberg-Martin, E. S., & Hikosaka, O. (2009). Midbrain Dopamine Neurons Signal Preference for Advance Information about Upcoming Rewards. *Neuron 63, 119–126.*

Brown, S. L. et al. (2009). Social closeness increases salivary progesterone in humans. *Hormones and Behavior 56, 108–111.*

Bucke, R. (1974). *Cosmic Consciousness, A Study in the Evolution of the Human Mind.* New York: Causeway Books.

Buckingham, M., & Clifton, D. (2001). *Now Discover Your Strengths.* The Free Press.

Burgdorf, J. & Panksepp, J. (2006). The neurobiology of positive emotions. *Neuroscience and Biobehavioral Reviews, 30,* 173-187.

Burns, R., & Gallini, J. (1983). The relation of cognitive and affective measures to achievement during an instructional sequence. *Instructional Science, 12,* 103-120.

Burow, P. (2007). *Core Beliefs: Harnessing the power.* Melbourne: Copernicus Publishing.

Cacioppe, R. (2000). *Creating Spirit at work: Re-visioning Organisation Development and Leadership - Part 1.* MCB University Press, Leadership and Organization Development Journal 21/2.

Cacioppe, R. (2000). *Creating Spirit at work: Re-visioning Organisation Development and Leadership - Part 2.* MCB University Press, Leadership and Organization Development Journal 21/2.

Cacioppo, J.T., & Bernston, G.C. (1992). Social psychological contributions to the decade of the brain: Doctrine of multilevel analysis. *American Psychologist, 47*(8), 1019-1028.

Cahill, L., et al. (1994). *Beta-adrenergic Activation and Memory for Emotional Events.* Nature.

Capra, F. (1984). *The Tao of physics: An exploration of the parallels between modern physics and eastern mysticism.* New York: Bantam. Capra, F. (1996). *The web of life.* New York: Doubleday.

Capra, F., & Steindl-Rast, D. (1975). *Belonging to the Universe.* San Francisco: Harper.

Casti, J.L. (2000). *Paradigms regained.* New York: William Morrow.

Cavanna, A. E., & Trimble, M. R., (2006). The precuneus: a review of its functional anatomy and behavioural correlates. *Brain (2006), 129, 564–583.*

Chalmers, D.J. (1996). *The conscious mind.* New York: Oxford University Press.

Chapman, E. et al. (2007). Fetal testosterone and empathy: Evidence from the Empathy Quotient (EQ) and the "Reading the Mind in the Eyes" Test. *Social Neuroscience, 1 (2), 135-148.*

Chatzkel, J.L. (2003). *Knowledge capital.* Oxford: Oxford University Press.

Chiron, C., Jambaque, I., Nabbout, R., Syrota, A., & Dulac, O. (1997). The right brain is dominant in human infants. *Brain, 120* (6), 1057-1065.

Chopra, D. (1993). *Ageless body, timeless mind: The quantum alternative to growing old.* New York: Harmony.

Chopra, D. (1989). *Quantum healing: Exploring the frontiers of mind/body medicine.* New York: Bantam.

Chopra, D. (2003). *Synchro Destiny.* Harmony Books.

Christman, S. D. (1994). The many side of the two sides of the brain. *Brain and Cognition, 26.*

Ciaramelli, E., Muccioli, M., Làdavas, E., & di Pellegrino, G. (2007). Selective deficit in personal moral judgment following damage to ventromedial prefrontal cortex. *Scan, 2,* 84-92.

Clark L. (1997). *Essential Celtic Mythology.* San Francisco: Thorsons.

Cogill, S. R., Caplan, H. L., Alexandra, H., Robson, K. M., & Kumar, R. (1986). Impact of maternal postnatal depression on cognitive development of young children. *British Medical Journal, 292* (6529), 1165-1167.

Colby, A., Kohlberg, L., Gibbs, J., & Lieberman, M. (1983). *A longitudinal study of moral judgment. Monographs of the Society for Research in Child Development,* 48, Nos. 1-2.

Colin, V. L. (1996). *Human attachment.* New York: McGraw-Hill.

Colinvaux, P. (1980). *The fate of nations: A biological theory of history.* New York: Simon and Schuster.

Collins, J. C., & Porras, J. I. (1996). Building your company's vision. *Harvard Business Review, September-October.*

Cope, M. (2000). *Know your value? Manage your knowledge and make it pay.* London:

Prentice Hall.

Cordoso, C. (2012). *Acute Intranasal Oxytocin Improves Positive Self-Perceptions of Personality.* A Thesis in the Department of Psychology. Presented in Partial Fulfillment of the Requirements for the Degree of Master of Arts (Psychology) at Concordia University, Montreal, Quebec, Canada.

Covey, S. (1992). *Principle Centred Leadership.* New York: Fireside.

Covey, S. R. (1990). *Principle Centred Leadership.* New York: Fireside.

Covey, S.R.W. (1989). *The seven habits of highly effective people.* New York: Free Press.

Cozolina, L. J. (2002). *The neuroscience of psychotherapy: Building and rebuilding the human brain.* New York: WW Norton and Company.

Craig, A.D. (2002). How do you feel? Interoception: the sense of the physiological condition of the body. *Nature Reviews Neuroscience, 3,* 655-666.

Craig, A.D. (2009). How do you feel – now? The anterior insula and human awareness. *Nature Reviews Neuroscience, 10,* 59-70.

Creem, S.H. & Proffitt, D.R. (2001). Defining the cortical visual systems "What", "Where" and "How". *Acta Psychologica, 107,* 43-68.

Crick, F. (1994). *The astonishing hypothesis: The scientific search for the soul.* New York: Scribner's Sons.

Crowe, E., & Higgins, T., (1997). Regulatory Focus and Strategic Inclinations: Promotion and Prevention in Decision-Making. *Organizational Behaviour and Human Decision Processes, 69, No. 2, 117–132.* Academic Press.

Csíkszentmihályi, Mihály (1990). *Flow: The Psychology of Optimal Experience.* New York: Harper and Row.

Damasio, A. R. (1994). *Descartes' error.* New York: Putnam.

Damasio, A. R. (1999). *The feeling of what happens.* New York: Harcourt Brace.

Damasio, A. R. (2003). *Looking for Espinoza.* Harcourt Inc.

Daniels, D. & Price, V. (2000). *The Essential Enneagram: The Definitive Personality Test and Self-Discovery Guide.* HarperCollins: San Francisco. Daruna, J.H. (2004). *Psychoneuroimmunology.* Elsevier .

Davis, C., Kleinman, J.T., Newhart, M., Heidler-Gray, J. & Hillis, A.E. (2006). Speech and language functions that depend on Broca's area. *Brain and Language, 99,* 8-219.

Dawes, R.M. (1988). *Rational Choice in an Uncertain World.* Harcourt Brace Jovanovich.

Dawson, G., Panagiotides, H., Klinger, L. G., & Hill, D. (1992). The role of frontal lobe functioning in the development of self-regulatory behaviour. *Brain and Cognition, 20.*

Dêbiec, J. (2007). From affiliative behaviours to romantic feelings: a role of nanopeptides. *Federation of European Biochemical Societies Letters, 581,* 2580-2586.

Decety, J. (1994). Mapping motor representations with positron emission tomography. *Nature, 371.*

Decety, J., Jackson, P.L., Sommerville, J.A., Chaminade, T., & Meltzoff, A.N. (2004). The neural bases of cooperation and competition: an fMRI investigation. *NeuroImage, 23*(2), 744-751.

Decety, J. et al. (2008). Children Are Naturally Prone To Be Empathic And Moral. Who caused the pain? *An fMRI investigation of empathy and intentionality in children. Neuropsychologia*; DOI: 10.1016/j.neuropsychologia.2008.05.026

Decety, J. (2010). Dissecting the Neural Mechanisms Mediating Empathy. *Emotion Review, 3 (1), 92–108.*

Demartini, J. F. (2002). *The breakthrough experience.* Carlsbad: Hay House.

Department. Of Psychology, Florida State University. (2007). *Junkies, Adrenaline Junkies, and Pleasure,* 10.1371/journal.

Descartes, R. (1984). *The philosophical writings of Descarts* (J. Cottingham, R. Stoothoff, & D. Murdock, Trans.). Cambridge: Cambridge University Press.

De Waal, F. (1989). *Peacemaking among primates.* New York: Penguin.

Dennett, D. C. (1991). *Consciousness Explained.* Boston: Little, Brown.

Desimone, R. (1991). Face-selective cells in the temporal cortex of monkeys. *Journal of Cognitive Neuroscience, 3.*

DiAngi, L. (2002). *The Magic is in the Extra Mile.* Erie: Larry DiAngi Productions.

Diamond, J. (1979). *Behavioral Kinesiology.* New York: Harper and Row.

Diamond, J. (1979a). *Your Body Doesn't Lie.* New York: Warner Books.

Diamond, M. C., Krech, D., & Rosenweig, M. R. (1966). The effects of enriched environment on the histology of the rat cerebral cortex. *Journal of Comparative Neurology, 123.*

Diamond, M. C., Scheibel, A. B., Murphy, G. M., & Harvey, T. (1985). On the brain of a scientist: Albert Einstein. *Experimental Neurology, 88.*

Dickerson, S. & Kemeny, M. (2004). Acute Stressors and Cortisol Responses: A Theoretical Integration and Synthesis of Laboratory Research. *Psychological Bulletin, 130, No. 3, 355–391.*

Diversi, T. (2006). *The Correlation between HOS Types and Body Shape.* (unp).

Doidge, N. (2007). *The brain that changes itself.* Melbourne: Scribe Publications.

Dolan, R. J. (1999). On the neurology of morals. *Nature Neuroscience, 2*(11).

Doughty, D.D., Shin, L.M., Alpert, N.M., Pitman, R.K., Orr, S.P., Lasko, M. et al. (1999). Anger in Healthy Men: A PET study using Script-Driven Imagery. *Society of Biological Psychiatry, 46,* 466-472.

Dowse, R. & Ehlers, M. (2005). Medicine labels incorporating pictograms: Do they influence understanding and adherence?, *Patient Education and Counseling, 58, (1).*

Drake, R. A., & Seligman, M. E. P. (1989). Self-serving biases in casual attributions as a function of altered activation asymmetry. *International Journal of Neuroscience,* 45.

Duhaime-Ross, A. (2013). Empathy and Disgust Do Battle in the Brain: An injured rat helps us understand the struggle between empathy and disgust. *Scientific American, June 15, 2013.*

Dunphy, D., Turner, D. & Crawford, M. (1997). Organizational learning as the creation of corporate competencies. *Journal of Management Development, 16* (4).

Dunn, E. W. et al. (2008). Spending Money on Others Promotes Happiness. Science 319, 1687-1688.

Easterlin, R.A., & Crimmins, E.M. (1991). Private materialism, personal self-fulfillment, family life, and public interest: The nature, effects, and causes of recent changes in the values of American youth. Public Opinion Quarterly, 55, 449-533.

Edelman, G. (1992). *Bright air, brilliant fire.* New York: Basic Books.

Eddington, K. M., Dolcos, F., Cabeza, R., Krishnan, K. R., & Strauman, T. J. (2007). Neural correlates of promotion and prevention goal activation: An fMRI study using an idiographic approach. *Journal of Cognitive Neuroscience, 19, 1152–1162.*

Eddington, K. M., Dolcos, F., McLean, A. N., Cabeza, R., Krishnan, K. R. R., and Strauman, T. J. (2009). Neural correlates of idiographic goal priming in depression: goal-specific dysfunctions in the orbitofrontal cortex. *Soc.Cogn.Affect.Neurosci. 4, 238–246.*

Eggert, N. (1998). *Contemplative Leadership for Entrepreneurial Organizations: Paradigms, Metaphors, and Wicked Problems.* Westport: Quorum Books.

Ehlers, A., & Margraf, J. (1987). Anxiety induced by false heart rate feedback in patients with panic disorder. *Behaviour Research and Therapy, 26.*

Eisenberg, N.I., & Lieberman, M.D. (in press). *Why it hurts to be left out: the neurocognitive overlap between physical and social pain.* Submitted to *Trends in Cognitive Science.*

Eisenberger, N.I., & Lieberman, M.D. *Conflict and Habits: a social cognitive neuroscience approach to the self. 4004.* CRC Press.

Eisenberger, N.I., Lieberman, M.D., & Williams, K.D. (2003). Does rejection hurt? An fMRI study of social exclusion. *Science, 302,* 290-292.

Eisenberger, N.I., & Lieberman, M.D. (2004). Why rejection hurts: a common neural alarm system for physical and social pain. *Trends in Cognitive Sciences, 8*(7), 294-300.

Eisenhardt, K.M., Kahwajy, J. L., & Bourgeois, L. J. (1997). How management teams can have a really good fight. *Harvard Business Review, July-August.*

Emde, R. (1990). Mobilising fundamental modes of development: Empathic availability and therapeutic action. *Journal of the American Psychoanalytic Association, 38,* 881-913.

Epstein, D. (1994). *The 12 stages of healing: A network approach to wholeness.* San Rafael, CA: Amber-Allen Publishing.

Esch, T., & Stefano, G.B. (2004). The neurobiology of pleasure, reward processes, addiction and their health implications. *Neuroendicronology Letters, 25*(4), 235-251.

Esch, T., & Stefano, G. B. (2005). The Neurobiology of Love. *Neuroendocrinology Letters 26(3):175–192.*

Eslinger, P. J. (1998). Neurological and neuropsychological bases of empathy. *European Neurology, 39,* 193-199.

Farrer, C., & Frith, C. D. (2002). Experiencing Oneself vs Another Person as Being the Cause of an Action: The Neural Correlates of the Experience of Agency. *NeuroImage 15, 596–603.*

Fast, N., Gruenfeld, D. K., Sivanathan, N., & Galinsky, A. (2009). Illusory Control: A Generative Force Behind Power's Far-Reaching Effects. *Psychological Science.* Downloaded from pss.sagepub.com at UQ Library on July 14, 2013

Feist, G.J. (1998). A meta-analysis of the impact of personality on scientific and artistic creativity. *Personality and Social Psychological Review, 2,* 290-309.

Feldman, R., Greenbaum, C. W., & Yirimiya, N. (1999). Mother-infant affect synchrony as an antecedent of the mergence of self-control. *Developmental Psychology, 35* (1), 223-231.

FeldmanHall, O., Mobbs, D., & Dalgleish, T. (2012). Deconstructing the brains moral network: dissociable functionality between the temporoparietal junction and ventro-medial prefrontal cortex. doi:10.1093/scan/nss139. Oxford University Press.

FeldmanHall, O., Dalgleish, T., & Mobbs, D., (2013). Alexithymia decreases altruism in real social decisions. *SciVerse ScienceDirect, Cortex 49, 899-904.*

Fellows, L. K., & Farah, M. J., (2003). Ventromedial frontal cortex mediates affective shifting in humans: evidence from a reversal learning paradigm. *Brain, 126, 1830-1837.*

Fenwick, P. (2011). The Neuroscience of Spirituality. Royal College of Psychiatrists.

Field, T. M., Healy, B., Goldstein, S., Perry, S., & Bendell, D. (1988). Infants of depressed mothers show 'depressed' behaviour even with non depressed adults. *Child Development, 59* (6), 1569-1579.

Field, T. M. (1997). The treatment of depressed mothers and their infants. In L. Murry & P. J. Cooper (Eds.), *Postpartum depression and child development* (pp. 221-236). New York: Guilford.

Fields, C. (2011). From "Oh, OK" to "Ah, yes" to "Aha!": Hyper-systemizing and the rewards of insight. *Personality and Individual Differences 50 (2011) 1159–1167.*

Filoteo, J. V., et al., (in press). Cortical and Subcortical Brain Regions Involved in Rule-

Based Category Learning. *NeuroReport.*

Fischer, H., Wik, G., & Fredrikson, M. (1997). Extraversion, Neuroticism and Brain Function: a PET study of personality. *Person. individ. Diff. 23 (2), 345-352.*

Fisher, B. (1988). Wandering in the wilderness: The search for women role models. Signs: Journal of Women in Culture and Society, 13, 211–233.

Fisher, C.D. & Ashkanasy, N. M. (2000). The emerging role of emotions in working life: An introduction. Journal of Organizational Behavior, 21, 123-129.

Fisher, H. (2004). *Why We Love.* New York: Henry Holt.

Fivush, R., & Hudson, J. A. (1990). *Knowing and remembering in young children.* New York: Cambridge University Press.

Fivush, R. (1994). Constructing narrative, emotion, and self in parent-child conversations about the past. In U. Neisser & R. Fivush (Eds.), *The remembered self: Construction and accuracy in the self-narrative* (pp. 136-157). New York: Cambridge University Press.

Fliessbach, K. et al., (2007). Social Comparison Affects Reward-Related Brain Activity in the Human Ventral Striatum. *Science, 318, 1305-1308.*

Focquaert, F., et al., (2007). Empathizing and systemizing cognitive traits in the sciences and humanities. *Personality and Individual Differences 43, 619–625.*

Focquaert, F., et al., (2010). Mindreading in individuals with an empathizing versus systemizing cognitive style: An fMRI study. *Brain Research Bulletin 83, 214–222.*

Fogassi, L., & Rizzolatti, G. (2013). The Mirror Mechanism as Neurophysiological Basis for Action and Intention Understanding. I*s Science Compatible with Free Will?: Exploring Free Will and Consciousness in the Light of Quantum Physics and Neuroscience, DOI 10.1007/978-1-4614-5212-6_9, Springer Science & Business Media, LLC, 117-134.*

Fonagy, P., Steele, M., Steele, H., Moran, G. S., & Higgitt A.C. (1991). The capacity to understand mental states: The reflective self in parent and child and its significance for security of attachment. *Infant Mental Health Journal, 12*(3), 201-218.

Fontana, D. (1993). *The Secret Language Of Symbols.* London: Pavilion Books.

Forrester, J. (1994). *Learning through systems dynamics as preparation for the 21st century.* MIT Systems Dynamics Education Project.

Forrester, J. (1956). *The beginning of systems dynamics.* MIT Systems Dynamics Education Project.

Foster, B. & Seeker, K. (1997). *Coaching for Peak Performance.* San Francisco: Jossey-Bass Pfeiffer.

Fox, N. A. (1994). Dynamic cerebral processes underlying emotion regulation. In N. A. Fox (Ed.), *The development of emotion regulation: Biological and behavioural considerations. Monographs of the Society for Research in Child Development, 59* (2-3, Serial No. 240).

Frackowiak, R.S.J. (Ed.). (2004). *Human brain function, 2nd edition*. San Diego: Elsevier Academic.

Freyd, J. J. (1987). Dynamic mental representations. *Psychological Review, 94*, 427-438.

Frijda, N. H. (1986). *The Emotions*. Cambridge, UK: Cambridge University Press.

Frith, C. (2002). Attention to action and awareness of other minds. *Consciousness and Cognition, 11*, 481-487.

Frith, C.D., & Frith, U. (1999). Interacting minds: A biological basis. *Science, 286*, 1692-1695.

Fritz, R. (1984). *The Path Of Least Resistance*. New York: Fawcett Columbine.

Gaillard R, Dehaene S, Adam C, Clémenceau S, Hasboun D, et al. (2009). *Converging Intracranial Markers of Conscious Access*. PLoS Biol 7(3): e1000061. Doi:10.1371/journal.pbio.1000061.

Gallagher, H.L. & Frith, C.D. (2003). Functional Imaging of Theory of Mind. *Trends in Cognitive Sciences, 7*, 51-96.

Gallese, V., Fadiga, L., Fogassi, L., & Rizzolatti, G. (1996). Action recognition in the premotor cortex. *Brain, 119*, 593-609.

Gauther, I., et al., (1999). Activation of the middle fusiform 'face area' increases with expertise in recognizing novel objects. *Nature Neuroscience 2 (6), 568-573*.

George, C., & Solomon, J. (1996). Representational models of relationships: Links between caregiving and attachment. *Infant Mental Health Journal, 17* (3), 198-216.

Gigerenzer, (1996). The psychology of good judgment: Frequency formats and simple algorithms. *Journal of Medical Decision Making, 16*.

Goel, V., Grafman, J., Sadato, N., & Halletta, M. (1995). Modelling other minds. *NeuroReport, 6*, 1741-1746.

Goldenfeld N., Baron-Cohen, S., & Wheelwright, S. (2005). Empathizing and Systemizing in Males, Females and Autism. *Clinical Neuropsychiatry 2 (6), 338-345*.

Goldberg, E. (2001). *The Executive Brain*. Oxford University Press.

Goldberg, E. (2005). *The wisdom paradox*. London: Pocket Books.

Goldberg, E., & Costa, L. D. (1981). Hemispheric differences in the acquisition and use of descriptive systems. *Brain and Language, 14*.

Goleman, D. (1995). *Emotional Intelligence*. New York: Bantam Books.

Goleman, D. (2000). Leadership That Gets Results. *Harvard Business Review, March-April*.

Goleman, D. (1998). *Working with emotional intelligence*. London: Bloomsbury Publishing.

Goleman, D. (2006). *Social intelligence: The new science of human relationships*. New York, NY: Bantam Books.

Goleman, D., Boyatzis, R., & McKee, A. (2002). *Primal leadership: realizing the power of emotional intelligence.* Boston: Harvard Business School Press.

Gonzalez-Liencres, C. Shamay-Tsoory, S. G. & Brune, M. (2013). Review Towards a neuroscience of empathy: Ontogeny, phylogeny, brain mechanisms,context and psychopathology. *Neuroscience and Biobehavioral Reviews 37, 1537– 1548.*

Goodworth, C. (1988). *The secrets of successful leadership and people Management.* Heinman Professional Publishing.

Grafton, S. T., Arbib, M. A., Fadiga, L., & Rizzolatti, G. (1996). Localisation of grasp representations in humans by positron emission tomography. 2: Observation compared with imagination. *Experimental Brain Research, 112* (1), 103-111.

Graham, G. (2002). If you want honesty, break some rules. *Harvard Business Review, April.*

Graham, A. M., Fisher, P. A., & Pfeifer, J. H. (2013). What Sleeping Babies Hear: An fMRI Study of Interparental Conflict and Infants' Emotion Processing. *Psychol Sci. 24(5): 782–789. doi:10.1177/0956797612458803.* NIH-PA Author Manuscript.

Greene, R. & Elffers, J. (1998). *48 Laws of Power,* New York: Viking Press.

Greenfield, S. (2000). *The private life of the brain.* London: Penguin Books.

Grisaru, N., Chudakov, B., Yaroslavsky, Y., & Belmaker, R. H. (1998). Transcranial magnetic stimulation in mania: A controlled study. *American Journal of Psychiatry, 155*(11).

Gunnar, M. R., & Stone, C. (1984). The effects of positive maternal affect on infant responses to pleasant, ambiguous and fear-provoking toys. *Child Development, 55,* 1231-1236.

Gunnar, M. R. (1992). Reactivity of the hypothalamic-pituitary-adrenocortical system to stressors in normal infants and children. *Pediatrics, 90* (3), 491-497.

Gurdjieff, G. (1950). *Beelzebub's Tales To His Grandson.* London: Broadway house.

Han, S., & Northoff, G. (2009). Understanding the self: a cultural neuroscience approach. *Progress in Brain Research, 178, 203-212.*

Hanson, J. L., et al., (2012). Structural Variations in Prefrontal Cortex Mediate the Relationship between Early Childhood Stress and Spatial Working Memory. *The Journal of Neuroscience, 32(23):7917–7925.*

Harackiewicz, J. M., Barron, K. E., & Elliot, A. J. (1998). Rethinking achievement goals: When are they adaptive for college students and why? *Educational Psychologist, 33,* 1-21.

Harbaugh, W. T. et al. (2007). Neural Responses to Taxation and Voluntary Giving Reveal Motives for Charitable Donations. *Science 316, 1622-1625.*

Hariri, A. R., & Holmes, A. (2006). Genetics of emotional regulation: the role of the serotonin transporter in neural function. *Trends in Cognitive Sciences, 10*(4), 182-191.

Hariri, A.R. et al. (2000). Modulating Emotional Response: Effects of a Neocortical Network on the Limbic System. *NeuroReport, 8,* 11-43.

Harlow, J. (1868). Recovery from the passage of an iron bar through the head. *Publication of the Massachusetts Medical Society, 2.*

Harris, M., & Butterworth, G. (2002). *Developmental Psychology.* London: Psychology Press.

Harris, T. (1976). *I'm OK - You're OK: A practical guide to transactional analysis.* London: Pan Books.

Harter, S., Bresnick, S., Bouchey, H. A., & Whitsell, N. R. (1997). The Development of multiple role-related selves during adolescence. *Development and Psychopathology, 9,* 835-854.

Hasselmo, M. E., Rolls, E. T., & Baylis, G. C. (1989). The role of expression and identity in the face-selective responses of neurons in the temporal visual cortex of the monkey. *Behaviour Brain Research, 32* (3), 203-218.

Hawkins, D.R. (1995). *Power versus Force: An Anatomy of Consciousness.* Carlsbad: Hay House.

Heim, S., Eickhoff, A.B. & Amunts, K. (2008). Specialisation in Broca's region for semantic, phonological, and syntactic fluency? *NeuroImages, 40,* 1362-1368.

Herald, J. (2004). *What are you waiting for?* Crows Nest: Allen & Unwin.

Hesse, E. (1999). The adult attachment interview: Historical and current perspectives. In J. Cassidy & P. R. Shaver (Eds.), *Handbook of attachment: theory, research, and clinical applications* (pp. 395-433). New York: Guilford.

Hill, G. W. (1982). Groups versus individual performance: Are N+1 heads better than one? *Psychological Bulletin, 91.*

Hirschhorn, L. (2002). Campaigning for change. *Harvard Business Review, July.*

Hirosawa, T. et al., (2012). Oxytocin attenuates feelings of hostility depending on emotional context and individuals' characteristics. *Scientific Reports, 2, 384.* DOI: *10.1038/srep00384*

Hofer, M. A. (1994). Hidden regulators in attachment, separation, and loss. *Monographs of the Society for Research in Child Development, 59* (2-3), 192-207.

Horney, K. (1945). *Our Inner Conflicts.* New York: Norton.

Houf, H. (1945). *What religion is and does: an introduction to the study of its problems and values.* New York: Harper and Brothers.

Hout, T. M., & Carter, J. C. (1995). Getting it done: New roles for Senior Executives. *Harvard Business Review, November-December.*

Howard, G. S. (1991). Culture tales: A narrative approach to thinking, cross-cultural psychology, and psychotherapy. *American Psychologist, 46*(3), 187-197.

Hoyle, R. L., Bromberger, B., Groversman, H. D., Klauber, M. R., Dixon, S. D., and Snyder, J. M. (1983). Regional anesthesia during newborn circumcision: Effect on infant pain response. *Clinical Pediatrics (Philadelphia), 22*. http://en.wikipedia. org/wiki/Neuroscience retrieved 20/5/2007.

Hubel, D.H. (1967). Effects of distortion of sensory input on the visual system of kittens. *Physiologist, 10*(1), 17-45.

Hudson, K. (1999). *Transforming a Conservative Company - One Laugh at a Time.* Harvard Business School Press.

Hurlemann, R. et al., (2010). Oxytocin Enhances Amygdala-Dependent, Socially Reinforced Learning and Emotional Empathy in Humans. *The Journal of Neuroscience, 30(14):4999 –5007.*

Huskinson, L. (2004). *Nietzsche and Jung: The Whole Self in the Union of Opposites.* Hove.

Huxley, T. (1874). On the hypothesis that animals are automata. In *Collected Essays.* London, 1893-94.

Izuma K., Saito, D., & Sadato, N. (2008). Processing of Social and Monetary Rewards in the Human Striatum. *Neuron 58, 284–294, April 24, 2008.* Elsevier Inc.

Jack I. J., et al., fMRI reveals reciprocal inhibition between social and physical cognitive domains. *NeuroImage 66, 385–401.*

James, W. (1890). *The Principles of Psychology.* New York: Holt.

Janoff-Bulman, R. (1992). *Shattered assumptions: Towards a new psychology of trauma.* New York: Free Press.

Jantsch, E. (1975). *Design for Evolution.* New York: George Brazillier.

Jason, G., & Pajurkova, E. (1992). Failure of metacontrol: Breakdown in behavioural unity after lesions of the corpus callosum and inferomedial frontal lobes. *Cortex, 28.*

Jauch, J. M. (1968). *Foundations of Quantum Mechanics.* Reading, Mass.: Addison-Wesley.

Jaynes, J. (1976). *The origins of consciousness in the breakdown of the bicameral mind.* Boston: Houghton Mifflin.

Jeannerod, M., Arbib, M. A., Rizzolatti, G., & Sakata, H. (1995). Grasping objects: The cortical mechanism of visuomotor transformation. *Trends in Neuroscience, 18* (7), 314-320.

Jeffers, S. (1987). *Feel The Fear and do it Anyway.* Butler Bowdon.

Jeffers, S. (1992). *Dare to connect: Reaching out in romance, friendship and the workplace.* New York: Fawcett Columbine.

Jordan, J., Sivanathan, N., & Galinsky, A. (2012). Something to Lose and Nothing to Gain: The Role of Stress in the Interactive Effect of Power and Stability on Risk Taking. *Administrative Sceince Quarterly 2011 56: 530.* Sage Publications. http://asq.sagepub.com/content/56/4/530 retrieved 14/7/2013.

Johnson, Dr S. (1999). *Who moved my cheese?* London: Vermilion.

Johnson, M. (1987). *The body in the mind.* Chicago: University of Chicago Press.

Johnson, M., et al., (2006). Dissociating medial frontal and posterior cingulate activity during self-reflection. *SCAN 1, 56-64.* Oxford University Press.

Joseph, R. (1996). *Neuropsychiatry, neuropsychology, and clinical neuroscience.* Baltimore: Williams and Wilkins.

Judith, A. (1996). *Eastern body, western mind: Psychology and the chakra system as a path to the self.* Berkley, CA: Celestial Arts.

Jueptner, M., & Weiller, C. (1998). A review of differences between basal ganglia and cerebellar control of movements as revealed by functional imaging studies. *Brain, 121*(8), 1437-1449.

Jung, C. (1969). *Aion.* Princeton: Princeton University Press.

Kahneman, D. (2003). A perspective on judgment and choice: Mapping bounded rationality. *American Psychologist, 58*(9), 697-720. Kagan, J. (1994). *Galen's Prophecy,* New York: Basic Books.

Kalbe, E. et al. (2010). Dissociating cognitive from affective theory of mind: A TMS study. *ScienceDirect Cortex 46, 769–780.*

Kalin, N.H., Shelton, S.E., & Lynn, C.M. (1995). Opiate systems in mother and infant primates coordinate intimate contact during reunion. *Psychoneuroimmunology, 20,* 735-742.

Kaplan, R.S., & Norton, D.P. (1996). *The balanced scorecard: Translating strategy into action.* Boston: Harvard Business School Press.

Keenan, J.P., McCutcheon, B., Freund, S., Gallup, G.G. Jr, Sanders, G.,*Pascual-Leone, A. (1999). Left hand advantage in a self-face recognition task. *Neuropsychologia, 37*(12), 1421-1425.

Kehoe, P., & Blass, E.M. (1989). Opioid-mediation of separation distress in 10-day-old rats: Reversal of stress with maternal stimuli. *Developmental Psychobiology, 19*(4), 385-398.

Kekes, J. (1995). *Moral Wisdom and Good Lives.* Ithaca, NY: Cornell University Press.

Kelley, R. E. (1998). *How to be a star at work.* New York: Times Books.

Kelner, S., Rivers, C.A., & O'Connell K.H. (1996). *Managerial Style as a Behavioural Predictor of Organisational Climate.* Boston: McBer and Company.

Keltner, D., & Haidt, J . (2003). Approaching awe, a moral, spiritual, and aesthetic emotion. *Cognition and Emotion, 17,* 297-314.

Kemp, A. H. et al. (2012). Oxytocin Increases Heart Rate Variability in Humans at Rest: Implications for Social Approach-Related Motivation and Capacity for Social Engagement. *PLOS One 7 (8) e44014.*

Kehoe, P., & Blass, E. M. (1989). Conditioned opioid release in ten-day-old rats: Reversal of stress with maternal stimuli. *Developmental Psychobiology, 19*(4).

Kersey, D., & Bates, M. (1984). *Please Understand me (Sth Ed.).* Prometheus Nemesis

Books Co.

Keverne, E. B., Martens, N. D., & Tuite, B. (1989). Beta-endorphin concentrations in cerebrospinal fluid of monkeys are influenced by grooming relationships. *Psychoneuroendocrinology.*

Kim, D. (1993). *The Systems Thinker.* Pegasus Communications.

Klein, S. (2006). *The Science of Happiness.* Carlton North, Vic: Scribe publications.

Klein, E., Kreinin, I., Chistyakov, A., Koren, D., Mecz, L., Marmur, S. et al. (1999). Therapeutic efficacy of right prefrontal slow repetitive transcranial magnetic stimulation in major depression. *Archives of General Psychiatry, 56* (4), 315-320.

Knowles, P.A., Conner, R.L., & Panksepp, J. (1989). Opiate effects on social behaviour of juvenile dogs as a function of social deprivation. *Pharmacology, Biochemistry and Behaviour, 33* (3), 533-537.

Koban, L., Pichon, S., and Vuilleumier, P. (2013). Responses of medial and ventrolateral prefrontal cortex to interpersonal conflict for resources. Oxford University Press. doi:10.1093/scan/nst020

Koestler, A. (1967). *The Ghost in the Machine.* London: Hutchinson.

Kosfeld, M. et al. (2005). Oxytocin increases trust in humans. *Nature, 435, 673-676.*

Kotter, J. P. (1999). What Leaders Really Do. *Harvard Business Review.* Cambridge .

Kotter, J. P. (1995). Leading Change: Why Transformation Efforts Fail. *Harvard Business Review, March-April.*

Kouzes, J., & Posner, B. (1993). *Credibility, How Leaders Gain and Lose It, Why People Demand It.* San Francisco: Jossey-Bass.

Krapp, A., & Fink, B. (1992). The development and function of interests during the critical transition from home to preschool. In K.A Renninger, S. Hidi, & A. Krapp (Eds.), *The role of interest in learning and development* (pp. 397-430). Hillsdale, NJ: Lawrence Erlbaum.

Krause, D. (1995). *The Art of War for Executives.* Perigee Book.

Kretschmer, E. (1925). *Physique and Character. International Library of Psychology.* Routledge. Great Britain.

Kubler-Ross, E. (1970). *On Death and Dying.* New York: MacMillan.

Kuhn, T.S. (1962). *The Structure of Scientific Revolutions.* Chicago: University of Chicago Press.

Lamm, C., Decety, J., & Singer, T. (2010). Meta-analytic evidence for common and distinct neural networks associated with directly experienced pain and empathy for pain. *NeuroImage 54 (2011) 2492–2502.*

Langer, E. J. (1978). Rethinking the role of thought in social interaction. In J. H. Harvey, W. Ickes, & R. F. Kidd (Eds.), *New directions in attribution research, 2,* pp. 35-58). Hillsdale, NJ: Erlbaum.

Lapid-Bogda, G., (2004). *Bringing Out the Best in Yourself at Work: How to Use the*

Enneagram System for Success. Santa Monica: McGraw-Hill.

Larsen, R.J., Kasimatis, M., & Frey, K. (1992). Facilitating the furrowed brow: An unobtrusive test of the facial feedback hypothesis applied to unpleasant affect. *Cognition and Emotion, 6,* 321-338.

Le Doux, J. (1998). *The emotional brain*. Phoenix: Orion Books Ltd.

Lerner, J. S. & Keltner, D. (2000). Beyond valence: Toward a model of emotion-specific influences on judgement and choice. *Cognition and Emotion, 14 (4), 473-493.*

Levine, S., Haltmeyer, G. C., Karas, G. G., & Denenberg, V. H. (1967). Physiological and behavioural effects of infantile stimulation. *Physiology and Behaviour, 2*(1).

Levy, J. (1969). Possible basis for the evolution of the human brain. *Nature, 224.*

Lewicki, P., Hill, T., & Czyzewska, M. (1992). Non-conscious acquisition of information. *American Psychologist, 47*(6).

Lewis, C.S. (1960). *Four Loves*. Harvest Books.

Lieberman, M.D., & Eisenberger, N.I. (2004). Conflict and habits: a social cognitive neuroscience approach to the self. In Tesser, A., Wood, J., Stapel, D. (Eds.), *On Building, Regulating and Defending the Self: a Psychological Perspective* (pp. 77-102). New York, NY: Psychology Press.

Lieberman, M.D., & Eisenberger, N.I. (2009). Pains and pleasures of social life. *Science, 323,* 890-891.

Lieberman, M.D., Gaunt, R., Gilbert, D.T., & Tope, Y. (2002). Reflexion and reflection: A social cognitive neuroscience approach to attributional inference. *Advances in Experimental Psychology, 34,* 199-249.

Lieberman, M.D., Schreiber, D., & Ochsner, K.N. (2003). Is political cognition like riding a bicycle? How cognitive neuroscience can inform research on political thinking. *Political Psychology, 24*(4), 681-704.

Lieberman, M. et al. (2005). A Pain by Any Other Name (Rejection, Exclusion, Ostracism) Still Hurts the Same: The Role of Dorsal Anterior Cingulate Cortex in Social and Physical Pain. In J. Cacioppo et al. (Eds.), *Social Neuroscience: People Thinking About Thinking People.* Cambridge, Mass.: MIT Press.

Liebert, R.M., & Liebert L.L. (1998). *Personality: Strategies & Issues Eighth Edition.* New York: Brooks Cole Publishing.

Liotti, M., & Tucker, D. M. (1992). Right hemisphere sensitivity to arousal and depression. *Brain and Cognition, 18,* 138-151.

Llinas, R. R. (1990). Intrinsic electrical properties of mammalian neurons and CNS function. *Fidia Research Foundation Neuroscience Award Lectures, 4.*

Loewenstein, G.F. (1994). The psychology of curiosity: A review and reinterpretation. *Psychological Bulletin, 116*(1), 75-98.

Lord, C. G., Ross, L., and Lepper, M. (1979). Biased assimilation and attitude polarisation: The effects of prior theories on subsequently considered evidence. *Journal of Personality and Social Psychology, 37* (11), 2098-2109.

Lorenz, E. N. (1963). *Deterministic nonperiodic flow.* J. Atmos. Sci. 20: 130–141.

Lowen, A. (1958). *Language of the Body.* New York: Collier Books.

Lupien, S. J., et al., (2009). Effects of stress throughout the lifespan on the brain, behaviour and cognition. *Nature Reviews, Neuroscience, 10, 434-445.*

MacLean, P.D. (1985). Brain evolution relating to family, play, and the separative call. *Archives of General Psychiatry, 42,* 405-417.

MacLean, P. D. (1985). The psychobiological functions of dissociation. *American Journal of Hypnosis, 26*(2).

Maier, S.F., & Seligman, M.E.P. (1976). Learned helplessness: Theory and evidence. *Journal of Experimental Psychology: General, 105,* 3-46.

Main, M. (1995). Attachment: Overview, with implications for clinical work. In S. Goldberg, R. Muir, & J. Kerr (Eds.), *Attachment theory: Social , developmental, and clinical perspectives* (pp. 407-474). Hillsdale, NJ: Analytic Press.

Main, M., & Goldwyn, R. (1984). *Adult attachment scoring and classification system.* Unpublished manuscript, University of California at Berkeley.

Main, M., & Goldwyn, R. (1984). *Adult attachment scoring and classification system.* Unpublished manuscript, University of California at Berkeley.

Main, M., & Solomon, J. (1990). Procedures for identifying infants as disorganised/disorientated during the Ainsworth Strange Situation. In M. T. Greenberg, D. Cicchetti, & E. M. Cummings (Eds.), *Attachment in the preschool years: Theory, research, and intervention* (pp. 121-160). Chicago: University of Chicago Press.

Main, M., Kaplan, N., & Cassidy, J. (1985). Security in infancy, childhood, and adulthood: A move to the level of representation. In I. Bretherton & E. Waters (Eds.), Growing points of attachment theory and research. *Monographs of the Society for Research in Child Development, 50* (1-2), 66-104.

Malinkowski, B. (1984). The role of myth in life. In A. Dundes (Ed.), *Sacred narrative* (pp.193-206). Berkeley: University of California Press.

Markovits, Y., et al., (2008). Regulatory foci and organizational commitment. *Journal of Vocational Behavior 73, 485-489.*

Martin-Araguz, A., Bustamante-Martinez, C., Fernandez-Armayor, A., & Moreno-Martinez, J. (2002). Neuroscience in al-Andalus and its influence on medieval scholastic medicine. *Revista de neurología, 34* (9).

Maslow, A. H. (1964). *Toward a psychology of being.* Princeton, NJ: Van Nostrand.

Matthews, J. (1991). *The Celtic Shaman: A Practical Guide.* London: Rider.

McAndrew, F. T., (2009). The interacting roles of testosterone and challenges to status in human male aggression. *Aggression and Violent Behavior.* Elsevier Ltd.

McCarthy, G. (1995). Functional neuroimaging of memory. *The Neuroscientist, 1*(3).

McCaskey, M. B. (1979). The hidden messages managers send. *Harvard Business Review, November-December.*

McCraty, R. (2002). Influence of cardiac afferent input on heart-brain synchronization and cognitive performance. *International Journal of Psychophysiology, 45*(1-2), 72-73.

McCraty, R., Atkinson, R., & Tiller, W. (1999). The role of physiological coherence in the detection and measurement of cardiac energy exchange between people. Paper presented at the Tenth International Montreux Congress on Stress, Montreux, Switzerland.

McCraty, R., & Watkins, A. (1996). *Autonomic Assessment Report Interpretation Guide,* Boulder Creek, California: Institute of HeartMath.

Meaney, M., Aiken, D. H., Viau, V., Sharma, S., & Sarrieau, A. (1989). Neonatal handling alters adrenocortical negative feedback sensitivity and hippocampal type II glucocorticoid receptor binding in the rat. *Neuroendocrinology, 50.*

Meaney, M. J., Diorio, J., Francis, D., Weaver, S., Yau, J., Chapman, K., & Seckl, J. R. (2000). Postnatal handling increases the expression of CAMP-inducible transcription factors in the rat hippocampus: The effects of thyroid hormones and serotonin. *The Journal of Neuroscience, 20*(10).

Mehta, P. H., & Josephs, R. A., (2006). Testosterone change after losing predicts the decision to compete again. *Hormones and Behavior 50, 684–692.*

Melchizedek, D. (1990). *The Ancient Secret of the Flower of Life.* Flagstaff: Light Technology Publishing.

Meyer, M. (2009). How Culture Shapes Our Mind and Brain. Weblog *http://brainblogger.com/2009/10/10/how-culture-shapes-our-mind-and-brain.*

Meyers, C. A., Berman, S. A., Scheibel, R. S., & Hayman, A. (1992). Case report: Acquired antisocial personality disorder associated with unilateral left orbital frontal lobe damage. *Journal of Psychiatry and Neuroscience, 17*(3), 121-125.

Miller, H., Alvarez, V., & Miller, N. (1990). *The psychopathology and psychoanalytic psychotherapy of compulsive caretaking.* Unpublished manuscript.

Miller, P.J., & Sperry, R.W. (1988). Early talk about the past: The origins of conversational stories of personal experience. *Journal of Child Language, 15*(2), 293-315.

Mintzberg, H., Ahirstrand, B., and Lapel J. (1998). *Strategy Safari.* New York: The Free Press.

Mitchell, K. J., et al., (2009). Age-Group Differences in Medial Cortex Activity Associated with Thinking About Self-Relevant Agendas. *Psychol Aging. 2009 June ; 24(2): 438–449.* NIH Author Manuscript.

Moll, J., et al., (2005). The neural basis of human moral cognition. *Nature Reviews, Neuroscience, 6, 799-809.*

Mölle, M., Marshall, L., Lutzenberger, W., Pietrowsky, R., Fehm, H.L., & Born,

J. (1996). Enhanced dynamic complexity in the human EEG during creative thinking. *Neuroscience Letters, 208*(1), 61-64.

Moore, T. (1992). *Care of the Soul.* HarperCollins Publishers.

Moore, T. (1994). *Soul mates: Honoring the mysteries of love and relationship.* New York: Harper Perennial.

Moskovitz & Grant (2009). *The Psychology of Goals.* New York: The Guildford Press

Moriguchi, Y., et al., (2006). Impaired self-awareness and theory of mind: An fMRI study of mentalizing in alexithymia. *NeuroImage 32, 1472 – 1482.*.

Moriguchi, Y., et al., (2007). Empathy and Judging Other's Pain: An fMRI Study of Alexithymia. *Cerebral Cortex 17:2223-2234.*

Myss, C. (2002). *Sacred Contracts: Awakening Your Divine Potential.* Harmony.

Myss, C. (1996). *Anatomy of the spirit: The seven stages of power and healing.* New York: Crown Publishers.

Nataraja, S. (2008). *The blissful brain: Neuroscience and proof of the power of meditation.* London: Gaia Publications.

Nelson, C. A., (Eds.). (1993). *Minnesota symposia on child psychology: Vol.26. Memory and effect in development.* Hillsdale, NJ: Erlbaum.

Nelson, K. (1993). Events, narratives, memory: What develops? In C.A. Nelson (Ed.), *Minnesota Symposia in Child Psychology: Vol. 26. Memory and affect in development* (pp. 1-24). Hillsdale, NJ: Lawrence Erlbaum Associates, Inc.

Nelson, R. J. & Trainor, B. C. 2007. Neural mechanisms of aggression. *Nature Reviews Neuroscience, 8,* 536-546.

Nichols, K., & Champness, B. (1971). Eye gaze and the GRS. *Journal of Experimental Social Psychology, 7.*

Nichols, R. G., & Stevens, L. A. (1957). Listening to people. *Harvard Business Review,* September-October.

Nisbett, R. E., & Ross, L. D. (1980). *Human Inference: Strategies and Shortcomings of Social Judgment.* Englewood Cliffs, NJ: Prentice-Hall.

Nishitani, N., & Hari, R. (2000). Temporal dynamics of cortical representation for action. *Proceedings of the National Academy of Science, 97*(2), 913-918.

Nix, G. A., Ryan, R. M., Manly, J. B., & Deci, E. L. (1999). Revitalization through self-regulation: The effects of autonomous and controlled motivation on happiness and vitality. *Journal of Experimental Social Psychology, 35,* 266-284.

Noriuchi, M., Kikuchi, Y., & Senoo, A. (2008). The Functional Neuroanatomy of Maternal Love: Mother's Response to Infant's Attachment Behaviors. *Society of Biological Psychiatry, 63,* 415- 423.

O'Connel, B. (1997). *Mindreading.* Cox & Wyman Ltd.

O'Doherty, J., Kringelback, M. L., Rolls, E. T., Hornak, J., & Andres, C. (2001). Abstract reward and punishment representations in the human orbitofrontal cortex. *Nature*

Neuroscience, 4(1), 95-102.

Oatley, K. (1992). Integrative action of narrative. In D. J. Stein & J. E. Young (Eds.), *Cognitive science and clinical disorders* (pp. 151-172), New York: Academic. Ochs, E., & Capps, L. (2001). *Living narrative: Creating lives in everyday storytelling.* Cambridge, MA: Harvard University Press.

Ochsner, K. et al. (2004). For Better or for Worse: Neural Systems Supporting the Cognitive Down- and Up-regulation of Negative Emotion. *NeuroImage, 23,* 483-99.

Ochsner, K. et al. (2006). How Thinking Controls Feeling: A Social Cognitive Neuroscience Approach. In P. Winkleman, & E. Harmon-Jones (Eds.), *Social Neuroscience.* New York: Oxford University Press.

Ochsner, K. N., Bunge, S. A., Gross, J. J., & Gabrieli, J. D. (2002). Rethinking feelings: an FMRI study of the cognitive regulation of emotion. *Journal of Cognitive Neuroscience, 14(8), 1215-1229.*

Oei, N. Y. L., et al., (2012). Stress shifts brain activation towards ventral affective areas during emotional distraction. *SCAN (2012) 7, 403-412.*

Oppenheim, D., Nir, A., Warren, S., & Emde, R.N. (1997). Emotion regulation in mother-child narrative co-construction: Associations with children's narratives and adaptation. *Developmental Psychology, 33,* 284-294.

Ornstein, R. (1997). *The right mind: Making sense of the hemispheres.* New York: Harcourt Brace.

Osman, M. (2012). The role of reward in dynamic decision making. *Frontiers in Neuroscience 6 (35).*

Overmier, J.B., & Seligman, M.E.P. (1967). Effects of inescapable shock upon subsequent escape and avoidance behaviour. *Journal of Comparative and Physiological Psychology, 63,* 23-33.

Pagano, B., & Pagano, E. (2004). *Transparency Edge: How Credibility Can Make Or Break You In Business.* New York: McGraw-Hill.

Palmer, H. (1998). *Inner Knowing: Consciousness, Creativity, Insight, and Intuition.* New York: Jeremy Tarcher/Putnam.

Palmer, H. (1998). *The Enneagram Advantage: Putting the 9 Personality Types to Work in the Office.* New York: Harmony Books.

Palmer, H. (1995). *The Enneagram in Love and Work: Understanding Your Intimate & Business Relationships.* San Francisco: Harper/Collins.

Palmer, H. (1988). *The Enneagram: The Definitive Guide to the Ancient System for Understanding Yourself and the Others in Your Life.* San Francisco: Harper/SF.

Palmer, H. (1995). *The Pocket Enneagram.* San Francisco: Harper/SF.

Panksepp, J. (1998). *Affective neuroscience: The foundation of human and animal emotions.* New York: Oxford University Press.

Panksepp, J., Nelson, E., & Siviy, S. (1994). Brain opioids and mother-infant social motivation. *Acta Paediatrica Supplement, 397*, 40-46.

Parkes, C. M., Stevenson-Hinde, J., & Marris, P. (1991). *Attachment across the life cycle.* London: Routledge.

Pascarella, P. (2003). Workers Without Borders: Creating Bonds When Workers Have No Loyalty. In *Business: the Ultimate Resource.* China Citic Press.

Pascual-Leone, A., Nguyet, D., Cohen, L.G., Brasil-Neto, J.P., Cammarota, A., Hallett, M. (1995). Modulation of muscle responses evoked by transcranial magnetic stimulation during the acquisition of new fine motor skills. *Journal of Neurophysiology, 74,* 1037–1045.

Pascual-Leone, A., et al., (1996). The role of the dorsolateral prefrontal cortex in implicit procedural learning. *Exp Brain Res 107:479-485.* Springer-Verlag.

Pavot, W., Diener, E., & Fujita, F. (1990). Extraversion and happiness. *Personality and Individual Differences, 11,* 1299-1306.

Pearsall, P. (1999). *The heart's code: Tapping the wisdom and power of our heart energy.* London: Bantam.

Perls, F. S. (1969). *Ego, Hunger and Aggressio.* New York: Vintage Books.

Perner, J., & Ruffman,T. (1995). Episodic memory and autonoetic consciousness: Developmental evidence and a theory of childhood amnesia. *Journal of Experimental Child Psychology, 59*(3), 516-548.

Perry, A. et al., (2010). Intranasal oxytocin modulates EEG mu/alpha and beta rhythms during perception of biological motion. *Psychoneuroendocrinology (2010) 35,* 1446—1453.

Perry, B.D., Pollard, R.A., Blakley, T.I., Baker, W.L., & Vigilante, D. (1995). Childhood Trauma, the Neurobiology of Adaptation and 'Use-Dependent' *Infant Mental Health* Development of the Brain – How 'States' become 'Traits'. *Journal, 16* (4), Winter.

Peterson, C.I. & Seligman, M.E.P. (2004). *Character strengths and virtues: A handbook and classification.* Washington, DC: APA Press and Oxford University Press.

Phillips, H. (2004). The cells that make us human. *New Scientist, 2452*(19), 32-36.

Pierrehumbert, B., et al., (2012). Adult attachment representations predict cortisol and oxytocin responses to stress. *Attachment & Human Development, 14 (5),* 453–476.

Pinel, J.P.J. (2009). *Biopsychology* (7th ed.). Boston, MA: Allyn and Bacon.

Plato. (2000). *The Republic.* Mineola, NY: Dover Publications.

Platt, M. L., & Glimcher, P. W. (1999). Neural correlates of decision variables in parietal cortex. *Nature, 400.*

Plotsky, P. M., & Meaney, M. J. (1993). Early, postnatal experience alters hypothalamic corticotropin-releasing factor (CRF) MRNA, median eminence CRF content and stress-induced release in adult rates. *Molecular Brain Research, 18.*

Poldrack, R.A., & Foerde, K. (2007). Category learning and the memory systems debate. *Neuroscience and Biobehavioural Reviews, 32,* 197-205.

Porges, S. W., Doussard-Roosevelt, J. A., & Maiti A. K. (1994). Vagal tone and the physiological regulation of emotion. *Monographs of the Society for Research in Child Development, 59* (2-3), 167-186.

Porter, M. (1998). *Competitive strategy: Techniques for analysing industries and competitors.* London: Free Press.

Radojevic, M. (1994). Mental representations of attachment among prospective Australian fathers. *Australian and New Zealand Journal of Psychiatry, 28.*

Raine, A., Buchsbaum, M. S., Stanley, J., Lottenberg, S., Abel, L., & Stoddard, J. (1994). Selective reductions in prefrontal glucose metabolism in murderers. *Biological Psychiatry, 36.*

Rameson, L.T., & Lieberman, M.D. (2009). Empathy: A social cognitive neuroscience approach. *Social and Personality Psychology Compass, 3*(1), 94-110.

Rasoal, C., Danielsson, H., & Jungert, T. (2012). Empathy among students in engineering programmes. *European Journal of Engineering Education, 37 (5): 427*

Ratey, J. (2002). *A User's Guide to the Brain.* London: Vintage Books.

Recanzone, G. H., Schreiner, C. E., & Merzenich, M. M. (1993). Plasticity in the frequency representation of primary auditory cortex following discrimination training in adult owl monkeys. *Journal of Neuroscience, 13.*

Reich, Wilhelm. (1949). *Character Analysis.* New York: Farrar, Straus, and Giroux.

Richard, J. & Nelson, C.H. (2007)., *Accounting of change in declarative memory: a cognitive neuroscience perspective: Developmental Review, 27,* 349-373.

Richmond, J., & Nelson, C.H. (2007). Accounting for change in declarative memory: A cognitive neuroscience perspective. *Developmental Review, 27,* 349-373.

Rizzolatti, G., & Arbib, M. A. (1998). Language within our grasp. *Trends in Neuroscience, 21* (5), 188-194.

Rizzolati, G., & Craighero, L. (2004). The mirror-neuron system. *Annual Review of Neuroscience, 27,* 169-192.

Robbins, A. (1991). *Awakening the Giant Within.* New York: Simon & Schuster.

Robbins, S., Millet, B., Cacioppe, R., & Waters-Marsh T. (1998). *Organizational Behaviour: Leading and Managing People In Australia and New Zealand.*

Roethlisberger, F. (1941). *Management and Morale.* Cambridge: Harvard University Press.

Rogers, C., and Farson, R. E. (1957). Active Listening. In R. G. Newman, M. A. Danziger, & M. Cohen (Eds.) (1987), *Communication in Business Today.* Washington C.C.: Heath and Company.

Rolls, E. T. (2000). The orbitofrontal cortex and reward. *Cerebral Cortex, 10*(3).

Ross, E. D., Homan, R. W., & Buck, R. (1994). Differential hemispheric lateralisation of primary and social emotions: Implications for developing a comprehensive neurology of emotions, repression, and the subconscious. *Neuropsychiatry, Neuropsychology and Behavioural Neurology, 7,* 1-19.

Rothbart, M. K., Taylor, S. B., & Tucker, D. M. (1989). Right-sided facial asymmetry in infant emotional expression. *Neuropsychologia, 27.*

Rowan, A. (2003). *The lore of the Bard.* St Paul: Llewellyn Publications.

Russek, L. G., & Schwartz, G. E. (1996). Energy cardiology: A dynamical energy systems approach for integrating conventional and alternative medicine. *Advance, 12.*

Sagi, A., van Ijzendoorn, M. H., Scharf, M. H., Koren-Karie, N., Joels, T., & Mayseless, O. (1994). Stability and discriminant validity of the adult attachment interview: A psychometric study in young Israeli adults. *Developmental Psychology, 30.*

Saling, L.L., & Phillips, J.G. (2007). Automatic behaviour: efficient not mindless. *Brain Research Bulletin, 73,* 1-20.

Sassa, Y., et al., (2012). The correlation between brain gray matter volume and empathizing and systemizing quotients in healthy children. *NeuroImage 60, 2035–2041.*

Saxe, G. N., Chinman, G., Berkowitz, R., Hall, K., Leiberg, G., Schwartz, J., & van der Kolk, BA. (1994). Somatization in patients with dissociative disorders. *American Journal of Psychiatry, 151*(9).

Saxe, R., & Haushofer, J. (2008). For love or money: A Common Neural Currency for Social and Monetary Reward. *Neuron, 58,* 164-165.

Saxe, R., & Wexler, A. (2005). Making sense of another mind: The role of the right temporo-parietal junction. *Neuropsychologia, 43*(10), 1391-1399.

Saxe, R. (2006). Uniquely human social cognition. *Current Opinion in Neurobiology, 16:235–239*

Schaefer, M. et al., (2013). Mirror-like brain responses to observed touch and personality dimensions. *Frontiers in Human Neuroscience., 7 (227).*

Schacter, D. L. (1996). *Searching for memory: the brain, the mind and the past.* New York: Basic.

Schacter, D. L., Alpert, N. M., Savage, C. R., Rauch, S. L., & Albert, M. S. (1996). Conscious recollection and the human hippocampal formation: Evidence from positron emission tomography. *Proceedings of the National Academy of Sciences USA, 93.*

Schacter, D. L. (1992). Understanding implicit memory: A cognitive neuroscience approach. *American Psychologist, 47.*

Schaffer, R. H. (1988). *Breakthrough Strategy.* New York: Harper Business.

Schedlowski, M. & Tewes, U. (1996). *Psychoneuroimmunology.* Kluwer Academic / Plenum Pub.

Schmitter, A. M. (2010). Ancient, Medieval and Renaissance Theories of the Emotions.

17th and 18th Century Theories of Emotions. *The Stanford Encyclopedia of Philosophy (Winter 2010 Edition).*

Schore, A. N. (1991). Early superego development: The emergence of shame and narcissistic affect regulation in the practicing period. *Psychoanalysis and Contemporary Thought, 14,* 187-250.

Schore, A. N. (1994). *Affect regulation and the origin of the self: The neurobiology of emotional development.* Hillsdale, NJ: Erlbaum.

Schore, A. N. (1997). Early organisation of the non-linear right brain and development of a predisposition to psychiatric disorders. *Development and Psychopathology,* 9(4), 595-631.

Schore, A.N. (2003). *Affect Regulation and the Repair of the Self.*

Schore, A.N. (2003). *Affect Regulation and Disorders of the Self.* Norton & Co. Ltd.

Schultheiss, O. C., Wirth, M. M., & Stanton, S. J. (2004). Effects of affiliation and power motivation arousal on salivary progesterone and testosterone. *Hormones and Behavior 46, 592– 599.*

Schuman, J. (1997). *The neurobiology of affect in language,* Malden, MA: Blackwell.

Scientific American, October, 1994.

Searle, J. R., *Minds, brains, and programs,* Behavioural and Brain Sciences, 3: 417-24, 1980.

Searle, J. R. (1984). *Minds, brains, and science.* Cambridge: Harvard University Press.

Searleman, A. (1977). A review of right hemisphere linguistic capabilities. *Psychological Bulletin, 84*(3), 503-528.

Seligman, M., & Peterson, C. (2004). *Character Strengths and Virtues: A Handbook and Classification.* Oxford University Press.

Seligman, M.E.P. (1975). *Helplessness: On depression, development, and death.* New York: Freeman.

Seligman, M.E.P., & Maier, S. F. (1967). Failure to escape traumatic shock. *Journal of Experimental Psychology, 74,* 1-9.

Senge, P. (1994). *The fifth discipline field book.* London: Nicholas Brealey Publishing.

Serven-Schreiber, D. (1996). *Healing Without Prozac.*

Serven-Schreiber, D. (2004). *Healing Without Freud or Prozac.* Rodale International.

Servan-Schreiber, D. (2005). *Healing without Freud or prozac: Natural approaches to curing stress, anxiety and depression without drugs and without psychotherapy.* London: Rodale International.

Shamay-Tsoory, S. G., et al. (2009). Intranasal Administration of Oxytocin Increases Envy and Schadenfreude (Gloating). *Society of Biological Psychiatry 66:864–870.*

Sheldon, W.H. (1942). *The Varieties of Temperament: A Psychology of Constitutional Differences.* USA: Harper & Brothers.

Sheldon, W.H. (1954). *Atlas of Men.* USA: Harper & Brothers.

Shepard. G. M. (1994). *Neurobiology,* 3rd edition. Oxford University Press.

Shaw, G., Brown, R. & Bromley, P. (1998). *How 3M Is rewriting business planning, May-June.*

Sheldrake, R. (1981), *A New Science of Life: The Hypothesis of Formative Causation,* Los Angeles: JP Tarcher.

Shepherd, S. V. et al., (2009). Mirroring of attention by neurons in macaque parietal cortex. *PNAS 106 (23) 9489–9494.*

Sherman, G., et al., (2012). Leadership is associated with lower levels of stress. *PNAS Early Edition, 1-5.*

Shine, B. (1999). *The Infinite Mind.* Harper Collins Publishers.

Shnabel, N., et al., (in press). Demystifying Values-Affirmation Interventions: Writing About Social Belonging Is a Key to Buffering Against Identity Threat. *Personality and Social Psychology Bulletin.* Downloaded from psp.sagepub.com at Columbia University on March 12, 2013.

Siegel, D. J. (1995). Perception and cognition. In B. Kaplan and W. Sadock (Eds.), *Comprehensive textbook of psychiatry,* (6th edition) (pp. 277-291). Baltimore: Williams & Wilkins.

Siegel, D. (1999). *The developing mind: How relationships and the brain interact to shape who we are.* New York: Guilford Press.

Sigelman, C., & Rider, E. (2006). *Lifespan human development* (5th ed.). Belmont, CA: Thompson Wadsworth.

Simon, H. A. (1983). Human Nature in Politics: The Dialogue of Psychology with Political Science. In (Jun., 1985), *The American Political Science Review, 79* (2), 293-304.

Simons, J. (2011). What really happened? Sharp memories tied to brain crease. *msnbc. com contributor.*

Smither, R., Houston, J., & McIntire, S. (1996). *Organisation Development, Strategies for Changing Environments.* New York, NY: Harper Collins.

Sperduti, M., et al., (2011). Different brain structures related to self- and external-agency attribution: a brief review and meta-analysis. *Brain Struct Funct, 216:151–157.*

Sperry, R. W. (1969). A modified concept of consciousness. *Psychological Review, 76,* 532-36.

Squire, L.R. (1987). *Memory and the brain.* New York: Oxford University Press.

Squire, L.R., & Zola-Morgan, S. (1991). The medial temporal lobe memory system. *Science, 253*(5026), 1380-1386.

Squire, L. R., Knowlton, B., & Musen, G. (1993). The structure and organisation of memory. *Annual Review of Psychology, 44.*

Stafford, L. D., et al., (2010). Bolder, happier, smarter: The role of extraversion in positive mood and cognition. *Personality and Individual Differences 48, 827–832.*

Stanovich, K.E., & West, R.F. (2000). Advancing the rationality debate. *Behavioral and Brain Sciences, 23,* 701-726.

Stapp, H. P. (1993). *Mind, matter, and quantum mechanics.* Berlin: Springer-Verlag.

Stich, S. (1990). *The Fragmentation of Reason.* Cambridge: MIT Press.

Strauman, T. J., et al., (2013). What shall I be, what must I be: neural correlates of personal goal activation. *Frontiers in Integrative Neuroscience, 6, Article 123.*

Szekely, E. B. (1973). *Creative Yoga, Karma Yoga.* San Diego: Academy Books.

Stuss, D.T., Gallup, G. G., & Alexander, M. P. (2001). The frontal lobes are necessary for 'theory of mind'. *Brain, 124*(2), 279-286.

Summerfield, C., et al., (2005). Mistaking a House for a Face: Neural Correlates of Misperception in Healthy Humans. *Cerebral Cortex doi:10.1093/cercor/bhi129.* Oxford University Press.

Sweeney, P. J., Matthews, M. D. & Lester, P. B (2011). *Leadership in Dangerous Situations.* Naval Institute Press: Annapolis, Maryland.

Tabibnia, G., and Lieberman, M. D. (2007). Fairness and Cooperation Are Rewarding: Evidence from Social Cognitive Neuroscience. *Ann. N.Y. Acad. Sci. 1118: 90–101. New York Academy of Sciences. doi: 10.1196/annals.1412.001*

Takeuchi et al. (2013). White matter structures associated with empathizing and systemizing in young adults. *NeuroImage 77, 222–236.* Elsevier Inc.

Takeuchi, H. et al. (2013). Resting state functional connectivity associated with trait emotional intelligence. *NeuroImage (in press).*

Takeuchi, H. et al., (2013). White matter structures associated with empathizing and systemizing in young adults. *NeuroImage, 77, 222-236.*

Tamir, D. I., & Mitchell, J. P. (2012). Disclosing information about the self is intrinsically rewarding. *PNAS Early Edition.* www.pnas.org/cgi/doi/10.1073/pnas.1202129109

Taylor, G. J. (2000). Recent developments in alexithymia theory and research. *Canadian Journal of Psychiatry, 45.*

Taylor, M. A. (1999). *The fundamentals of clinical neuropsychiatry.* Oxford, UK: Oxford University Press.

Taylor, S. E., & Brown, J. D. (1988). Illusion and well-being: A social psychological perspective on mental health. *Psychological Bulletin, 103*(2), 193-210.

Teneback, C. C., Nahas, Z., Speer, A. M., Molloy, M., Stallings, L. E., Spicer, K. M., Risch, S. C., & George, M. S. (1999). Changes in prefrontal cortex and paralimbic activity in depression following two weeks of daily left prefrontal TMS. *The Journal of Neuropsychiatry and Clinical Neurosciences, 11*(4), 426-435.

Thatcher, R. W., Walker, R. A., & Giudice, S. (1987). Human cerebral hemispheres develop at different rates and ages. *Science, 236*(4805), 1110-1113.

Thelen, E. (1989). Self-organisation in developmental processes: Can systems approaches work? In M. Gunnar & E. Thelen (Eds.), Minnesota Symposium on Child Psychology, 22, *Systems and development* (pp. 77-117). Hillsdale, NJ: Erlbaum.

Thibodeau, G.A., & Patton, K. T. (1997). *Structure and Function of the Body.*

Topps, M. (2009). Oxytocin: Envy or Engagement in Others? *Society of Biological Psychiatry 67:e5–e6.*

Tracy, B. (2004). *Goals! How to get everything you want – Faster than you ever thought possible.* San Francisco, CA: Berrett-Koehler Publishers, Inc.

Treffil, J. (1992). *Sharks have no bones.* New York: Simon and Schuster.

Tremblay, L., & Schultz, W. (1999). Relative reward preference in primate orbitofrontal cortex. *Nature, 398,* 704-708.

Trevarthen, C. (1993). The self born in intersubjectivity: the psychology of an infant communicating. In U. Neisser (Ed.), *The perceived self: Ecological and interpersonal sources of self knowledge* (pp. 121-173). Cambridge, UK: Cambridge University Press.

Trevarthen, C. (1996). Lateral asymmetries in infancy: Implications for the development of the hemispheres. *Neuroscience and Biobehavioural Reviews, 20,* 571-586.

Tucker, D. M., Luu, P., & Pribram, K. H. (1995). Social and emotional self-regulation. *Annals of the New York Academy o f Sciences, 769,* 213-239.

Tulving, E. (1985). How many memory systems are there? *American Psychologist, 40*(4).

Tulving, E. (1993). Varieties of consciousness and levels of awareness in memory. In A. Baddeley & L. Weiskrantz (Eds.), *Attention, selection, awareness and control: A tribute to Donald Broadbent* (pp. 283-299). London: Oxford University Press.

van der Kolk, B. A., Pelcovitz, D., Roth, S., Mandel, F. S., McFarlane, A., & Herman, J. L. (1996). Dissociation, somatization, and affect dysregulation: The complexity of adaptation to trauma. *American Journal of Psychiatry, 153*(7), 83-93.

van Ijzendoorn, M. H. (1995). Adult attachment representations, parental responsiveness, and infant attachment: A meta-analysis on the predictive validity of the Adult Attachment Interview. *Psychological Bulletin, 117*(3), 387-403.

van Ijzendoorn, M. H. (1992). Intergenerational transmission of parenting: A review of studies in con- clinical populations. *Developmental Review, 12.*

van Ijzendoorn, M. H., & Bakermans-Kranenburg, M. J. (1996). Attachment representations in mothers, fathers, adolescents and clinical groups: A meta-analytic search for normative data. *Journal of Consulting and Clinical Psychology, 64*(1), 8-21.

Veccio, R. P. (1988). *Organizational Behaviour.* The Dryden Press.

Wada, J. (1961). Modification of cortically induced responses in brainstem by shift of attention in monkeys. *Science, 133.*

Walsh, V., Ashbridge, E., & Cower, A. (1998). Cortical plasticity in perceptual learning demonstrated by transcranial magnetic stimulation. *Neuropsychologia, 36* (1), 45-49.

Walton, M. E., & Baudonnat, M., (2012). The value of competition in the rat race. *Nature Neuroscience, 15, 9, 1182-1183.*

Watanabe, M. (1996). Reward expectancy in primate prefrontal neurons. *Nature, 382* (6592), 629-632.

Waytz, A., Zaki, J., Mitchell, J. P. (2012). Response of Dorsomedial Prefrontal Cortex Predicts Altruistic Behavior. *The Journal of Neuroscience, 32(22):7646 –7650.*

Wenzlaff, R.M. (1993). The mental control of depression: Psychological obstacles to emotional well-being. In D.M. Wegner & J.W. Pennebaker (Eds.), *Handbook of mental control* (pp. 239-57). Englewood Cliffs, NJ: Prentice Hall.

Westbrook, C., et al., (2013). Mindful attention reduces neural and self-reported cue-induced craving in smokers. SCAN (2013) 8, 73-84.

Westphal, M., Seivert, N. H., & Bonanno, G. A. (2010). Expressive Flexibility. *Emotion, 10, No. 1, 92–100.*

Wheeler, M. A., Stuss, D. T., & Tulving, E. (1997). Toward a theory of episodic memory: The frontal lobes and autonoetic consciousness. *Psychological Bulletin, 121,* 331-354.

Whitmore, J. (1992). *Coaching for Performance: GROWing People, Performance and Purpose.* London: Nicholas Brealey.

Wike, T., & Fraser, M. (2009). School shootings: Making sense of the senseless. *Aggression and Violent Behaviour, 14*(3), 162-169.

Wilber, K. (2000). *A Theory of Everything: An Integral Vision for Business, Politics, Science, and Spirituality.* Shambhala.

Wilber, K. (1982). *Eye to Eye: The Quest for the New Paradigm.* New York: Doubleday/ Anchor.

Wilber, K. (2000). *The Collected Works of Ken Wilber.* Boston: Shambhala.

Wilber, K., Engler, J. Y., & Brown, D. (1986). *Transformations of Consciousness: Conventional and Contemplative Perspectives on Development.* Boston: Shambhala.

Wilber, K., Anthony, D., & Ecker, B. (Eds.). (1987). *Spiritual Choices.* New York: Paragon House Publishers.

Wilber, K. (Ed.). (1987). *Quantum Questions: Mystical Writings of the World's Great Physicists.* Shambhala.

Wilber, K., & Wilber, Treya Killam. (1991). *Grace and Grit: Spirituality and Healing in the Life and Death of Treya Killam Wilber.* Shambhala.

Wilber, K. (1995). *Sex, Ecology, Spirituality: The Spirit of Evolution.* Boston, MA: Shambhala.

Wilber, K. (1996). *A Brief History of Everything.* Boston, MA: Shambhala.

Wilber, K. (1999). *One Taste: Daily Reflections on Integral Spirituality.* Shambhala.

Wilber, K. (1998). *The Essential Ken Wilber: An Introductory Reader.* Shambhala.

Wilber, K. (1997). *The Eye of Spirit: An Integral Vision for a World Gone Slightly Mad.* Shambhala.

Wilber, K. (1998). *The Marriage of Sense and Soul: Integrating Science and Religion.* Shambhala.

Wilber, K. (1977). *The Spectrum of Consciousness.* Wheaton: Quest.

Wilber, K. (1979). *No Boundary: Eastern and Western Approaches to Personal Growth.* Los Angeles: Center Press (new edition: Shambhala, 1981).

Wilber, K. (1980). *The Atman Project : A Transpersonal View of Human Development.* Wheaton: Quest.

Wilber, K. (1981). *Up from Eden: A Transpersonal View of Human Evolution.* New York: Doubleday/Anchor.

Wilber, K. (1982). *A Sociable God.* New York: McGraw-Hill. Note: this book is currently out of print as a separate book, and only available in Collected Works, Volume 3.

Williams. W. M., & Sternberg, R. J. (1988). Group intelligence: Why some groups are better than others. *Intelligence 12.*

Winnicott, D. W. (2002). The capacity to be alone. In *Maturational Processes and the Facilitating Environment* (pp. 29-36). New York: International Universities Press, 1958.

Winston, J. S. et al. (2002). Automatic and Intentional Brain Responses During Evaluation of Trustworthiness of Faces. *Nature Neuroscience, 5*(3). Winston, R. (2003). *The Human Mind.* Bantam Books.

Witelson, S. F., Kigar, D. L., & Harvey, T., (1999). The exceptional brain of Albert Einstein, *The Lancet, 353*(9170), 2149-2153.

Wolf, N.S., Gales, M., Shane, E., & Shane, M. (2000). Mirror neurons, procedural learning, and the positive new experience: A developmental systems self psychology approach. *Journal of the American Academy of Psychoanalysis and Dynamic Psychiatry, 28,* 409-430.

Wolf, N. S., Gales, M. E., Shane, E., & Shane, M. (2001). The developmental trajectory from amodal perception to empathy and communication: The role of mirror neurons in this process. *Psychoanalytic Inquiry, 21*(1), 94-112.

Worden, J.W. (1983). *Grief counselling and grief therapy.* London: Travistock Publications Ltd.

Xue, G., et al., (2009). Functional Dissociations of Risk and Reward Processing in the Medial Prefrontal Cortex. *Cerebral Cortex, 19, 1019-1027.*

Xue, G., et al., (2008). Risk And Reward Compete In Brain: Imaging Study Reveals Battle Between Lure Of Reward And Fear Of Failure. *Science Daily.* University of

Southern Califsornia. Retrieved August 7, 2013, from http://www.sciencedaily.com/ releases/2008/10/081009144325.

Yong, E. (2012). The Hype About the Love Drug Is Dangerous. One Molecule for Love, Morality, and Prosperity? *Slate.com/articles/health_and_science*

Zak, P. J., Stanton, A.A., & Ahmadi, S. (2007). Oxytocin increases generosity in humans. *PLoS ONE 2*(11), e1128, 1-5.

Zak, P. J., Kurzban, R., Matzner, W. T. (2005). Oxytocin is associated with human trustworthiness. *PLoS ONE 2(11): e1128*

Zeki, S. (2007). The neurobiology of love. *Federation of European Biochemical Societies Letters, 581,* 2575-2579.

Zeltzer, L. K., Anderson, C. T. M., & Schecter, N. L. (1990). Pediatric pain: Current status and new directions. *Current Problems in Pediatrics, 20*(8).

Zenger, J. H. & Perrin, C. (1993). *Leading teams: Mastering the new role.* Irwin Professional Publishing.

Zhu, Y., et al., (2007). Neural basis of cultural influence on self-representation. *NeuroImage, 34, 1310–1316.*

About the Author

As an author, coach and consultant, I have been fortunate to have had a life that has enabled me to work with people, at their very best and their very worst.

When participants have attended my *NeuroPower* Transformational Leadership programs and have experienced significant breakthroughs, often they want to know a little about my story.

Peter Burow

B.Bus Comm Dip. M.MHH,
NS.NLP, AFAIM

To this end the following thumbnail sketch of my life will give you a deeper insight into my personal and professional journey.

Let me introduce myself...

I was born on Boxing Day to two young teachers in the small town of Bundaberg in Queensland, Australia. Mum was the only one in her family to have gone to university. She came from a pioneering family with eight children; times were tough, and the whole family worked and saved to send her off to be educated. She held the aspirations of her whole family. Mum taught me the power of patience and strategy. Her aspiration was to marry anyone but a farmer, which is where my father comes into the scene.

While Mum was a country girl, Dad was from town. He moved schools frequently when he was in his early teens and, in his words, never really caught up. He wanted to be an electrician but my grandfather thought that teaching was better – so he became a teacher. His only career advice to me was to try anything but teaching. Dad taught me to question everything and test the boundaries of authority. One of his sayings is 'People only seem to get upset if they know about it.' He taught me how to manage my fear in a way he has always found difficult. One of my earliest memories was when I was about three, and involved a ritual ladder climbing that took place every afternoon when Dad returned home from work. He would set up the aluminium ladder and I had to climb a step higher every day. One day I could stand on the very top. We were both very proud.

Mum, as most mums do, wanted to be the perfect mum and constantly fought with the fact that she was supposed to be using the education her family had given her rather than being at home with her child. She contented herself by giving me a full education from the moment I could talk. My first storybooks were ones that Mum thought would give me a good Christian perspective on life and introduced me to the Old Testament biblical characters. For some reason I loved Moses although Jesus was a bit of a mystery to me.

I have very clear memories of when I was three, discussing if Jesus was a normal man filled with the Holy Spirit or if he was God. I decided he was a man filled with the Holy Spirit, which meant that I too could do what Jesus did if I could work out how to be filled with the Holy Spirit. I loved Sunday School, where Mum was the Superintendent, but couldn't work out why everyone wanted to colour in and not discuss the theological issues behind the stories. I quickly became a behaviour management issue.

When I was five my parents bought me a keyboard. Such a thing of amazement and magic I had never seen. I started with lessons and decided that I would be the best organist in the world. I've never dreamt small. Every morning from 6.30am until 7.15am I would practise with the headphones on. It drove me mad but taught me about how to keep doing something until it's mastered.

At school I couldn't work out what the other children were doing. I couldn't see the point to 'tiggy' or any of the other games they played. I remember asking Dad what the point of tennis was; he said I'd understand when I was older.

In Year Two I wrote my first book. I proudly took it to school for show and tell. I presented my work but to my amazement I was told by my teacher that I couldn't possibly have written it and that I was obviously an attention-seeking liar. I had been so excited about showing it too!

My reaction to this was to get busy. In Grade Three I fell in love with *Dr. Who* and *The Investigators* books, both of which were banned from the school library. My response was to bond with the second in charge of the library, and create a puppet show, which ran at lunchtimes. I charged the children an entrance fee and drummed up business by volunteering for tuckshop duty and convincing the children to use their money for the puppet show rather than ice creams. Back in 1973 I made $165.00 profit over a three-month period. The money was spent on *Dr. Who* books and the entire series of *The Investigators* books for the library. For an eight-year-old this was a great victory.

Each day I had so much to do and so little time to do it. At a parent-teacher interview my Year Five teacher explained that he felt as if he was interrupting me to ask me to do schoolwork. By Year Six I had a puppet show that was taken to other schools with no less than twenty Year Six helpers – a third of the class. At lunchtime my friend Nigel and I ran a second-hand shop that sold anything kids could find from home – we made good money and donated it to the class for art materials.

When I was eleven I broke my leg at a school camp and was in hospital for 100 days. My mother says that I went in as a child and came out about forty years old. The children back at school were all put on roster to visit. Each visitor had to bring a present! This was fantastic. Imagine an eleven-year-old receiving three presents a day for 100 days! Suddenly I felt very popular.

I bonded with the nurses and the doctors, playing cards and arguing theology with the Anglican nurse and the Seventh Day Adventists who would visit me. I watched daytime television. At home I was only allowed one hour per day, but in hospital I watched TV night and day. I also discovered social politics and helped the nurses I liked get even with the nurses we didn't. For me, hospital was lonely but fantastic. It also gave Mum the opportunity to discover that I was way behind academically at school. From that day on I had after school work every day until I went to university. In the words of Jim Hacker from *Yes, Prime Minister*, I received a comprehensive education – to make up for my comprehensive education.

High school was excellent because I had the chance to start all over again. My academic results were average at best but I decided to position myself as a top student. I found out who the top students were, dressed like they did, studied harder than they did and competed at every opportunity. It was on my first day of high school that I met a curly haired chap who seemed popular and had a very endearing turn of phrase. I decided that he would also be good to get to know. Robert and I became good mates and he was good to compete with in maths and woodwork. He was always better at maths, which is just as well because today we are fellow Directors in a number of companies and for the last fifteen years he has looked after all my accounts and legal issues. I trust him implicitly.

I was fairly focused on studying at high school, although a few character forming events took place during secondary school that spring to mind. The first involved winning the state championship of Jaycees Youth Speaks for Australia. This was a national speaking competition for senior Secondary School students that focused on a seven-minute inspirational and a two-minute impromptu speech. Back then the finals were televised. For me, this involved travelling to Brisbane (about a day's trip away) and performing in a television studio. I was terrified. Much to my amazement I returned home a winner. For a fortnight after the finals Brisbane radio stations, newspapers and magazines rang me for comments about a range of topics from politics to school standards. In Bundaberg people would stop me in the street to ask my advice about how their children could grow up into a 'nice young man' like I was, or to give me advice about my hair or my clothes. I was a no-name one day and suddenly known to everyone the next.

At lunchtimes I worked with one of the church Elders down at the local piano shop. I was also President of the Young Organists' Association and was invited to be a guest concert organist by the Wurlitzer Corporation. (At the time, home organs were all the rage.) I still have a bright red (YOA) uniform blazer with sequins and diamantes on it that I wore on stage for my final eye-raising number, *The Flight of the Bumblebee*.

When I wasn't helping down at the piano shop at lunchtime, I visited elderly people from the church who had no visitors and needed the company. I helped at the local Sunday School, volunteered as an usher and ticket sales person at the local amateur playhouse (and even acted in some of their plays), MC'ed the Mayor's Concert, was on the local judging panel for baby shows, played piano at church on Sundays and for local dances and weddings on weekends for pocket money. At school I set up the drama club, the reading club in the library and was voted a School Prefect. I had an absolute ball.

At church I teamed up with a talented English girl who was a gifted mime. She taught me this engaging little skit where we mimed that we wallpapered a room over the door and couldn't find the way out. We entered the skit into the state Youth For Christ drama competition. The audience loved it and my family and I were given the funding to attend the Christian music and drama camp in Cooma down south. This is where I learned about how to play in a band, something that I didn't really use until I played keyboard in a university band called *The Surrogate Mothers*.

On Australia Day 1984, the Bundaberg City Council awarded me the Young Citizen Award. I was not expecting it at all. I was there at the invitation of the local Member of Parliament. I can remember being so amazed that I was completely speechless. I couldn't say a word. It doesn't happen often but when it does, it does. I remember receiving the award and looking at the people in the park applauding and feeling so unworthy of their applause. I had enjoyed everything I had done. I remember the local Member of Parliament saying, 'Surely you have something to say,' and me just shaking my head and his hand in silence.

I moved to Brisbane when I was eighteen and started my undergraduate degree in Business Communications. The year before I graduated I started a small communications consultancy specialising in work for not-for-profit organisations. I was the Parish Council Secretary in the Uniting Church and believed that one day I would be an ordained Minister. In the meantime, however, I would run a consultancy.

It was hard. For the first two years my business partner and I survived by taking it in turns to collect the dole and split it between us for food. Our team was made up of volunteers who turned up for the coffee and biscuits and the education they could receive. I quickly learned that the moment deadlines needed to be met or the environment became too intense, they would all take the day off. This gave me great insight into the motivations of employees and the importance of having a corporate vision, to which they would commit even if only for their own reasons.

To make ends meet during this time I played piano and did stand-up comedy. This was excellent experience. It was as a stand-up comedian that I first realised that there are very different humours. Almost inevitably if I made one half of the group laugh, the other half would be offended. If the offended folk found something funny, the others would be bored. It was where I first started becoming aware of the six different ways people process information and started exploring how they combined to form personality.

About this time I started working with a Spiritual Director. In case you're wondering what a Spiritual Director looks like, mine was an eighty-four-year-old Catholic nun who didn't let me get away with anything. As I got to know her better I discovered that, while she allocated herself an allowance of just $50 per month, she had made some excellent business decisions over the years and was a multi-millionaire. Like me, she had a love of God and business. I worked with her for four years developing an awareness of emotional reactivity which was important for the professional coaching and leadership work I had ahead of me.

I built the consultancy for the following thirteen years into one of the state's largest, and most awarded marketing and media consultancies. During this time I specialised in helping leaders from all sectors, (including church leaders and State Premiers) to lead and communicate effectively during times of change and crisis.

My media training and presentation clients varied from conservative groups like Coopers and Lybrand, and Woolworths through to multi-level marketing companies and politicians. It was with the executives of these companies that I refined *NeuroPower*. Each participant in my training would complete a questionnaire before attending the course and would receive a print-out of their profile. During the training I would ask participants to cross out any information about their profile in the paragraphs I supplied them that they felt was inaccurate and add in data about their personality they felt had been left out. Over a five-year period we had more than 2000 responses, which made up the base line research for the *NeuroPower* Profiler.

During the thirteen years I ran the consultancy I also owned a travel agency, a property development firm, investment company, a disabled workshop for collation and packaging, a graphic design firm, a gardening service employing intellectually disabled folk, an IT software development company and also managed a serviced office centre.

I retired from this in my thirteenth year of operation after a nasty go-cart accident, and to recuperate financially and emotionally from a disastrous property project (and a broken heart). I also wanted to focus more on studying personality and transformation. In particular I was interested in the amazing insight held by the Maya Lenca people from Central America who conducted a 10,000 year longitudinal study into personality. This lead to four years' study of the Maya Lenca under the personal guidance of His Excellency Leonel Antonio Chevez, the last royal Maya Lenca Prince from Eastern El Salvador, who at the time lived in Brisbane, Australia in exile. In 2004, the Maya community awarded me a Diploma in Maya Studies for my work of collating and helping to preserve the Maya Health and Personality System and in June, 2005, in the rain forest of El Salvador, the *NeuroPower* framework was blessed by Her Excellency Francisca Romero Guevara.

After leaving the consultancy in Brisbane I formed a smaller specialist team of consultants who worked in Sydney with some of Australia's largest public companies and government instrumentalities providing strategic advice in leadership development and organisational transformation.

Since 1987, my team and I have coached thousands of executives Australia-wide using the frameworks and methodologies in this book. The success of this approach has helped to change the culture and performance of some of Australia's most recognised organisations. My role, as coach or adviser, has been to focus the individual on accessing their Genius and their noble side and to help them, as leaders, bring out the nobility in others. These noble qualities are available only to those who can hold the natural tension caused by competing polarities. While this is a simple concept, it is not easy, and requires enormous discipline and determination.

Like all of us, my personal journey has had highs and lows, good times and bad times. I know what it's like to have enormous influence and power and what it's like to break down completely emotionally and physically with broken dreams and a broken heart. What this journey has provided me with has been the perfect opportunity to refine a process for converting pain to power, naivety to nobility, hell to heaven.

Today I work with teams experiencing the stress that comes immediately before success. I share the *NeuroPower* methods for converting the daily s**t that comes across their desks into fertiliser that grows nobility and power.

Looking back I would change nothing in my past. Instead I am overwhelmingly grateful for the way my life has emerged and the opportunities and privileges it has afforded me.

And of course... the best is yet to come.

29586711R00193

Printed in Great Britain
by Amazon